Interlitteraria

Supplement 1 – 2015

Taming World Literature

In honorem Jüri Talvet

The publication of *Interlitteraria* is supported by the Cultural Endowment of Estonia (Eesti Kultuurkapital) and the University of Tartu.

Interlitteraria is indexed in ERIH PLUS (European Reference Index for the Humanities), CEEOL (Central and Eastern European Online Library) and DOAJ (Directory of Open Access Journals), and is scheduled to be included in EBSCO Publishing's databases.

Language editing for this issue:
Daniel Edward Allen (English), ***Dieter Neidlinger*** (German),
Jean Pascal Ollivry (French)

ISSN 1406-0701
ISBN 978-9949-32-938-0 (print)
ISBN 978-9949-32-939-7 (pdf)

Contents – Matières – Inhalt – Contenido

Introduction

This year, we are celebrating the 70th birthday of our colleague and good friend Jüri Talvet. This year is, in addition, the 35th anniversary of the discipline of World Literature at the University of Tartu: in 1980, the Chair of Foreign Literature (now World Literature) was founded as an independent discipline with its own study track. The Chair was first led by Professor Harald Peep, with Professors Yuri Lotman and Jüri Talvet among his co-workers. Jüri Talvet became Professor of World Literature after Estonia regained its independence in 1991, and he has played a crucial role in securing the discipline's independence within the university and in broadening its horizons internationally. Thanks to his initiative and hard work, the Chair of World Literature and the Estonian Association of Comparative Literature have established a rich tradition of biannual international conferences as well as the journal *Interlitteraria*. Although we call our discipline "comparative literature" in English, Jüri Talvet has insisted upon the use of the term *maailmakirjandus* – "world literature" – in Estonian.

In the world of comparative studies, these two notions are not always perceived as synonymous. World literature and comparative literature can be viewed as complementary disciplines or even as opposing or incompatible concepts. The various definitions reflect the diversity of a discipline that deals with literary traditions and practices that transcend one particular monolingual culture in its local space. The variety is due to the fact that even the broadest view, taking in the world in its great complexity, is always dependent on a vantage point. To better understand different vantage points and the various meanings of our discipline, we have invited scholars from diverse academic and cultural backgrounds to reflect upon world literature and comparative literature in this celebratory special issue of *Interlitteraria*.

In the first part of the volume the focus is on the terms themselves, on the formation, the current state and challenges within the discipline. European comparative literature demands good knowledge of several languages and cultures and reading works of literature in the original; newer tendencies that have emerged in the USA encourage the 'distant' and translation-based reading of texts of diverse origin in order to reach more generalised and universally relevant conclusions. The dilemma of the global accessibility of texts *versus* their 'untranslatability' is discussed from various perspectives by European and American scholars who are all looking for ways to settle neither for studying only a fraction of the world in all its diversity nor for studying only an undiversified version of the world.

DOI: http://dx.doi.org/10.12697/IL.2015.S1.1

The articles in the second part concentrate on the perspective of small literatures at the periphery of larger cultural spaces. In these literatures, the concept of world literature, as well as the comparative approach, has been instrumental in the construction of their own local tradition. Having developed in constant contact with, and in awareness of others, these literatures have long experience with taming the diversity of the surrounding world for their own purposes, while also recognising the infinite capacity of this diversity to resist and to re-emerge. A closer look at this dynamics has been taken by Estonian, Slovenian and Luxemburgish scholars on the example of their respective literary traditions.

The third part offers a series of individual case studies on authors and works ranging from Renaissance literature to fiction about the Holocaust. The variety of topics in this section represents the refusal of world literature to be truly tamed to fit any generalising frame, but there is also an underlying common theme to these essays: they all focus on literature as a means of reflection upon ethical questions related to the human experience, to history or to the discipline itself.

When we launched the call for this special issue, a *Festschrift* prepared as a surprise gift to *Interlitteraria*'s editor-in-chief Jüri Talvet, we aimed at maximal creative and scholarly freedom for the authors. The way the individual voices, initially unaware of each other's contribution, came together in a true discussion was an additional surprise gift to us, which we now can share with our readers. Although, in truth, there was no reason to be surprised at this gift. The achievements we set out to celebrate have always stemmed from capacity for dialogue, from collegial understanding and from friendship based on shared values. This volume brings together writings from three continents and eleven countries; from eminent scholars whose expertise and friendship has been an invaluable help to Jüri Talvet's work, up to the very existence of this journal, and from young researchers who have benefited from Jüri's support on their way to the discipline and, most importantly, to the world full of literature(s).

Liina Lukas, Katre Talviste

Ajalooline vaatlus tõendab, et vaevalt leidub elujõule kindlamat tagatist kui kultuuri suhtlus teiste kultuuridega ja kõige laiemas mõttes maailmakultuuriga. Ka suurimad kultuuriruumid pole läbi saanud tiheda suhtluseta neist väljaspool paiknevate kultuuriruumidega. Tõsi, mingitel kuldajastutel on mõne suurkultuuri „seest" ikka siginenud enesekindlaid kujutelmi kultuuri isepüsimisest, kuid paraku ei ole need kultuurid ega kujutelmadki kestma jäänud kauem kui sajandiks või paariks.

Jüri Talvet,
„Maailmakirjanduse kodustamise küsimusi"

Historical observations confirm that nothing really grants vitality more surely than a culture's communication with other cultures and with the world culture in the broadest sense. Even the largest cultural spaces haven't managed without active communication with cultural spaces situated outside of them. It is true that at certain golden epochs self-assured fantasies of autosufficience have emerge from "inside" of some great cultures, but unfortunately neither these cultures nor these fantasies have lasted longer than a century or two.

Jüri Talvet,
"The Reception of World Literature in Estonia.
Some Preliminary Remarks"[1]

[1] The mottos for the three sections of this volume are taken from Jüri Talvet's article "Maailmakirjanduse kodustamise küsimusi" ("Some Questions Regarding the Taming of World Literature") published in 2005 in the Estonian journal *Keel ja Kirjandus,* and in 2006 in *Interlitteraria* under the title "The Reception of World Literature in Estonia. Some Preliminary Remarks". The latter version is used as the source of the English quotes.

Time as a Moral Quality: A Confession

JAAN UNDUSK

Abstract. What is a (morally) significant deed? The one which is done in due time. There are various morals in us fighting for the right to represent the „significant deed“ of the moment: family moral, working moral, Christian moral. To choose between them seems to be a cognitive rather than a moral task because they are all "good" morals. Yet we often tacitly know which is the just moral of the moment, although we choose another.

Keywords: moral philosophy, time, good deed, magic word

Time as a moral category was studied in several 20th-century philosophies. For Emmanuel Lévinas (1906–1995), the French philosopher of Lithuanian-Jewish origin, time is a measure of responsible existence: the more time I have the more responsibly I exist. The meaning of being is not an existential loneliness, but to be face to face with the Other, which presupposes a fundamental ethical relationship. And this relationship is temporal in essence. I exist responsibly as much as I have time for the Other. The man whose leitmotif is 'I do not have time', does not exist ethically. An early essay by Lévinas, "Time and the Other" (1947), begins with an eloquent claim: "Time is not a fact of an isolated and lonely subject, but it is the very relation of one subject with another." (Levinas 1947: 126).

Another French philosopher of Jewish origin from the same generation, Vladimir Jankélévitch (1903–1985), asserts in his book *Le Pardon* (1967, translated into English as "Forgiveness") seemingly quite the opposite. "Bare time has no moral significance" (Jankélévitch 1998: 1031), he writes, arguing that if one is guilty of something, the simple flow of time – be it a ten- or hundred-year period – is not enough to rehabilitate him. One has to break off the fluent flow of time and make one's excuses. So what Jankélévitch means is that to let time go does not correct any mistake, any fault; time in itself has no reconcilable power.

I on my part shall try to show that the simple flow of time can still have moral qualities, and in this sense I am moving in the general line of Lévinas; to let the time flow and miss the right moment, or inversely, to try to anticipate the time, can both be symptoms of moral conflict. This does not actually contradict

DOI: http://dx.doi.org/10.12697/IL.2015.S1.2

Jankélévitch, so much the more that I am speaking of a primary deed, and he is speaking of a secondary correction of it, that is, of pardoning.

For some of the readers, perhaps, I shall begin like a pastor in church, because my question is: what is a good deed? Or, to put it in a more specific way: what is a morally significant deed? And the answer in this paper will be as naïve as the question was: a good deed, be it big or small, is a deed which is done in due time, at the right moment. So simple is my definition. A major deed is not necessarily a good deed, if it is done too early or too late. Time counts if we try to evaluate the moral quality of an undertaking.

The claim sounds too absolute to be reliable but I hope to explain it in the course of this discussion.

Referring to language, the foremost instrument of our work as men and women of letters, the situation seems at first to be different. Because language typically comes into play before or after deeds, before and after action. Language in its essence is precisely the tool used to deal with things that are absent, that is, with the things not yet here, or no longer here. Language is a sign system, which means that it consists of things that stand for other things not present at the moment. One can speak of a cat in a room where there are never any cats. One can speak of freedom, of love, when there is neither love nor freedom. Language is a tool for things that are missing.

Our rare aim however, both as human beings and writers, is to grasp, at some perfect moment, a real cat just by saying it. To pronounce 'freedom' which stops being missing at the very moment. To express love, not in order to narrate, but to welcome its presence by the same speech act of love. In these magic moments, the linguistic sign stops designating, designating objects, and begins to connect, to connect living subjects, such as you and me. This is the appearance of the magic power of language no longer bound to the restrictions of a system, yet bound up with another person.

A powerful word is similar to a good deed. They can both be dangerous. At the right moment, when doing something really good, calling something into existence, we are unable to control the future. Everything is born to be free. We step out of the system of signs, of conventions, and face uncertainty. The impact of the magical power of words, as well as good deeds, is not predictable. This sounds like a paradox, and it really is. I shall return to this later.

My proposition was that a good deed is done in due time, at the right moment. And here an immediate question arises, of course: what is this "due time"? Who has competence enough to tell us when the right time is for a significant deed? It seems as if I am attributing to expressions like "due time", "the right time", and so on, a religious status, as in the New Testament where God himself fixes the right moment. Peter the Apostle says: "Humble yourselves therefore under the mighty hand of God, that he may exalt you in due time." (1 Pt 5,6). The Greek equivalent for "due time" in such cases is the famous *kairos*, the blessed time, the divine moment, guaranteed by God's intervention. In this sense, the discussion about the "right time" might seem theological. But, of course, my aim is not to speak like a priest in the name of God. I am meditating upon our everyday skill in perceiving the "right time".

I assume – and this is my other fundamental claim – that in many cases we recognise the right moment for a good deed almost infallibly. We often tacitly know the just moral of a particular moment, and we do not need the authority of God for that. We are aware of the right deed which must be done at this very moment, sometimes surprisingly well. The next question is, of course, shall we really follow this first, instinctive (or intuitive), moral impulse, or resist it; shall we carry out the good deed of the moment, or do something else that is also needed? The example is given by an old story.

It is a parable of two men walking along a narrow mountain path. Suddenly one man stumbles and slips over the edge of the abyss. He stays there, hanging over the abyss, holding himself only with his trembling hands. Without doubt, this can last only some seconds, not more; then he will fall. The other man recognises at once the right moral of the moment, and the only deed that can be significant just now: to extend his hand to the falling man, in order to help him. But it is dangerous, in all probability they will fall both; there will be two corpses instead of one. Still the other man holds out his hand, only he does so a second or two later, when the man over the abyss is already going to fall and can hardly seize the helping hand. Now, the willing helper is safe. One man falls into the abyss because there was no remedy to avoid it, the other stays alive.

How could we analyse the helper's behaviour in this situation? He unmistakably recognised the only moral thing he had to do – to offer his hand to another in trouble. So he did. He did it in order to show it to God who sees everything and in whom he perhaps believes, or to show it to the falling man as the last sign of mercy, or in order to convince himself that, as a human being, he is willing to act properly. Offering his hand was an evidence for that. Yet he did it belatedly. And what is more important, he did it consciously (or half-consciously) belatedly, in order to save his own life. He acted deliberately with a minimal belatedness and instead of a good deed, only a sign of it remained. Which means that he stayed within the boundaries of a system. Or simply, he was safe.

Most likely, in a similar situation a fair number of people would behave in quite the same way as the man in the mountains did. His companion on the edge of the abyss had no big chances any more – this was, unfortunately, true. In all probability, the helping man, when accomplishing his morally significant deed, might have killed himself as well. Two corpses instead of one, is this a morally more perfect result? And perhaps the helping man was married and had little children at home, so his first moral duty was to stay alive. Perhaps he was not even allowed to risk his life and we must evaluate his lack of doing as a morally brave deed?

The only weak point in this reasoning is that the first spontaneous idea of the man in the mountains was to help his brother in arms, to help him immediately and really. He knew he must do it. And this argument is watertight. Psychologists in their professional language say that when the time to cognitively control the first moral response is lacking, the likelihood of deontological response increases (Suter, Hertwig 2011: 457), which roughly means that our first instinctive reactions in problematic situations do not maximise a good outcome, but rather follow some 'non-profit' moral rule.

You may think I am imagining an extreme case here because it ends with a dramatic death. However, it is not impossible that the situation reflects – pointedly, of course – our often typical everyday behaviour: to produce the signs of willingness rather than the deeds themselves, that is, to do things a bit earlier or a bit later than the right, and often dangerous, moment. The difference between a moral sign and a moral deed is exactly time: signs appear before and after the deed, they are untimely – too soon, or belated. Signs stand for the missing part of life, as I said already, they appear 'before' and 'after'. In the middle of existence, one faces something unpredictable. Signs anticipate good deeds (which means that they also avoid them) and they ask forgiveness for not having done them. To feel sorry about something, to express regret at something, to warn against something, to ask pardon for something – these are unavoidable elements of our civilised human lifestyle. There is no reason to mock them. Some thinkers, like the above-mentioned Vladimir Jankélévitch, value forgiveness as an essential part of normal social life. It is worth keeping in mind, however, that each request for forgiveness is a signifier of some good deed left undone. Feeling regret, or asking for forgiveness, are signs of our willingness to do something good, and at the same time, of our inability to do it in a real way.

I run over my main statements up to now. First, time is a decisive factor in defining a (morally) significant deed; this deed is to be done in due time, not earlier or later. Secondly, 'in due time', 'at the right moment', etc., these are not ontological, or theological, or ethnographic concepts, but the realities of our subjective consciousness; on many occasions we recognise quite well the right moment for a particular deed, or the right deed for this particular moment. Thirdly, although we recognise the right moment, we often act untimely or belatedly, too early or too late. Instead of a significant deed at the height of the right moment, we produce a sign of it before or afterwards.

Why do we miss the right moment so often?

We want to stay alive, to feel safe and satisfied and undisturbed. A significant deed is at least uncomfortable, embarrassing, unpleasant, but it can be terrifying or dangerous as well. You need to be brave to perform it. It breaks the routine every time one gets in touch with it. While doing good you are always risking your present lifestyle.

A good deed, like a magic word, binds. If the man in the mountains offers his hand immediately, the two men will remain fatally bound. If one of them falls, the other will fall with him; if they are saved, they'll remain together as friends forever. How nice it is to say 'I love' before real passion overcomes you. And how difficult it is to bring forth something fundamental in the heart of the hurricane when the words simply will not come. The magic word is left unsaid so often because nobody knows what will come after that: maybe the fall into the abyss; in any case, a fatal connection until death, and beyond. Paradoxically, one cannot sell good deeds, one buys them, and pays a high price for them.

Even more interesting than our emotions of self-defence is that there are always rational weapons with which to fight against the good deed. Different morals standing side by side, fight for the right to represent the good deed of the moment: family moral, working moral, Christian moral, etc. These are all 'good' morals, aiming at the better lot for mankind, which only complicates the situation further. Because they prefer decisions in contradicting directions. Take the accident in the mountains: from the viewpoint of family morals, the helping man's behaviour was impeccable. At the same time, we suspect him to be a coward. Which means that there are other morals which do not approve of his behaviour.

There is a well-known novel by the grand master of horror fiction Stephen King titled *It* (1986); the work was turned into a film by Tommy Lee Wallace in 1990. A group of children in a little American town decide to fight against some evil principle called It. It appears in the costume of a clown and offers bright balloons to children, killing them afterwards. We can surmise that It is a collective projection of childish fears. It comes back every 30 years to find its victims in the new generation, especially, the children who fear the most. At first, the aforementioned group of children seems to be successful in keeping It away, and they swear to one another that when It returns, in the future, they will come together anew to fight against it. Now 30 years have gone and one of the members of this group still living in the old hometown calls up the others: come together immediately, It is back. The guys are all 40 years old now, living in various places in the United States, or in England. And now they must leave their homes, their life companions, their work at once, without saying why and for how long. They made a promise 30 years ago, so they must keep it. There are various morals contradicting it, and insisting that they stay at home. For example, there is a man whose wife is heavily pregnant. Of course, he is afraid to leave his home – but it is scary to stay as well. Ten minutes later, his wife finds him dead in the bathroom. The men who fear, will die first. Stephen King is not only the number one living horror fiction author in the world but a great moralist as well. Although the man in his novel knew that it was highly advisable to stay at home beside his pregnant wife, he still felt that when doing so he was acting falsely. That's why he died, according to the will of Stephen King.

The accident in the mountains I told you about had a much milder outcome: the man who refused, stayed alive. At any rate, the conflict in the stories is the same between the two 'good' morals, one of them original, instinctive, natural, the other an emotional or intellectual re-interpretation of it.

Avoiding the good deed might also save your life, that's true. Perhaps it is often 'practical' to act belatedly. One of the most famous teachers of mankind, Balthasar Gracián, writes in *The Art of Worldly Wisdom* (*El oráculo manual y arte de prudencia*, 1647; translated into Estonian by Jüri Talvet in 1993): "It's a sign of a noble heart dowered with patience, never to be in a hurry, never to be in a passion. First be master over yourself if you would be master over others. You must pass through the circumference of time before arriving at the centre of opportunity. A wise reserve seasons the aims and matures the means. Time's crutch effects more than the iron club of Hercules. God Himself chasteneth not with a rod but with time. He [= Charles V] spake a great word who said, 'Time and I against any two.' Fortune herself rewards waiting with the first prize." (Gracian 1904: 32–33) This is not an apology of plain immoralism; we can take it for an explication of the wise ambivalent intuition of the man in the mountains. What has been said about belatedness, is valid when speaking of acting too early as well; in this case the fact of fleeing from the responsibility, or anticipating the situation of responsible action, is sometimes even more obvious.

Precisely this very human ability to miss the right moment, to act in an anticipatory or belated manner, to postpone the significant deed and make a remarkable sign of it instead – this is the great source of all psychological fiction. And the great problem of our everyday lives as well. I mind the situations where the right choice is immediately recognised, and still postponed. When I urgently feel that I must go just now and play with my children, just now and not later, because *vita brevis est*, life is short, and we shall all die tomorrow some day, and if I – in this situation – open the window (not the door!) and shout: "Dear children, tomorrow we shall play together all day, not now!", then, at this very moment, I am missing my good deed for today, although I give a willing sign of it. The problem is not described as "to do or not to do", but rather as "to do, or to give a sign of doing something". It seems to us that a positive sign of a particular deed is not a negation of the deed just because it is positive. Actually, it is a negation, especially in the situations where the robust deed, and not the sympathetic sign, is urgently needed.

Let us look at the situation in the mountains once more, a parable of two men, one of them falling but hanging still some seconds over the abyss. From the standpoint of art and literature, several typological variants can be described.

First: the second man looks at the event indifferently or even enjoys it, says something ironic, turns his back towards the sinking man, or even clicks his fingers. This is the paradigm of sadistic psychology. You can come across this kind of episode on almost every page in Marquis de Sade and his followers, but occasionally, of course, in other types of texts as well when malevolent figures are characterised.

Another variant: the second man is in terror, crying, weeping, flinging his arms, etc., but daring not to help his friend in the fear of falling into the abyss himself (and he feels right). This you can call the paradigm of animal psychology although I do not want to hint at any animal. Dramatic scenes of this kind we can find masses of in thrillers, but in realistic novels as well.

In the third case, the second man behaves like a hero: without hesitating, he attempts to help his friend, risking his life and offering his hand. This is the paradigm of heroic psychology, no matter how it ends, with one corps, two corpses, or zero corpses because heroism is a power in itself. The outcome can be a tragedy or a James Bond story.

One can guess that there is a paradigm of some absurdist psychology as well. For example, the second man, when observing that his companion is going to fall, jumps himself into the abyss to be the first corpse at the bottom.

So you can stage the dramatic event in the mountains in different psychological paradigms and try various stylistic systems. I still insist that the psychologically mature effect can be achieved mostly only then, when the second man is behaving in such a way as depicted at the beginning: holding out his hand to help his friend – but with an almost unnoticed shift in time. I do not want to underestimate other aesthetic solutions. But if speaking of grown-up human psychology, only this type of behaviour will satisfy the highest demands of art. And therefore I call it simply the paradigm of human psychology. This cannot lead to the simplistic conclusion that in every psychological novel or movie there is a belatedly stretched-out hand somewhere in the background. In any case, it is a kernel motif of all psychological fiction.

One of the great plays of all time is Samuel Beckett's *Krapp's Last Tape* (1958). In this little text of twelve pages, an old and unsuccessful writer, Krapp, is listening to a tape with the recordings of his own life told by himself: Krapp at sixty-nine is listening to Krapp at thirty-nine summarising an event ten or fifteen years earlier. He was lying beside his beloved woman then, on the bottom of a boat floating silently over the waters of some mountain lake. Krapp looked into the eyes of the woman and put his head onto her breast, but did nothing more because he had decided to miss a deed that might appear significant in her eyes, and therefore binding for him. The undoing is marked with a sudden present tense in the telling of the story, as if to make the moment everlasting. "We drifted in among the flags and stuck. The way they went down, sighing, before the stem! (*Pause.*) I lay down across her with my face in her breasts and my hand on her. We lay there without moving. But under us all moved, and moved us, gently, up and down, and from side to side." (Beckett 1984: 44) The boat floated and time flowed, and very soon the significant – everlasting, yet short – moment was over. Many years after this silent event Krapp is listening to the tape again and again, with a growing understanding that after that day, it was not possible for him to be lucky any more. The play seems to be like an archetype of all psychological writing.

This reasoning has its political facet as well. There are two fields of activity where the language of 'befores' and 'afters', of warnings and reproaches, seems to be foregrounded, used and over-used. These are politics and education. Parents, teachers and politicians all warn in advance and blame afterwards. Everybody knows from their personal experience, from sunny childhood above all, that this kind of usage is generally not very binding. It can even be called democratic because one criticises the rules of the Other, but does not violate the Other's private freedom. Befores and afters leave the dangerous 'right moment' out of sight.

Take for example politics. Most professional politicians do not prefer to act 'at the right moment' because it equals abandoning the slang of political correctness and stepping into the realm of uncontrollable, unpredictable consequences. At the right moment, one runs the risk of losing the whole game. The right moment for a good deed can be the right moment for the worst one as well, 'good' and 'bad' are the extremes of the same moral series. The Greek *kairos* designated the omnipotent critical moment which might result either in glory or doom. Every medicine is poison. Remember the accident in the mountains. The moment was not only brilliant to fulfil a good deed but also to do something terrible: the helping man could kick the fingers of his comrade in order to be sure of his falling. Taking it into account, the parents and politicians could be forgiven for their often careful style of handling.

This explains perhaps, why during the last 100 years approximately the advantages of the right moment were often taken by political dictators. I am not speaking only of Hitler and Stalin. They were not scared of treading on that risky ground which the correct politicians, staying within the system of fair play, prefer to avoid – to act at the right moment. Of course, from the democratic point of view, dictators do not hold out their hand to help the man in trouble, they rather crush his fingers. Their successful use of the magic of words can be called irresponsible. However, their courage, or rather, their reckless disregard for the incalculable results, is still worth analysing, even if for one reason: they are able to bind the masses to their person. They are not afraid of being binding. They are not left alone as Krapp was. The people are prone to appreciate leaders who take risks on a razor's edge.

But let us return to good deeds and writers in conclusion. At the beginning of the 1950s, when most Western writers kept silent on the political destiny of the Baltic lands, there remained one courageous voice at the right moment whose message was very clear: Estonia, Latvia and Lithuania are a part of Europe, not of Soviet military pretensions or pipedreams. This was the voice of German author Edzard Schaper, who lived in Estonia before World War II and also married there, a voice barely known today, but one of the most popular prose writers in Germany in the 1950s. His appeal to the Germans for the freedom of the Baltic countries in *Radio Berlin* (1952, published in Schaper 1956: 53–61) is becoming even more and more important as the years go on.

Sometimes there is no need to write or speak at all, even if you are a writer. There are other means to influence the public opinion. The first Estonian president after the Soviet occupation was Lennart Meri, a distinguished man of letters, an author of lyrically conceptualised travelogues. Before he became president in 1992, he worked as the Estonian minister of foreign affaires from 1990 on. During this time, the Estonian delegation led by prime minister Edgar Savisaar and including Lennart Meri, visited the White House in Washington. Estonia had not yet recovered its independence. After the audience with the US president George Bush, probably on October 12, 1990 (Jaakson 2011: 255–256), Meri noticed a magnificent ancient globe nearby, walked over to it, took out his ink pen, and placed an X with it on the spot somewhere in Siberia. Here, he said to president Bush, we can go fishing and catch a really big salmon. The act remained absolutely illogical and incomprehensible in a delicate diplomatic situation. Of course, some people, like writer Mihkel Mutt, who himself was the member of the Estonian delegation then, are of the opinion that Meri said it not to the US president, but to the secretary of state, James Baker.[1] Some stress

[1] According to my private conversation with Mihkel Mutt.

that the ink-marked spot was not in Siberia but on the Kamchatka peninsula, in the Russian Far East. According to another version, Meri defaced the venerable globe of American presidents not only once, but twice: several months later, Meri returned to the Oval Office, this time as the representative of an Estonia that had recovered its independence, walked to the globe – which had been repaired in the meantime – took out his pen and placed an X just where he had before. President Bush laughed, and the friendship was sealed. (Goble 2006). The popular version says president Meri placed an X not only on one spot, but on all spots in Siberian rivers where one can fish well and catch a crab (Raun 2000: 117). In any case, president Meri committed an act of diplomatic vandalism at least once. Yet this kind of "managed indiscretion", as Paul Goble labels the tricks Meri was often fond of (Goble 1999), was absolutely the best at this very moment a politician could do for the sake of his regenerating land, Estonia.

The right moments for good deeds happen all the time, every day. A good deed is not necessarily a major deed – and not all major deeds are necessarily good ones. A good deed is done in due time, at the right moment, that's all. We recognise the right moral for the moment almost infallibly. A good deed is the deed we are just waiting for – one must simply be the first to do it. Be simply the first to risk some good with unexpected results.

Jaan Undusk
jaan@utkk.ee
Eesti Teaduste Akadeemia Underi ja Tuglase Kirjanduskeskus
Roosikrantsi 6
10119 Tallinn
EESTI / ESTONIA

References

Beckett, S. 1984. *The Collected Shorter Plays*. New York: Grove Press.

Goble, P. A. 1999. The managed indiscretions of Lennart Meri. – *Eesti maailmas 21. sajandi künnisel. Eesti Vabariigi presidendi Lennart Meri 70. sünnipäevale pühendatud konverentsi kogumik*. Tartu: Tartu Ülikooli Kirjastus, 13–22.

Goble, P. A. 2006. *Estonia: The 'Managed Indiscretions' of Lennart Meri*. – http://www.rferl.org/content/article/1066680.html (01.08.2015).

Gracian, B. 1904. *The Art of Worldly Wisdom*. Trans. J. Jacobs. London: Macmillan and Co.

Jaakson, E. 2011. *Eestile. (Eesti mälu, 48)*. Tallinn – Tartu: Eesti Päevaleht – Akadeemia.

Jankélévitch, V. 1998. Le Pardon. – V. Jankélévitch, *Philosophie morale*. Éd. F. Schwab. Paris: Flammarion, 997–1149.

Levinas, E. 1947. Le Temps et l'Autre. – *Le choix. Le monde. L'existence: Cahiers du Collège Philosophique*. Grenoble – Paris: B. Arthaud, 125–196.

Raun, O. 2000. *Test*. Tallinn: SE&JS.
Schaper, E. 1956. *Untergang und Verwandlung. Betrachtungen und Reden*. Berlin: Ullstein Bücher.
Suter, R. S., Hertwig, R. 2011. Time and moral judgement. – *Cognition*, vol. 119, 454–458.

Against Cultural Imperialism: World Literature, Comparative Literature, and 'Generalism'

LIISA STEINBY

Abstract. In contrast to what is commonly thought, modern, historical literary studies were not originally restricted to a national – even less, nationalist – perspective, but already in Herder and Goethe we find the idea of a world community of literatures. Nevertheless, in the course of the nineteenth century literary studies narrowed to the study of literature in national frames. This approach was contested only after WWII, when some seminal works, such as those of Auerbach and Curtius, established the unity of European literature. In the end-of-the-twentieth-century discussion concerning the globalisation of culture, the Eurocentrism of Comparative Literature was criticized and a study of world literature in the broad sense of the word called for. However, the approaches emphasizing globalisation, (post)colonialism, multiculturalism, marginalization etc. are themselves criticized for a cultural imperialism in the manner how theoretical concepts are imposed on the subject of study. The question how to face world literature as a whole is given different answers of which Moretti's and Damrosch' are here briefly discussed. At the end of the article, an approach is proposed which stresses the necessity of developing theoretical concepts in close contact with the subject of study. The synthetic view on the subject enabled by such concepts results however in a merely elliptic presentation of the whole.

Keywords: World Literature, Comparative Literature, 'generalism', Herder, Goethe, Auerbach, Curtius, Damrosch

That we live in an era of cultural globalisation is obvious. What this actually means, however, is contestable: it can mean an unprecedented uniformity of culture, in which (American) commercial popular culture has attained global domination (cf. Moser 2013: 161); or it can mean an inconceivable plurality of different cultures and sub-cultures, which now have entered the global cultural scene.[1] We may ask what these two alternatives would mean for the discipline of Comparative Literature – or, as it is called in Estonia, 'world literature'. The

[1] To avoid a concept of globalisation connected to capitalism and cultural uniformity, Gayatri Spivak suggests replacing the term with 'planetarity'; cf. Spivak 2003: 72.

DOI: http://dx.doi.org/10.12697/IL.2015.S1.3

former would mean that literary scholarship would lose its identity as one of the central humanist disciplines and turn into a sociology of marketing and consumption, possibly with an ideology-critical intention, while under the latter the field of literature to be studied would suddenly have expanded to encompass an uncountable number of diverse literatures, a plethora which we cannot possibly encompass as a single whole. It is as though we were being punished for our imposture in claiming to be studying world literature: now we cannot avoid facing the fact that what we have called 'world literature' was in practice merely a few European (and American) literatures. It is as though we were now being taken at our word and proffered the literature of the whole world as an object of study.

How to deal with this situation? Today almost every literature department embraces scholars whose subject of study are non-European – African and Asian – literatures, from countries which define their cultural identity through their colonial past and postcolonial present. This is just part of the diversification of the subject of study, since today the emphasis is often on the literatures of different sub-cultures or local cultures, rather than on the 'great' authors and the development of national literatures (in relation to each other). How does this expansion and diversification of the scope of study change the practices of Comparative Literature? This discipline originally developed from the same root as national philologies, which means that command of the language of the target culture was a *sine qua non* of the study. Now 'world literature', rather than referring to a few European and American literatures, comprises a great magnitude of different languages and cultures; how do we deal with the basic requirement of linguistic proficiency for the scientific study of literature? This question arises at a time when we are witnessing, in the United States in particular but in European universities as well, an alarming decline in students' interest in learning any foreign language (except English), to the point that foreign languages departments are being closed or are operating with a reduced programme as parts of a larger unit.

We can start by asking how the new concept of world literature is related to the original idea, as developed in the thinking of Herder and Goethe. Moreover, this is not the first time that comparative literature is said to be in crisis; rather, throughout its existence as an academic discipline it has struggled to define its specific approach. I am therefore also inquiring into the history of the discipline, asking specifically whether the great 'classics' of Comparative Literature, Erich Auerbach and Ernst Robert Curtius, offer a possible model to be heeded in the comparative study of literature. In the last section of the article, I briefly discuss David Damrosch's redefinition of World Literature, as a phenomenon and a field of research intended to replace Comparative Literature.

Herder and Goethe on world literature and the comparative study of literature

We are used to thinking that the comparative study of literature emerged later than the study of national literatures, which started during the period of Romanticism around 1800. This is true insofar as the study of national literatures was established at European universities (and in the United States) during the nineteenth century, while in the case of comparative literature this took place only after World War II (cf. Solte-Gresser 2013; Gymnich 2013; Zymber 2013). The comparing, transnational approach, however, in fact emerged as part of the new, literary-historical way of thinking at the end of the eighteenth century. The modern, historical study of literature, whose founding father is Johann Gottfried Herder (cf. e.g. Lempicki 1968: 360), was born in the context of the comparison of literatures and cultures (cf. May 1969; Gossens 2011: 54–56). Herder was also the first to develop the idea of a world literature, which is more comprehensible than the main tradition of European literature, although he does not use this term (cf. Gillies 1931–33; Gossens 2011: 62). Herder claimed that valuable literature – oral or written – is found among all peoples, and that everywhere it has a unique character. This conception contested and soon replaced the traditional view of classical European literature as providing the universal measure of excellence (cf. Casanova 2004: 75–81).

Herder's claim is that languages, cultures and literatures have developed differently under different geographical and social circumstances. Poetry (or literature, *Dichtung*) expresses the lived world of a culture and a period: it is through its poetic imagery that a culture understands itself. The literary scholar is invited to become acquainted with this world by learning the language, becoming well versed in the literature and contextualising it in its circumstances. By so doing, (s)he helps the poets and the literary public in his or her native country to gain access to foreign works of literature, leading to the enrichment of literature in the scholar's own country (e.g., Herder 1985: 187).

One method in Herder's historical and contextualising approach is comparison (cf., e.g. Herder 1985). For example, he compares Greek and German epigram writers, trying to pin down the peculiar character of each of them (Herder 1994). The comparison extends from the details of rhythm, metre, and imagery to comparisons of cultures and eras, which, however, he does not see as monolithic but as internally diversified and open to mutual influence. Most of the literatures which Herder discusses are European – including the folk poetry of peoples who lack a written literature, such as the Serbs and the Finns –, but one of his main works is a comprehensive study of the Old Testament as poetry (*Vom Geist der Ebräischen Poesie*, 1782–83). (This is a particularly interesting work for the modern reader, since in it the lived world of the ancient Hebrews, in which religion held a central place, is featured as created by Hebrew poets on the basis of the natural and social living conditions of the people. This means that the Old Testament is claimed to consist not of the words of God but of those of the Hebrew poets, who have also themselves created the image of God; cf. Steinby (in press).) When Herder remarks that Greco-Roman poetics does not suit the study of the poetry of the Old Testament (e.g., Herder 1993: 1194–1196), he is explicitly leaving Eurocentric thinking behind. Another example of Herder's critique of Eurocentrism is his faulting of Winckelmann, the scholar of Greek art whom he greatly admired, for representing Greek art as though it were without precedent, ignoring its roots in Egyptian culture (Herder 1984: 221). Herder's collection of folk poetry likewise includes examples from other than European countries. His conception of literature is thus not confined to the European literatures but is in principle global, or transnational (cf. Gossens 2011: 49–62). In practice, it is our knowledge of languages that sets the limits for our profound understanding of another culture.

The Romantic literary histories written on this new basis were initially, in the works of the brothers Schlegel (August Wilhelm Schlegel's *Über dramatische Kunst und Litteratur,* 1809–1811; Friedrich Schlegel's *Geschichte der alten und der neuen Litteratur,* 1815), comprehensive, encompassing the history of the most important European literatures from antiquity to the present; in addition, Friedrich Schlegel was one of the pioneers of the study of Sanskrit in Europe. By the middle of the nineteenth century, however, the normal form of literary history was the history of the literature of a single nation. Both the transnational and the national study of literature thus have their origin in Herder. In the nineteenth century the latter became overwhelmingly more important, since it chimed in with the political nationalism emerging during and after the Napoleonic wars. As is well known in Northern Europe, literature became a particularly important part of the identity construction of small nations striving for political self-determination, such as the Finns and the Estonians.

Along with Herder, Goethe has been named as a founding father both of comparative literature (cf. e.g. Guillén 1993: 40; Said 2004: 95) and of the transnational view of literature (cf. e.g. Pizer 2000: 214). From the 1770s onward, Goethe heeded Herder's ideas of an anticlassicist poetry, and acknowledged Herder as the most important instigator of the rise of historical thinking in Germany (cf. Nisbet 1993: 116). Early on, Goethe had adopted Herder's view of poetry as a possession belonging to all peoples and cultures. His interest in non-European cultures is displayed, for example, in his *West-östlicher Divan* (1819), written in imitation of the fourteenth-century Persian poet Hafiz.

The idea of a 'world literature' appears for the first time in Goethe's conversation with Eckermann on 31 January 1827. Goethe says that in his vision the time of national literatures has now passed by: we are at the threshold of the era of world literature, and it is now our duty to hasten its coming.[2] He says this after describing to Eckermann a Chinese novel he has just been reading. This, he says, is merely a small part of the valuable literature of China. Nevertheless, he also says that ancient Greek literature remains the paragon of literature (ibid.). Although Goethe introduces the notion of 'world literature' in a context that makes it clear that he is not thinking merely of Europe, there are notes of his in which he equates world literature with European literature (cf., e.g., Goethe 1999: 500). The context in which he introduces the idea is different from that in which Herder had developed it following the 1760s: the 1820s were an era of political nationalism. Goethe refused to engage in nationalist activities or to see literature as a means of nationalist politics (cf. Weber 1977: 541–554). In first speaking to Eckermann of the idea of world literature, Goethe was referring primarily to the building of connections among authors in different (European?) countries, which is facilitated by new, increasingly rapid forms of communication (Eckermann s.a. 180; cf. also, e.g., Birus 1995). In a wider sense, however, the notion refers to the (Herderian) idea of literature as a universal possession and treasure of humanity, an idea that comprises both an acknowledgement of the endless diversity of literature and our participation in the same humanity (*Humanität*; cf. Gillies 1931–33: 63–67; Birus 1995: 17, 23).

Conceiving of literature both as a transnational, global phenomenon and simultaneously as nationally, historically, generically and individually variable, and considering it as bound to the language and the lived world of a culture, are thus fundamental elements of Herder's and Goethe's view of literature. Literature is approached by acquiring a knowledge of the language and of the cultural and historical context. At the turn of the millennium, comparative research has in some respects meant a return to these views, in opposition to national and biographical – and more recently 'text-immanent' (and deconstructivist) – approaches to literature.

2 *"National-Literatur will jetzt nicht viel sagen, die Epoche der Welt-Literatur ist an der Zeit und jeder muß jetzt dazu wirken, diese Epoche zu beschleunigen."* Eckermann s.a. 180.

Against nationalism: the problems in Auerbach and Curtius as a paradigm for comparative study of literature

Herder had seen in the European states of his time primarily a mechanical, repressive apparatus, and perceived a cleft between the people's cultural creativity and the coercion practiced by the rulers (cf. e.g. Herder 1989: 333–4; Barnard 1964: 84–86). In the nineteenth century, literary history was commonly conflated with the aims of political nationalism. The philologies of the modern European languages and literatures were established alongside classical philology. The approach was in principle similar to that in classical philology: the texts were scrutinised with respect to language, content, author and context. In practice, the biographical approach was emphasised more than in classical philology. The comparative, transnational approach found its place in the universities much later. Its institutionalisation began in France and Switzerland, where the first Chairs of Comparative Literature were set up in the second half of the nineteenth century (cf. Solte-Gresser 2013: 25). In French comparativism, the focus was on individual authors or literary phenomena and their reception in another national literature, meaning, as Claudio Guillén has remarked, that this study was based on a national literature as the primary unit (Guillén 1993: 47). Departments of Comparative Literature were generally established in Europe and the United States only after World War II. In the United States in particular, these departments soon became the cradles of theoretical and methodical discussion concerning the study of literature in general (cf. e.g. Gymnich 2013: 32–34). While Comparative Literature in the United States was originally oriented towards (West-)European literatures, from the 1970s onward the target area expanded so as to cover non-European literatures too, as well as the literatures of hybrid, marginal or multicultural groups (ibid. 33–34).

The rise of Comparative Literature in the 1950s took place in a historical situation in which nationalist politics in Europe had ended in catastrophe. German nationalism had destroyed half of Europe and had made the whole idea of European culture questionable. It is no coincidence that the rise of Comparative Literature is connected with anti-nationalism, and that among its founding fathers are three German Romanists: Leo Spitzer, Erich Auerbach and Ernst Robert Curtius. Spitzer and Auerbach had to leave National Socialist Germany, and after a period in Istanbul they ended up in the United States, where they contributed crucially to the creation of Comparative Literature (cf., e.g., Apter 2006: 47). All three demanded a literary scholarship that transcended national boundaries; the perspective was primarily a pan-European one – which is in accord with the view that nationalism was a particularly European phenomenon – although in Istanbul Spitzer broadened his view to include Turkology as well (cf. Apter 2006: 27, 46–56). Spitzer was a scholar of style, who in his essays proceeded from linguistic and stylistic traits to deep cultural meanings, but who never wrote a comprehensive, synthesising study (cf. Spitzer 1928, 1948). Auerbach and Curtius, in contrast, have become renowned in far wider circles than those of Romanists alone through their monumental works, which have set an example for transnational literary study. Auerbach's *Mimesis: Dargestellte Wirklichkeit in der abendländischen Literatur* (1946) demonstrated for a wide audience what a comprehensive comparative study can achieve, while Curtius' *Europäische Literatur und lateinisches Mittelalter* (1948) was most influential in the German-speaking countries, where it gave rise to the study of literary topoi. Both works, like Spitzer's stylistic studies, follow the philological method; but the remarkable differences between the works show that there are many versions of this method. In what follows I briefly discuss Auerbach's and Curtius' works, to determine the extent to which these milestones of comparative study can be taken as methodological models.

Auerbach's *Mimesis* comprises twenty chronologically ordered chapters, ranging from Homer and the Old Testament to the author's own time. The development of European literature is followed through the analysis of exemplary texts derived from Greek, Hebrew, Latin, Italian, Spanish, French, English and German literature from different centuries; Auerbach regrets not being able to include Russian literature in his study, as he does not know Russian (Auerbach 1967a: 459). The method in each chapter is to start with a fragment of the exemplary text, which is analysed down to its linguistic and stylistic details; the scope is then broadened by references to other texts so as to cover the whole picture of the literary period, thus opening up the world as seen in that particular culture. The theme which Auerbach follows in particular is the representation of reality, giving some scholars cause to view him as a participant in the debate over the nature of realism (cf. Wellek 1954). He distinguishes in the representation of reality between two lines crisscrossing in Western literature: the separation of styles according to topic (*Stiltrennung*) and the mixing of styles (*Stilmischung*). In the Greco-Roman tradition, and in the classical tradition which adhered to it, the tragic and the comic were kept apart, and certain kinds of characters and events were considered fitting only to one of these: people of humble origin or otherwise inferior belong to comic genres, while those of noble origin or of superior character have their place in tragic or serious genres (cf. Aristotle 1448a). In the tradition of the mixed style, which Auerbach traces back to the Old Testament, anyone can be spoken of in either comic or tragic tone – or both. For Auerbach, the latter obviously means recognition of the fundamental equality of human beings. The motive behind *Mimesis* was apparently not only to show that national borders are of minor importance in

European literature – which despite its great variability and profound historical change is a single whole –, but also to emphasise human equality, which of course was a most topical theme in a Europe overshadowed by National Socialism.

Auerbach's method can be called philological, if we interpret this in a broad sense: comprising the ability to take into account everything, from linguistic details to the cultural and social world of the era (cf. Saariluoma 1993). But does Auerbach in this work provide a methodological example for comparative literature to follow? I think that we have two reasons to answer in the negative. First, Auerbach does not define any method that would bring us from textual fragments to the very broad conclusions he attains. He of course argues for his conclusions using textual analysis and comparisons to other texts, but in a manner that implies the availability of an extraordinary amount of knowledge. For example, when he talks about the *Chanson de Roland,* he does not actually derive everything from the text fragment analysed, but makes use of his vast knowledge of the literature, culture and society of the period. It is true that this is how a philologist works; but this procedure cannot be reduced to any set of defined methodical rules, the following of which would ensure coming to the same conclusions that he does. The second problem in seeing *Mimesis* as a methodological model is its exceptional character as a philological study, to which Auerbach refers in the epilogue. He states that he wrote the book in Istanbul, where he did not have the relevant secondary literature available; therefore he does not follow the normal practice of due reference to the sources used. He also thinks that under normal conditions he would probably never have written the book, since the topic is far too vast for a study which takes into consideration all relevant secondary materials (Auerbach 1967a: 518). Thus the work that to many of us appears as a paragon of comparative literature is paradoxically an anomaly, born under exceptional conditions; an anomaly that because of the lack of the normal reference practices could be even considered unscientific.

Several of Auerbach's individual analyses have been criticised, but this has not shaken the classic status of *Mimesis.* Facing the problem of how such an enormous topic as world literature in the era of globalisation can be addressed – a topic far exceeding even European literature in scope (cf., e.g., Damrosch 2003: 111; Moretti 2013: 48–49, 65–70) –, we may ask how Auerbach succeeded in combining a vastness of scope with a sensitivity to the unique character of a particular text. He posed the question in an essay, suggesting that due to the immensity of the material a historical synthesis is possible only intuitively; or rather, that the principle (*Ansatzpunkt*) followed in a synthesising presentation is found by intuition (Auerbach 1967b: 306). In *Mimesis,* such principles are the representation of reality, the separation of styles, and the concept of the figura, which Auerbach introduces in his analysis of Dante's *Divina commedia* (cf. Auerbach 1967a: 515–6). These are all found in the subject of study itself: Auerbach is convinced that general concepts borrowed from others and developed in another context cannot lead to a profound understanding of the subject (1967b: 309). Auerbach does not consider his view of synthesis in relation to the Herderian and Early Romantic concepts of fragment and totality, although his concept shows an affinity with their views: he demands a synthesis which comprises the whole field (cf. 1967b: 306), although such a synthesis is necessarily elliptic.

Curtius was allowed to continue his work in Nazi Germany, but his *Europäische Literatur und lateinisches Mittelalter* is a protest against a study of literature and culture confined to the scope of a single nation only. European literature is one, and ancient and modern literatures are connected by a shared medieval Latin literature; Curtius is convinced that national philologies go astray when they disregard this common basis (Curtius 1973: 22). He says that he uses analytical methods (229) or "philological microscopy" (235) in revealing this common foundation, or rather common trunk. What, then, does this common foundation consist of? Latin was throughout the Middle Ages the language of education and the Church; from this shared cultural tradition derive a great number of shared forms of thought and verbal presentation, which survive and continue through the centuries. Curtius addresses rhetoric as the most important channel through which a great number not only of literary forms, but also of topics – unvarying, fixed ideas, which he calls topoi, appropriate for use in different connections – have been transferred from antiquity to modernity; Curtius wishes to create a basis for the scholarship of topoi (*Toposforschung*; 92). Such topoi include, for example, the portrayal of the hero as strong and wise (176–190), an idyllic ideal landscape (191–209) and the use of the metaphor of a book when speaking of the 'reading' of someone's countenance, of the human mind, or of nature (306–352). The reader, however, may doubt whether Curtius succeeds by such means in demonstrating the unity of European literature. Does the recurrence of certain modes of presentation, or the continuous presence of certain topoi from ancient through medieval to modern literature, suffice to prove its unity? These recurring elements certainly do not prove that European literature remained essentially the same through the millennia. Curtius operates with details; his method of approaching European literature can be called episodic or erratic. As such, it is insufficient as a method for the comparative study of literature.

Curtius' research nevertheless brought new perspectives to the study of literature, not only with its pan-European thesis but also through his linking of literature back to education and learnt modes of literary expression. He is convinced that new content and forms are produced in a culture far more seldom than we customarily think (395) – we can add: more seldom than Herder and expressivist aesthetics after him supposed. Curtius shows the author as being far less autonomous than Herder assumed, indeed in a shape that seems familiar to us who live in a post-Foucauldian era. We can also say that Curtius paved the way for the study of recurring elements in texts, such as has been carried out exemplarily in the New Historicism.

From specialist to generalist? Damrosch's 'world literature' as a new form of American cultural imperialism

The reader of *Handbuch Komparatistik: Theorien, Arbeitsfelder, Wissenspraxis* from 2013, edited by Rüdiger Zymner and Achim Hölter, is soon convinced of the point the editors mention at the beginning (Zymner & Hölter 2013b: 1–2): that there is no method or theory applicable solely and specifically to comparative literature (cf. also Bernheimer 1995a: 2), but that the appropriate theoretical and methodological approaches are in fact the same as in the study of literature in general. The different approaches presented in the book are familiar to all scholars of literature. Some recent issues and phenomena, however, such as postcolonial, multicultural, migrant and hybrid literatures, concern comparative literature in particular, or at least constitute a challenge to national literary studies. I do not intend to discuss here what each of these could mean from the perspective of the comparative study of literature (cf., e.g., Gillespie 1995; Schmeling et al. 2000; Zymner & Hölter 2013a: 145–262). I confine myself to a brief discussion of what this broadening of scope, to encompass not only Europe and the Americas but Africa and Asia as well – in principle, the whole world –, means for comparative literature. In particular I discuss David Damrosch's suggestion as to how, by revising the concept of world literature and creating a new programme based on it, a programme obviously meant to replace the 'old' comparative literature, we can solve the problem arising from the immensity of materials.

The Goethean origin of the concept of 'world literature' has often been mentioned in criticising comparative literature for its Eurocentrism, starting in the 1970s. The broadening of scope took place under very different political and cultural circumstances compared to the rise of comparative literature as against national literatures in the work of a Spitzer, Auerbach or Curtius in the 1940s. While they took the philological approach for granted in widening the scope of study, at the turn of the millennium we are in a situation in which a common requirement in literary studies is to approach the topic using specific theoretical and methodical concepts; the scholar is supposed to choose his or her conceptual apparatus from among a relatively wide range of theories currently considered applicable. Some of these theories, such as those of postcolonialism, hybridity and multiculturalism, have been developed particularly for the new situation. But do these theories in fact furnish the scholar with a workable toolkit – or more than one – for dealing with world literature?

The weakness of such theoretical toolkits becomes obvious at every conference that brings together literary scholars from different corners of the world. It soon becomes apparent that regardless of the topic, which might be from any literature, they all speak the same language of literary theory; they all apply the theories of some of about forty theoretical gurus of that decade – Foucault, Bakhtin, Derrida, Bhaba, Said or some of the thirty-five others. The encounter of different cultures and literatures is endangered or made impossible when any literature whatsoever is set within the hegemonic framework of a theory – notwithstanding the extent to which the intention of that theory is to deconstruct existing hegemonic structures. Dorothy Figueira (2013: 198) writes of (American) postcolonial studies that they are practiced by scholars who do not know the language of the target literature and who have only a superficial knowledge of the target culture. Instead of investigating the culture from the vantage point of that culture, these scholars repeat familiar conceptions, highlighting the demand for tolerance and the target subjects' subdued position. Again and again the scholar demonstrates that power is unevenly distributed and certain groups are marginalised, and continues deconstructing metaphysical presuppositions – instead of analysing the variety of contents and forms found in the literary works (199; similarly Siebers 1995: 198; Gillespie 1995). Christian Moser (2013: 161–162) claims that in literary study carried out from a perspective of globalisation, the target is mostly severed from its context and placed in a simplifying global context; he poses as a desideratum a form of research that takes into account the diversity of literatures and literary works, at the same time that they are seen in a global connection. This critique of literary studies adopting a perspective of postcolonialism or globalisation naturally does not concern these approaches alone, but any approach that gives preference to theoretical constructions and underrates the complexity of the particular literary phenomenon. It merely seems to be the case that the challenge of globalisation makes visible the inadequacy of any theoretical approach – despite the fact that theories tend to present themselves as universally valid.

According to Franco Moretti, those of us engaged in literary studies cannot deny that the object of our research comprises the literature of the whole world, and he asks how a whole of this magnitude can be the subject of scholarship (Moretti 2013: 45). He envisages the era of text analysis as now past. To be able to perceive any pattern in the immense mass of global literature, we have to look at it from a distance, mediated by special studies by other scholars who offer a general characterisation of a phenomenon; our task then is to proceed at even higher levels of abstractions, in order to identify general trends in literature (48–49). The question that arises, then, is of course whether this kind of further generalising on the basis of the generalisations of others can be called the study of literature at all. In his different writings Moretti suggests various ways of modelling the development of literature: for instance by means of a sociological 'world-systems theory' (the concept derives from Immanuel Wallerstein; cf. Moretti 2013: 43), or more traditionally, using the metaphor of the tree or wave, of which he considers the former better suited for modelling the 'organic' development of national literatures and the latter for describing transnational phenomena ('currents') (60–61). He also presents quantitative and 'topographic' descriptions of literary phenomena: graphs, maps and trees (Moretti 2007). There is no indication that Moretti is able to prove that his methods can be used to reveal important phenomena in the development of literature, any more than previous quantitative approaches that were introduced to raise the level of 'scientificity' of literary studies (for a critique of Moretti, cf., e.g., Arac 2002).

Likewise, David Damrosch proposes, in his *What is World Literature* (2003), a solution to the problem of how to deal with the unfathomable amount of literature produced all over the world. The solution is a redefinition of world literature: world literature is not the sum of all local or national literatures, nor even the most significant part of it, but is now "all literary works that circulate beyond their culture of origin, either in translation or in their original language" (4). At one blow, the requirement of knowledge of the language of the target literature is abolished: 'world literature' is no longer all literatures in their original contexts but literature in the new context into which it has been imported. Damrosch acknowledges that this means that every culture has its own 'world literature', comprising those works that originate from another culture but 'circulate' in this one, and he admits that he is speaking only of his own, i.e. 'foreign' literature in English in the United States. He pays no attention to the question of how this principle of the plurality of 'world literatures' will affect the global perspective on literature. In practice, his stand means that a scholar in the United States need not bother with any discussion elsewhere: he or she can focus merely on what a work of foreign literature means in its contemporary American context.

Damrosch avows that knowledge concerning the original context is useful for an understanding of 'world literature', but the extent of this knowledge is "less than is needed for a full contextual understanding of a work within its home tradition. [...] To read Bei Dao's poems in English we should be alive to relevant aspects of the context or their production, but we don't finally need the Chinese context in all its particularity." (22) Damrosch is here speaking of what the reader needs in order to appreciate the "power and beauty" of a work (85).

It goes without saying that a so-called ordinary reader need not be a specialist in order to gain much from reading foreign literature. The matter is completely different, however, when we are speaking of the scholarly study of literature. With his new definition of world literature – as 'foreign literature read from the perspective of one's own culture' – Damrosch is abolishing the difference: "Why settle for reading at a cultural and linguistic remove when we can spend our limited time on works from our own language and immediate tradition?" "World literature [...] is experienced as what is available to read, in classrooms and on bookstore shelves, on course syllabi and in anthologies for students and general readers"; and he is fully confident that we can find "new ways of assessing and working with texts that now range from the earliest Sumerian poetry to the most recent fictional experiments of the Tibetan postmodernists" (111). Rather than a specialist, the scholar of world literature is a 'generalist'. Damrosch demonstrates this 'generalist' approach by discussing examples ranging from *Gilgamesh* to Kafka.

Damrosch's analyses show, against his purpose, how such superficial and general knowledge of the original context, which to his mind can be beneficial for the reader of 'world literature', in fact reduces the target to a familiar pattern and effectively prevents an encounter with anything different. For example, in reading Aztec poetry, according to Damrosch, we ought to recognise that

> the poems were always closely tied to urgent religious and political concerns, and by this very engagement their meaning altered radically with the Conquest. The same images and verses that aided and even heightened the brutality of the imperial regime were turned to a new purpose some years later: to strengthen the resolve of a conquered people to resist their total destruction. Understanding this sort of shift helps us to read their poems more fully [...] (97).

The concepts whereby the poetry is clarified are very general and do not convey anything specific in the text or its context: expressions such as "the brutality of the imperial regime", "the resolve of a conquered people to resist their total destruction" are sweeping, abstract expressions that belong to the vocabulary of the observer only. The reader is allowed to remain in the framework of what is familiar and safe, without encountering anything that might offer something new or different that might challenge one's view of things. The great opportunity that art offers us in challenging our views and forcing us to widen our horizon, of which Gadamer speaks in his *Truth and Method* as the legitimation of existence of art, is lost. Likewise, when Damrosch discusses at length a four-line Egyptian poem, pondering how the garment mentioned in the poem should be translated, the result of the analysis is nothing but a most trivial and general meaning.

Exoticism is added by also giving the poem in hieroglyphs, which the reader, of course, cannot decipher.

The most disagreeable thing in Damrosch's approach, however, is its untroubled cultural imperialism. The literary scholar no longer needs to take pains to understand the target literature and its world in depth. Damrosch emphasises that a text can appear very different in its new context in 'world literature' (read: in the eyes of the reading public in United States) to in its original context, but that it is the task of the literary scholar precisely to determine the meaning of the work in this new context (e.g. 22). It is cultural imperialism to claim to be discussing a work from a foreign culture but to not even try to understand it from its own vantage point, approaching it in translation and merely as part of the culture of the United States. The Other has been silenced, and what the scholar is interested in is merely what is going on in his or her own mind. The hope to be understood from one's own perspective is lost for good for everyone 'outside'.

Comparative literature has cause to maintain the requirement of knowledge of the language of the target literature and of specialist knowledge of the culture in question. The so-called Bernheimer report from 1993 concerning the state of Comparative Literature at US universities emphasised that knowledge of foreign languages is still the basis of the discipline (Bernheimer 1995b: 43). The requirement of knowledge of foreign languages is now to be extended from the main European languages – French, German, Spanish, Italian – to include all encounters with a foreign culture (similarly, Spivak 2003: 5). The report also calls attention to the inner diversity of a culture and tensions within it, and underlines the importance of a contextualisation of literature that also observes ideological and power structures (42–45). Moreover, literature and literary study are seen as important in determining one's cultural identity. This is an aspect which Gayatri Spivak has reformulated by saying that the comparative study of literature is a process in which the individual and collective identity of oneself and the Other are reciprocally determined: what is one's "own" has to be seen also through the Other's eyes (2003: 25–29, 70).

The Bernheimer programme looks in many respects like an extended version of Herder's and Goethe's ideas as to how foreign literatures should be understood both as part of common human culture and in their specificity; the latter is possible only by achieving deep insight into that particular culture, for which a prerequisite is the command of the language. A return to Herder's and Goethe's ideas as a whole, however, is impossible. Culture and language now look – if not less homogenous, since Herder and Goethe were sensitive to cultural and linguistic differences – inherently more controversial. After Marx, Freud, Nietzsche and Foucault, we recognise that language and culture contain ideological and manipulative elements and a power struggle in general, which was not recognised in the eighteenth and early nineteenth century. Culture and politics no longer appear as separate domains but as deeply intermingled. On the other hand, Herder's and Goethe's ideas of historicism, contextualism and accurate, particularising reading are followed not only by Auerbach but also, for example, by Edward Said (61–62, 70–74, 96–97), who asks the literary scholars not to start with general, theoretical concepts defined by others in other contexts but to form their key concepts on the basis of an encounter with the texts, keeping close to them.

Liisa Steinby
liisaa@utu.fi
Yleinen kirjallisuustiede
FI-20014 Turku
Turun yliopisto
SUOMI / FINLAND

References

Apter, E. 2006. *The Translation Zone. A New Comparative Literature.* Princeton: Princeton University Press.

Arac, J. 2002. Anglo-globalism? – *New Left* Review, 16, 35–45.

Aristotle. 1997. *Aristotle's Poetics.* Ed. John Baxter & Patrick Atherton, trans. George Whalley. Montreal, Buffalo: McGill-Queen's University Press.

Auerbach, E. 1967a [1946]. *Mimesis. Dargestellte Wirklichkeit in der abendländischen Literatur.* Bern und München: Francke Verlag.

Auerbach, E. 1967b [1952]. Philologie der Weltliteratur. – *Gesammelte Aufsätze zur romanischen Philologie.* Bern und München: Francke, 301–310.

Barnard, F. M. 1964. *Zwischen Aufklärung und politischer Romantik. Eine Studie über Herders soziologisch-politisches Denken.* Berlin: Erich Schmidt Verlag.

Bernheimer, C. 1995a. Introduction: The Anxieties of Comparison. – Bernheimer 1995b, 1–17.

Bernheimer, C, ed. 1995b. *Comparative Literature in the Age of Multiculturalism.* Baltimore and London: The Johns Hopkins University Press.

Birus, H. 1995. Goethes Idee der Weltliteratur: Eine historische Vergegenwärtigung. – M. Schmeling, Hrsg., *Weltliteratur heute. Konzepte und Perspektiven.* Würzburg: Königshausen und Neumann, 5–28.

Casanova, P. 2004. *The World Republic of Letters,* trans. M. B. DeBevoise. Cambridge, Mass., London: Harvard UP.

Curtius, E. R. 1973 [1948]. *Europäische Literatur und lateinisches Mittelalter.* Bern und München: Francke.

Damrosch, D. 2003. *What Is World Literature?* Princeton and Oxford: Princeton University Press.

Eckermann, J. P. s.a. *Gespräche mit Goethe in den letzten Jahren seines Lebens* (1836–48). Leipzig: Max Hesse's Verlag.

Figueira, D. 2013. Postkolonialismus und Komparatistik. – Zymner & Hölter 2013a, 197–199.

Gillespie, G. 1995. Auf den multikulturellen Irrwegen der amerikanischen Komparatistik: Kontrast und Mahnbild für ein junges Europa. – M. Schmeling, Hrsg., *Weltliteratur heute. Konzepte und Perspektiven*. Würzburg: Königshausen und Neumann, 85–99.

Gillies, A. 1931–1933. Herder and the Preparation of Goethe's Idea of 'Weltliteratur'. – *Publications of the English Goethe Society*, N.S. 9, 46–67.

Goethe, J. W. von. 1999. Vorarbeiten und Bruchstücke. – *Werke*, Weimarer Ausgabe, Bd. 42.2 (1890). Nachdruck: Verlag Hermann Böhlaus Nachfolger, Weimar, 397–516.

Gossens, P. 2011. *Weltliteratur. Modelle transnationaler Literaturwahrnehmung im 19. Jahrhundert*. Stuttgart und Weimar: Metzler.

Guillén, C. 1993. *The Challenge of Comparative Literature*. Trans. Cola Franzen. Cambridge: Harvard UP.

Gymnich, M. 2013. Anglo-amerikanischer Sprachraum (UK, Irland, USA, Kanada, Neuseeland, Australien) [part of the chapter „Räumlich-sprachliche Ausrichtungen"]. – Zymner & Hölter 2013a, 29–34.

Herder, J. G. 1984. *Über die neuere deutsche Literatur. Fragmente*. – *Werke*, hg. v. Wolfgang Pross, Bd. I. München, Wien: Hanser.

Herder, J. G. 1985. *Über die neuere deutsche Literatur* [erste bis dritte Sammlung von Fragmenten, 1767]. – *Werke*, Bd. 1: *Frühe Schriften 1764–1772*, hrsg. v. Ulrich Gaier. Frankfurt am Main: Deutscher Klassiker Verlag.

Herder, J. G. 1989. *Ideen zur Philosophie der Geschichte der Menschheit*. – *Werke*, Bd. 6, hrsg. v. Martin Bollacher. Frankfurt am Main: Deutscher Klassiker Verlag.

Herder, J. G. 1993. *Vom Geist der Ebräischen Poesie*. – *Werke*, Bd. 5: *Schriften zum Alten Testament*, hrsg. v. Rudolf Smend. Frankfurt am Main: Deutscher Klassiker Verlag.

Herder, J. G. 1994. „Anmerkungen über das griechische Epigramm" [1773]. – *Werke*, Bd. 4: *Schriften zu Philosophie, Literatur, Kunst und Altertum 1774–1787*, hrsg. v. Jürgen Brummack und Martin Bollacher. Frankfurt am Main: Deutscher Klassiker Verlag.

Lempicki, S. 1968. *Geschichte der deutschen Literaturwissenschaft bis zum Ende des 18. Jahrhunderts*. Göttingen: Vandenhoeck & Ruprecht (2. Aufl.).

Moretti, F. 2007. *Graphs, Maps, Trees. Abstract Models for Literary History*. London, New York: Verso.

Moretti, F. 2013. *Distant Reading*. London, New York: Verso.

Moser, C. 2013. Globalisierung und Komparatistik. – Zymner & Hölter 2013a, 161–164.

Nisbet, H. B. 1993. Goethes und Herders Geschichtsdenken. – *Goethe-Jahrbuch*, 110, 115–133.

Pizer, J. 2000. Goethe's 'World Literature' Paradigm and Contemporary Cultural Globalization. – *Comparative Literature*, 52, 213–227.

Saariluoma, L. 1993. Erich Auerbachin *Mimesis* 1990-luvulla. – *Toiseuden politiikat. Kirjallisuudentutkijain Seuran vuosikirja* 47, toim. Pirjo Ahokas ja Lea Rojola. Helsinki: SKS.

Said, E. W. 2004. *Humanism and Democratic Criticism*. New York: Columbia University Press.

Schmeling, M., Schmitz-Emans, M., Walstra, K., Hrsg. 2000. *Literatur im Zeitalter der Globalisierung*. Würzburg: Königshausen und Neumann.

Siebers, T. 1995: Sincerely Yours. – Bernheimer 1995b, 195–203.

Solte-Gresser, C. 2013. Frankreich und französischer Sprachraum [part of the chapter „Räumlich-sprachliche Ausrichtungen"]. – Zymner & Hölter 2013a, 24–29.

Spitzer, L. 1928. *Stilstudien I: Sprachstile*. München: Max Hueber.

Spitzer, L. 1948. *Linguistics and Literary History. Essays in Stylistics*. Princeton, NJ: Princeton University Press.

Spivak, G. C. 2003. *Death of a Discipline*. New York: Columbia University Press.

Steinby, L. [in press]. *Mythopoiesis, Offenbarung, Aufklärung. Die alttestamentarische Gottesvorstellung Herders in* Vom Geist der Ebräischen Poesie.

Weber, P. 1977. Die Herausbildung des Begriffs Weltliteratur. – G. Klotz, W. Schröder, P. Weber, Hrsg., *Literatur im Epochenumbruch. Funktionen europäischer Literaturen im 18. und beginnenden 19. Jahrhundert*. Berlin und Weimar: Aufbau, 531–614.

Wellek, R. 1954. Auerbach's Special Realism. – *Kenyon Review*, 16, 299–307.

Zymner, R., Hölter, A., Hrsg. 2013a. *Handbuch Komparatistik. Theorien, Arbeitsfelder, Wissenspraxis*. Stuttgart, Weimar: J. B. Metzler.

Zymner, R., Hölter, A. 2013b. Einleitung: Konturen der Komparatistik. – Zymner & Hölter 2013a, 1–4.

INTERLITTERARIA 2015, SUPPL. 1: 36–42

Against Otherworldly World Literature; For Worldly Comparative Studies

GERALD GILLESPIE

Abstract. In this paper I will describe the new international standards of Comparative Literature as of the present century and contrast these to the movement calling itself World Literature. I believe the evidence shows the latter is a by-product of recent widespread retrogression in American higher education, unwary imitation of which in newer programs in other countries will largely slow down the development of our field. A principal aim will be to distinguish sounder broad-gauged approaches called World Literature, such as upheld by Jüri Talvet, from the shallower substitutes; and to define and affirm the desirability of a natural alliance between international and local efforts to engage in comparative studies.

Keywords: World Literature, Comparative Literature, General Literature, Eurocentrism, teaching and research programs

The title of my paper is not aimed against generous views of World Literature in the broader Goethean tradition, such as the practices which Jüri Talvet has long and ably practiced and which distinctly embrace contemporary international standards of Comparative Literature. I have no quarrel with the use of World Literature (henceforth WL) as an umbrella label over a variety of scholarly practices housed in a particular department or program – for example, a juxtaposition of more demanding Comparative Literature (CL), General Literature (GL), translation studies, cultural studies, literary theory, etc. – if the components are clearly defined to the students and public. Nor is it objectionable to employ WL as a kind of banner, a general indicator of openness to foreign cultures in one's own home territory. Rather, my concern is with the contemporary proliferation of retrogressive tendencies harmful to comparative studies, hidden under the label WL as a convenient mask. That is, I worry about the attempt to co-opt the older term WL as camouflage for a simultaneous dumbing down of comparative studies and for the promotion of anthology sales by riding on the back of English as a global lingua franca.

The promoters of what I deem retrogression need to count extensively on diverting attention by manipulating the term WL. But more than a confusion

DOI: http://dx.doi.org/10.12697/IL.2015.S1.4

of terminology is involved, because their efforts increase the danger that newly constituted programs, and shaky older ones seeking a restart, will miss out on an already achieved, now contemporary international level of CL practice. Especially the blandishments of newfangled American-style WL may divert local programs wastefully in various parts of the globe, if the local educational entities and aspiring students fail to grasp that their local cultural environment can be better aligned intellectually with regional and global phenomena. The best defence for institutions and students is to define rigorously what constitutes an adequate contemporary CL, even if they cannot yet materially realise all that CL involves, because the evolved picture of CL in the early twenty-first century is the surest guide to excellence on a global level; whereas, in effect, though touted as supposedly new, the more recent American WL concept promotes cultural narrowness. A brief review of the higher aspirations of the post-war pioneers will help clarify why.

To begin with, here is a statement published fifty years ago by Henry Remak, the opening words of his famous essay "Comparative Literature: Its Definition and Function":

> Comparative Literature is the study of literature beyond the confines of one particular country, and the study of the relationship between literature on the one hand and other areas of knowledge and belief, such as the arts (e.g., painting, sculpture, architecture, music), philosophy, history, the social sciences, religion, etc., on the other. In brief, it is the comparison of one literature with another or others, and the comparison of literature with other spheres of human expression.

Remak's formulation received an important enhancement in 1990 in a book titled *Comparative Poetics: An Intercultural Essay on Theories of Literature* by Earl Miner. Miner demonstrated in some detail why international comparative literature needed to pay due attention to the major non-European poetic systems and traditions which antedated modernism and were shaped over centuries in ways not congruent with European categories.

Remak's and Miner's generous view of a robust bigger world framework for comparative studies excludes no culture of any dimensions or its particular history and already encompasses conceptually every activity which various later proponents of interdisciplinary approaches have sought to elevate to a primary status. Two tendencies in early debates of the 1950s and 1960s within the International Comparative Literature Association (ICLA) stand in pronounced contrast. These tendencies are still widespread today, and are well represented in the institutional life of many actual teaching and research programs. One tendency – voiced for example by the eminent Soviet academician Victor

Girmounski in the 1960s – is the call for comparatists worldwide to agree, first, on the laws by which societies function and then to apply this understanding to all literary life worldwide. The other tendency is the attempt to assimilate all aspects of geocultural reality worldwide into one's own dominant culture, based on belief in the explanatory efficacy of Eurocentric theories for mastering all cultural phenomena. These two tendencies have sometimes merged in movements in Europe and the Americas, for example, when self-styled innovators tried to replace a much more ambitious CL approach with so-called cultural studies and multiculturalism. I believe these two polarities recur dressed in today's latest fashion, a supposedly renewed World Literature. My colleagues Franco Moretti and David Damrosch serve to represent these polarities, in rough terms, in North America. In Europe, a number of General Literature programs incorporate many of the prominent features: in their curricula and research programs they cultivate a potpourri of philosophical and political inquiries alongside formalistic analyses of works, rely heavily on translations of works not originally produced in the dominant local language or closely related languages, and depend on Eurocentric theorising, including intra-systemic European criticism of European societies and European imperialism. I have spoken about these issues in detail in several essays of the past decade.

It makes good sense that quite a few academic programs, societies, and journals combine the terms "general" and "comparative" in their titles, because the ideas and activities behind the labels are naturally related. However, the problem encountered widely both in Europe and in the Americas is that groups that ostensibly are practicing "general and/or comparative" literary studies either are located in or captive to, and thus too often are suffocated by, the local department in charge of the dominant cultural language and literatures written in it – by English departments in the USA or Britain, by French departments in France or Québec, by German departments in Germany and Austria, by Spanish departments in Spain and Argentina, and so forth.

Let me say at once that I have no complaint whatever against General Literature (GL) in its own right. The point I am making is different. It is not invidious to remind ourselves of the fact that for at least the past half century Comparative Literature (CL) has been striving to elaborate both interdisciplinary and cross-cultural approaches that are truly international in scale, truly open and accommodative to non-Eurocentric participants, whereas GL is inherently circumscribed by its local cultural mission everywhere. On closer inspection, the same proposition applies to the diffuse successor, WL redux. If we sum up this relationship, we can say that modern CL encompasses a plethora of particular General Literatures in the plural, but no local or regional GL can contain CL, although it is clearly beneficial if GL in any local variation interacts reasonably with more ambitious CL and a productive relationship can be established. In my view, however, it has ceased to be reasonable to pretend not to know that for several decades the International Comparative Literature Association has been forming global research teams to tackle projects which obviously exceed the capacity of individual researchers in Eurocentric regions and countries.

By the 1980s, ICLA had moved onto an intercontinental level of active collegial collaboration. Thus to contemporary international comparatists there is a disconcerting old-fashioned ring to the definition of WL as "a mode of reading, a detached engagement with a world beyond our own," which we find in Damrosch (297). This sense of detachment goes hand in hand with a reiteration of one of the standard Eurocentric notions of GL, except now applied to WL, as a "large and multilayered group of foreign works that circulate in a given culture" (298). It reflects an unambitious cultural self-cocooning, in contrast to the demands of active interchange which CL poses. Hence, in my view, to adopt American-style WL amounts to a regrettable lowering of sights.

This judgment of systemic challenges takes nothing away from the high-level individual accomplishments of the individual scholars, Moretti and Damrosch, whom I have chosen to represent the general WL direction. I admire many traits and specific aperçus in their critical writings, and perhaps above all I find it happily positive that both recognise the importance of historical processes and flows, and that neither falls into a blind fixation on some particular synchronic slice out of literary history. As in the slim book *Graphs, Maps, Trees*, Moretti strives toward abstract instrumentalities with which to describe literary history, whereas Damrosch crisscrosses from one cultural moment to another over several millennia in his engaging book *What is World Literature?* While Moretti stretches for some political-logarithmic paradigm and Damrosch is content with temporal bricolage, both display the virtue of wanting to interest us in literary events of all magnitudes from tiny to large. Their fascination for genetic questions contrasts in some measure with that of the semiotician Itamar Even-Zohar. Even-Zohar subordinates literature as merely one realm of codes to a totalizing semiotic general system, reversing the key focus of CL, insofar as CL looks out from within literary life at other elements and dynamics in cultural systems. In my estimation, Damrosch and Moretti want to keep literature as their chief lens or instrument, but it is the desire for a pseudo-scientific grasp, the purported distancing for the sake of objectivity, which undermines the potential of WL in both cases. Because so-called WL, whether as a neo-Marxian 'materialist' or a neo-humanist 'cultural' approach, fails to respect the local expression of extra-European and non-European cultures in their linguistic actuality and contexts, it remains captive to its own Eurocentric narrowness. Thus it exudes an 'otherworldly' arbitrariness both in Eurocentric and non-Eurocentric environments.

CL demands more – demands so much, in fact, that even the best equipped comparatists who have acquired serious acquaintance with several cultural super-systems and many of their languages recognise that every comparatist is just a partial comparatist. Modern international CL encourages teams of partial comparatists, with partially or extensively overlapping expertise, to tackle complicated aspects of cultural life beyond the local or regional level. My concern is that new-fashioned WL promotes a continuation of one or another of the favourite poses of Western intellectuals. In the case of Moretti, the approach is rooted in Marxian materialist dogma, as in his early book *Signs Taken for Wonders*, which argues in ingenious permutations that "in its deepest foundations form is always an ideology" (Moretti, 10, citing Lukácz). In the case of Damrosch, WL is more modestly deemed to be a "great conversation that takes place" both among authors closer culturally and in the minds of readers who are distant culturally (298) – in other words, events which semioticians call "interferences" or acts of "reception" occur. This is a state of affairs which semiotics on the one hand and CL on the other, with such offshoots as reception aesthetics, translation studies, and related fields, have been noting for decades. We are indeed fortunate to have in the European tradition a number of people like Goethe to exemplify the great genius whose mind really does transcend boundaries and obstacles. But a horde of lesser lights imagine to deal with a much expanded world picture, when in fact they eschew the sort of effort Goethe took for granted: the learning of non-European languages, thought, and mores.

The pursuit of this passive sort of WL retards realisation of what is needed in a genuinely global, multidirectional, polycentric meta-discourse such as today's international CL proposes and pursues. Of course, a terrible temptation for students in countries around the globe who wisely acquire a mastery of English is to see how to exploit this lingua franca as a shortcut, to hang out with WL people, and to avoid the kind of hard work learning foreign tongues and codes which Goethe accepted as the proper norm. As a merely partial comparatist, exploring only several cultural streams in Europe and the Americas, I recognise that there is a shortage of colleagues from the several continents whose knowledge truly bridges the cultural realms intensively enough to get us beyond something like a regional level of GL or a transoceanic Eurocentrism. It is also clear that even these multi-dimensional people must work in cross-hatched teams to elaborate a genuinely international CL which addresses more than Eurocentric audiences. And reciprocally, if the new-fashioned WL approach, which is in reality only a relabelled GL, takes hold in non-European regions, that will slow down the enormous progress which the ICLA has promoted in recent decades in building teams that look at the world from more than one centre, for example, look from East Asia at South America, or from Scandinavia at South Asia, and so forth, alongside reciprocal research partners from various other parts of the globe.

I recognise that it is highly ambitious to desire the promotion of a polycentric pursuit of CL, rather to accede to the exportation of a Eurocentric approach to all the world under the guise of newfangled WL. At least, in the interim, we can insist on honesty in advertising, so that, once they are better clarified, the terms of the choice will empower more colleagues on all continents to aspire to a seriously worldly discipline.

Gerald Gillespie
gillespi@stanford.edu
Division of Literatures, Cultures, and Languages
School of Humanities & Sciences
Pigott Hall, Building 260
450 Serra Mall,
Stanford, California 94305
USA

Selected References

Damrosch, D. 2003. *What is World Literature?* Princeton and Oxford: Princeton University Press.

Even-Zohar, I. 1990. *Polysystem Studies*. Special issue of *Poetics Today*, 11.1.

Gillespie, G. 2003. Comparative Literary History as an Elitist Metanarrative. – *Neohelicon*, 30.2, 59–64.

Gillespie, G. 2004. Part Three: "The Global Scope of Comparative Literature Today." – *By Way of Comparison: Reflections on the Theory and Practice of Comparative Literature*. Paris: Honoré Champion, 154–267.

Gillespie, G. 2005. Literary Studies: General and Comparative. – *Neohelicon*, 32.2, 337–41.

Gillespie, G. 2013. Das scheinbar 'neue' Weltliteraturkonzept im Dienste restaurativer Beschränkung kultureller Kompetenz. – *KulturPoetik*, 13, no. 3, 1–8.

Girmounski, V. 1969. Les courants littéraires en tant que phénomènes internationaux. – *Actes du Ve Congrès de l'Association Internationale de Littérature Comparée: Proceedings of the Vth Congress of the International Comparative Literature Association, Belgrade 1967*. Ed. by Nikola Banašević. Amsterdam: Swets & Zeitlinger.

Miner, E. 1990. *Comparative Poetics: An Intercultural Essay on Theories of Literature*. Princeton: Princeton University Press.

Moretti, F. 1988. *Signs Taken for Wonders: Essays in the Sociology of Literary Forms*. London, New York: Verso.

Moretti, F. 2000. Conjectures on World Literature. – *New Left Review*, 1, 56–67.

Moretti, F. 2005. *Graphs, Maps, Trees: Abstract Models for a Literary History*. London, New York: Verso.

Remak, H. H. H. 1971. Comparative Literature: Its Definition and Function. – N. P. Stallknecht, H. Frenz, eds., *Comparative Literature: Method and Perspective*. Carbondale and Edwardsburg: University of Southern Illinois Press.

World-weary Of Academic Worldviews

DOROTHY FIGUEIRA

Abstract. Using the structuring metaphor of an imaginary meeting between Walt Whitman and Jose Martí, the author examines the relationship between American formulations of World Literature and Comparative Literature and investigates how each discipline 'welcomes' the other. She distinguishes between what a European comparatist such as Jüri Talvet might envision when he thinks about the relationship between the two disciplines. Talvet sees them as working together in a symbiotic relationship to engage in passive and active canon reform. He takes a neutral attitude to the recent American marketing of World Literature. The author, however, places World Literature within the US context, discusses its origins in Area Studies, its relationship to the American academic model of multiculturalism and ultimately, its relationship to the management of diversity on US campuses.

Keywords: Comparative Literature, World Literature, Jüri Talvet, Area Studies, alterity studies, diversity in US academe

In a recent article published in *The Comparatist*, the Cuban-American critic Alfred Lopez discussed Jose Martí's reading of Walt Whitman. From this article, I learned that Whitman was a cursory reader, perusing a dozen books at any time, reading a few pages here and there, seldom getting sufficiently interested in any volume to read it in its entirety, dipping into various genres and reading no language but English. Although he never travelled beyond North America, it did not prevent him from envisioning the many places he evokes in *Salut au Monde* though, as Lopez notes "his own mystical, abstracted vision of an America is at once generalized and exceptional" (Lopez 2011: 5). The world Whitman presented in this poem was populated by undifferentiated Others "facilely reduced to 'Camarados' in turn subsumed into his Hegelian vision of America as an ever-expanding end-of-History" (Lopez 2011: 6).

Lopez compares the American poet to the Cuban Martí and speculates on their possible encounter at a reception following a lecture on Abraham Lincoln by Whitman at Madison Square Theater in 1887. If Martí and Whitman did, in fact, speak, it would have been in English, although Martí could have spoken in Spanish and French. Martí might have broached any number of interesting topics, since he was learned in the Classics and had advanced degrees in law and

DOI: http://dx.doi.org/10.12697/IL.2015.S1.5

philosophy, was a renowned journalist, editor, novelist and playwright. One does not want to belittle Whitman, but Martí's considerably larger intellectual scope was grounded, as Lopez notes, in "a keen awareness of cultural and material difference" (Lopez 2011: 7). While Whitman did not possess expertise in a broad range of subjects and disciplines, one certainly would not guess it from the expansive and expansionist claims of his poetry. Whitman did not seem to be aware of his parochial vision or his provincial experience of the world. Certainly, none surface in poems such as "Starting from Paumanok", in which the American poet imagines himself "sailing to other shores to annex the same, yet welcoming/every new brother... Coming among the new Ones myself to be their companion/and equal." At no point does the poet ever pause to wonder how he proposes to accomplish this encounter in English. One might even question how his prospective new "brothers" might feel about being "welcomed" in their own homeland by some interloper (Lopez 2011: 10).

Perhaps, by now, you suspect where I am going with this train of thought. Whitman's inverted logic of welcoming new brothers as long as they speak English presents a crystallisation of American exceptionalism that serves as an apt metaphor for what I see at work in recent American formulations of World Literature. Martí's interdisciplinarity, in-depth knowledge of other cultures and languages, and his awareness of cultural difference calls to mind Comparative Literature at its disciplinary best. I fear that Whitman's claims to "welcome" ("annex") the world reflect far more World Literature's rather imperialistic vision of a world to be packaged and consumed in English, the ever-increasing hegemonic language of academe. It is telling that one approach to the Other is theorised today in America as a democratising force and the other conception, deemed by some as elitist, is espoused by actual others, Hispanics like Martí, Lopez, or myself. In fact, this other approach is also embraced by a theorist such as Jüri Talvet, who also stands outside the American mainstream and who recognises the limitations that the American model of World Literature might pose in an international setting.

Like Martí, the proto-comparatist of our metaphor, Talvet realises the importance of interdisciplinarity, focus on language, and cultural specificity in the comparative study of literature. While Talvet values the idea of World Literature, he feels it needs the input of comparatists in order to hold its own against the institutional power of the sciences. Talvet worries, in particular, about the increasing trend to make the humanities more science-like (and to make literature a beggarly appendix to the real/hard sciences) through a widespread mechanical application of theories. He envisions World Literature and Comparative Literature working together, but acknowledges the unique capacity of comparatists to study literature in its widest possible context. In Talvet's estimation, Comparative Literature alone offers the necessary detailed treatment of literary phenomena as a substantial factor for a national literature in its linguistic and social dimensions. World Literature depends on translation and canon formation. Moreover, from his position in Estonia, Talvet wonders about the exile position that a World Literature translated into English really means for certain languages and literatures. Beyond such ideological and political concerns, Talvet also recognises the role specific genres might play in the World Literature canon. Talvet places value in a pedagogy of World Literature only insofar as it can avoid what he terms a passive canon and adopt active and diligent canon reform (Talvet 2014). Talvet is speaking from his particular stance as an Estonian critic, author, translator and theorist. As such, he calls for an expansive and open cooperation between World Literature and Comparative Literature as a means of strengthening both fields. In other words, Talvet would like to see a more symbiotic relationship between World Literature and Comparative Literature. Like other European and Asian comparatists, however, he views the recent American marketing of World Literature in rather neutral terms. It does not carry for these scholars any historical and pedagogical baggage, nor do they see it as serving any specific political aims for its American practitioners. This is an important point. World Literature is not something new that has arisen in the wake of Comparative Literature's 'demise'. It has a history and serves a purpose. Its arrival on the theoretical and pedagogical scene is not an accident.

It is this trajectory that I wish to examine in the following discussion. Specifically, I would like to investigate how, beyond American World Literature's laudable aims of re-envisioning how we fashion ourselves in relation to geopolitical location, there are individuals who dwell outside the comfort zone of the American "we" who might think otherwise. I, for one, view the theorising about World Literature as a means whereby the American "we" co-opts the Other. It is my thesis that World Literature, as it is formulated and practiced in the US, reflects how the American academic fashions him/herself with respect to the Other. As the poetry of Whitman suggests and as trends in literary theory of the past forty years amply show, it is quite easy to level out this Other. Poets and academics often work from a self-image that does not correspond to social reality. Sometimes, their fanciful creations tell us more about those constructing the categories than about anything else. With this thought in mind, allow me to extend my metaphor a bit further.

Just as in Whitman's poem, so too for World Literature as it is theorised and practiced in the US, there is no imperative to truly encounter (and hence respect) the 'other' population. As in the case of Whitman, World Literature's messianic mission of welcoming the Other is not a reflection of humanism, but an attempt at cultural appropriation. Sometimes it is merely enough to evoke the existence of Others (as Whitman did) and offer nominal representation and a selectively partial exploration (as we do today in American World Literature anthologies). It is really not necessary to grasp the intellectual history and contextualise the Other or broaden its significance by drawing any associations that might extend knowledge beyond the master narrative that one has responsibly engaged the world. In fact, by appropriating the Other in this manner, American World Literature sanctions a selectively fragmented exploration, ensuring a general failure of real engagement. As we saw in the case of Whitman, so too in American World Literature, there is considerable hubris involved when one speaks for the Other.

Presented as an ideal toward which literary studies should aspire, American World Literature falls prey to an overriding impulse to homogenise, taking for granted that there is a common conception of the verbal/linguistic act, what constitutes a classic in a given society, and differing definitions of literature across cultures. It assumes that the codes of communication that a given system uses to address its intended readers are easily available in other cultures and times (Chanda 2013a: 7). American World Literature's reframing through translation and new cultural contexts reflects far more the translator's framing through his/her hegemonic language and theoretical jargon rather than that of the local language's writer (Chanda 2013b: 3). Although American World Literature affects a respect for the Other as a reified object of cultural difference, it only delivers a superficial and unidirectional overview, with Anglophone culture as the one recognising the non-Anglophone and (often) non-white culture. In order "to be" or "speak out", the non-white and/or non-Anglophone culture must seek legitimacy and recognition from white culture and use the language of white culture to produce itself (Rizvi 1994: 63). In this manner, the Other preserves its own heritage, only as long as it speaks English (Prashad 2000: 112) or is translated into it.

American World Literature does not adequately address this basic problem of translation upon which it largely depends. Translation into Western languages usually does not strive to transform the essence of the text in its source language. However, in translation, a text becomes different, something commensurate in the target language. You make English what is not English. It is a one-way street: your ensuing English text does not become changed by the experience of the encounter. Rather, the Other becomes changed. In terms reminiscent of Herder's vision of *Humanität,* the translation in a World Literature anthology becomes the true mediator of genius. This notion presupposes impartiality on the part of the English translator whose geography, political situation and eclectic character lend themselves to the tasks of ordering the genius of other cultures and building new creations from them. On a more personal level, such mediation is an application of the English translator's/editor's presence in the world (*Hiersein*).

What is it about the American World Literature translator/editor that allows him/her to assume another mode of thinking or feeling? In the act of translation, there is not only the expropriation of the Other's artistic production and the communication of knowledge from one tradition to another, but an implicit claim of improving upon it. These are common traits of translation practice (Figueira 1991: 29). No matter how sensitive or talented the translator may be, a translation is an independent work, altered from the original. A translation accommodates a text *à la française* or *à l'anglaise*, etc. – removing foreign elements that might impede comprehension and sometimes even perfecting the original. Faithfulness in translation has historically been seen as a disservice to the reader who expects an agreeable reading experience in which he/she need not question nor be surprised by a text. Translations seek general accuracy rather than complete fidelity. Making the foreign intelligible often encourages a pedestrian style and idiom (Figueira 1991: 31). A translation is, therefore, not a practical intermediary but an interpretation. For these reasons, translations are seen to provide a default reading, certainly not the preferred mode and certainly not the mode on which to base a pedagogy. Institutionalising the study of the Other in a format that relies on translation promotes assimilation with domesticating egalitarian demands attached. American World Literature does not adequately acknowledge this aesthetic concern, nor does it consider fully the political ramifications.

It should not be forgotten that World Literature has its origins in Area Studies, a field that was a Cold War Pentagon construction for managing the global situation. The new World Literature advocates have not quite figured out that Area Studies was not only discredited as racist and illegitimate a few decades ago, but has bequeathed to World Literature many of the problems that brought it into disfavour. Both Area Studies and World Literature tend to ignore the local in favour of the interests of an abstract universal humanity. Both view notions such as the 'nation' or 'foundational values' as homogenous and universal. One of the most damning criticisms levelled against Area Studies was its dependence on government funding that presumably compromised its objectivity. While World Literature does not carry the stigma of US State Department sponsorship, it is bankrolled by private corporations (such as universities) and large publishing conglomerates whom some might find just as sinister as the government! The only difference between Harvard and the US government these days is that Harvard has more money! Whereas Area Studies produced strategic documentation compiled by US State Department personnel from data collected by a peon class of exploited native informants, World Literature appears in anthologies, edited by Western/Western-based scholars, but often translated by new native informants. It is the same old, same old. The West still interprets the rest. Instead of the baksheesh formerly doled out to Area Studies' native informants, one hopes that their

World Literature successors get to share a bit in the royalties, especially since the resulting anthologies are required reading in thousands of World Literature courses throughout the US and are bought by tens of thousands of students.

American World Literature is not only modelled after Area Studies, it is also indebted to the theories and pedagogies that have arisen in the past forty years. Due to a radicalisation of theory and the ensuing paradigm shift from the aesthetic to the political, it has become acceptable to view literature as an outmoded form of cultural capital belonging to the bourgeoisie. An important stage in this process of radicalisation involved the rejection of the canon of dead white males in favour of the cultural studies model. However, it soon became apparent that dismantling the canon often had less to do with installing a more immediate and less conservative hierarchical format and more to do with establishing a new authority, grounded in ideology and seeking reification by identifying and marketing marginalised populations. In the case of American universities, these commodity populations were packaged and marketed first under the rubric of multiculturalism, then under the umbrella of postcolonial literatures and now, it appears, as World Literature. All these pedagogies of alterity claim to bring the literatures from the margins to the centre when, in fact, all they really do is allow critics from the centre to co-opt the margins.

World Literature shares American multiculturalism's mission to recognise the contributions of neglected groups and offer a reform project heralding diversity and promoting a progressive politics. Like postcolonial criticism, American World Literature pretends to uncover occluded and submerged identities and to liberate the oppressed. Yet, the samples of under-represented and repressed literatures offered by this brand of World Literature do not in any way problematise a Euro-Amero-centric perspective. Rather American World Literature promotes an ethos of recognition without adequately questioning Euro-centric definitions of knowledge. Like other pedagogies of alterity before it, American World Literature ultimately consolidates control. Like these preceding pedagogies, it also obscures issues of power and privilege, by rendering the Other tokenistic (Chow 2002: 113). As Gerald Gillespie has shown, the current interest in World Literature does not harken to anything new (Gillespie and Figueira 2014), but in its present configuration begs the question of what purpose its resurgence might possibly serve in today's academe? On a primary level, we can speculate that American World Literature as a new theory and practice serves those who teach courses on World Literature. People who teach World Literature may do so because they are not skilled to teach national or comparative literature. By rendering one's parochialism and limitations into something grandiose, more "inclusive" and humanitarian, one can recruit those very values that drive one's parochialism and limitations into reverse and claim a more noble universalism (Chanda 2013a: 9).

As I have noted elsewhere, it is quite possible that the recent American interest in World Literature betokens an effort on the part of scholars to refashion themselves now that other theories and pedagogies of alterity have played themselves out. Unifocal scholars often feel the need to retool themselves, in order to make their mark. The "new" World Literature scholar whose formation has been almost exclusively in English literature can pretend to reinvent the wheel, do what the comparatist has been doing for decades and claim, in the process, to be non-elitist because he or she does not bother to learn foreign languages. But I ask you, what is more elitist than practicing a brand of criticism that claims to champion a voiceless and under-represented world but does so only in the English language? Since when does the imposition of Western ways of thinking on the non-West make us non-elite? I suspect there is a lesson to be learned from the proliferation of theories and pedagogies that promise to improve the world (and, in the process, assuage white Western guilt) and that lesson is that we should not take at face value academic projects that blithely claim to engage in a reform process. Have Comparative Literature's standards of cultural and linguistic specificity really been lost, as some critics contend? Or are certain theorists just claiming they have disappeared in order to support the hegemony of the English language and their own positions as experts in the field? I am very suspicious of solutions to the supposed death of our discipline when what certain critics propose is far less than what some comparatists have delivered for decades. I am even more suspicious when academics claim thereby to be striking a blow for democracy.

In my book, *Otherwise Occupied* (2008), I make the case that academic theories and pedagogies of the Other (identity studies, multiculturalism, post-colonial criticism and now we might add World Literature) were constructed and used in America to undermine Affirmative Action by influencing institutional policies for recruitment. I investigate how these various theoretical constructions of the Other proliferated in the US in direct proportion to the failure of statistical evidence to support the success claims of institutional diversity. I contend that these theories and pedagogies, in effect, aid in masking the continued marginalisation and containment of America's minorities within academe. I also show how such initiatives dovetail very nicely with university marketing concerns. I analyse how American universities have in the past occluded low numbers in diversity by establishing various ethnic studies programs and peopling them with under-represented ethnics. Identity Studies first contributed to the balkanisation of ethnics into fields for which they were deemed biologically and culturally suited. In other words, minorities were allowed to enter the ivory tower only if they are willing to settle for studying themselves. Minorities were thus neutralised and contained in such placements. Now, with multiculturalism, postcolonialism and World Literature, American universities need not even hire minorities. Viewed in this light, alterity initiatives are, in fact, strategies of containment that obscure the stasis of power and privilege rather than redistribute rights and rethink recognition. Under the guise of inclusion and hospitality, they mask a racialist agenda. Such pedagogies deflect attention away from social issues such as real discrimination, real unequal access, and real hierarchies of ethnic privilege that are far from being resolved (Huggan 2000: 126) in academe today. Under the guise of promoting tolerance, American World Literature, like the other pedagogies of alterity before it, enables academic elites to displace, diffuse, and thus intensify class, gender, and racial contradictions.

Such pedagogies serve a demographic purpose in American academe of contributing to the representation of diversity. Multiculturalism and postcolonialism allowed an often privileged Asian and Middle Eastern diasporic professoriate to speak on behalf and in lieu of their supposedly mute brethren. With World Literature, the most recent bureaucratic institutionalisation of Othering, we can now witness the process of 'taking back' the American university from both the minorities housed in identity studies and Third World model minorities supervising multicultural and postcolonial studies. We have come full circle back to Whitman. We too can now embrace and celebrate linguistic limitations and fragmentary knowledge. With World Literature, we too can now engage in a quasi-mystical endeavour that glorifies nothing but good old American exceptionalism. Whitman was able to indulge his fancies because he lived in an openly imperialistic age, in an America that revelled in its belief in white supremacy and gloried in an aura of rural utopianism. Our modern theorists of the world must be more subtle. And here, as in all scholarly justifications for shady political postures (from academic Marxism to the moral relativism of deconstruction), we call upon theory to assuage our consciences. Rather than examining the economic and political forces at work during the final stages of decolonisation and its aftermath, literary theory has focused on postmodernist views of a hybridised and syncretic world.

The work of Baudrillard has proven particularly useful in this regard, especially his notion that travel can be viewed as a spectacular form of amnesia. According to such a theory, any part of the world can be recreated or made to stand for another. In a world of third-order simulacra, encroaching pseudo-places merge to eliminate geographical or ethnic space entirely. This levelling out of the world has contributed to theoretical creations of metaphorical space in which critics might dwell that are separate from the real space they inhabit. In this metaphorical space, critics can voice ideologies of subversion and rebellion that are simply too unsettling, if voiced from their own actual space. Their delicate balancing acts stem from the paradox of their inhabiting a space of bourgeois comfort, while needing at the same time to distance themselves from global capitalism. When critics appropriate the metaphorical space of the Other, whether it be postcolonial, the nomad, the exile, or now even the entire world, they hope to exonerate themselves for all the benefits they receive from this same capitalism. In this process, we find the meeting of incommensurables, a deep seated need for the experience of political engagement coming out of the 1960s meeting a 1990s' need to be media savvy, and the new millennium's desire to package and market intellectual capital. There is no small irony in how easily these three conceptual frameworks have melded. If the belief in criticism as a viable intervention is a relic of the 60s that has proven itself bankrupt, we might want to view 'new' purportedly 'cutting-edge' pedagogies as responses to this socio-political impotence. Potency, when it exists, resides in the critic's relationship to colleagues as it is constructed through the coinage and the use of new systems, accompanying jargon and business collaborations with university administrators and publishers.

In American institutions today, the marketing concerns are, therefore, twofold. First, there is marketing to and through university administrators who buy into the idea that an initiative such as World Literature (like multiculturalism and postcolonial criticism before it) provides the most advanced and 'logical' approach to the miasma of competing cultures and ethnicities. Through an 'innovation' such as World Literature, American institutions can recruit and pretend to 'restructure' with supposedly radical responses to new socio-economic realities. However, amidst all of World Literature's talk of multilingualism, translation, reframing, flows, and inclusivity, there is really no discussion about the relations of power, the market, canon formation and even the notion of 'literature' in the moment of global capital (Chanda 2013b: 7).

The American brand of World Literature has thus entered into the fray as the latest avatar of earlier theories and pedagogies purporting to engage the Other that have sprung up on American campuses in the last four decades. Like the earlier fads in multiculturalism and postcolonial studies, the newly-minted World Literature Programs are practical in that they are all are relatively easy 'specialisations', demanding no in-depth knowledge of another culture or foreign languages, a skill that has fallen by the wayside among American students. In fact, one of the explicit justifications for the creation of World Literature departments is the difficulty of adequate language training eroding the competency of many Comparative Literature programs in the States. The inability to train students in languages and literatures derives from a decline in learning and standards beginning in the 70s. World Literature's solution to these lower standards, to quote Gerald Gillespie, is to universalise them (Gillespie and Figueira 2014). World Literature claims to eschew the 'elitism' of Comparative Literature's mandate to learn foreign languages. With World Literature, students who are not trained in elite American universities, deemed the only real sites where one can study languages like Sanskrit and Nahuatl, can still 'welcome' the world's literature in their midst. Moreover students who, because of their content-light training, have not studied even common foreign languages and their literatures can do World Literature. Likewise students whose training prevents them from doing broad-based comparative or theoretical study can do World Literature and they can pretend to 'do' the Other 'better' than Comparative Literature does.

As we saw in the case of Whitman, so too with World Literature, co-optation can be achieved under the pretence of democratising. The reality is that World Literature feeds the same brand of American isolationism of which Whitman sings. Like Whitman, all these pedagogies of alterity claim to engage the Other. However, the resounding global education that such pedagogies actually offer literature students can consist of nothing more than snippets from endless recycled 'representative' authors writing or translated into the English language. In the case of World Literature, there is a sense of *noblesse oblige* in formulating a field that demands so little from its future practitioners just as it is odd to call Comparative Literature elitist (especially given the immigrant status of many of its practitioners) because it demands knowledge of foreign languages. (Are statisticians deemed elitist for needing to know calculus?) What is really going on here? Eliminating standards does not democratise anything. It only points to American cultural provincialism, triumphalism, and a deep indifference to the world. It may just reflect a little bit of racism. It certainly betokens a privileging of the Self to 'speak for' the Other.

In literary studies today, we have become rather promiscuous ventriloquists. Spivak muted the subalterns to make a place for the critic (herself) to speak on their behalf. She filtered Mahasweta Devi who herself is a high-caste spokesperson for tribals. The Indian critic Jasbir Jain draws a fundamental distinction regarding this issue of spokespersonship when she compares what she has termed a "literature of empathy" to a "literature of experience". She asks where the lack is located in the "empathetic" privileged writer or critic that enables him or her to speak for others? In posing this question, I feel that Jain has cut to the heart of what is at issue here: there *is* no lack that ethically renders spokespersonship legitimate. In academe, to cite Aijaz Ahmad, textual culture can only pretend to be activist culture. Theory and criticism do not change the condition of the disenfranchised. Critics who claim otherwise are fooling themselves and others. When academics speak, they usually do so for personal gain, something as simple as a new job or 'proper' recognition. One speaks for the Other to co-opt that Other, to take his or her apportioned voice and sometimes, as a wonderful consequence, the place allotted for that Other by the system that tries to or, more often, pretends to redress past discrimination.

In all these attempts to 'speak for' the Other, I cannot help but think of Walt Whitman blithely welcoming his "camarados" in their own land. We must be wary of those who undertake the task of speaking for others and articulating their experience. The motivations behind such acts of masquerade and collaboration are not noble. Just as it is unsavoury for middle-class whites to speak for Blacks, Native Americans and Chicanos, those institutions that promote such performances are no less odious. Similarly, there is just something silly about monolingual Western or Western-trained World Literature scholars packaging the world. Nevertheless, this marketing of empathy and representation has become standard in American academe. It is possible because (again a legacy of the 60s) in the university setting (perhaps more than elsewhere) we can be whatever we say we are. What counts are not one's actions but the narrative about the action that one constructs. One can certainly speak for the Other, regardless of one's own subject position. Yet, in the outside world, the last decade has taught us some harsh lessons. The willed failure in the US to grasp the essential role played by source contexts and languages has led to failures of interpretation and understanding among peoples. The academic postmodern tendency to treat all literatures as a kind of meta-language that can be lifted out of their natural linguistic context and examined on the a-historical specimen tray of contemporary theory has proved to be woefully inadequate. What is urgently needed is not a continuation of these cynical and Lilliputian exercises but a commitment to understanding the world's literatures' connection to and elucidation of the socio-cultural context of the cultures from which they spring. It is clear that students in the twentieth-first century need to be able to experience and interrogate this totality of the world's literatures, not just the constricted and diluted product packaged and marketed by the self-serving managers of American academe.

Dorothy Figueira
figueira@uga.edu
University of Georgia
121 Joseph Brown Hall
Athens, Georgia 30602-6204
USA

References

Ahmad, A. 1992. *In Theory: Classes, Nations, Literatures*. London: Verso.

Chanda, I. 2013a. *Comparative Literature/World Literature: An Indian Perspective*. [Paper presented at the International Comparative Literature Association.]

Chanda, I. 2013b. *PostWorld Literature: Thoughts from a Comparatist from a 'Post' Colony*. [Unpublished paper presented at George Mason University.]

Chow, R. 2002. Theory, Area Studies, Cultural Studies: Issues of Pedagogy in Multiculturalism. – *Learning Places: The Afterlives of Area Studies*. Eds. Masao Miyoshi and H. D. Harootunian. Durham: Duke UP, 103–18.

Figueira, D. 1991. *Translating the Orient*. Albany, NY: SUNY P.

Figueira, D. 2008 *Otherwise Occupied: Theories and Pedagogies of Alterity*. Albany, NY: SUNY P.

Gillespie, G., Figueira, D. 2013. Das scheinbar neue Konzept des *World Literature* im Dienst restaurativer Beschränkung kultureller Kompetenz. – *KulturPoetik*, 13, no. 3, 9–19.

Huggan, G. 2000. Exoticism, Ethnicity, and the Multicultural Fallacy. – *"New" Exoticism: Changing Patterns in the Construction of Otherness*. Ed. Isabel Santaolalla. Amsterdam: Rodopi, 91–96.

Lopez, A. J. 2011. Translating Interdisciplinarity: Reading Martí Reading Whitman. – *The Comparatist*, 35, 5–18.

Lopez, A., Marzec, R. P. 2010. Postcolonial Studies at the Twenty-Five Mark. – *Modern Fiction Studies* 56(4), 677–688.

Prashad, V. 2000. *The Karma of Brown Folk*. Minneapolis: U of Minnesota P.

Rizvi, F. 1994. The Arts, Education and the Politics of Multiculturalism. – *Culture, Difference and the Arts*. Eds Sneja Gunew and Fazal Rizvi. St, Leonards, Australia: Allen and Unwin, 54–68.

Spivak, G. 2003. *Death of a Discipline*. New York: Columbia UP.

Talvet, J. 2014. Comparative Literature and World Literature: Toward a Symbiotic Co-existence. – D. Figueira, C. Mohan, eds., *Translation and Literary Culture: New Aspects of Comparative Literature* [in press].

La littérature comparée contemporaine : un paradigme alternatif

MONICA SPIRIDON

Abstract. *Well-Tempered Relativism or How to Compare the Incomparable.* Our study points to the fact that contemporary comparative studies run the risk of ending up in a babel-like relativism, following in the footsteps of self-styled 'scientific anthropology' and defended by scholars in the name of an unlimited diversity. As outlined by us the object of study of comparative literature can also seen as a dynamic network of minimal elements, transgressive aggregates, which can migrate both across socio-cultural contexts and across diverse media: fictional worlds, genres, narrative configurations, the empty recyclable containers of myth, and many others. On inspection, they present two sides: one which is open to descriptive and empirical research and the other which is formal and requires coherent and persuasive demonstrative scenarios. This theoretical and methodological option could successfully address a series of stubborn fractures in the area of comparative studies: morphological versus functional, text versus cultural context, synchronic versus diachronic and, last but not least, empirical versus theoretical.

Keywords: contemporary comparative studies, babel-like relativism, transgressive aggregates, fictional worlds, narrative configurations, genres

Se donnant comme objet d'étude une territorialité – *die Welt* (Goethe 1988) –, la littérature comparée est venue au jour dans un système centrifuge de références, qui privilégiait une source prestigieuse de modèles, censés être imités dans ses périphéries les plus lointaines. Dans l'horizon plus vaste d'un monde réel géopolitiquement centré, la pratique comparatiste a vite breveté un symbolisme spatial cohérent, riche en métaphores cartographiques.

Comme il convient tout de même de l'admettre, au-delà de tous ses dérapages, la littérature comparée traditionnelle de souche gœthéenne était au moins parvenue à lancer un défi à la différence babélienne qui menaçait de rendre légitime un adage du type : *À chaque littérature, son discours théorique et sa pratique particulière de recherche.*

Elle s'était mise à échafauder un système de référence où les similitudes se feraient perceptibles, tandis que les différences se laisseraient ériger en objets d'analyse. Convertie par la suite en essence, la catégorie *d'universalisme* – sa

DOI: http://dx.doi.org/10.12697/IL.2015.S1.6

clef de voûte et son outil théorique cardinal – avait abouti à une synonymie inconfortable avec l'eurocentrisme oppressif.

À l'abri d'une déconstruction diligente, qui visait à bouleverser de fond en comble l'état de la question, et tout en soulignant le glissement de leur objet d'étude vers le planétaire, les comparatistes contemporains se sont obstinément cantonnés dans une sorte de *néo-territorialité* métaphorique. Je renvoie brièvement à quelques exemples, illustrant surtout le tournant méthodologique des années quatre-vingt-dix, stimulé par le rapport Bernheimer. (Bernheimer 1995)

Pour Michael Riffaterre, la réhabilitation théorique du comparatisme a l'air d'une ample *transgression territoriale*. À son avis, le nouveau comparatisme devrait mener tambour battant une offensive censée dépasser toutes les *failles* survenues entre les langues et les cultures. (Riffaterre 1995 : 67–68) (Je remets à plus tard sa suggestion du partage méthodologique entre le comparatisme – spéculatif – et les études culturelles – empiriques – portant, elles, surtout sur les identités et les différences.)

Afin de réduire à un dénominateur commun les nombreuses métaphores agricoles proposées par Marie Louise Pratt, on pourrait dire que le *décloisonnement radical* reste au centre de son projet théorique. (Pratt 1995 : 60) (Voilà une métaphore spatiale de plus.)

Même si elle fut le produit d'une critique sévère du territorialisme traditionnel, la nouvelle *géométrie littéraire* envisagée par le David Damrosch des années quatre-vingt-dix (Damrosch 1995), mais aussi par le David Damrosch de deux mille trois (Damrosch, 2003 : 128), s'avère elle aussi bien ancrée dans un système spatial, pour y projeter un monde littéraire *elliptique et poly-centré*.

En dépit de toute une décennie qui s'était théoriquement appliquée à battre en brèche la spatialité (voir surtout le nouveau tournant méthodologique déclenché par le rapport Saussy de deux mille cinq (Saussy, 2005)), il est toutefois évident que les plus récentes catégories en circulation – *littérature-monde / world literature* – nous proposent une reviviscence de la dimension territoriale. Devenu planétaire et pluri-centré, leur horizon d'étude incommensurable court, par principe, le risque de compromettre axiomatiquement le dialogue et la comparaison. Quant aux paradigmes méthodologiques légitimés par leur découpage, ils sont à trouver dans l'empirisme d'inspiration anthropologique (sinon ethnologique tout court) que Michael Riffaterre, par exemple, nous avait suggéré d'éviter. (Riffaterre 1995 : 72)

Il me semble donc qu'en théorie, les recherches actuelles où se fait jour le thème de la *littérature-monde* puissent nous installer dans une vision polaire inconfortable : *ou bien* l'approche abstraite, spéculative, produisant bon nombre de modèles et de métaphores épistémologiques spatiales, *ou bien* la territorialité empirique et historicisante.

Y a-t-il quand même une option alternative ? Comment identifier un niveau d'analyse ouvrant à la démarche comparatiste la voie du relativisme et de la diversité, mais en même temps lui assurant le statut d'approche paradigmatique et intégrative ? Ou tout au moins, comment projeter une charpente théorique à la fois cohérente et non réductionniste (voire oppressive) ?

En tant que produit culturel, tout Soi littéraire rend possible une communication avec Autrui. Un Soi et un Autrui qui, dans la pratique historique, ne se trouvent que rarement – voire jamais – en contact. Dans ce cas-là, « une médiation peut quand même survenir, qui les fasse entrer en communion et se rencontrer en un troisième point qui leur soit ouvert ». (Bruner 2002 : 216) Une médiation qui reste indispensable « à la saisie partagée du sens ». Par le biais conceptuel de la sémiotique et dans les termes bien connus de Charles Saunders Peirce, il serait bon de concevoir cette instance médiatrice comme un *interprétant* et notamment comme une *communauté interprétative.* (Bruner 2002 : 219)

Voila une catégorie dont je vais tirer profit dans ce qui suit, en érigeant la congrégation des comparatistes en communauté interprétative. Celle-ci serait appelée à gérer un amas (ou plutôt un entrepôt) d'éléments minimaux, empiriquement observables et en même temps théorisables. Dans ce qui suit, je vais les appeler *des agrégés morpho-fonctionnels à vocation migratoire multiple* : transculturelle, transhistorique et trans-médiatique. Je vais en mentionner quelques exemples.

Le premier nous est fourni par les configurations discursives qui, dans des cultures et dans des temps variables, projettent des univers alternatifs par rapport au monde accepté comme (le) Réel. Il s'agit de la *Fiction,* telle qu'elle est identifiée par de nombreuses collectivités de dimensions fort variables. *Les mondes fictionnels* définis par Thomas Pavel représentent des entités strictement formalisées et en même temps soumises à une ample variation géographique et historique. (Pavel 1988 : 56) Leur étude comparatiste impliquerait un côté intégratif, trans-individuel, voire normatif et en même temps un côté factuel et descriptif. La synchronie et la diachronie, l'information factuelle et l'approche spéculative, les données textuelles directement observables et la mise en perspective contextuelle s'y mêlent profitablement.

Il y en a un autre, en provenance d'une aire fort vénérable des études littéraires, réputée conservatrice et abstraite : *la Narration.* Dans la lignée théorique de Paul Ricœur et de Jonathan Culler (Ricoeur 1985 ; Culler 1981 : 170) par rapport au temps et à la focalisation, la catégorie maîtresse de voix narrative serait ouvertement orientée vers le récepteur, et vers ses attentes de lecture historiquement instables. D'ailleurs, les développements les plus significatifs connus par les théories de la narration (Chatman 1987; Bal 1985; Altman 2008) se laissent concevoir comme un glissement progressif de l'intérêt spéculatif et des modèles logiques biplans (de souche aristotélicienne) vers des modèles intégratifs de communication, orientés vers trois points de repère : *l'univers raconté, les configurations discursives* qui en rendent compte mais aussi *l'activité interprétative* de la communauté réceptrice qui entreprend de « *reconfigurer* » les projections narratives. (Ricoeur 1985 : 20) Tout compte fait, le thème de la narration comme activité culturellement relative – dont on devrait tenir compte non seulement théoriquement mais aussi empiriquement – se fait jour dans les scénarios démonstratifs les plus serrés en la matière.

Un des exemples les plus révélateurs nous en est offert par les *Genres.* Conçus comme des moules de la création culturelle, et en même temps comme des modèles de réception, les genres donneraient aux lecteurs les plus différents le moyen d'aboutir à des interprétations identiques sinon très voisines. Le policier, le mélodrame, la biographie, la confession, l'histoire d'amour – en anglais « *romance* », tellement prisée à travers les temps et les espaces – voilà des configurations trans-textuelles, acceptées comme significatives par de nombreuses catégories de récepteurs, par les cultures et dans les contextes historiques les plus variés. On peut certainement les formaliser, mais on peut aussi les aborder empiriquement, et on l'a déjà fait. (Altman 2008)

Tout comme la fiction ou comme les configurations narratives, les genres sont eux aussi aptes à traverser le discours verbal, non verbal ou visuel, et à se faire employer par tous les médias : la littérature, le film, les bandes dessinées, les jeux vidéo, les produits télévisuels, et plus récemment les *new media.* D'après nous, c'est surtout la *vocation trans-médiatique* de ce type d'agrégés morpho-fonctionnels qui est à même de certifier leur capacité *transgressive.*

Pour ceux qui en doutent encore, le transfert de fourniture conceptuelle et méthodologique entre la littérature et les autres médias est tout à fait légitime. Dans la recherche culturelle actuelle, le rapport traditionnel entre la littérature et les médias tend à s'équilibrer, sinon à être mis à l'envers. La littérature cesse d'être la source et la banque privilégiée d'emprunt des médias, qui parviennent à lui rendre le statut de récipiendaire de leur fourniture conceptuelle et méthodologique.

Les recherches empiriques portant sur les genres médiatiques révèlent leur capacité à entraîner le public le plus hétérogène dans un type particulier de contrat récepteur. D'après Tamar Liebes et Elihu Katz, la stabilité des attentes génériques de lecture ne serait même pas bousculée par les variables identitaires des récepteurs. Apte à transgresser le contexte socioculturel différentiel dans lequel chacun des récepteurs définit son identité nationale, de genre, de race, de classe, d'âge ou de catégorie socio-économique, ce type de contrat générique et non référentiel est appelé par les deux chercheurs mentionnés ci-dessus *engagement métalinguistique.* (Katz, Liebes 1984 ; 1993)

Même les commentaires critiques de leurs recherches (comme ceux du sociologue Armand Mattelart) ne font que souligner une fois de plus la forte vocation trans-contextuelle des contrats génériques. (Mattelart, Neveu 2003 : 53)

Il n'entre pas dans mon propos d'insister davantage là-dessus. Je me limite donc à mentionner simplement les modèles collectifs sous-tendus par la catégorie du mythe, telle qu'elle est définie par des études récentes portant sur la littérature et sur les cultures médiatiques. Dans les termes de Ruth Amoisy, par exemple, il y a des représentations sociales qui s'imposent à l'imaginaire des communautés culturelles les plus diverses, grâce à des schémas discursifs figés, aptes à traverser tous les nouveaux supports de communication. (Amoisy 1991 : 9)

Une pareille tentative d'offrir au comparatisme littéraire un champ d'étude à mi-chemin entre des antipodes l'érigerait en *archi-* ou en *méta-discipline* : en un discours qui jouisse d'un fondement empirique solide mais qui soit aussi prêt à accepter des postulats, des concepts et des modèles méta-historiques explicites.

De nos jours, dans la recherche socio-humaine, la catégorie d'archi-discipline (ou de méta-discipline ?) est épistémologiquement tombée en disgrâce. On pourrait expliquer la dépréciation de ce concept tout d'abord par l'extension infinie de son champ empirique – une extension dont les disciplines humaines se méfient dernièrement. (Keley 2002 : 243–245) Il nous faut aussi admettre que depuis quelque temps, le fondement paradigmatique des disciplines culturelles a radicalement changé. Si l'on fait crédit aux épistémologues, elles témoignent maintenant d'un scepticisme, sinon d'un athéisme cognitif robuste, se montrant fort sensibles aux charmes de la discipline-pilote du moment : l'anthropologie. (Keley 2002 : 245)

On se rappelle bien que, mise en branle par son ambition de surclasser l'ancienne anthropologie (dite tantôt de fauteuil, tantôt de bibliothèque), la recherche contemporaine du domaine s'est mise à étaler des velléités de discipline scientifique rigoureuse. Pour une telle démarche, qui joue emphatiquement la carte de l'investigation empirique (*field work*), les moindres différences socio-historiques sont à prendre en compte, et le détail le plus trivial devient pertinent.

Mais, heureusement, il n'y a pas qu'une anthropologie.

Même si l'anthropologie factuelle, descriptive et non problématique y fait toujours figure de vedette, sur la scène actuelle de la recherche il y a aussi l'anthropologie interprétative, dans la lignée de Clifford Geertz, taxée couramment d'archi- ou de méta-anthropologie. (Inglis 2000 : 108) Le dessein déclaré de ce type de démarche, qui s'efforce de modeler le matériau factuel pour le rendre intelligible, serait de mettre en place des cadres conceptuels situés à une altitude moyenne et de forger des métalangages adéquats portant sur la diversité culturelle. Car pour Geertz et pour ses disciples, afin de devenir pertinent, le matériau doit être rapportable à un système de références construit par le chercheur. (Geertz 1983)

Une des affirmations de Geertz, à trouver dans son livre *After the fact. Two Countries, Four Decades, One anthropologist* (*Après le Fait. Deux Pays, Quatre décades, Un anthropologue*), me semble particulièrement pertinente pour la congrégation des comparatistes intéressés par la *littérature-monde* : « Sur le terrain infini qui s'ouvre aujourd'hui devant nous, la vraie recherche implique un haut degré d'auto-analyse : une réflexion du chercheur portant sur soi et sur ses outils, traduite dans un discours théorique se réfléchissant. » (Geertz 1995 : 125, ma traduction)

En guise de conclusions

La logique néo-territorialiste impliquée par des catégories comme *littérature-monde / world literature* menace par principe de pousser le comparatisme vers un relativisme babélien, instauré au nom de la diversité infinie et qui se donne comme modèle d'une prétendue anthropologie scientifique.

Pour citer un éloquent historien des idées, de cette façon « on risque de se laisser surpasser par des données, d'être mal guidés par les vanités et les conventions des traditions historiques et d'être tentés par la conviction hyper empirique que tout jugement, toute évaluation devraient être mis de coté jusqu'au tarissement des sources, sinon supprimé tout court. » (Keley 2002 : 244–245, ma traduction)

Comme les lignes précédentes l'ont déjà suggéré, il convient de retenir que l'objet d'étude du comparatisme s'impose plutôt comme un réseau dynamique dont les éléments minimaux sont des agrégés morpho-fonctionnels doués *d'une vocation migratoire* à travers les contextes socioculturels, ainsi qu'à travers les médias : les mondes fictionnels, les genres, les configurations narratives, les récipients vides et récupérables du mythe et du stéréotype. Ceux-ci prêtent à l'analyse deux visages : un versant ouvert à la recherche empirique, descriptive, et en même temps un versant formel apte à légitimer des scénarios démonstratifs cohérents et persuasifs.

Dans une perspective sémiotique, ce découpage méthodologique correspond, à peu de choses près, aux *formes du contenu*. Telles qu'elles sont définies par l'école sémiotique danoise et notamment par Louis Hjelmslev, *les formes du contenu* sont aptes à circonscrire un plan d'élévation spéculative placé à mi-distance entre les *formes* (abstraites) *de l'expression* et les *substances* (brutes) *du contenu.* (Hjelmslev 1963)

Ce type de découpage serait apte à dépasser des polarités ou des fractures telles que morphologique versus fonctionnel, texte versus contexte culturel, synchronique versus diachronique et surtout empirique versus théorique. Tout en conservant son point d'appui solide dans la diversité socio-historique, la démarche comparatiste saurait ainsi s'offrir comme dessein la projection des paradigmes signifiants, des catégories analytiques aptes à modeler l'évidence empirique. Mais, en tout premier lieu, *elle parviendrait à soumettre sa propre démarche à la métaréflexion.*

En fin de compte, je me demande bien si cela n'a pas l'air un peu utopique ; mais on sait tous que depuis toujours, les utopies ont mis en train l'esprit inquisitif...

Monica Spiridon
mspiridon@ines.ro
Universitatea din București
Facultatea de Litere
Str. Edgar Quinet nr. 14
București
ROMÂNIA / ROMANIA

Bibliographie

Altman, R. 2008. *A Theory of Narrative.* New York: Columbia University Press.

Amoisy, R. 1991. *Les idées recues. Sémiologie du stéréotype.* Paris: Nathan.

Bal, M. 1985. *Narratology: Introduction to the Theory of Narrative.* Toronto: University of Toronto Press.

Bernheimer, C. 1995. The Bernheimer Report. – C. Bernheimer, ed., *Comparative Literature in the Age of Multiculturalism.* Baltimore: John Hopkins University Press, 39–51.

Bruner, J. 2002. La Culture, le Soi et l'Autre. – F. Rastier, S. Bouquet, eds., *Une Introduction aux Sciences de la Culture.* Paris: PUF, 91–104.

Chatman, S. 1978. *Story and Discourse: Narrative Structure in Fiction and Film.* Ithaca: Cornell University Press.

Culler, J. 1981. Story and Discourse in the Analysis of Narrative. – J. Culler, *The Pursuit of Signs. Semiotics, Literature, Deconstruction.* Ithaca: Cornell University Press, 169–188.

Damrosch, D. 1995. Literary Study in an Elliptical Age. – Bernheimer, ed. 1995, 122–134.

Damrosch, D. 2003. What *is World Literature?* Princeton: Princeton University Press.

Godzich W. 1994. After the Storyteller. – V. Godzich, *The Culture of Literacy.* Cambridge MA: Harvard University Press, 96–106.

Geertz, C. 1983. *Local Knowledge. Further Essays in Interpretive Anthropology.* New York: Basic Books.

Geertz, C. 1995. *After the Fact. Two Countries, Four Decades, One Anthropologist.* Cambridge MA: Harvard University Press.

Goethe, J. W. von. 1988. *Conversations de Goethe avec Eckermann.* Paris: Gallimard.

Hjelmslev, L. 1963. *Prolegomena to a Theory of Language.* Madison: University of Wisconsin Press.

Inglis, F. 2000. Portrait of a Method. – *Clifford Geerz, Culture, Custom and Ethics.* London: Polity Press, 107–133.

Katz, E., Liebes, T. 1993. *The Export of Meaning. Cross Cultural Readings of "Dallas".* London: Polity Press.

Katz, E., Liebes, T. 1984. Dallas and Genesis: Primordiality and Seriality in Popular Culture. – W. Carey, ed., *Media, Myths and Narratives. Television and the Press,* 113–126.

Keley, D. R., 2002. *The Descent of Ideas. The History of Intellectual History.* Burlington: Ashgate Publishing.

Mattelart, A., Neveu, E. 2003. *Introduction aux Cultural Studies.* Paris: La Découverte, 52–53.

Pavel, T. 1986. *Fictional Worlds.* Cambridge MA: Harvard University Press. [Trad. *L'Univers de la Fiction.* Paris: Seuil, 1988.]

Pratt, M. L. 1995. Comparative Literature and Global Citizenship. – Bernheimer, ed., 1995, 58–66.

Ricoeur, P. 1985. *Time and Narrative,* vol. 2. Chicago and London: The University of Chicago Press.

Riffaterre, M. 1995. On *the Complementarity of Comparative Literature and Cultural Studies.* – Bernheimer, ed., 1995, 66–77.

Saussy, H. 2005. Chiasmus – *Comparative Literature, Responding to the Death of a Discipline: An ACLA Forum,* Vol. 57, No. 3, 234.

Saussy, H. 2006. Exquisite Cadavers Stiched from Fresh Nightmares. – *Comparative Literature in the Age of Globalization.* Baltimore: The John Hopkins University Press, 3–42.

The Human Need for Ethopoesis: Toward an Apologetics for World Literature

HARVEY L. HIX

Abstract. There is a way of understanding contemporary life that sees technology as having displaced poetry, rendering it irrelevant or at best compensatory. I propose a contrary view. The predominance of technology, I contend, has made poetry more urgent than ever before, so urgent that it is a condition for the continued survival of the human species. My case for this contrarian understanding has two elements. First, I note two aspects of contemporary life that testify to our want of poetry, and then I sketch a conception of ethopoesis as a response to the want revealed by these two aspects of contemporary life. This conception of the ethopoetic gestures toward (without pretending fully to achieve) a cultural understanding that recognises the urgency, even the necessity, of poetry, and toward a vision of a poetry that might be adequate to this cultural need.

Keywords: poetry, technology, global economy, agency, poesis

There is a way of understanding contemporary life that sees technology as having displaced poetry, rendering it irrelevant or at best compensatory. We live in the information age, according to this view, under the sign of Moore's Law, and poetry, as Wittgenstein observed even before digital supplanted analogue, "is not used in the language game of giving information" (§ 160). According to this understanding, poetry's absence from popular culture confirms its reduction to insignificance. Gaming and film and television reach billions of people worldwide, and generate billions each year in revenue. Poetry reaches only a tiny, tenuous, negligible audience, and operates at a loss, needing to be propped up by patronage, burdening rather than bolstering economic growth.

I propose a contrary view. The predominance of technology, I contend, has made poetry more urgent than ever before, so urgent that it is a condition for the continued survival of the human species. The exclusion of poetry from popular culture is a symptom not of *poetry's* illness but of *culture's*. The situation is not that poetry is dying for want of an audience, but that humanity is dying for want of poetry. As Charles Bernstein succinctly formulates the matter: "What is to be regretted is not the lack of mass audience for any particular poet but the lack of poetic thinking as an activated potential for all people" (225).

DOI: http://dx.doi.org/10.12697/IL.2015.S1.7

My case for this contrarian understanding has two elements. First, I note two aspects of contemporary life that testify to our want of poetry, and then I sketch a conception of 'ethopoesis' as a response to the want revealed by these two aspects of contemporary life. This conception of the ethopoetic gestures toward (without pretending fully to achieve) a cultural understanding that recognises the urgency, even the *necessity*, of poetry, and toward a vision of a poetry that might be adequate to this cultural need.

Our want of poetry

Technology and economy now are global in ways, and to a degree, far beyond what they ever have been before. Transportation has overcome regional limitations to the movement of goods; digital technology has overcome the limits distance once imposed on communication; corporations now have worldwide market reach; natural resources from any region are accessible to exploitation by entities in other, far-distant regions; and so on. Our economy has raced toward total globalisation, but our cultures and our concepts of citizenship have not globalised at the same pace, instead remaining local and sectarian. Corporations are now multinational, but political institutions remain stubbornly national; natural resources and manufactured products move easily from one place to another, but the movement of humans is tightly restricted by national boundaries; those with capital can find safety and security for their *money* more readily than those without capital can find safety and security for their *persons*; and so on.

This disparity between a global economy and local cultural and civic values has as its upshot structural violence, which Paul Farmer defines as "acts of violence are perpetrated, usually by the strong against the weak, in complex social fields," fields in which "a set of historically given and, often enough, economically driven conditions... guarantee that violent acts will ensue" (9). Farmer argues that political democracy cannot be had without the attainment also of economic democracy, that in other words cultural and civic values must also check, not only be checked by, economic forces.

Though Farmer does not identify poetry as an ally in this cause, I here contend that poetry urges, and furthers, the revaluation for which he calls. Until we are able to construct, and begin to enact, a global *culture* and global *citizenship*, our global *economy* will only be destructive: exaggerating the disparity between rich and poor, exhausting resources and generating waste faster and faster, prompting ever more terrorism and war and genocide. There are many ways to articulate why this is so. Janet Dine gives one especially lucid way in her article "Rigging the Risks", which explains, as its subtitle suggests, "why commercial law kills". Capitalism, she affirms, in its essence is simple ("goods are traded by humans to try to alleviate their needs or wants" (47)), and its primary tool, the contract, is functional and ethically sound. But "like any other human institution it [the contract] can be corrupted," and the dominant contractually-based institutions, namely multinational companies (e.g. banks) and international financial institutions (e.g. the IMF), have been corrupted. "The role of commercial law in a market economy", Dine posits, "is to allocate risk" (48), but it has not done so equitably. Instead, both international and national laws, "written", Dine reminds us, "mostly by wealthy élites", have participated in creating poverty the results of which include: more than one of every eight humans is undernourished; one of every eight humans does not have access to safe drinking water; two of five do not have access to adequate sanitation. That combination – unclean water and poor sanitation – kills 1.4 million children every year (4000 every day, one every 20 seconds) (46). In creating laws about contracts, commercial law establishes rules defining and protecting property, regulating how it is acquired and disposed of, but Dine emphasises that "property rights are not rights over *things* but, on the contrary, rights against other people", specifically the right to *exclude* them (51). Laws constructed by and for those who already own property (and in modern capitalist states nearly everyone involved in making laws does own property) will pursue "the widest concept of property and freedom to trade" without regulatory control, thus encouraging "accumulations of property without imposing countervailing responsibilities" (51).

Dine's analysis depicts the current global economy as not merely out of step with, but dependent upon the suppression of, valid conceptions of global culture and citizenship. Such an exposition of the global situation suggests a condition for any suitable response to it. To mitigate the structural violence of our economy, we need cultural and civic parameters – our checks on economic activity – able to stand up to, and to modify, the nature of the economic activity taking place. My case for what I call here the 'ethopoetic' is that without it our attempts even to envision, much less to implement, such parameters would be impoverished and futile.

That impoverishment and futility is revealed by contrasting the medium of economic exchange with the medium of cultural and civic exchange. Along at least one vector, the contrast is stark. The medium of economic exchange, currency, homogenises and distorts value. It makes everything fungible: by means of it, anything can be rendered equivalent to anything else. So many tons of rice are equivalent to, and can be traded for, one automobile; so many hours of a person's labour at a certain job are equivalent to one month's rent on an apartment. The medium of cultural exchange, language, recognises value in its full variety and particularity. Its differentiating capacity enables it to resist and to limit fungibility, to preserve uniqueness from equivalence.

Currency performs its generalising by substituting price for value. Implied by the substitution is an erasure of the distinction between price and value. Currency, in other words, pretends that price *just is* value. But it is not. Henry K. H. Woo gives a concise exposition of the fact that price and value differ. Although economists all would agree on the importance of price theory, Woo says, many mainstream economists would find no interest in a theory of value. In particular, neoclassical economists "might consider the problem of value largely a pseudoproblem that has been dissolved" because value is "a subjective concept, and the classical search for an absolute standard is nothing but a futile enterprise" (1). Besides, even the pseudoproblem "has been ingeniously solved" within the neoclassical framework by stipulating that value is "identical to price in the state of market equilibrium and is measured by it" (1). To reassert value's distinction from price, we need a medium in which the substitution of price for value can be challenged, and language is such a medium. This recognition grounds both an apology for poetry and an ideal for poetry. That is, it helps explain why poetry is necessary and also what poetry at its best might be.

In her book *Lyric Philosophy*, Jan Zwicky fulfils this recognition of language's capacity for challenging the substitution of price for value. She does so by proposing a literary way of seeing that she calls "lyric comprehension", which "does not distinguish between a thing's being and that-it-is-valuable" (102). In other words, lyric comprehension, by maintaining a thing's being as integral to its valuation, contrasts with – is the opposite of – pricing, which performs its valuation by substituting a uniform measure for a thing's being. Lyric comprehension opposes the economic comprehension manifest through currency. Zwicky expands on this position in *Wisdom and Metaphor*, by speaking of "ontological attention", a correlative of "lyric comprehension", as "a response to particularity: *this* porch, *this* laundry basket, *this* day. Its object cannot be substituted for, even when it is an object of considerable generality ('the country', 'cheese', 'garage sales'). It is the antithesis of the attitude that regards things as 'resources', mere means to human ends. In perceiving *this*ness, we respond to having been addressed" (52). That the object cannot be substituted means that its value has been preserved in distinction from price, which makes anything substitutable for anything else. In contrast to the voracious equivalences imposed by price (this porch, which costs $1000, is worth 100 of these laundry baskets, which only cost $10 apiece), *this*ness insists that no porch can substitute for this laundry basket, and no laundry basket for this porch. Such linguistic and literary comprehension – such poesis – pushes back against the homogenising of economic comprehension.

The capacity of language to particularise, to retain the uniqueness of a thing as integral to its identity and the being of a thing as integral to its valuation, is a *capacity*, one we can realise effectively or not. Which suggests an ideal for poetry: to be that language use in which the particularising capacity of language, its resistance to the economic substitution of price for value, is most fully realised. The ideal receives concise and elegant formulation in Wyslawa Szymborska's Nobel Prize acceptance speech: "In daily speech", she says, "where we don't stop to consider every word, we all use phrases such as 'the ordinary world', 'ordinary life', 'the ordinary course of events'". But in poetry, which realises the particularising capacity of language by weighing every word, "nothing is usual or normal. Not a single stone and not a single cloud above it. Not a single day and not a single night after it. And above all, not a single existence, not anyone's existence in this world" (xviii). In Szymborska's terms, nothing is usual or normal; in Zwicky's terms, nothing can be substituted. In either formulation, poetry is at work resisting the global economy's pressure to make anything substitutable for anything else, and thus to make *everything* susceptible to market exchange.

It is not only that technology and economy have changed our world, the context in which we live and think and act; they also have changed us. We are in different circumstances than ever before, and we ourselves are different. Humanist and posthumanist accounts concur in the assessment that our reach now exceeds our grasp, and that this exceeding is not the unqualified, heavenly good that Browning's Andrea del Sarto imagined it to be.

Martha Nussbaum formulates the difference elegantly in her humanist manifesto *Not for Profit*: "We live in a world", she declares, "in which people face one another across gulfs of geography, language, and nationality. More than at any time in the past, we all depend on people we have never seen, and they depend on us" (79). Our most pressing problems are global, and "have no hope of being solved unless people once distant come together and cooperate in ways they have not before". This global interdependency encompasses us all, Nussbaum says. "The global economy has tied all of us to distant lives. Our simplest decisions as consumers affect the living standards of people in distant nations who are involved in the production of products we use. Our daily lives put pressure on the global environment" (80). To some small extent, of course, it was ever so. Hunter-gatherers pressured other species, and left behind them a rubble of tools and shelters. A northerner wearing a cotton blouse in the antebellum US subsidised the enslavement of an African-American on a plantation down south. The difference in degree, though, is now so great as to amount to a difference in kind. My shoes subsidise child labour in Singapore, the car I drive sanctions the circumstances in which female factory workers are routinely raped and killed at the US/Mexico border, my trash is dumped into a dead zone in the Pacific, and on and on. Nussbaum says it would be irresponsible of us "to bury our heads in the sand, ignoring the many ways in which we influence, every day, the lives of distant people". In the absence of my reckoning with that influence, my human interactions will be "mediated by the thin norms of market exchange in which human lives are seen primarily as instruments for gain" (80). I will only continue and increase my harm to distant others.

If Nussbaum's humanist manifesto emphasises the synchronic extension of our reach, its expansion across space, Timothy Morton's posthumanist manifesto *Hyperobjects* emphasises the diachronic extension of our reach, its expansion across time. Morton distinguishes, as the fields through which our reach has come to extend, three timescales, which he names "the *horrifying*, the *terrifying*, and the *petrifying*" (59). The horrifying is the scale of five-hundred years. Five-hundred years ago is beyond the time of Shakespeare's *Henry VIII* to the time of the events the play depicts, which even to Shakespeare and his contemporaries were "historical". Yet, Morton notes, I am participating in creating effects that will affect humans as far into the future as Henry VIII is in the past: "75 percent of global warming effects will persist until five hundred years from now" (58). What holds at the "horrifying" timescale holds also at the "terrifying" timescale of thirty-thousand years. This is the distance into the past of the Chauvet Cave paintings, and yet, again, the effects of my current actions will continue to have effects that far into the future: 25 percent of the carbon compounds my car releases the next time I drive it will still be in the atmosphere thirty thousand years from now, and "the half-life of plutonium-239 is 24,100 years" (59). Even at the timescale Morton calls the "petrifying", my effects will linger. Even then, "7 percent of global warming effects will still be occurring", and "form built structures (skyscrapers, overpasses, garnets for lasers, graphene, bricks)" of "the new 'minerals' such as concrete, created with extreme rapidity by humans (we have doubled the number of such minerals on Earth)" will have created "a layer of geological strata" (60).

Morton's point is that "the future hollows out the present", by which he means that the three timescales "are truly humiliating" because "they force us to realize how close to the Earth we are" (60). Because it *can* be imagined, infinite duration – eternity – is forgiving. Because it *can't* be imagined, time at the scales Morton considers, the time of "very large finitude" rather than of infinity, is unforgiving. Morton describes contemporary humanity collectively, and each of us individually, as participating in the construction of "hyperobjects" such as global warming, which exist in very large finitude, and which therefore starkly reveal the degree by which my reach now exceeds my grasp. By helping cause global warming, "I am directly responsible for beings [a hundred-thousand years] into the future, insofar as two things will be true simultaneously: no one then will meaningfully be related to me; and my smallest action now will affect that time in profound ways". Even the most trivial-seeming of my mundane decisions/ actions affects others far into the horrifying, terrifying, and petrifying futures: "A Styrofoam cup will outlive me by over four-hundred years" (60).

Ethopoesis in answer to our want

Our changed circumstances and our changed selves entail that our responsibilities have changed. My indirect actions now are more potent than my direct actions, and consequently the unintended consequences of my actions always and necessarily exceed the intended consequences. The asymmetry between effect and control has switched. Insofar as others' effects on me exceed my control – the old situation – the result is tragedy: *my* destruction looms. For the Greek tragedians, my agency is inadequate to my circumstances (a fact that receives personification as Fate, Necessity, and so on). My effects are too small to fulfil my intentions. For us, now, my agency is *over*adequate. My effects are too large for my intentions to manage. Insofar as my effects on others exceed my control – the new situation – the result is disaster (war, ecological violence, structural violence, and so on): our destruction looms. To put this another way, the state in which contemporary mechanical and digital technology and the contemporary global economy have placed us differs from the "state of nature" from which Hobbes tries to help us remove ourselves. In Hobbes, we are each threatened with destruction. Any human might be destroyed. In current circumstances, we are *all* threatened with destruction. Humanity might be destroyed. In Hobbes, the bind is the prisoners' dilemma: we need a way to remove agency from the individual. Now the bind is the Midas touch: we need a way to restrain the agency of the individual.

To theorise this new situation, this inversion of the relationship between agency and volition calls for a contrast between approaches I will call 'ethotechne' and 'ethopoesis'.

The following chart schematises the distinction I mean, and the brief glosses that follow the chart open the process of exposition.

	Ethotechne	Ethopoesis
Exemplum	Only YOU can prevent forest fires.	Only YOU can prevent global warming.
Positive agency	I can cause a forest fire by myself.	I cannot cause global warming by myself.
Negative agency	I can *decide* not to cause a forest fire.	I cannot decide not to cause global warming.
Determinant	Occasion is primary.	Conditions are primary.
Cause/effect relationship	Simple.	Complex.
Range	Local.	Global.
Reducibility	A rule is adequate. ("Don't put your elbows on the table.")	No rule is adequate. ("Be a good parent.")
Demand	Calls upon (calls for) a particular behaviour.	Calls upon (calls for) full personhood.
Possibility	There is an interpretation of the charge that makes my fulfilling it possible to me.	No interpretation of the charge would make fulfilling it possible to me.
Divisibility	Either/or.	Continuum.
Unifying Principle	Summation.	Wholeness.
Essential Quality	Private.	Civic.
Attribute required	Obedience.	Citizenship.
Efficacy	Immediate: decision=>action=>outcome	Mediated: decision(s)=>action(s)=>other variables=>outcome
Character	Problem.	Mystery.
Means	I can *discover* a *solution.*	I must *imagine* an *alternative.*
Capacity invoked	Calls for *techne.*	Calls for *poesis.*

Exemplum: One of the longest-running and most successful advertising campaigns ever in the United States depicts an anthropomorphised bear named Smokey, whose insistent message has been "Only YOU can prevent forest fires". So familiar is this campaign that, according to the Ad Council, "Smokey Bear is recognized by 97% of adults [in the U.S.], and 3 out of 4 adults are able to recall his message without prompting." I mention the ad campaign here because its motto helps to draw an important distinction. "Only YOU can prevent forest fires" has proven extraordinarily effective as a campaign slogan, but it is also patently false. Many forest fires will occur in the coming year, and there is nothing you or I can do to prevent them. There is, however, a way to register the slogan such that it makes sense, and the Forest Service can employ the literally false motto in full confidence that we the audience will 'translate' it readily into the imperative mode, as the commands, "Stamp out cigarette butts, and do not leave campfires unattended". (The ad campaign leaves aside consideration of forest fires caused by extra-human factors, such as lightning, and expects its audience to 'translate' the slogan in ways that leave aside such fires. For the purposes of this paper, I follow that lead.)

The point I wish to make here, though, is that the ad campaign's slogan works for forest fires, but would not work for all difficulties created by and affecting humans. For example, it would make no sense to say "Only YOU can prevent global warming". Melty Glacier would not be able to adapt Smokey Bear's motto, because the adaptation would, like the original, be patently false, but unlike the original the adaptation would not be amenable to 'translation' into a true statement, one that offers positive guidance. Admonished by Smokey, I will diligently monitor my decisions and actions when I go camping this year, and as a result of that diligence I will cause no forest fires. There will be one forest fire less than there might otherwise have been. Admonished by Melty, though, there is no due diligence for me to perform. I can take measures to reduce my carbon footprint, but global warming will continue inexorably, not measurably or discernibly slowed. The part I play in – my relationship to – forest fires differs from the part I play in global warming, and the difference between the two exemplifies the difference between what I am here calling ethotechne and ethopoesis.

Positive agency: This term names one axis along which the relationship between agency and intention varies. In ethotechne, my intention governs my agency: I can, for example, cause a forest fire by myself. In contrast, in ethopoesis my intention does not govern – is not adequate to – my agency. For example, I cannot cause global warming by myself. In the ethotechnical realm, intention and effect merge; in the ethopoetic realm, they diverge. Consequently, in the ethotechnical, teleological and deontological approaches to ethical concerns will tend to concur, and in the ethopoetic, they will tend to contrast. My having good intentions will suffice in relation to forest fires, because those intentions, since they govern my agency, will yield effects consonant with the intentions. My having good intentions will not suffice in relation to global warming, because, absent their governing my agency, effects consistent with them need not attend them.

Negative agency: Here, too, the distinction is straightforward. In ethotechne, my intention and agency are related to one another in such a way that I can decide not to cause a forest fire, but in ethopoesis, my intention and agency relate to one another differently: I cannot simply decide not to cause global warming. This distinction tracks the positive agency distinction, but applies to the 'negative' rather than the 'positive' domain: the domain in which I seek not to have a given effect. Positive agency concerns my capacity to cause a forest fire or global warming, and negative agency concerns my ability not to cause – my ability to avoid causing – those phenomena.

Determinant: In ethotechne, the occasion is primary, but in ethopoesis the conditions are primary. What is essential about my starting a forest fire is the occasion, and it is what I do on that occasion that brings about the results. I can start a forest fire only when I am on a camping trip, in the forest, not when I am at home in the city. In ethopoesis, though, the conditions are primary. I live in a time period and within a human social arrangement in which hydrocarbons are the primary energy source, as a result of which carbon is being released into the atmosphere faster than it can be absorbed by natural processes. Consequently, it is not a specific occasion on which I cause global warming; it's the conditions in which I move and live that cause global warming. I might wake up one morning and decide that the time is right – i.e. this is the occasion – for setting a forest fire. There is no occasion, though, for my bringing about global warming: I am engaged in doing so continually, not occasionally.

Cause/effect relationship: The forest fire can be described in a clear and adequate way by a simple causal chain. I decide to leave a campfire burning when I'm not watching it, or I carelessly throw a cigarette butt out the window of my car as I drive through Yellowstone; that action lights dry leaves on fire and that fire expands into a large area. I do one thing, and because I did that one particular thing another particular thing follows. But in ethopoesis, the cause/effect relationship is not a simple causal chain, but a complex causal network. It's not that I, or any single human, decided to burn hydrocarbons as a primary energy source, but that many things –the invention of the internal combustion engine, the mass production of motor vehicles, and the burning of coal for energy, and so on – decisions made by various people, in various times, in various circumstances, all are engaged in a complex nexus of causes and effects, plural, that create the phenomenon we describe as global warming.

Range: The simple cause/effect chain occurs at a local level. I light my cigarette in one place, and I throw it out the window in one place. The fire begins in that place and spreads to a region continuous with that place. The event begins as, and remains, local. But in ethopoesis, the cause/effect nexus and the event or phenomenon is global rather than local. Although I am currently seated at my computer, drawing electricity, that electricity was produced somewhere else, and the emissions from the production of that electricity are not being released here in my home office, but instead where the energy was produced. The food that I eat is not itself, here at my dinner table, releasing hydrocarbons, but I purchased it at a grocery store, which got it from a distributor, which procured it from farms in Mexico, so it was shipped by train or truck from Mexico, over great distance. Hydrocarbons were burned during the shipping, rather than at the moment of my meal, and released across that distance, rather than being released here. The effects of global warming don't follow me around like the rain cloud in a comic strip; they alter the climate of the entire globe. The strengthened storms and higher temperatures might more directly affect someone on the other side of the planet than they affect me.

Reducibility: I distinguish ethotechne and ethopoesis along the axis I call reducibility by noting that for ethotechnical concerns, a rule is adequate. For example, the rule not to leave unattended campfires is adequate, in contrast to the rule not to use fossil fuels. Or, again, the rule don't put your elbows on the table is an adequate rule, in contrast to the rule be a good parent, which needs so much further interpretation and amplification that in an important sense it's no help. It's a good principle, in that it would be a good thing if one did fulfil it, but it's no good at all in the sense that it's no help: it offers no guidance. In ethotechne there is an applicable rule that is meaningful and can be enacted; in ethopoesis, there is not. In this regard, the contrast between ethotechne and ethopoesis resembles that in Christian theology between law and grace. Law seeks to enumerate the rules that will be adequate to guide me through any and every occasion; grace changes my condition.

Demand: The ethotechnical calls upon or calls for a particular behaviour. In relation to forests, I am called upon not to leave campfires unattended, and not to discard cigarette butts that have not been fully extinguished. The ethopoetic calls upon or calls not for a particular behaviour but for an altered or elevated personhood. My particular behaviour of raking up leaves manually, rather than using a motorised leaf blower, may be positively inflected, but it is so minuscule as to be invisible, utterly ineffective. In the ethopoetic, my whole person is called into question, and called to involvement. I am under the sign of the maxim at the end of Rilke's "Archaic Torso of Apollo": "You must revise your life."

Possibility: In the ethotechnical, there is an interpretation of the given charge that makes my fulfilling that charge possible to me. But this is not so in the ethopoetic, where no interpretation of the charge would make it possible for me to fulfil it adequately and fully. For instance, I have to this point done what I will continue to do until I die: fulfil the ethotechnical call not to cause forest fires. I have never caused a forest fire, and I never will cause a forest fire. I will never leave a campfire unattended, nor will I ever throw an unextinguished cigarette butt out of a car window. But it is clear that I could not prevent global warming. It's not that I am failing to do something that would prevent global warming, but that there is nothing I can do that would prevent global warming. Global warming ought to be prevented, but no interpretation of that call results in its being possible for me to fulfil the call.

Divisibility: The ethotechnical offers itself in either/or terms. Either I have or I have not left a campfire unattended. Either I have or I have not thrown a cigarette butt out of the window. The ethopoetic offers itself as a continuum. I might participate more actively or less actively in the creation of global warming. I might participate more self-consciously or less self-consciously, more reflectively or less reflectively. I might maximise my complicity in global warming, or minimise it. I might, for instance, regularly drive my very large SUV to and from the market or on long cross-country drives, which would increase my complicity, or I might walk to work or take shared commuter transit, which would decrease my complicity.

Unifying Principle: Here the contrast I wish to draw is that the ethotechnical offers itself as, or purports to work by, summation. If all park visitors to national parks in the United States next year act according to Smokey's advice, then the sum of those separate and individual decisions will be that no human-caused forest fires will occur. If the first visitor acts according to Smokey's advice, and the second visitor, and the third, and so on through all the visitors, then no one will cause a forest fire, and no human-caused forest fires will occur. Matters of ethopoetic concern operate according to wholeness, a wholeness that exceeds or is not identical to summation. It is plausible to think that every human being might decide not to leave campfires unattended; it is not plausible in current social conditions to think that humans will cease to burn fossil fuels.

The greater the number of individuals who follow the appropriate rules, the smaller the number of forest fires caused by humans. In the ethotechnical realm, individual decisions can add up in an effective way. In contrast, in ethopoetic matters such as global warming, even the decisions by a great many people to stop using hydrocarbons would not stop the process of global warming. I might myself cut my carbon footprint to a tenth of its current size, and I might convince a thousand of my closest Facebook friends to do so also, but global warming would not cease as a result. A larger whole would have to be changed, rather than the sum of many individual parts changing, in order for that to happen.

Essential Quality: By calling the essential quality of ethotechne 'private', I mean that it is a matter of conscience, that even insofar as it impacts others, it remains something that I do individually and am responsible for individually. Whether it does or does not affect other people, whether or not other people are aware of it, I am responsible. Even in a circumstance where no one else knows that I set the forest fire, I still am accountable for setting it. By the ethopoetic, I mean something like I take it Socrates means in his argument with Crito. My life formation is inseparable from the larger human community and my place in it, so that it is not a matter of individual conscience alone. Even though Socrates was condemned for something he didn't do, the condemnation applies. He ought to accept the penalty imposed on him, because it is a part of, or is an effluence of, the whole in which his life has been and is enmeshed. The larger-than-himself, the entirety, is definitive, rather than he himself, the part. Socrates has an individual conscience, which he is very concerned to follow, but it is not what governs in this matter.

Attribute required: In ethotechnical matters I am called on to obey. The rule not to leave campfires unattended describes something I should simply do. I am duty-bound to obey that principle. I am essentially passive in relation to it, and my obedience occurs, for all practical purposes, in isolation from anything else. The attribute required of me by the ethopoetic is something larger, what I'm calling here 'citizenship', but by which I mean something that is not exhausted by obedience to a rule, but includes my own judgment in relation to natural constraints, the judgments of others, and so on. I am in active, reciprocal, *responsible* relationship with global warming, a relationship is inextricably linked to other aspects of my thought and life.

Efficacy: The contrast along the axis I'm calling 'efficacy' is that the cause/effect relationship in ethotechne is immediate. I make a decision, I perform an action, and something results immediately from that action. I decide to carelessly toss my cigarette butt, I do so, the dry pine needles on which it falls light, and a forest fire begins. In contrast, in ethopoetic concerns, the cause/effect relationship is mediated. I decide to compose this book at a computer, rather than writing it out longhand. I make that decision and perform the action, but then other things take place. The electricity that I use is drawn from somewhere else, so the outcome, global warming, is mediated by other factors and other agencies. It is not a direct, immediate outcome of my action. My typing this book at my computer does not initiate, nor would my writing longhand have stopped, global warming. In contrast to my throwing out a cigarette butt, which if I do it causes a forest fire, and if I don't doesn't cause a forest fire.

Character: I mean to apply here a distinction drawn by Louis Mackey, between a problem and a mystery:

> In the nature of the case, a problem can be solved. The terms in which it is stated define what will count as a solution. Confronted on a math test with a problem that cannot be solved, the student has every right to complain that it "isn't really a problem." Like a problem, a mystery is an indeterminate situation that begs to be made determinate. But its indeterminacy is such that the description of the mystery does not specify conditions of resolution and closure. For that matter, the mystery itself cannot be fully described. Faced with a mystery, you can never be sure what will count as a solution, or even that there is one. (247)

My observation in this essay is that the ethotechnical offers itself to us in the form of a problem, and the ethopoetic offers itself to us in the form of a mystery. As a result of which, in the ethotechnical there is a solution available, at least potentially or in principle, but in the ethopoetic, because it is a mystery it is not offered in terms of a problem and a solution.

Means: Confronted with a problem, I can discover (or in principle I can discover, or I seek to discover) a solution. How do I keep from causing forest fires, I ask myself. Oh, I see: I will thoroughly douse my campfire before I leave my campsite, and I will carefully stub out each of my cigarette butts. I need only be adequate to an occasion. Confronted with a mystery, though, I cannot simply find the right switch to flip. No occasion offers itself; I and my conditions must be remade. When I ask how I can keep from causing global warming, I must imagine an alternative self and alternative conditions.

Capacity invoked: It is the combination of all these factors that gives the name to the two categories that I am identifying here, because in relation to forest fires I ought to exercise my capacity for what the Greeks called *techne*, but in relation to global warming techne is inadequate, and I ought to draw on my capacity for what they called *poesis*. The techne/poesis distinction in Greek bears some resemblance to the craft/art distinction in English, and indeed *techne* is often translated 'craft'.

The invocation of the capacity for poesis offers at last a succinct way to state the case toward which this paper has aimed. The Greek word *techne* is of course the etymological root of the English word technology, and *poesis* the root of poetry. The understanding of contemporary life I seek to contest, the one which holds that technology has displaced poetry, takes for granted that everything can be treated as a problem. If that were true, then indeed techne is the appropriate means for addressing our concerns, and it is right that technology, as a useful aid to problem-solving, should displace poetry. If, however, as I contend, the most pressing current concerns of humankind (such as global warming) and the perennial concerns of humankind (such as war) and the most important concerns of human individuals (such as love) are not problems but mysteries, then our greater need is not technology but poetry, and the increased prominence of technology in contemporary society is deceptive, masking the continuing greater importance of poetry.

Harvey L. Hix
hhix@uwyo.edu
Philosophy Department 3392
University of Wyoming
Laramie, WY 82071
USA

References

Ad Council web page. http://www.adcouncil.org/Our-Work/Current-Work/Family-Community/Wildfire-Prevention. Accessed 20 October 2013.

Bernstein, C. 1992. *A Poetics*. Cambridge: Harvard Univ. Press.

Dine, J. 2011. Rigging the Risks: Why commercial law kills. – *Irish Pages*, 6:1, 46–63.

Farmer, P. 2003. *Pathologies of Power: Health, Human Rights, and the New War on the Poor.* Berkeley: Univ. of California Press.

Mackey, L. 2002. *An Ancient Quarrel Continued: The Troubled Marriage of Philosophy and Literature.* Lanham: Univ. Press of America.

Morton, T. 2013. *Hyperobjects: Philosophy and Ecology after the End of the World.* Minneapolis: Univ. of Minnesota Press.

Nussbaum, M. 2010. *Not for Profit: Why Democracy Needs the Humanities.* Princeton: Princeton Univ. Press.

Szymborska, W. 1998. *Poems New and Collected: 1957–1997.* Trans. Stanislaw Baranczak and Clare Cavanagh. Harcourt: Harvest Books.

Thoreau, H. D. 1989. *Walden.* Ed. J. Lyndon Shanley. Princeton: Princeton Univ. Press.

Wittgenstein, L. 1970. *Zettel.* Ed. G. E. M. Anscombe and G. H. von Wright. Trans. G. E. M. Anscombe. Berkeley and Los Angeles: Univ. of California Press.

Woo, H. K. H. 1992. *Cognition, Value, and Price: A General Theory of Value.* Ann Arbor: Univ. of Michigan Press.

Zwicky, J. 1992. *Lyric Philosophy.* Toronto: Univ. of Toronto Press.

Zwicky, J. 2003. *Wisdom & Metaphor.* Kentville, N. S.: Gaspereau Press.

World Poetry in a Socio-Political View[1]

ARTURO CASAS

Abstract. On the horizon of World Literature and paying special attention to Jüri Talvet's Estonian Elegy, this paper presents for consideration the consequences of the functional instability of the subject/author in the constitution of the poetic-I and the projection of this onto the inter-subjective and public domains. The aim is to move towards a socio-cultural and political reading of contemporary poetic production.

Keywords: canonicity, event, Jüri Talvet, public sphere, world poetry

A Jüri Talvet, benquerido amigo,
en recoñecemento do seu maxisterio e
estímulo intelectual

The institutionalisation of the lyric as a modern literary category in the West did not bring about, unlike the case of other genres, the more or less foreseeable development of a theoretic tradition from the classical period. In fact, this tradition was not firm before the Renaissance. On founding it, the commentators of Aristotle and Horace introduced profound adjustments aimed at ending the diffuse fundamental genericity, although they still operated with vacillations. Expressed in relational perspective, in the mid-16th century Antonio Minturno and Giulio Cesare Scaligero observed the differences and interdependencies of the lyric with the other two main genericities in play, the narrative and the dramatic. In the case of Minturno, incidentally, granting pre-eminence to the old Aristotelian notion of medium (*hois*), reinterpreted in the sense that could be described as perfomative (Guerrero 1998: 81).

The subsequent course of aesthetic investigations into the lyric, particularly during Romanticism, redirected the treatment of this subject towards the basic spheres of discursiveness and subjectivity activated by the poem itself. We therefore speak of modifications in two of the main operations associated, in rhetorical and pragmatic terms, to the poetic enunciation. Or, before that, to its

1 This paper is linked to the research project *La poesía actual en el espacio público. Intervención, transferencia y performatividad*, with public funding from the Spanish Government (FFI2012-33589). Translated by Desmond Joyce and revised by the author.

DOI: http://dx.doi.org/10.12697/IL.2015.S1.8

own possibility of materialising as a discourse *in* and *for* a specific historic and sociocultural context, i.e. in a certain public space, according to the studies by Roger Chartier (1990) on the cultural background of the French Revolution. Let us consider in this regard, in operative terms, the following description by Daniel Innerarity (2006: 15–16):

> The public space is a place where problems are pointed out and interpreted, where tensions are experienced and the conflict is turned into debate, where the problematization of social life is staged.

Consider, on the other hand, the fact that from the 18th century onwards there are significant examples of how aesthetics and hermeneutics privilege the poem as an object of knowledge, thereby anticipating genuinely modern positions that, to avoid any misunderstanding, could be specified by mentioning, among others, the thinking of Martin Heidegger, María Zambrano, Jacques Rancière or Giorgio Agamben.

Modernity, in effect, brought with it a series of enunciative readjustments that affected the non-intimate or relatively private dimensions of the poem and the possibility itself of poetry's appearance in the public sphere, even in a transnational public sphere. In this journey, the lyric aspect of poetry was institutionalised, although at the same time there remained open a favourable space for other poetic variants, often not exclusive in the full sense of lyricism as such. For the want of a more precise label, we can call these variants non-lyric.

As has just been suggested, the lyric and non-lyric specifications of modern and post-modern poetry are interconnected discursive domains, with a distribution of functionalities subject to permanent re-examination, especially in the aspect of cultural practices and perhaps not so much on a merely theoretic or poetological level. Something similar has occurred in other discursive domains. This is the case of fictional prose, the genre of the essay or theatre forms. However, in these fields a permanent theoretic reflection has often materialised regarding the limits between the fictional and the non-fictional, the argumentative or the sentimental or, for example, the series of anti-bourgeoisie theatre practices that gave rise in France to the label of *antithéâtre*.

What is truly interesting about this emergence of new pacts of discursive production-reception, lies in the redirecting of the perspective on the literature genre to what is its most characteristic place: that of the existence of a relational complex in which the genres are defined by their pragmatic-enunciative functions and by their links and networks within certain historic and cultural coordinates. Among these, it is necessary to consider those of an international or, strictly speaking, worldwide nature, with all the semantic values (Landrin 2010) that this latter adjective has acquired starting from Goethe, when it is applied to the noun literature and activates the concept of *Weltliteratur* (Martí Monterde 2011; Jurt 2014: 15–48).

It seems obvious, on the other hand, that little has been done by means of comparatism to consolidate the possible meanings of a World Poetry. Probably because the textual references that American and French traditions, to mention the two most dynamic or at least most commonly cited, have been working with in relation to World Literature have been overwhelmingly narrative. Both Franco Moretti (1993) and Pascale Casanova ([1994] 2004), for example, have especially privileged, in their approaches to the matter, the novel. This is not the case, however, for another of the most reputed champions of the conceptual emergence of World Literature, North America's David Damrosch (2003, 2009); with regard to poetry, he usually concentrates on comparisons between Western, pre-colonial American, Egyptian, Chinese, Sanskrit and Mesopotamian traditions, paying special attention to thematic dimensions and to the perception and apprehension of the surrounding world. Something similar to the first point is also perceived if we consider recent titles, but of great influence in this academic field, such as *The Routledge Companion to World Literature* (D'haen, Damrosch & Kadir 2012), *World Literature: A Reader* (D'haen, Domínguez & Thomsen 2013) or, to introduce another perspective, *Against World Literature* (Apter 2013).

It is necessary, nonetheless, to return to the matter that we were beginning to develop. It goes without saying that difficulties exist in order to attain an agreement about the specificity of the lyric. Such (supposed) specificity has been explained more by literary history and its academic, educational and institutional projections than by other disciplines. This has frequently been done starting from a canon and a canonicity[2] that have been protected in a critical and aesthetic sense, with clear social, ideological and also national implications.

On the other hand, the promotion of a (supposedly) non-intermediated expressiveness of the subject and his/her particularity – Fichte, Hegel – promoted the culmination of the poetry-lyric confusion, persistent in the present time as a frequent requirement of canonicity. It is therefore evident that the institutionalising authorities of culture have been granting a charter of aesthetic privileges to certain poetics, to the exposition of certain subjectivities and representations, to specific constructions of the historic subject and of his/her own historicity, as opposed to concurrent alternatives. The explanation of this process is complex. It involves cultural, social and, naturally, political factors

2 By canonicity I mean the organic series of different features that uphold a certain canon.

that have to do with what Pierre Bourdieu (1979) studied as distinction and the social basis of taste.

Should any doubt remain, we could revise what Jean-Marie Schaeffer (1980), called in a paper of notable influence, the *doxa romantique*, based on five propositions directly and almost exclusively aimed at the truth, dignity, autotelism and specificity of a language established as "non-common". As the theoretician himself acknowledged, this series of propositions determined a specific poetic ontology, whose validity can be questioned.

As a consequence, the alternative expressions to the poetic have sometimes been reduced to cultural marginality and exceptionality. The determination by negation that appears when speaking about non-lyric poetry requires, for this very reason, a somewhat detailed clarification. The delimitation between lyric and non-lyric has depended on the conditions constituting each cultural system, and the discursive institutionalisation of poetical expression within it. It has also depended on the specific conflict between literary repertoires, prioritised forms of consumption and other key factors that dynamise cultural emergence to a greater or lesser degree.

In general, with the aforementioned precautions, we could define as non-lyric – or post-lyric, or post-poetic, as has also been said – poetry that does without the centrality of an enunciating subject marked by the features that, based on the Hegelian revision of the system of genres, are usually recognised as characteristic of the lyric discourse (Casas 2012): expression of a coherent individual awareness, applied to the constitution of a subjectivity expressed by way of existential introspection; tendency towards presentness in the introduction of referred emotions and perceptions, with which the use of narrative developments is moderated; mimicking enunciation of the conditions of a transcribed soliloquy,[3] which is not perceived as fictional; reduction of the features associated with dialogism in relation to the comprehension and construction of a world and also to that of expression, which tends to dilute the heteroglossia, polyphony or hybridisation; and, in short, requirement of a special disposition in relation to the reception, above all by allowing the poetry to incorporate an unusual informative and communicative density, which requires a fairly defined mediality, formulable as intimate reading of a printed text.

In rhetorical terms, non-lyric poetry highlights the priority of discursive marks such as narrativity and dialogism; it even experiences an essay-argumentative expansion of what has traditionally been described as poetic diction. In general, it involves breaks with a discursivity and performativity that

3 Which is used to appeal in simultaneousness to the key 'writing', in evident opposition to orality.

fall within the private – with all the exceptions that should be introduced here – and that explore, on the other hand, the public, conflicts, dialogue and direct interaction. And moreover, once again, the hybridisation of media and repertoires (Pons & Reynés 2012). A direct result is the postulation of another subjectivity, of other subjects of enunciation and of another disposition for reception.

In a way, it also stresses the turn from the identity and from what idealism consecrated as spirit to an area that exposes the difference and manifests the body, voice, material and tangible presence of another self or of another us. Naturally, underneath this debate is another of undeniable importance and validity, that which refers to the author–authorship pair (Barthes, Foucault, Blanchot, Deleuze, Derrida) and, with it, the complex ontological scenography of modernity, from Nietzsche to Heidegger; this still appears in a definition of the lyric that is the result of most of the characteristics that we have accumulated with regard to mimesis-representation, subjectivity, privacy, non-fictionality, distinction or transcendence.

As a complement to what has been developed up to now, it will be useful to consider the series of features that Werner Wolf has systematised. He proposed reconceptualising the lyric from a cognitive point of view, based on the observation of certain plurifactorial prototypes delimited above all as enunciative and functional options. As we shall see, some of the features adduced by Wolf (2005) have a counterpoint in the notes that we have considered with regard to non-lyric poetry. And we will return to this straightaway.

But let us now consider his proposal, based on nine recurrent characteristics in the lyric poem: 1) brevity, 2) potential orality and performativity with an absence of dramatisation, 3) deviated use in relation to everyday language and to discursive conventions, resulting in the maximal semanticisation of the textual elements, 4) sound/visual versification and exploitation of the language's acoustic properties, 5) outstanding self-referentiality and self-reflexivity, 6) existence of an apparently non-mediated awareness or agenciality as the basis of the lyric enunciation or experience (foundation of the monological effect of the lyric discourse), 7) emotional horizon with centrality not of the object but of the subject and of his/her perception, 8) irrelevance or absence of exterior action and narrative plot, 9) no referenciality or absoluteness of the lyric enunciate (Wolf 2005: 38–39). As we shall see, these are notes that sufficiently reflect a real theoretical torrent that has accumulated over more than two centuries.

If this is what the lyric is, could the category of the non-lyric be defined by simply inverting these notes? I do not think so. As I have tried to suggest, we would have to begin by assuming the relational nature of these two discursive spheres, their dialectics and adaptation to the cultural conditions onto which they are projected. In fact, one of the greatest mistakes of theorisation regarding the lyric is that it is usually detached from these factors; it tends to detach itself from the referential semiotic-historic coordinates, it even has a tendency to absolutise the lyric genericity, ignoring the system of genres in which it is included or acts by carrying out certain functions. Therefore, although it would not be complicated to do so, I will not now proceed to invert or negate, point by point, what has been attained by Wolf. However, it is essential to take him into account – his position or an equivalent one – regarding what I will now proceed to expound.

First of all, that the series of literary, para-scenic, inter-artistic and sometimes intermedial practices that we encompass here under the label of 'non-lyric poetry', by means of their agents, their readers, receivers or publics and of their own analysts, is adverse to the theoretic impulse of unification that, despite all of the alternatives experienced by the lyric, is usually shared by their correlative agents, readers and scholars or theorisers. This is important because it presupposes, in general terms, a desisting of any standardisation or rarefaction (as defined by Foucault) aimed at preserving a uniqueness that is meant to be avoided. It could be said that while the lyric, as an exercise and as a theoretic object, seeks a form of essentiality, of retraction or, in another context, of absolutisation, the non-lyric is characterised by quite the opposite. And this is not due to any kind of exclusive peculiarity, but rather precisely because in the canonical and orderly distribution of enunciative and textural practices, the non-lyric has been the outside, the disorder, the unstable.

Having considered the multiple registers of non-lyric poetry, even the inciting fact of the simultaneous coexistence of lyric and non-lyric registers in a single book of poems, I would like to observe and point out some regularities in relation to the characteristic subjectivity and discursivity of non-lyric poetic enunciation. These are regularities that, although they do not unite this field of practices, they do enable us to refer to it – understanding each other – as a diffuse domain of forms of social intervention and cultural consumption. There are three such regularities. I will immediately refer to them by mentioning the same number of concepts that have been developed in political philosophy, critical theory and sociology. These are subjectivation, the event and what we will identify as art/poetry for the public or for the political.[4] Therefore, we are going to direct our attention to thinking non-lyric poetry in culture and in the political.

Moreover, in order to reinforce the idea of the non-exclusion of lyric and non-lyric registers in a single poetic composition, I would like to refer, to illustrate

4 If we want to view it this way, these three references would respectively answer Wolf's points six and seven (for subjectivation), points one and eight along with the customary mention of the instant (for the event) and points two, five and nine (for the public dimension of non-lyric poetry).

some of my reasonings, to one of Jüri Talvet's most famous texts as a poet, his "Eesti eleegia", composed in October 1994 and published three years later.[5] It goes without saying that Talvet's highly recognisable poetics, even taking into account the undeniable modulations that it has experienced with the passing of time, incorporates many of the notes that have become customary when it comes to defining the specific domain of World Literature or World Literatures.[6] This must be influenced by his position as an academic, comparatist and translator, as well as the verifiable fact that many of his poems are linked to the simultaneously cosmopolitan and localised experience of the journey, the fine reference to cultural contrast and the multiple insinuations derived from the verification – also experiential – that not all of us feel the same, live the same or read the same.

The concept of subjectivation has been developed by Jacques Rancière in the context of his thinking on politics viewed as an activity "that has equality as a principle" (Rancière 1995: 7) and that understands emancipation as a process by means of which new subject spaces are gained, which consist of a reassigning of the pre-political (*police*, according to Rancière) relationship between place and body. In harmony with this, he postulates that subjectivation consists of the production of an enunciation capacity not identifiable beforehand in a given field of experience. As María De Gandt (2004: 88) has highlighted, Rancière

---

5 I will do so despite being aware that the poet has repeatedly declared his lyric affiliation. For example, in a dialogue with the translator Alberto Lázaro-Tinaut (2010: 160), he pointed out the following: "Every genre has its nucleus. In poetry, this nucleus is above all the intimate and the lyric. If we depart a lot from this and we adapt to something that is located in the surroundings or in the sphere of another nucleus, of another genre, we will end up writing bad poetry or something that would barely be identified with poetry." The poem that I will use in my analysis was included in the volume *Eesti eleegia ja teisi luuletusi* (Talvet 1997). I will use the bilingual edition *Eesti eleegia ja teisi luuletusi/Elegía estonia y otros poemas*, translated into Spanish by Alberto Lázaro-Tinaut and the author himself (Valencia: Llambert Palmart, 2002). I will likewise use the English translation by Harvey L. Hix and the author, accessible – the same as the Estonian original and the Spanish and Italian versions – on the poet's website http://talvet.edicypages.com/en, which I will cite (consultation: October 5, 2014).

6 Although it has circulated a lot, Damrosch's (2003: 281) well-known proposition that I cite below is probably somewhat reductive: "family resemblances can be found among the different forms of world literature circulating today, emergent patterns that lead me to propose a threefold dimension focused on the world, the text, and the reader:
1. *World literature is an elliptical refraction of national literatures.*
2. *World literature is writing that gains in translation.*
3. *World literature is not a set canon of texts but a mode of reading: a form of detached engagement with worlds beyond our own place and time.*"

constitutes the political subject on an implicit model, none other than that of literary enunciation; and, incidentally, keeping Mikhail Bakhtin very much in mind.

Certainly, the use of Bakhtinian conceptual networks centred on authority, heterology and all kinds of overcome boundaries is clear. It re-emerges with even greater force in *Le Spectateur émancipé* (2008), a compilation book that begins with generational and autobiographic declarations regarding the interventionist and self-sufficient position of the politically committed intellectual (Rancière 2008: 23). The paradox of the relationship between politics and art is highlighted in the following terms by Rancière (2008: 67):

> Art and politics support each other as forms of dissent, operations of reconfiguration of the common experience of the sensitive. There are aesthetics in politics in the sense that acts of political subjectivation redefine what is visible, what can be said about it and which subjects are capable of doing so. There are aesthetic politics in the sense that the new forms of circulating the word, of showing what is visible and of producing emotions determine new capacities, breaking with the old configuration of the possible.

Well, it could be said after what is attributed to the mention of Auschwitz, that one of the tasks assumed by poetry (by its authors and its publics) is precisely the exploration of subjectivity in relation to the historicity of the experience (Casas 2010). To a very important extent, in order to resolve in which way the subject instituted by the poem says, represents, documents or witnesses history. Even *his/her* history within the historic.

It is clear in Talvet's "Estonian Elegy" the way in which, from the first verses, he introduces the purpose of witnessing immediate history, resulting in the merging of an entire series of expectations, undoubtedly also – perhaps above all – those related to the recent achievement of national independence after long decades of Soviet rule. The poem begins with several lines of prose, which are reproduced below:

> Shortly after midnight on 28 September 1994, in an area of the Baltic Sea sailors call "the ship cemetery," the passenger ferry *Estonia*, en route from the Estonian capital Tallinn to the Swedish capital Stockholm, sank, taking with it to the seafloor more than 900 human lives. No other peacetime shipwreck on the Baltic has claimed so many victims. Technical failure and human error are among the possible causes of the wreck, as is a criminal act. The only certain conclusion of the investigating commission is that the huge ship was brought down by water.

After this text come the following verses, which reflect the correlation between them (the dead), on the one hand, and me/us (the witnesses) on the other, the latter being self-represented as political subjects of a complex and very slow historical process of national emancipation:

> No, it cannot be true.
>
> Cramps of disbelief constricted throats that morning.
> Legs turned to lead, as if earth were dragging us to its roots,
> the way water tore them, naked children,
> suddenly from their dreams to her iron-cold breasts.
>
> No, it cannot be true.
>
> Liberty should have meant warmth at last, and joy.
> As always, among the first, Estonia pushed forward proudly.
> The tether tied to us from twilit past times
> could be forgotten finally, and the dark Middle Ages
> with their foolish taboos could withdraw.

Just as Rancière elaborates his concept of subjectivation, it is clear that he places us before a political subject, to which, naturally, one can incorporate notes of those customarily considered non-universal from a Eurocentric perspective. This explains the conditions of subordination, coloniality or others. What is important, in relation to his reasoning, is understanding subjectivation as an expression of dissent since, as Rancière has expounded at different times, politics works to configure its own space, making its subjects and operations manifest, seen and heard. Opposite it would be the *police* and post-politics. And in addition, along with dissent, democracy.

Just think, apart from the specific value granted by stylistics and structuralism, the idea of lyric subject became established in modern aesthetic thinking with Kantian foundations subsequently revised by the Romantic poets. It is true that, starting from this revision, the enunciative movement of the lyric subject tends to found its own space of demonstration or investigation of the self, or in other cases of an us, frequently based on political difference or social dissent. It is also true that Romanticism explored in depth the correlation between these subjects, their identities or communities and history. What is therefore the characteristic of what we postulate here as non-lyric poetry? I think that precisely the fact that subjectivation emerges to produce a new relationship between the subject and his/her space of intervention and enunciation.[7] A basically political relationship that founds a new subject space. And in this regard, far from the functional stability of the lyric subject and of his/her discourse, which even affects the decision regarding the poet's cultural and political place as a public individual.

It is clear that all of the above appears in Talvet's poem by appealing to the Estonian people's historic sentiment, and to the contrast between this small Baltic nation and the great imperial powers in its geographical surroundings. Although also, in passing, by pointing out that there is a different and very old way of being Europeans, unrelated to any colonising projection: "For thousands of years already we have been Europeans:/ early tillers, at a time when others, the stronger,/ consumed their neighbors, like an insatiable swarm of grasshoppers." In this way, there appears in the poem a vindication, not exempt of irony, regarding the spiritual strength of Europe's small nations, set in parallel as the verses advance with the innocence of the ferry's young passengers who were swallowed up by the Baltic. I would add that, in my opinion, one of the most attractive lines of research into World Literature is the possibility of comparing it with research into international relations, into world politics and so-called World-systems. In this regard, I would like to point out the interest of Roland Bleiker's (2012) proposals,[8] which now is not the time to discuss.

In second place, the comprehension of the event is a point of multiple frictions in postmodernity. The contributions of Michel Foucault, Gilles Deleuze and Alain Badiou, among other thinkers, are not always consistent with each other in conceptual terms. For part of recent political philosophy, there is an unquestionable affiliation with Louis Althusser, as Slavoj Žižek (1999) has outlined, not only in relation to Badiou but also to Ernesto Laclau and Chantal Mouffe, to whom we will immediately refer. In Deleuze, the event points to the otherness. From Foucault we would now be interested, above all, in the relationship between event, enunciation and discursive formations.

At this time, the only thing that I can outline is the proposition that, essentially, non lyric poetry makes use of the event as a discourse. It consists in turning the

---

7 The reference to spatiality should not be understood only in a metaphorical sense. It also has a literal sense by means of which poetry and place are solidly linked together. This explains the frequency of the spatial and deictic highlighting of the non-lyric discourse; sometimes, even its location expressed and required in a public space that is once again literal (the square) or figurative (the network), not so suitable for the kind of reception associated with lyric poetry.

8 A sufficiently contextualised presentation of such are located in Gerard Holden's chapter "World Literature and World Politics: In Search of a Research Agenda" (D'haen, Domínguez & Thomsen 2013: 218–238).

event into discourse, if you like. Well, just like this effect, it seems undeniable that Jüri Talvet's poem "Estonian Elegy" explores the borders of lyric and non-lyric expression by granting value to the event of the shipwreck and the loss of almost a thousand human lives. In fact, in it there is an alternation of references of notable lyric density[9] and others of a completely different kind centred on the historic dimension and appealing to the disaster. And all of this almost always, moreover, in immediate positions with each other,[10] often marked by the use of the verse "No, it cannot be true" as a refrain. But the event value is formulated, above all, by the comparison between the ship and the nation, undoubtedly favoured by the ferry's name:

> Now Estonia sank again to a common grave,
> so suddenly there was no time to divine
> who in the mist of times had been master and who slave,
> who until the death hour had fornicated in the bed of pleasure
> and who had loved the homeland.

As we see, there where, in an epochal way, modern discursivity and subjectivity located the structurising strength of the lyric instant and presentness – or at a different level, the poetics of duration and *devenir* – lyric poetry chooses instead another kind of treatment for temporality, historicity and historic awareness itself. This other treatment is directed at a diversity of manifestations of change and repetition, among which it is not insignificant that which aspires at affecting the participants in this communicative act.[11]

Finally, the mention of Ernesto Laclau and Chantal Mouffe, made in relation to Žižek's replies to his dialectic opponents in the context of the debate on the political subject, leads to the consideration of poetry for the public (or for the political). It is a line of reflection that has to be interpreted in opposition to what so-called 'political poetry' could mean, undoubtedly, in other times different to those of the present. The difference shares points of contact with the one dealt with by Jacques Rancière between political and *police*, and has a clear precedent in Carl Schmitt's thinking. It appears in Laclau and Mouffe's initial collaborations on the concepts of democracy and hegemony. Mouffe has re-elaborated them

---

9 Such as, among others, the one directed at the 19th-century poet Lydia Koidula, not exempt in any case of counterpoints featuring almost expressionist nuances.

10 Particularly representative of what I am suggesting is the series of verses with which the poem ends.

11 It is obvious that this directly influences the increase in presence-based and para-scenic poetic practices, in live practices. It therefore also works to the probable detriment of the reading.

in his book *On the Political* (2005). And Laclau has done something similar in *Debates y combates*, with a chapter centred on criticism of Badiou's theorisation regarding the event, resolved by arguing that all universality is, of necessity, hegemonic (Laclau 2008: 67–99).

The main key in Laclau and Mouffe's comprehension of the hegemony concept is understanding conflict as inseparable from human societies, and antagonism as a constituent element of the political. As opposed to what is postulated by neoliberal thinking based on the idea of consensus, the political for Mouffe would be precisely that dimension of antagonism that constitutes societies. Politics would be, on the other hand, "the series of practices and institutions by means of which a certain order is created, organizing human coexistence in the context of conflictivity derived from the political" (Mouffe 2005: 16).

Logically, this tendency is not always verified, but I believe that it can be said that, in general, the non-lyric poem is postulated to a far greater extent than the lyric poem as a production for the political (Casas 2010). If you want, as an investigation of antagonism and dissent. This is again evident in the composition that we are discussing by Talvet, who, on the other hand, is an intellectual frequently referred to by critics and the prologue writers of his poetry books as annoyingly independent.[12] In conversation with his colleague, the American professor and poet Harvey L. Hix, recalled in the book *A Call for Cultural Symbiosis* (Talvet 2005b), originally published in Estonian that same year, our author reflected on the frequently studied paradox of the great power and the null power of the poetic word. His exact terms are the following (Talvet 2005b: 53–54):

> Finally I would like to answer one more question Harvey asked me. I had thought about it while preparing for the interview, but when we came to it, I forgot about it. The question: Shelley has said: "Poets are the unacknowledged legislators of the world." W. H. Auden has said: "Poetry makes nothing happen." How to explain such a radical difference in the evaluation by two outstanding poets of the social role of poetry? My answer: In principle there is a little difference. Shelley's poets are legislators only ideally. Shelley himself admits that in the real world they are not acknowledged. On the other hand, Auden's saying that "poetry makes

[12] "Jüri Talvet, un poeta «molestamente independiente»" ["Jüri Talvet, an 'annoyingly independent' poet"] is the title of the postface written by Janika Kronberg for the aforementioned volume published by the Spanish publishing house Llambert Palmart (pages 101–106). In this volume, the poem "Eesti eleegia" appears on pages 6 to 25. It is therefore a long poem, a category whose discursive comprehension requires the theoretical–critical proposals of María Cecilia Graña, particularly the volume coordinated by her *El poemetto. Un esempio novecentesco di ricerca poetica* (Graña 2007).

> nothing happen" could also be interpreted in the sense that poetry preserves the world's balance. It secretly undermines materialistic and political radicalism, which really are the only forces that want to "make something happen" in the world. Thus poets or "interior people," the great American thinker Ralph Waldo Emerson defined them, are useful to the world only in the sense that they keep the world's heart where it should be.

May I add that, occasionally, that the aforementioned investigation of antagonism becomes manifest even in the graphic layout of the poem in printed format; in its insubordination against thematic, rhythmic and elocutive restrictions; in its rejection of the mutual seclusion between the declarative and the fictional; but, above all, in the choice of an unstable and hybrid discursivity that does not comply with lyric canonicity (something of this last point appears in "Estonian Elegy"). By means of this impulse, non-lyric poetry seeks the expansion of its genericity, blending with other literary, artistic or medial modalities. It becomes narrative poetry, essay poetry, dramatic poetry;[13] it merges with visual arts, other times with dance. And it therefore locates other publics and claims a very different kind of communication, of community and of inter-subjectivity. As separate from the characteristic ones of lyric poetry as those outlined by the paths of poetry historically recognised as political.

Arturo Casas
arturo.casas@usc.es
Teoría da literatura e Literatura comparada
Facultade de Filoloxía – Campus Norte
Universidade de Santiago de Compostela
15782 Santiago de Compostela
Galicia
ESPAÑA / SPAIN

References

Apter, E. 2013. *Against World Literature: On the Politics of Untranslatability*. London: Verso.
Bleiker, R. 2012. *Aesthetics and World Politics*. Hampshire: Palgrave Macmillan.
Bourdieu, P. 1979. *La Distinction*. Paris: Éditions de Minuit.

[13] There are some examples of this in Jüri Talvet's poetry as a whole. I am thinking respectively of poems such as "Maroko reisikirjad", "Mälestusi Leidenist" and several from the 1986 book *Ambur ja karje*. The opening up of these examples to generic hybridisation is, in any case, nuanced in Talvet by the unquestionable centrality of an irrefutably poetic discursivity.

Casanova, P. 2004 [1999]. *The World Republic of Letters.* Trans. M. B. DeBevoise. Cambridge (Mass.): Harvard University Press.

Casas, A. 2010. Antagonism and Subjectification in the Poem of Resistance. – *Cosmos and History. The Journal of Natural and Social Philosophy*: 6/2, 71–81. Available at http://www.cosmosandhistory.org/index.php/journal/article/viewFile/202/311 (25.10.2014).

Casas, A. 2012. Non-lyric poetry in the current system of genres. – B. Baltrusch & I. Lourido Eds. *Non-Lyric Discourses in Contemporary Poetry.* Munich: Martin Meidenbauer Verlag, 29–44.

Chartier, R. 1990. *Les origines culturelles de la Révolution française.* Paris: Le Seuil.

Damrosch, D. 2003. *What Is World Literature?* Princeton: Princeton University Press.

Damrosch, D. 2009. *How to Read World Literature.* Malden: Wiley-Blackwell.

De Gandt, M. 2004. Subjectivation politique et énonciation littéraire. – *Labyrinthe,* 17, 87–96.

D'haen, Th., D. Damrosch & Dj. Kadir Eds. 2012. *The Routledge Companion to World Literature.* London: Routledge.

D'haen, Th., C. Domínguez & M.R. Thomsen Eds. 2013. *World Literature: A Reader.* London: Routledge.

Graña, M.C. Ed. 2007. *Il poemetto. Un esempio novecentesco di ricerca poetica.* Cagliari: Cooperativa Universitaria Editrice Cagliaritana.

Guerrero, G. 1998. *Teorías de la lírica.* Mexico City: Fondo de Cultura Económica.

Innerarity, D. 2006. *El nuevo espacio público.* Pozuelo de Alarcón: Espasa Calpe.

Jurt, J. 2014. *Naciones literarias. Una sociología histórica del campo literario.* Córdoba (Argentina): Eduvim.

Laclau, E. 2008. *Debates y combates. Por un nuevo horizonte de la política.* Buenos Aires: Fondo de Cultura Económica.

Landrin, X. 2010. La sémantique historique de la *Weltliteratur*: genèse conceptuelle et usages savants. – A. Boschetti dir. *L'Espace culturel transnational.* Paris: Nouveau Monde, 73–134.

Lázaro-Tinaut, A. 2010. Diálogo con Jüri Talvet, poeta. – J. Talvet. *Del sueño, de la nieve (Antología 2001–2009).* Zaragoza: Olifante.

Martí Monterde, A. 2011. *Un somni europeu. Història intel·lectual de la Literatura Comparada. De la* Weltliteratur *a la Literatura Comparada.* Valencia: Publicacions de la Universitat de València.

Moretti, F. 1993. *Opere mondo: Saggio sulla forma epica dal «Faust» a «Cent'anni di solitudine».* Turin: Einaudi.

Mouffe, C. [2005] 2007. *En torno a lo político.* Trans. S. Laclau. Buenos Aires: Fondo de Cultura Económica.

Pons, M. & J. A. Reynés Eds. 2012. *Lírica i deslírica. Anàlisis i propostes de la poesia d'experimentació.* Palma: Universitat de les Illes Balears.

Rancière, J. [1995] 2007. *El desacuerdo. Política y filosofía.* Trans. H. Pons. Buenos Aires: Nueva Visión.

Rancière, J. [2008] 2010. *El espectador emancipado.* Trans. A. Dilon & J. Bassas. Castellón: Ellago Ediciones.

Schaeffer, J.-M. 1980. Romantisme et langage poétique.– *Poétique*: 42, 177–194.
Talvet, J. 1997. *Eesti eleegia ja teisi luuletusi*. Tallinn: Kupar.
Talvet, J. [2005] 2005. *A Call for Cultural Symbiosis: Meditations from U.* Trans. H.L. Hix. Toronto: Guernica.
Wolf, W. 2005. The Lyric: Problems of Definition and a Proposal for Reconceptualisation. – E. Müller-Zettelmann & M. Rubik Eds. *Theory Into Poetry: New Approaches to the Lyric*. Amsterdam: Rodopi, 21–56.
Žižek, S. 1999. *The Ticklish Subject: The Absent Centre of Political Ontology*. London: Verso.

"Un incendio de rosas que nos perturba": 4 poemas gallegos contemporáneos[1]

JAVIER GÓMEZ-MONTERO

Abstract. ***"A Fire of Roses that Disturbs Us": Four Contemporary Galician Poems.*** The essay presents four Galician poets (M. Rivas, X. Valcárcel, M. A. Fernán-Vello, X. M. Alvarez Cáccamo) through some of their representative works, confronting the questions of individual and collective identity in light of a globalised world that threatens to uproot our conscious bonds to childhood and nation, history and society. Another focal point is the literary discourse of Galicia, a region in north-western Spain, in the larger context of Spanish-language literatures. These poems have been translated into English and German by friends and members of the Workshop for literary translation called Taller de Traducción Literaria, at Kiel University.

Keywords: Galician poetry, identity, translation, minority literatures

En su novela publicada en 1994 *En salvaxe compaña* (*En salvaje compañía*) Manuel Rivas enlaza con la tradición oral de su tierra natal, Galicia, esa región del noroeste español, cuyos paisajes, montañas y bosques la caracterizan no menos que el Atlántico con sus escarpadas costas. Con imágenes altamente poéticas el autor cuenta al principio sobre Don García, el último rey de Galicia, quien, a mediados del siglo XI, fue encadenado por su propio hermano, que lo tuvo preso durante dieciocho años. El rey pidió que tras su muerte lo enterrasen como había vivido, encadenado. Según cuenta la leyenda, alguno que otro habría visto

[1] El artículo retoma el posfacio "Los nietos de Rosalía de Castro", publicado en la antología *Ein Rosenfeuer, das uns verstört. 4 Dichter aus Galicien (Miguel Anxo Fernán-Vello, Manuel Rivas, Xulio L. Valcárcel y Xosé Maria Álvarez Cáccamo)*, coordinada por Luciano Rodríguez y Javier Gómez-Montero, que resultó de un proyecto del Centro de Estudos Galegos de Kiel de la mano de las lectoras Uxía Iglesias Tojeiro y Paz Huete Iglesias. Está en curso de preparación otra antología paralela *6 Dichterinnen aus Galicien – 6 poetas galegas*, coordinada actualmente por la lectora Antía Marante Arias desde el Centro de Estudos Galegos de Kiel que dirijo. Paz Huete Iglesias tradujo para este artículo la primera parte de aquel posfacio redactado en alemán (pp. 109–114). Las traducciones al alemán que cierran este artículo proceden de aquella misma publicación mientras que las traducciones al inglés han sido redactadas expresamente para esta entrega de *Interlitteraria* por John Rutherford.

DOI: http://dx.doi.org/10.12697/IL.2015.S1.10

desde entonces un cuervo blanco "con grillos de plata y una bola negra como el carbón". Y algo que está siempre presente en la mitología popular es el séquito del rey, esos 300 cuervos negros de Xallas que no eran guerreros, sino poetas (según la leyenda, el rey se había rodeado de un ejército de trovadores). Poesía, leyendas y mitos conforman en la cultura gallega una unidad inseparable, son el fundamento sobre el que los poetas de hoy en día escriben sus versos. Y esto lo hacen en gallego, su lengua desde siempre estigmatizada como lengua de los pobres e ignorantes, y ellos escriben contra su pérdida, siendo conscientes de la amenaza de la omnipresencia de lenguas extendidas tan universalmente como el español y portugués, con las que el gallego compite en la Península Ibérica.

Esta decisión de los escritores gallegos tiene sin duda alguna también componentes emocionales, pues ellos escriben contra una minorización cultural que arrastra ya muchos siglos en su propio país, pero con la certeza de unirse a una importante tradición de la literatura europea. Antiguamente las cantigas galego-portuguesas gozaban de una alta reputación como una forma de la lírica trovadoresca medieval, entre los siglos XII y XIV fueron recitadas por juglares y trovadores cortesanos de toda la Península Ibérica. Entre sus grandes joyas se encuentran las célebres cantigas de amigo de Martín Códax o los poemas del rey Alfonso X el Sabio (1221–1284) y de Dom Diníz de Portugal (1261–1325). No obstante, Galicia se convierte desde el Medievo (hasta muy entrado el siglo XX) en un país tremendamente atractivo en cuanto a su patrimonio paisajístico, o cultural en general, pero terriblemente pobre en lo económico, patria de campesinos y pescadores, cuyos hijos e hijas muy a menudo se tuvieron que buscar la vida en el extranjero: largo tiempo como jornaleros en Castilla; como trabajadores en las fábricas, taxistas o criados en las grandes ciudades españolas; como emigrantes en América del Sur; o, sobre todo durante la dictadura franquista, también como trabajadores emigrados a Francia, Alemania, Inglaterra o Suiza.

Da la impresión de que el país siempre dejó el poder en manos de otros, sin embargo, desde la muerte de Franco en 1975 y a partir de esta matriz de dolorosas experiencias históricas, se ha desarrollado una autoconciencia de comunidad, vigorosa y valiente, que durante los últimos treinta años también ha involucrado cada vez más a los discursos literarios. Este proceso se ha llevado a cabo en su mayor parte sin conocimiento por parte del lector alemán, para quien así como para muchos viajeros toda esa región atlántica era *terra incognita*, una mancha blanca en el mapa turístico de España, lo que no obstante comenzó a cambiar hace algún tiempo cuando en los años 80 del siglo pasado se redescubrió el Camino de Santiago y esa ruta peregrina tras las huellas del Apóstol ramificada por toda Europa que conduce a la capital gallega, Compostela se convirtió en un fenómeno turístico de masas.

Ya una vez el Camino hacia Santiago estuvo en boca de todos cuando, durante la Edad Media, multitudes de peregrinos, bajo los auspicios del monasterio de Cluny, emprendieron la marcha hacia la tumba del Apóstol e integraron así en la Europa cristiana la zona noroeste de la Península Ibérica, hasta entonces aislada y sólo conectada con la etnia celta de las Islas Británicas y de la Bretaña francesa. Ya en aquellos tiempos, tanto los dignatarios eclesiásticos como la alta nobleza de principios de la Edad Moderna, eran de procedencia extranjera y las élites dirigentes de la sociedad, en la administración, economía, jurisdicción y ejército, utilizaban desde siempre el español, mientras que el gallego era relegado como lengua de los pobres y más míseros. Se consiguió mantener en algunas zonas, fuera de los pocos centros urbanos que gestionaban las congregaciones monásticas y los nobles de rango inferior, igual que en las regiones costeras. En este menosprecio sistemático de la lengua regional, la Reina Católica Isabel tuvo ciertamente algo que ver. Cuenta la tradición que, irritada por culpa de una insubordinación, la regente se empeñó en "domesticar" a sus súbditos y ordenó medidas drásticas, que su cronista oficial Gerónimo de Zurita denominó con la famosa fórmula: "Doma y castración de Galicia". La marginalización empezó a cambiar levemente y en primer lugar con el crecimiento económico de la ciudad portuaria de Vigo, cerca de la frontera con Portugal, que se transformó en una ciudad industrial a partir de comienzos del siglo XX y más tarde, en los años 60, gracias a un impulso de modernización y al éxodo del campo a la ciudad de gran parte de la población que esta trajo consigo. Por aquel tiempo, en los ámbitos proletario e intelectual, se desarrolló a nivel social un movimiento dinámico de defensa de la lengua y cultura gallegas, organizado a través de células aisladas de la resistencia al régimen de Franco, que había prohibido el uso del gallego en todos los campos. Sin los resultados de tal movimiento sería imposible imaginarse el panorama literario, artístico y musical actual gallegos.

¿Pero qué significa que se identifique a Galicia como "Terra de Poetas", tal y como puso de relieve hace poco el premio Cervantes Antonio Gamoneda? Con esto el poeta leonés no se refería ni mucho menos a una desproporcionada cifra de autores y autoras, sino a su calidad intrínseca y a una característica fundamental del carácter popular, que se define como conciencia poética. Un indicio para tal conciencia es la identificación colectiva con el concepto emocional de *saudade*, ese sentimiento indeterminado de una nostalgia crónica, atravesada de tristeza, del que no se puede nombrar ningún referente preciso y que más bien se podría definir como una especie de depresión poética. Otro indicio podría ser la amplia proyección de la persona individualmente y de la idea de nación en mitologías marinas y telúricas, en formas de ver el mar y el paisaje, así como el propio reflejo íntima y colectivamente en leyendas tradicionales (sean estas de carácter popular, a menudo ancladas en supersticiones, o de origen literario, como los numerosos ejemplos de leyendas bretonas). Si esta es toda la verdad o no, otros lo decidirán. En todo caso el apego del pueblo gallego por su territorio bajo el signo de la melancolía es proverbial, y los etnólogos han esbozado un perfil psicosocial de la cultura gallega que se relaciona estrechamente con el proceso de desarrollo de la idea de una nación propia desde el Romanticismo. De especial relevancia es el hecho de que ningún rey, ningún santo o ningún político carismático aparezca como figura identificadora en el horizonte del imaginario cultural de los gallegos, sino una mujer, poeta y madre de siete hijos. Rosalía de Castro (1837–1885) ha conseguido formular esta experiencia de comunidad que determina la identidad de todo un pueblo, al principio solamente en su lengua materna gallega y después también en castellano, de gran calidad estética y fruto de un desgarro emocional muy arraigado. La hija de un sacerdote y de una joven de la nobleza rural, que vivió un matrimonio más bien poco feliz con su marido, el historiador gallego Manuel Murguía y a la que además se le murieron varios hijos de forma prematura, es el icono indiscutible, la figura carismática cultural a la que se remiten las generaciones de poetas más jóvenes hasta el día de hoy. Los méritos de Rosalía de Castro en la lírica gallega son muy variados; por ejemplo leyó el paisaje gallego como texto de su alma y libro de la nación, creó toda una galería de tipos costumbristas, definió poéticamente un conjunto de estructuras emocionales de la colectividad emocional y cantó en sus *Cantares Gallegos* (1863) en misteriosas tradiciones de su patria. Rosalía siempre supo encontrar versos que abundan insistentemente en la pena de la emigración, de la vida en la pobreza, y encontró las palabras precisas para formular la represión de la gente sencilla en su propia tierra, pero también se asomó a los abismos, lesiones y enredos de la existencia individual, como muestran las obras *Follas novas* (1880) y en *En las orillas del Sar* (1884). Sin duda por esto último se reconoce hoy en día a Rosalía de Castro como a la mayor poeta española, pues fue una precursora del discurso poético moderno en lengua castellana. Además dejó a un lado el enfático retoricismo hasta entonces vigente y confió en la naturalidad genuina de su escritura poética, buscando crear una intimidad con el lector mediante un ritmo discreto y con una dicción muy próxima al lenguaje en uso, emocional y reflexivo a un tiempo. En su época, las estructuras lingüísticas y compositivas de la representación del sujeto en el discurso poético de Rosalía de Castro fueron rompedoras para la lírica moderna española y, estilísticamente, hasta hoy en día continúan asumiendo una función performativa en los lenguajes poéticos del alma ibérica.

Por todo esto es lógico que el verso que da título a esta sucinta visión de la poesía gallega contemporánea – tan bien conocida al profesor Jüri Talvet, gran amigo de Galicia – proceda de un poema-homenaje en el que el autor más joven de los que aquí mostramos retrata al referente más elemental del universo literario gallego. El poema con el título *Rosalía* retoma a su vez un verso de

Antón Avilés de Taramancos, que se antepone como lema y contiene un juego de palabras con el nombre de la poeta: "Rosalía" – "fuego de rosas". Aún con todas las diferencias de las distintas voces y temperamentos líricos, los cuatro autores se tienen por nietos de Rosalía de Castro, por herederos de su legado poético, y escriben en el rastro que la poeta ha ido dejando. A los motivos fundamentales pertenecen, tanto hoy como antaño, la nación gallega y sus gentes, el mar y el paisaje con matices siempre nuevos, pero también tanto los deseos, impotencias y rebeliones de cada uno como una intimidad que cada vez se vuelve más frágil dentro de la rutina urbana. Son las mismas fuentes de inspiración, pero en el contexto estético y civilizatorio urbano del siglo XXI por parte de Manuel Rivas, enmarcada en una obsesión de espacio por parte de Miguel Anxo Fernán-Vello o en el gesto de un compromiso civil por parte de Xosé María Álvarez Cáccamo y finalmente inscrita en una experiencia íntima de la existencia por parte de Xulio L. Valcárcel. A su manera, sus voces prolongan también la estirpe de aquellos aves-poetas (los cuervos de Xallas) que guardaban antaño los feudos de Don García en Galicia, como M. Rivas inmortaliza en la novela En salvaxe compaña.

* * *

Estas páginas de homenaje a Jüri Talvet me sugieren concitar cuatro poemas escogidos del libro *Ein Rosenfeuer, das uns verstört,*[2] la aludida antología de poesía gallega y en traducción alemana publicado el 2010 en Kiel. "Rosalía" es el título del primer texto, y su autor –el editor y crítico literario además de articulista, Miguel Anxo Fernán-Vello– puede ser definido como un buscador de trascendencia, como un oteador de la plusvalía de toda realidad humana proyectada en los paisajes, los cuerpos y en la conciencia colectiva de nación. En concreto, y al igual que toda su obra, el poema "Rosalía" muestra la íntima ligazón entre existencia personal y creación artística. Parafraseando el núcleo del poema, Rosalía de Castro testimoniaría cómo la vida se intensifica y autentifica gracias al arte, a la literatura, y de ahí la conexión entre escritura y verdad que el poema proyecta con la poeta gallega por excelencia cuya semblanza poética gravita sobre la conjunción de vida y poesía, una fusión capaz de imponerse a todo destino personal o –dicho de otra forma– justo ése sería el propio destino personal.

También los otros tres poetas compartirán con Fernán-Vello la necesidad de interpelar a la sociedad contemporánea acertando a combinar resistencia civil y

---

[2] *Ein Rosenfeuer, das uns verstört. 4 Dichter aus Galicien/ 4 poetas galegos.* Übersetzt von Petra Strien-Bourmer, Victor Andrés Ferretti, Frank Nagel und dem Taller de Traducción Literaria zu Kiel in Zusammenarbeit mit Karina Gómez-Montero. Herausgegeben von Javier Gómez-Montero und Luciano Rodríguez (Verlag Ludwig: Kiel, 2010).

refugio en la intimidad, digiriendo decepciones con una acendrada voluntad de intervención cívica. Pero cuando la realidad obliga al poeta a debatirse entre esos polos, la voz poética se hace reflexiva, sabiendo anclar la emoción más personal en los sentimientos colectivos y trasladando la impronta de un territorio local en la dimensión más universal. Así ocurre en las novelas y poemas de Manuel Rivas donde las señas de identidad sobreviven al desgaste de la globalización y, particularmente en su poesía, una conciencia mítica de la realidad se entrevera con los imaginarios urbanos y la cultura de masas. Así no extrañe que "O pan negro" apunte a un momento de la historia familiar del autor y esté dedicado al abuelo y al hijo del escritor a un tiempo, rememorando un hecho que se proyecta líricamente hacia la generación futura. En las imágenes del poema se superponen dos momentos distintos en un único espacio: la mísera periferia de A Coruña en los años que siguieron a la contienda civil (36–39) y esos mismos lugares convertidos ya en el idílico entorno rural de la infancia del poeta, la casa aldeana de labranza, en los años sesenta. Además implícitamente allí, en ese *topos* íntimo de la memoria, planea la sombra de un acontecimiento determinante en la vida de la familia: el abuelo Manuel Barrós, de Corpo Santo, había escapado de su ejecución durante la Guerra Civil, al ser salvado del paredón por el párroco del pueblo que *in extremis* supo hacer ver al cabecilla del pelotón de fusilamiento la desgracia que se cernía sobre aquella familia y el desastre en que, en caso de matarle, quedaría abocada una mujer con diez hijos. En las vigorosas imágenes del poema, sin duda, se verán inscritas las huellas traumáticas de una vivencia, en carne propia o en su rememoración, que refleja las heridas de todo un pueblo, la hemorragia de vidas provocada durante aquellos años.

Introvertida nos resulta la voz de Xulio L. Valcárcel, siempre cercana y que parece hacer a veces acopio del tono de las *Lieder* de compositores románticos. Como una obsesión recorre el tiempo las pautas de sus versos y una sed insaciable de salvación del pasado íntimo anima sus poesías, concebidas ciertamente como piezas musicales, concentradas e intensas en su modestia. En el motivo poético de la casa, emblema de una irrecuperable patria existencial, resuenan los ecos de una conciencia personal tensada hasta el extremo, que se constituye como nostalgia y que consigue así recomponer la sima que media entre lo más duradero y lo más fugitivo del instante. La estructura del discurso poético se hace entonces plenamente elegíaca y la escritura acapara una y otra vez momentos de pérdida. Pero si la infancia y la casa familiar en la campiña lucense son motivos centrales en la obra de Xulio L. Valcárcel, jurista y crítico de arte activo, su función en poemas como "A chamada" (o "Casa baleira") es reclamar una toma de conciencia de lo cotidiano para encontrar en él las apoyaturas necesarias, adecuadas garantías de identidad. Ese paradigna es también válido para el discurso identitario de Xosé María Álvarez Cáccamo que no es sólo de carácter individual, sino que también adquiere una trascendencia social en el sentido de que la voz poética asume una acendrada valencia y responsabilidad civiles. Su voz, por ejemplo, se convierte en el grito de los asesinados y desaparecidos durante la Guerra Civil española, aquellos siniestros 15.000 días en los que "Fue la tiniebla norma exacta..." como reza el comienzo del poema que luego sigue. Una y otra vez, sus versos dan visibilidad a los hitos de la resistencia política tanto en la Galicia víctima de la represión franquista como los intentos de aquel régimen de frenar los movimientos de protesta estudiantil a finales de los años sesenta, de los que el poeta fue testigo siendo universitario en Santiago de Compostela.También en este caso, como en el discurso poético de los tres autores anteriores, el lenguaje y el tratamiento de las imágenes transportan acontecimientos históricos de ubicación local y vivencias personales a los contextos más universales de la experiencia humana, dándoles entonces transcendencia simbólica.

Así queda de manifiesto que la poesía gallega – por *négligeable* que pudiera parecer y a pesar de suponer un reducto discursivo quizá marginal en un noroeste poco visible de la península ibérica lejos del canon de la literatura europea o de otras literaturas nacionales de mayor proyección – ha dejado tras sí el márchamo de su tradicional condición subalterna y acierta a enriquecer –con la misma pujanza que la literatura estonia– la poesía universal con su propia forma de enfocar el presente y la historia con los temas más significativos para el futuro, sus modos y tonos particulares, sus mitologías poéticas y su específico imaginario así como por su irrefrenable voluntad de autoafirmación en tiempos de enorme carencia, por invocar una vez más aquel *Dichter in dürftiger Zeit* de Hölderlin. Estos poetas gallegos cumplen así hoy en día el sueño cabal de los trovadores galaico-portugueses – y no menos el deseo de Rosalía de Castro – de ver prolongadas sus voces en el tiempo y en el espacio, sueño que también ha sabido realizar de cara a su propia tradición literaria nacional el poeta estonio Jüri Talvet, el modelo de intelectual europeo y entrañable amigo homenajeado en estas páginas.

Javier Gómez-Montero
gomez-montero@romanistik.uni-kiel.de
Christian-Albrechts-Universität zu Kiel
Romanisches Seminar
Leibinzstr. 10
D-24098 Kiel
DEUTSCHLAND / GERMANY

MIGUEL ANXO FERNÁN-VELLO

ROSALÍA

Un incendio de rosas que nos perturba
Antón Avilés de Taramancos

A lúa negra dos seus ollos
fonda como un pozo
que garda o segredo escuro e ardente
da saudade.
E a boca grande
para o sorriso de ampla frescura
que acende o rostro.
Finas as mans que tocan a luz
das cousas
e delgados os dedos
que rozan o fío invisíbel da brisa.
Un aceno tinxido pola melancolía
ás veces brilla con súbito esplendor
e nas meixelas nace
a flor non común da ledicia.
E os andares tan leves,
sostendo no ar a lei dun desexo
e abrindo o camiño á transparencia.
Ela, como se o corpo fose unha arte
para sentir o mundo,
distinguida presenza
que impón un perfil de dozura.
Véxana ao lonxe
respirando a paz dos arboredos,
pensativa nun adeus
que lle preme nas tempas.
Véxana amordazando a dor,
punxida polos versos
nos que lle treme a vida.
Ela, que leva unha estrela na fronte
e nos queima.
Ela, que canta as raíces
do misterio
e ergue a voz por riba do tempo:
un incendio de rosas
que nos perturba.

(*Diccionario do estremecemento*, 2007)

ROSALÍA

Ein Rosenfeuer, das uns verstört
Antón Avilés de Taramancos

Der schwarze Mond ihrer Augen,
tief wie ein Brunnen,
bewahrt das dunkle, glühende Geheimnis
der Sehnsucht.
Der große Mund,
ihr unbeschwertes Lächeln
lässt das Gesicht leuchten.
Fein ihre Hände,
ertasten das Licht der Dinge,
und zart die Finger,
die unsichtbare Windsaiten streifen.
Auf ihren Zügen voller Schwermut
scheint manchmal ein plötzlicher Glanz auf,
und auf den Wangen erblüht
die seltene Blume der Freude.
Und der so leichte Gang
bewahrt in der Luft das Gesetz eines Begehrens,
bahnt sich Wege in die Klarheit.
Sie, ihr Körper, wie eine Gabe,
die Welt zu spüren,
noble Erscheinung,
deren sanfte Silhouette uns anrührt.
Seht sie dort in der Ferne,
atmend den Frieden des Hains,
ein Sinnen über den Abschied
liegt schwer auf ihren Schläfen.
Seht, wie sie den Schmerz bezwingt,
verdichtet in ihren Versen,
Pulsschlag des Lebens.
Sie ist es, ein Stern auf ihrem Haupt,
deren Brennen uns versengt.
Sie singt vom Ursprung
des Mysteriums
und erhebt ihre Stimme über die Ufer der Zeit:
ein Rosenfeuer,
das uns verstört.

(Traducción del Taller de Traducción Literaria de Kiel
bajo dirección de Frank Nagel)

ROSALÍA

A fire of roses that disturbs us
Antón Avilés de Taramancos

The black moon of her eyes
as deep as a well
that keeps the dark and burning secret
of *saudade*.
And her large mouth
for her smile of broad freshness
that lights up her face.
Slender the hands that touch the light
of things
and thin the fingers
that brush over the invisible thread of the breeze.
A look tinged with melancholy
sometimes shines with sudden splendour
and in her cheeks blossoms
the uncommon flower of joy.
And her walk, so light,
holding in the air the law of a desire
and opening the way for transparency.
She, as if her body were an art
for feeling the world,
distinguished presence
that imposes a profile of sweetness.
They see her in the distance
breathing the peace of the groves,
thoughtful in a farewell
that presses on her temples.
They see her silencing her pain,
pierced by the verses
in which her life quivers.
She, who bears a star on her forehead
and burns us.
She, who sings the roots
of mystery
and lifts her voice over time:
a fire of roses
that perturbs us.

(Traducción de John Rutherford)

MANUEL RIVAS

O PAN NEGRO

A Manuel Barrós, de Corpo Santo (Tabeaio),
e a Manuel Rivas, de Sigrás.
Meus avós. E tamén a Martiño, fillo.

En trementes humidades dunha memoria que non é a miña
estou a debullar o negro pan dos corenta,
o lume entrecortado por rezos e motores lonxanos como ouveos,
os panos bordados con dedos biqueiros na brancura,
e tamén o medo,
un medo que asubía infindo,
axexante nas hedras,
espido, terribelmente feble e pálido,
como os ollos por dentro.

Non é miña esta memoria.
Eu mirei as violetas empoleirarse aos xogos,
deixarse xenerosas nos valados secretos.
Mais esta chuvia cansa,
esa luz de limoeiro aterecido,
ese pouso de lúa sobre as tellas,
o muxido marelo que alenta polas lombas nabeiras...

Quen sexa o que recorde,
quen reteña o negro pan dos corenta,
a paciente criación dun mesmo nos bordados do liño,
o medo,
un medo omnipresente que pendura do teito,
quen sexa o que vos fale

da cerdeira tolleita por dentes de friaxe,
de motores lonxanos como ouveos, do medo,
dese medo orfo, aterecido,
que abre nos postigos e axexa pola fiestra.

Quen sexa o que recorde,
o que remova con agarimo a miña memoria de violetas
que abeiraban os xogos,
a miña memoria de columpios na rexa carballeira,
a miña memoria de prados musicais,

Quen sexa o que vos fale,
o que apouse os seus dedos de invernía
na miña memoria, o que aloumiñe coas súas mans de séculos
a miña memoria, o que con xeito doce apalpe na miña memoria
de pan branco con esas mans que debullaron o negro pan dos corenta.

Quen sexa o que recorde
ten un nome bordado na miña memoria de violetas,
na fresca vizosidade da mesta carballeira,
nos enredos, nos xogos, no pan branco,
nas memorias futuras que aloumiño, sen medo,
cos meus dedos de ensoño.

(*Balada nas praias do Oeste,* 1985)

SCHWARZES BROT

Für Manuel Barrós aus Corpo Santo (Tabeaio)
und Manuel Rivas aus Sigrás.
Meine Großväter. Und auch für Martiño, meinen Sohn.

In zitternder Feuchte einer Erinnerung, die nicht meine ist,
entkörne ich das schwarze Brot der Vierziger,
das Feuer, zerschnitten von Gebeten und Motoren, wie ein fernes Heulen,
das Weiß der Tücher, von zärtlichen Fingern bestickt,
und auch die Angst,
die Angst, die unaufhörlich pfeift
und die im Efeu lauert,
nackt, entsetzlich schwach und fahl,
wie das Innere der Augen.

Diese Erinnerung ist nicht meine.
Ich sah die Veilchen sich zu den Spielen recken,
freigebig blühen an verborgenen Mauern.
Doch dieser Regen ist ermüdend,
das Licht im starren Zitronenbaum,
der Bodensatz des Mondes auf den Dächern,
das gelbe Blöken, das über Rübenfelder streicht...

Wer es auch ist, der sich erinnert,
der aufbewahrt das schwarze Brot der Vierziger,
geduldiges Besticken, mit dem man auch sich selbst erschafft,
die Angst,
eine allgegenwärtige Angst, die von den Dächern hängt,
wer es auch ist, der zu euch spricht

vom Kirschbaum, den ein Kältebiss gelähmt,
von Motoren, fern wie ein Geheul, von Angst,
von der verwaisten Angst, vor Kälte starr,
die Läden öffnet und durchs Fenster späht.

Wer es auch ist, der sich erinnert,
und liebevoll mir die Erinnerung an Veilchen nimmt,
die unsere Spiele säumten,
meine Erinnerung an Schaukeln im mächtigen Eichenwald
meine Erinnerung an Wiesen voll Musik.

Wer es auch ist, der zu euch spricht
und seine Winterfinger
auf meine Erinnerung legt, der mit Jahrhunderthänden
meine Erinnerung liebkost, der meine Erinnerung an weißes Brot
berührt mit diesen sanften Händen, die das schwarze Brot der Vierziger
entkörnten.

Wer auch immer sich erinnert,
hat einen Namen, eingestickt in die Erinnerung an Veilchen,
in die dichtbelaubte Frische alter Eichen,
in Gewirr, in Spiele und in weißes Brot,
in künftige Erinnerungen, die ich sanft berühre, ohne Angst,
mit meinen träumerischen Fingern.

(Traducción del Taller de Traducción Literaria de Kiel)

BLACK BREAD

To Manuel Barros, from Corpo Santo (Tabeaio),
and to Manuel Rivas, from Sigrás.
My grandfathers. And to Martiño, my son.

In trembling moistness of a memory that is not mine
I am crumbling the black bread of the forties,
the fire with crepitations of prayers and distant engines like howls,
the cloths embroidered by kissing fingers in the whiteness,
and the fear,
a fear that whistles endlessly,
lurking in the ivy,
naked, dreadfully weak and pale,
like the inside of eyes.

It is not mine, this memory,
I watched the violets climb the games,
offer themselves generously in the secret walls.
But this rain is wearisome,
that light from a freezing lemon tree,
those dregs of the moon on the tiles,
the yellow lowing that blows over the turnip-covered uplands...

Whoever it is that remembers,
whoever keeps the black bread of the forties,
the patient creation of oneself in the embroidery on the linen,
the fear,
an omnipresent fear that hangs from the ceiling,
whoever it is that speaks to you

of the cherry tree crippled by teeth of cold,
of distant engines like howls of fear,
of that orphaned fear, numb with cold,
that opens the gates and lurks by the window,
whoever it is that remembers,
that fondly stirs my memories of violets
that fringed the stones,
my memory of swings in the thick oak grove,
my memories of musical meadows,

whoever it is that speaks to you,
that lays their winter fingers
on my memory, that caresses with their age-old hands
my memory, that sweetly feels in my memory
of white bread with those hands that crumbled the black bread of the forties,

whoever it is that remembers
has a name embroidered in my memory of violets,
in the fresh fertility of the dense oak grove,
in the home-made toys, in the stones, in the white bread,
in the future memories I caress, without fear,
with my fantasy fingers.

(Traducción de John Rutherford)

XULIO L. VALCÁRCEL

A CHAMADA

Escoito, casa, a túa chamada.
Houbo outras casas nas que fun
desennobelando os días un tras outro,
pero ningunha a ti comparábel,
casa na que abrín os ollos
ao asombro de estar vivo,
ser no mundo, e na que pensaba
tamén pechar o ciclo, apagando
a miña luz entre os teus muros.
Escoito, casa, a túa chamada,
nunca deixei de escoitala
por lonxe que estivese, por moito
que fose o tempo que faltase.
Fóra de ti, non estaba no meu,
pouco importaba a distancia.
Escoito, casa, a túa chamada.
É unha chamada de auxilio,
un S.O.S. urxente, angustioso.
Temes, quizais, que te desprece por vella,
como quen se avergoña dunha antiga amante,
ou que o tempo e a desgana
puxeran un veo de esquecemento
nos meus ollos.
Pero eu sigo prendido de ti, do teu recordo,
como de neno, cando xogaba
a facer casas tentando reproducirte
para recuperar o teu olor, camiñar a tentas
polas túas pezas, casa da alegría, casa
tamén das primeiras mortes.
Escoito, casa, a túa chamada...,
xa sen urxencia, resignada, mansa,
implorando, sen nada esixir.
Pero xa non poderei voltar.
Pecháronme os camiños do retorno.

(*Casa última*, 2003)

DER RUF

Haus, ich höre deinen Ruf.
Da gab es andere, in denen ich
die Tage nur herunterspulte,
doch keines war wie du.
Haus, wo ich die Augen aufschlug,
staunend, auf der Welt zu sein,
zu leben; wo ich gedachte,
meinen Kreis zu schließen,
mein Licht zu löschen, dort in dir.
Haus, ich höre deinen Ruf,
hab ihn immer schon gehört,
ganz gleich, wo ich auch war, egal
wie lang ich fort war.
Fern deiner Mauern war ich nicht bei mir,
selbst wenn mich nur ein Steinwurf von dir trennte.
Haus, ich höre deinen Ruf.
Es ist ein Hilferuf,
ein SOS, ein Notruf voller Angst.
Du fürchtest wohl, dein Alter könnte mich erschrecken,
als schämte ich mich einer alten Liebe,
als deckten Zeit und Unlust
meine Augen
mit dem Schleier des Vergessens.
Doch häng ich immer noch an dir, an der Erinnerung,
gleich jenem Kind, das spielte,
Häuschen baute, die dir glichen,
um deinen Duft zu spüren, durch deine Räume
mich zu tasten; Haus der Freude und auch
der ersten Toten.
Haus, ich höre deinen Ruf ...
nicht drängend mehr, ergeben, ruhig,
inständig, ohne Forderung.
Aber ich kann nicht mehr zurück.
Der Weg nachhaus ist mir versperrt.

(Traducción del Taller de Traducción Literaria de Kiel
bajo dirección de Victor Andrés Ferretti)

THE CRY

I listen, house, to your cry.
There have been other houses in which
I have unravelled the days one after another,
but none comparable to you,
the house in which I opened my eyes
to the amazement of being alive,
being in the world, and in which I planned
to close the cycle, too, extinguishing
my light between your walls.
I listen, house, to your cry,
I have never stopped listening
however far away I was, however
long a wait there was.
Away from you, I was not at my ease,
the distance mattered little.
I listen, house to your cry.
It is a cry for help,
an urgent SOS of distress.
You fear, perhaps, that I scorn you because you are old,
like someone ashamed of a former lover,
or that time and lack of interest
have placed a veil of forgetfulness
over my eyes.
But I am still in love with you, with your memory,
as, when a child, I played
at making houses trying to reproduce you
to recapture your smell, feel my way
through your rooms, house of good cheer, house
also of my first deaths.
I listen, house, to your cry...,
no longer urgent, resigned, meek,
imploring, demanding nothing.
But I can never return.
The roads back have all been blocked.

(Traducción de John Rutherford)

XOSÉ MARÍA ÁLVAREZ CÁCCAMO

FOI A TEBRA NORMA EXACTA DURANTE QUINCE MIL DÍAS
e houbo fillos que aprenderon a negar
a voz da despedida,
e fillos de pais mortos contra os muros de carbón
amnésicos traidores queimaron o fardo dos espectros
e déronse a berrar Viva Franco Viva Franco Arriba España.

Pero moitos cultivaron unha rosa secreta,
silenciosamente feridos,
orgullosamente firmes na conciencia sen quebra,
arrizadamente vivos polo alto dos montes,
duramente organizados,
subversivamente acesos de verdade,
explosivamente dispostos,
soñadoramente esperanzados,
sementadores da memoria e da razón
na vontade que herdamos
e será testamento inextinguíbel.

(*Os cadernos da ira,* 1999)

FINSTERNIS WAR DIE STRIKTE REGEL
FÜNFZEHNTAUSEND TAGE LANG

Es gab Söhne, die lernten, die Stimme
des Abschieds zu leugnen,
und Söhne von Vätern, die starben an der Kohlewand,
vergessliche Verräter verbrannten die Bürde der Gespenster
und brüllten nun Viva Franco, Viva Franco, Arriba España.

Doch viele hegten auch eine heimliche Rose,
pflegten im Stillen ihre Wunden,
stolz und standhaft, in unbeugsamer Redlichkeit,
waghalsig am Leben hoch oben in den Bergen
straff organisiert,
im Widerstand ehrlich entflammt,
stürmisch bereit,
voller träumerischer Hoffnung,
pflanzten sie Gedenken und Vernunft
in den Willen, den wir erbten,
unser untilgbares Testament.

(Traducción de Petra Strien-Bourmer)

THE EARTH WAS A PRECISE NORM FOR FIFTEEN THOUSAND DAYS

and there were sons who learnt to deny
the voice of farewell
and sons of fathers killed against walls of coal
amnesic traitors burned the bundle of ghosts
and started to yell Long Live Franco Long Live Franco Long Live Spain.

But many cultivated a secret rose,
silently wounded,
proudly firm in an unbroken conscience,
angrily alive in the heights of the hills,
rigidly organized,
subversively alight with the truth,
explosively at the ready,
dreamily hopeful,
sowers of memory and of reason
in the will that we inherited
and it shall be an inextinguishable testament.

(Traducción de John Rutherford)

Itinerarios de la poesía europea posmoderna

ALFREDO SALDAÑA

Itineraries of postmodern European poetry. Critical reading of the European poetry of the past decades involves overcoming the limited meanings of some concepts that have, for too long, been at the centre of literary debates and studies: nationalism, linguistic awareness and national identity, generation, canon, literary excellence, realism, etc. Critical reading of that poetry demands that we discard many cultural and aesthetic prejudices and enter a polyphonic landscape where it is necessary to distinguish the most singular voices from the epigones, to ultimately rewrite what has been written and canonised.

Keywords: contemporary European poetry, postmodernism, postnationalism, dissemination

Europa ha dado grandes nombres a la poesía universal a lo largo de estos dos últimos siglos. En el marco del primer romanticismo alemán Hölderlin y Novalis; Keats, Shelley y Blake en el romanticismo inglés, Leopardi en el italiano, Baudelaire, Nerval, Verlaine, Rimbaud y Mallarmé en el siglo XIX francés. Ya en la primera mitad del siglo XX, y en el conjunto de las diferentes lenguas europeas, Apollinaire, Gabrielle d'Annunzio, Marinetti, Maiakovski, Machado, J. R. Jiménez, Cernuda, Pessoa, Trakl, Benn, Breton, Valéry, Éluard, Yeats, Saint-John Perse, Stefan George, Rilke, Cavafis, Attila József, etc. Ahora bien, antes de dedicar alguna atención a otros poetas más próximos en el tiempo, quiero iniciar estas páginas planteando algunos interrogantes con la intención de generar reflexión y provocar el análisis: *¿es* la posmodernidad una suma de acontecimientos o *se presenta* como un conglomerado de discursos?, ¿se dan características específicas en nuestra época que permitan hablar de una *sensibilidad crítica posmoderna*?, ¿se esconde tras esa sensibilidad una particular ideología?, ¿cómo se manifiesta dicha sensibilidad en la poesía de estos últimos cincuenta años?, ¿es lícito hablar de un canon hegemónico en la poesía europea posmoderna?, o, por el contrario, ¿aconseja la variedad de formas que presenta esa poesía prescindir del canon y apreciar su singularidad en la suma de sus diferencias, en un paisaje polícromo caracterizado por la diversidad?, ¿requiere el análisis de dicha poesía una sensibilidad diferente?, ¿son necesarios nuevos modelos teóricos que se adapten a las especiales circunstancias con que se presenta el objeto poético

DOI: http://dx.doi.org/10.12697/IL.2015.S1.10

posmoderno? Ante este panorama, cabría suponer que la carencia de guías de comportamiento, la inconsistencia de algunos relatos surgidos en estas últimas décadas, la desconfianza frente a todos los discursos sistemáticos y la defensa de la independencia del artista como características inherentes de la posmodernidad pueden actuar como detonantes de una nueva sensibilidad crítica posmoderna.

En este contexto, leer críticamente la poesía europea de estas últimas décadas pasa por superar las limitadas acepciones de algunos conceptos que durante demasiado tiempo han ocupado el centro de los debates y los estudios literarios: nacionalismo, conciencia lingüística e identidad nacional, generación, canon, excelencia literaria, realismo, etc., vinculado este último únicamente a lo material, figurativo y sensorial de una realidad que ha dado la espalda a la imaginación. Se trataría de aceptar que esa realidad que acota el realismo es demasiado magra, intervenir en ella introduciendo cambios radicales, reconocer que la realidad y la imaginación constituyen ámbitos opuestos tan solo en lo formal, reivindicar una idea de *realidad* más amplia que la que ofrece el "realismo ingenuo" o "realismo literalista" (García 2005: 71), una realidad que dé cabida a sus diferentes versiones, incluidas aquellas que –desde determinados planteamientos morales– suelen considerarse más sucias y degradadas, y que acoja "la palabra de los sin rostro" (por decirlo con una expresión de los insurgentes zapatistas que podría servir como lema general de los desposeídos de la tierra), síntomas todos ellos que habrán de interpretarse como disonancia estética frente a un mundo política, económica y socialmente injusto. Vivir a la vez *en* y *contra* la realidad. Así, con un lenguaje desinflado de retórica innecesaria, deliberadamente coloquial y a menudo prosaico, algunos poetas han respondido a los conflictos que plantea el mundo contemporáneo con nuevas sensibilidades e ideas y han llevado a sus textos el compromiso social y la defensa de los valores ecológicos (Vladimír Holan, Yannis Ritsos, Josef Kostohryz, Edoardo Sanguineti, Jure Potokar y Bardhyl Londo son algunos ejemplos ilustrativos de estas corrientes).

De este modo, leer críticamente la poesía europea de estos últimos cincuenta años exige desprenderse de numerosos prejuicios culturales y estéticos, adentrarse en un paisaje polifónico en el que es preciso diferenciar las voces más singulares de los epígonos y recorrer de nuevo –libres de espurios intereses– los otros excesivamente transitados, reescribir, en definitiva, lo ya escrito y sancionado. Tal lectura supone, entre otras cosas, constatar la pérdida de importancia de conceptos como la *autoridad del sentido* o el *significado trascendental*, que han condicionado durante mucho tiempo nuestras sesgadas relaciones con los textos literarios, que se presentan ya como piezas de un monumental engranaje político, estético y cultural y en el que únicamente adquieren pleno sentido si son leídos a la luz de otros textos ya escritos, algo que favorece las prácticas interdiscursivas y metapoéticas puesto que si es verdad que el mundo ya no puede ser aprehendido de forma fiable en un texto literario, "Si la poesía ya no puede hablar del mundo, hablará, al menos, de cómo otros poemas han hablado del mundo. El discurso del método suplanta así al método del discurso" (Talens 1989a: 56). El mundo desaparece detrás del texto y solo tenemos acceso al texto del mundo.

Leer críticamente la poesía europea posmoderna implica contemplar un mosaico de culturas y tradiciones artísticas diversas a las que esa poesía acude de diferentes maneras y con distintos objetivos. Sin embargo, frente a la quiebra y la transgresión permanentes de una modernidad que se presenta como la *tradición de la ruptura* (O. Paz *dixit*), cierta sensibilidad artística posmoderna –desprovista de la capacidad crítica que acompañó a un buen número de manifestaciones modernas y asolada por una profunda crisis que afecta a la configuración de su paradigma estético– ha propiciado los contactos con una tradición a la que se siente estrechamente vinculada. Frente al deterioro experimentado por ciertos ritos artísticos consolidados en significativas actitudes modernas, desde algunos sectores artísticos de la posmodernidad se ha optado por reabrir los canales de comunicación con una usanza que ya no se contempla como algo impuesto sino que es aceptado con frecuencia de manera indiscriminada.

Tal lectura requiere ser conscientes de la crisis heredada de la modernidad, del estado de quiebra que asola a nuestros viejos y desgastados sistemas de pensamiento. Procede entonces partir de las complejas relaciones que se dan entre esa poesía y los elementos que actúan a su alrededor, transformar la negatividad resultante de la unidad descompuesta de los textos poéticos en agente de reflexión que fomente la crítica de esos mismos textos, valorar –como ya reclamara en un memorable ensayo Hugo Friedrich (1974) para la lírica moderna– la significación que adquieren algunas categorías negativas, entre las cuales ocupa un lugar destacado el fragmentarismo, que ha afectado tanto a la disolución de la estética sistemática en poéticas particulares como a la desintegración de la unidad de la obra artística. En estos últimos años, a la luz de algunas ideas planteadas en su momento por el propio Friedrich, algunos ensayos han abordado la complejidad del fenómeno poético europeo al margen de las fronteras nacionales; entre esos trabajos se encuentran algunas publicaciones coordinadas por Claude Le Bigot (2003; 2007) en las que se analizan cuestiones relacionadas con las principales líneas estéticas que confluyen en dicho panorama, las diferentes formas y estructuras empleadas, algunos de los temas y asuntos poéticos más relevantes, los recursos y modos de expresión utilizados con mayor frecuencia y los especiales tratamientos a que son sometidas las categorías pragmáticas del autor, el texto y el receptor; se resalta en alguno de esos trabajos la importancia concedida al ritmo, la musicalidad y el silencio como elementos prioritarios donde con frecuencia residen los valores estéticos del texto; se atiende al empleo de la ironía y el enmascaramiento como recursos distanciadores entre el sujeto y el objeto artístico; se alude también a la quiebra del yo biográfico como elemento referencial del texto, a la disolución de la subjetividad en fragmentos heterogéneos y a la destrucción de la realidad objetiva como referente inmediato y obligado del texto.

Tras Auschwitz la poesía europea continúa su camino. La herencia iconoclasta de la vanguardia se manifiesta en una considerable libertad formal y temática. Ese legado llega al Reino Unido con movimientos como el imaginismo, que defiende la supremacía de la metáfora sobre otros recursos, el vorticismo, partidario de una cierta abstracción, y el geometrismo, que da la espalda a la naturaleza y las emociones. En el desarrollo de todas esas corrientes desempeñarán papeles importantes Pound, un poeta que culminará gran parte de su monumental obra (*The Cantos*) en Europa (primero en Inglaterra y luego en Francia e Italia), y otro americano de origen que se convertirá en la gran figura de la poesía en inglés de la época, T. S. Eliot (1888–1965), autor de unos libros que reflejan la crisis de valores de la sociedad moderna con un lenguaje aparentemente coloquial y un notable sentido del ritmo: de la desolación de *The Waste Land* (1922) pasa al simbolismo espiritual de *Four Quartets* (1942). El mismo ambiente de vacío moral lleva a otros poetas al compromiso con la República en la Guerra Civil española. En cabeza del Grupo de Oxford, junto a Stephen Spender y Christopher Isherwood, se encuentra Wistan H. Auden (1907–1973), que busca con su poesía culturalista compensar la desolación espiritual. Ya en la posguerra destacan el vitalismo de Dylan Thomas (1914–1953), el intimismo cotidiano de Philip Larkin (1922–1985) y el romanticismo apasionado de Ted Hughes (1930–1998), quien fuese pareja de la poeta Sylvia Plath.

En la Francia de posguerra encontramos poetas relevantes, más o menos herederos de los grandes del XIX. Uno de ellos es Francis Ponge (1899–1988), cultivador de una poesía materialista centrada en un universo de objetos, a los que aplica su mirada impersonal (*Le Parti pris des choses*, 1942). Continuadores del surrealismo son Henri Michaux (1899–1984), también pintor, que refleja en su poesía viajes, experiencias con drogas y el lado oscuro del inconsciente, René Char (1907–1998), que pasa de un estilo aforístico a un enigmático simbolismo, y Edmond Jabès (1912–1991), de origen cairota y perteneciente a una familia judía procedente de Italia. La poesía alemana está dominada en el segundo tercio del siglo por la figura de Bertolt Brecht (1898–1956), quien, con un estilo distanciado y de emoción contenida y un lenguaje rico y al mismo tiempo accesible, expone los conflictos existenciales, políticos y sociales afrontados a partir de su militancia comunista. Otros poetas en lengua alemana son Paul Celan (1920–1970), una de las voces esenciales de la poesía universal del siglo XX, y la austríaca Ingeborg Bachmann (1926–1973), obsesionados por la impotencia comunicativa del lenguaje, mientras Hans M. Enzensberger (1929) representa el espíritu crítico de los setenta en *El hundimiento del Titanic* (1978). Un escritor radicalmente singular que también cultivó la poesía fue Thomas Bernhard (1931–1989), autor de *In hora mortis* y *Bajo el hierro de la luna*, publicados en 1958, dos obras fundamentales para comprender su atormentada personalidad, sus obsesiones temáticas y sus principales rasgos de estilo. Ambos libros presentan a un poeta que habita en el misterio y que recorre los caminos de una mística atormentada.

Entre los poetas rusos hay tres grandes figuras, además de Maiakovski. Anna Ajmátova (1889–1966), Osip Mandelstam (1891–1938) y Marina Tsvetáieva (1892–1941), víctimas los tres del terror stalinista. La poesía de Ajmátova se caracteriza por su introspección e intimismo, rasgos que se acentuaron con la consolidación de la literatura oficial del realismo socialista; censurada durante gran parte de su vida por las autoridades políticas de su país, escribió poemarios como *Caña*, *Versos líricos* y *Réquiem*. Mandelstam, autor de *Piedra*, *Tristia* y *Los cuadernos de Voronez*, fue uno de los máximos representantes del acmeísmo, movimiento que proponía la sencillez estilística frente a la estética simbolista. La literatura polaca, que contó con una activa vanguardia en los años veinte, ha dado posteriormente grandes poetas; entre ellos, Czeslaw Milosz (1911–2004), premio Nobel en 1980, que pasa de revisar la catastrófica historia reciente de su país en *Tres inviernos* (1936) a una lírica más evocadora y meditativa que reflexiona sobre el paso del tiempo y la experiencia, recogida en poemarios como *Ciudad sin nombre* (1969) y *Donde surge y donde se pone el sol* (1974). Y junto a Milosz, hay que destacar la voz de Wislawa Szymborska (1923–2012, galardonada asimismo con el Nobel en 1996), que a través de poemas de lenguaje sencillo y corte clásico aborda cuestiones de gran calado conceptual y metafísico. Nombres importantes de la poesía checa son Vitezslav Nezval (1900–1958), traductor de Rimbaud, Frantisek Halas (1901–1949), el reflexivo Vladimir Holan (1905–1980) y Jaroslav Seifert (1901–1986), premio Nobel en 1984, cantor de la revolución y del amor. La literatura griega contemporánea ha dado dos señalados poetas: Yorgos Seferis (1900–1971), de un clasicismo desesperanzado, y Odiseas Elitis (1911–1996), autor de una lírica comprometida con su pueblo.

La poesía europea de estas últimas décadas se caracteriza por la diseminación, que afecta a la escritura de poemas y poéticas que han de poner rostro lírico a una realidad social en la que, al parecer, hay más poetas que lectores de poesía (claro, estas estadísticas varían según los diferentes países y contextos lingüísticos). Sin embargo, esa diseminación ha generado un superávit productivo de un valor artístico cuestionable; la incesante elaboración de antologías (preparadas muchas veces con urgencia por mercaderes de la cosa literaria, sin haber sido suficientemente meditadas), el ritmo acelerado de publicación a que se someten muchos poetas (presionados o no por sus editores), los intereses extraliterarios a los que sirven algunas empresas editoras y de comunicación son otros rasgos característicos del paisaje poético europeo contemporáneo.

Dadas estas circunstancias, una parte considerable y en general muy bien valorada de la poesía posmoderna contempla la tradición como un pasado en ruinas dispuesto a ser revisitado sin atender a ningún criterio normativo. Es la *auctoritas* de una tradición sancionada por el uso y la reiteración lo que parece imponerse aunque esto, en sí mismo, no resulte novedoso ni perjudicial. Así, y dejando a un lado la atemperada actitud rupturista característica de algunos textos de los años sesenta (escritos a la luz de un intento de reactualización de la vanguardia histórica), esta recuperación del pasado artístico y cultural se materializa, entre otros aspectos, en el tratamiento de determinadas formas, estrofas, tendencias, temas y motivos tradicionales. Es la conocida práctica de la *imitatio*, basada en la recuperación de citas y lugares comunes más o menos literales, alusiones, parodias u homenajes, repetición de determinadas fórmulas estilísticas. En los casos más interesantes esta reactualización responde a una cierta actitud crítica, con lo que sus protagonistas renuncian a la elaboración de simples ejercicios de arqueología artística. En un plano más general, E. Milán (2004: 60) señala que el arte actual está atravesando "un momento de retroceso acrítico", vive preso del desencanto y el simulacro y basa buena parte de su actividad en la repetición de formas canonizadas, hasta el punto de haber hecho del *remake*, el *revival* y la recurrencia versiones de un cierto estilo posmoderno. Se trata, a menudo, de poetas afónicos; su voz es el altavoz –y no la voz más alta y elevada– de una determinada cultura.

El viaje realizado hasta aquí conduce al encuentro de la poesía europea de estas últimas décadas, un fenómeno complejo que se resiste a ser analizado desde un único punto de vista. Si en otros lugares he distinguido entre una posmodernidad acomodaticia, dócil, sumisa y acrítica, y una posmodernidad crítica, inconformista, inquieta y deseosa de cambios y transformaciones (Saldaña 1997; 2004; 2008; 2013), ahora conviene recordar que ambas actitudes encuentran sus respectivos desarrollos en diferentes tipos de poesía posmoderna. Así, frente a una poesía anclada en la tradición, extraordinariamente hábil en el manejo de unos cuantos recursos artísticos y culturales más o menos brillantes, ideológicamente conservadora, mitómana, culturalista y evasiva, se encuentra otra poesía que apuesta por el riesgo, la aventura, la innovación y la crítica. Dada esta situación, hay que esforzarse para investigar y valorar en su medida el alcance de las tendencias poéticas más desatendidas por la crítica oficial y académica, si queremos acceder a una visión clara y lo más completa posible de un determinado panorama poético (las editoriales, los suplementos culturales de los diarios, las antologías de poesía, los programas académicos de literatura y los premios literarios responden con excesiva frecuencia a muy concretos intereses que tienen que ver más con el mercado literario que con la estética literaria). Refiriéndose al panorama poético británico, Dietz (1984) denuncia la lamentable situación en que se encuentra, controlada desde unos escasos puntos estratégicos que detentan el poder y la información: las antologías de Penguin, editoriales como Faber y Chatto & Windus, críticos –poetas a su vez– que ejercen de editores y antólogos de poesía (Craig Raine, Andrew Motion, Blake Morrison), rasgos que, lejos de desaparecer, se han acentuado en estas últimas décadas. Los paralelismos con la situación poética española son más que evidentes, como muestra la siguiente afirmación de Dietz: "sociológicamente, en términos de incidencia social y editorial, la poesía británica actual depende de unos pocos resortes en manos de un grupo minoritario de personas" (1984: 7), y esas semejanzas podrían extenderse a otros ámbitos lingüísticos del continente europeo. En este sentido se encuentra la lectura que aquí propongo de la poesía postmoderna, en lo posible no contaminada por ningún tipo de agente extraliterario y que nos permita contemplar cómo se presenta y qué valores adquiere en dicha poesía eso que aquí denomino *sensibilidad crítica postmoderna*.

Si prestamos atención al panorama editorial, habría que mencionar un par de publicaciones recientes: doscientos setenta poetas europeos desde 1968 hasta la actualidad han sido seleccionados por los críticos estadounidenses Prufer y Miller para figurar en la antología *New European Poets* (2008), publicada en Estados Unidos. En ella se describe su obra como "ferozmente inteligente, a menudo irreverente, y comprometida con la historia y la política" y se recogen muestras escritas en lenguas minoritarias (euskera, gaélico, sami, etc.). Entre estos autores figuran los vascos Kirmen Uribe, con tres poemas, y Bernardo Atxaga, con dos. Sus autores aseguran que "es la primera antología en inglés de poesía europea actual" e incluye a poetas que escriben en inglés, francés, ruso y español, entre otras lenguas. Para muchos de ellos supone su primera traducción al inglés, aunque no es el caso de los dos escritores vascos.

Mil años de poesía europea (2009) reúne algunas voces canónicas de la poesía europea a lo largo de sus diez siglos de vida en una antología bilingüe, que ha corrido a cargo de Francisco Rico y Rosa Lentini, poeta, traductora y editora. La antología contiene desde las canciones de mujer de la Alta Edad Media hasta los grandes líricos del siglo XX. Son más de 80 poetas en una docena de idiomas, y de cada uno de ellos se han seleccionado los poemas más representativos en su lengua original y en su traducción al español, hasta completar 25 o 30 páginas por cada poeta. La *Chanson de Roland*, el romancero castellano, Dante Alighieri, Petrarca, Ausiàs March, Villon, Michele Marullo, Garcilaso de la Vega, Ronsard, Camoes, Góngora, Quevedo, Milton, Goethe, Blake, Novalis, Shelley, Keats, Leopardi, Hugo, Baudelaire, Verlaine, Rimbaud, Kavafis y Valéry son algunos de los poetas seleccionados en esta antología. Junto a ellos, cuatro españoles del siglo XX: A. Machado, J. R. Jiménez, J. Guillén y García Lorca.

Organizándose como oportunidades para la confrontación territorial, estética e ideológica, estas y otras antologías se presentan como síntesis descriptivas, más o menos neutrales y objetivas de un determinado panorama poético, y todas ellas ofrecen algunos de los itinerarios (sin duda, los más aplaudidos) que la poesía europea ha recorrido en estas últimas décadas. Ahora bien, y dado que, como denuncia Talens (1989b: 17), importan menos los *nombres* de los poetas que las *propuestas de escritura*, argumento que, dado la vuelta, retoma en otro lugar: "la circulación de nombres y títulos a través de los *mass media* ha sustituido la familiaridad dialógica con los textos" (Talens 1994: 2), ¿muestran las tendencias que encontramos en estos volúmenes la totalidad de registros que presenta la poesía europea de este período?, ¿recogen estas antologías –por separado o en conjunto– la diversidad de poéticas elaboradas durante estos años? Creo que la respuesta a ambas preguntas es la misma: no. Las antologías dedicadas a difundir la poesía escrita en Europa durante estos últimos años –en términos generales– adolecen de unos mismos defectos: los intereses, en ocasiones, extraliterarios a los que sirven y los prejuicios estéticos, ideológicos y morales con los que están planteadas. En algunos casos, el antólogo no solo hace su particular apuesta sino que –a la luz de la más pura tradición retórica y preceptista– también dicta los itinerarios futuros y los temas susceptibles de ser recreados artísticamente.

En cualquier caso, casi todas las antologías y, sobre todo, los particulares itinerarios por los que discurren las obras (antologadas o no en volúmenes colectivos) de los diversos poetas muestran un laberinto de tendencias en el que no resulta fácil orientarse, dados los diferentes planteamientos estéticos ensayados (a veces, incluso, por un mismo escritor durante la evolución de su propia obra). Por lo tanto, una descripción mínimamente rigurosa y profunda del panorama poético europeo de estos últimos cuarenta años requiere unas dosis de paciencia, serenidad y buen humor que raras veces reúnen los críticos que se han ocupado del asunto. Así, es necesario prescindir de intereses más o menos velados, tópicos y prejuicios de todo tipo, valorar los trabajos de la crítica no como dogmas absolutos de fe sino como propuestas más o menos adecuadas de análisis e interpretación y, sobre todo, volver a leer (o, en algunos casos, leer por vez primera) los textos poéticos si queremos acceder a un conocimiento crítico y exhaustivo de este panorama poético. En definitiva, contra la regla y la consigna que hacen de la inercia y la costumbre procedimientos de análisis e interpretación, la excepción de la lectura crítica de los textos poéticos liberada de la convención ciega y escandalosamente perpetuada. Así pues, un panorama poético como el que acabo de describir no puede ser analizado desde una única sensibilidad dominante y, de esta forma, la aproximación al conocimiento total de dicho panorama ha de emprenderse necesariamente desde la consciencia de su amplitud, complejidad y naturaleza contradictoria. El fragmento supone un modo de expresión teórica y artística extraordinariamente representativo de la crisis y la complejidad características de nuestro tiempo. De esta manera, el fragmentarismo proporciona –frente a todos los totalitarismos, integrismos, holismos, fundamentalismos y dogmatismos– una posición ideológica adecuada desde la cual abordar el análisis de una actualidad asimismo diversa, plural, mestiza, escindida y fragmentada; heredado de la crisis de la modernidad, el fragmento se presenta como una seña de identidad de nuestro tiempo ya que la *condition postmoderne* (Lyotard) es una categoría esencialmente fragmentaria (nada más lejos de mi intención que se aprecie este planteamiento antidogmático como un modo de *pensamiento débil*).

Buena parte de los poetas que han surgido en Europa en estas últimas décadas presentan un marcado perfil cultural, pero no en un sentido restrictivo pues en sus textos no hacen acopio solo de la cultura sancionada por la *auctoritas* de la tradición clásica (y decir *clásica* es decir, casi siempre, *grecolatina*), sino que incorporan –a veces, pudiera parecer, de manera indiscriminada– cualquier tipo de dato o información cultural. En el ámbito de la poesía española contemporánea, los novísimos (sinécdoque de un fenómeno artístico más amplio que aquí denominaré *poéticas de los setenta*) forman parte de un proceso internacional de renovación del lenguaje poético que se desarrolla a partir de la Segunda Guerra Mundial. Poetas griegos como Odiseas Elitis o Yorgos Seferis; norteamericanos como Charles Olson, Robert Creeley, John Ashbery o los *beats* Allen Ginsberg, Gary Snyder o Amiri Baraka (antes Leroy Jones); checos como Miroslav Holub o Jan Skacel; británicos como el galés David Jones, el escocés Kenneth White, el irlandés Seamus Heaney (premio Nobel en 1995) o los ingleses Ian Hamilton Finlay, John Riley o Andrew Crozier; italianos como Alfredo Giuliani, Edoardo Sanguineti, Elio Pagliarani, Antonio Porta o Nanni Balestrini (antologados –por cierto– en 1961 en *I Novissimi. Poesie per gli anni '60*, de donde tomó el título Castellet para su antología de 1970); españoles como Eduardo Chicharro, Carlos Edmundo de Ory, Pablo García Baena, Juan Eduardo Cirlot, Gabino-Alejandro Carriedo, Miguel Labordeta o Antonio Gamoneda, entre otros poetas extranjeros y españoles, representan algunos de los antecedentes supranacionales inmediatos de parte de la poesía –a mi juicio– más interesante que comienza a escribirse a mediados de los años sesenta, aquella parte que hizo del riesgo y la aventura, la experimentación y la osadía, la tensión y la crítica unas maneras de entender y practicar el lenguaje poético. Así, no resulta nada raro encontrar en muchos de los poetas mencionados fenómenos, técnicas y recursos poéticos como el *collage*, la fragmentación, el experimentalismo, la disolución del yo, la combinación de diferentes lenguas, el fin de la primacía del significado único en favor de la simultaneidad de distintos significados o la búsqueda de nuevos procedimientos expresivos, elementos todos ellos que ya habíamos encontrado en las vanguardias históricas.

Entre los poetas en lengua inglesa mencionados en el párrafo anterior, y ya en la segunda mitad del siglo XX, probablemente sea el irlandés Seamus Heaney (1939–2013) uno de los más influyentes. Como católico del Ulster, Heaney sufrió en primera persona la compleja y violenta historia contemporánea de su patria. Su obra, iniciada en 1965, está formada por títulos como *Death of a Naturalist* (1966), *Door into the Dark* (1969), *Wintering Out* (1972), *North* (1975). En su escritura se entrecruzan el pasado y el presente, la muerte y el amor, la poética y la política. Otro poeta muy bien valorado por críticos como Harold Bloom y Christopher Ricks es Geoffrey Hill (1932), autor de once libros de poesía, desde el inicial *For the Unfallen* (1958), pasando por *Mercian Hymns* (1971), un extraordinario libro de poemas en prosa, hasta el reciente *Without Title* (2006). Hill ocupa en la actualidad la cátedra de poesía de la Universidad de Oxford. Por último, y también originario de Irlanda del Norte, Paul Muldoon (1951), cuya obra no se despega de la realidad, surge de un compromiso con el mundo que le rodea con el que lleva a cabo una indagación personal de la realidad. Nada tan fantástico como el mundo real, parecen decir sus versos.

La lengua portuguesa también ha dado grandes nombres a la lírica europea contemporánea. Después del extraordinario caso de Fernando Pessoa, Eugénio de Andrade (1923–2005) posiblemente haya sido el poeta con mayor prestigio y repercusión internacional. *Materia solar, Blanco en lo blanco, Contra la oscuridad, El otro nombre de la tierra, La sal de la lengua* y *Los surcos de la sed* son muestras de la enorme capacidad de Andrade de llevar al poema el lenguaje mudo de las cosas que en verdad importan: la tierra y la infancia, el deseo y la sed, la luz que funde el cuerpo y la memoria. También de 1923 y lisboeta es Mário Cesariny (fallecido en 2006), una de las figuras más importantes del surrealismo portugués de estas últimas décadas tanto desde su faceta de pintor como con su obra poética, en la que recurre con frecuencia a inventarios caóticos, neologismos, diálogos inconexos y automatismos que convierten el resultado el algo poliédrico y sumamente vivaz. António Ramos Rosa (1924–2013), ensayista y traductor, poeta con una amplia obra (*Ciclo del caballo,* 1985, *La facilidad del aire,* 1998, *El aprendiz secreto,* 2001, *Acordes,* 2002) recibió el Prémio Pessoa en 1988 y el Premio Europeo de Poesía en 1991. José Viale Moutinho (Funchal, Madeira, 1945), periodista y traductor (en español puede leerse *Un caballo en la niebla,* 1992). José Agostinho Baptista (también nacido en Funchal, 1948), con once libros publicados hasta la fecha, su poesía ha sido reconocida como una de las más originales e innovadoras de la actualidad. Nuno Júdice (1949), autor de una ya amplia obra poética y ensayística que ha sido reconocida con importantes premios. Vergílio Alberto Vieira (Braga, 1950), autor de más de veinte títulos de poesía, ensayo, traducción y narrativa (en español puede leerse *Piedra de trance*, publicado en 1992).

Otros poetas importantes en otras lenguas europeas que han destacado en estas últimas décadas son, a mi juicio, el griego Kostas Steryópulos (Atenas, 1926), profesor de filología neohelénica en la Universidad de Atenas, de donde fue expulsado durante la dictadura de los coroneles (en español se puede leer *El sol de la medianoche*, 1999); el sueco Tomas Tranströmer (Estocolmo, 1931), galardonado en 2011 con el Nobel de Literatura; el finlandés Claes Andersson (1937), autor de títulos como *Desde que uno se ha jubilado* (1989) o *El buen burócrata* (1991); el francés Jean-Pierre Colombi (Marsella, 1941), autor de una poesía impresionista que parece perseguir la anotación pura y simple de las sensaciones; el esloveno Tomaz Salamun (1941), quien practica una escritura concebida a la luz de la imaginación y la libertad de la vanguardia; el checo Miloslav Ulicny (Praga, 1942), profesor en la Universidad Carolina y traductor de poesía española; el italiano Antonio Sagredo (Lecce, 1945), quien elabora una poesía tocada por las alas de la luz del mejor Rimbaud, alcanza un tono hermético modulado por una sintaxis y una imaginería léxica muy originales (en español puede leerse *Tortugas*, 1993); el ensayista polaco Adam Zagajewski (1945), exiliado en Francia y posteriormente en Estados Unidos, autor de *Lienzo* (1990), *Tierra de fuego* (1994), *Retorno* (2003) y, entre otros, *Deseo* (2005); la sueca Nina Burton (1946), autora de *La primera noche*; el albanés Rudolf Marka (1951); la búlgara Rada Panchovska (1952), traductora de poesía española y latinoamericana; el italiano Valerio Magrelli (1957), autor de *Ora serrata retinae* (1980) y *Nature e venature* (1987), uno de los más destacados de la gran promoción de poetas europeos posterior a la explosión de 1968; el francés Michel Houllebecq (1958), más conocido como narrador, autor de *Renacimiento* (2001) y *Supervivencia* (2007), donde parte de la observación de la realidad cotidiana en versos que a veces no son más que huellas de tal mirada: expresión tragicómica y lírica de una subjetividad implacable; el esloveno Alojz Ihan (1961), autor de *La moneda de plata* (1985), *Los jugadores de póker* y *Un Platón entre los dentistas* (1997).

Por razones obvias, párrafo aparte merece el estonio Jüri Talvet (Tartu, 1945), comparatista de prestigio internacional de la Universidad de Tartu, un poeta que vive a la intemperie, que se desplaza por el mundo como si fuese su casa sin un itinerario previamente marcado y escribe en libertad sobre las cosas que ve, sobre lo que ve en sus viajes –sean reales o imaginarios– por los caminos de la tierra o por los senderos de su conciencia; se traslada así sabedor de que su rumbo está escrito en el aire o “en el agua sonora del tiempo” y encuentra con frecuencia rostros de personas que le conmueven intensamente, comparte con los demás situaciones y experiencias no por más sencillas y domésticas menos extraordinarias; a veces viaja sin salir de casa y en esas ocasiones recorre laberintos por donde antes han transitado otros viajeros que hicieron de la imaginación la válvula de escape más potente. Y su poesía entonces es un artefacto dispuesto a recomponer los huesos amontonados de la realidad, renueva la memoria familiar (la existencia junto a los padres, los hijos, los escenarios compartidos con la gente querida), redescubre el mundo, reinventa la vida. Desde su primer libro de poesía publicado, *Despertares* (1981), Talvet se ha caracterizado por mantener una rigurosa y en el fondo radical independencia en el contexto de la literatura estonia contemporánea, una independencia marcada por un compromiso con el lenguaje entendido como una herramienta llamada a desvelar las miserias y contradicciones del mundo. Autor de una considerable y muy meritoria obra como comparatista y crítico literario, Jüri Talvet se supo desde el principio como un "arroyo cuyo destino era fluir"; en este sentido, ha sabido muy bien fundar una escritura poética depurada de todo elemento superfluo, una escritura en movimiento, en construcción, sin el lastre innecesario que un exceso de erudición podría acarrear, y ello a pesar de las frecuentes citas y alusiones de estirpe cultural o literaria que su poesía incorpora. Así, el texto poético se presenta al final como una encrucijada en la que confluyen –sin despegarse en exceso de la realidad más salvaje y destructiva de su tiempo (ahí está ese revelador poema rescatado del olvido titulado "1953")– un intenso lirismo y una radical incertidumbre, rasgos de una escritura elaborada por alguien que no deja de enfrentarse al mundo desde el cambio y la perplejidad permanentes. Una poesía concebida de esta manera no puede sino entenderse como un alegato en defensa del sueño y de la nieve (ese precisamente, *Del sueño, de la nieve*, fue el título de una antología de su poesía publicada en español en 2010), esos escenarios blancos y silenciosos amenazados por la vigilia y el fuego devastador de la historia, un arma de combate frente a las adversidades e inclemencias del mundo, un escenario de liberación y celebración de la luz, porque ahí fuera, traspasada la línea que la delimita, "el invierno persiste" (Talvet 2010: 15).

En este contexto, nos encontramos con que la poesía europea contemporánea se ha configurado como un paisaje en el que poetas, editores de poesía, críticos literarios y profesores de literatura están llamados a ser prácticamente sus únicos habitantes (dejo deliberadamente de lado a los "lectores" porque considero que estos se encuentran integrados en las especies que acabo de citar), un paisaje removido en los últimos años con excesiva frecuencia por la aparición de numerosas antologías poéticas, instrumentos ya no sé si de periodización, canonización o confusión literarias, un paisaje, en todo caso, en el que un buen número de antólogos, editores, críticos, profesores y poetas se ha esforzado por dibujar un panorama poético utilizando únicamente las etiquetas del realismo, la figuración, el sentimentalismo o la experiencia –en sus sentidos más alicortos y ramplones–, marcas que dan cuenta solo de algunos de los itinerarios por los que ha transcurrido la poesía europea contemporánea, con lo cual se han dejado al margen otros desarrollos basados en la recuperación de parte de la vanguardia histórica, o de tendencia minimalista, con una propensión hacia una poética conceptual o del silencio, o de la abstracción, o de aliento épico y registro marcadamente discursivo o narrativo, o, en fin, de intención política, aunque, claro, cabría preguntarse qué tipo de poesía no responde a una u otra intención política. En todo caso, y dado que la poesía europea posmoderna se presenta como un panorama en cualquier caso más heterogéneo de lo que a menudo se ha querido presentar, conviene distinguir las diferentes líneas que recorren ese panorama, entre las que se encuentran esas otras situadas en sus márgenes, desplazadas del centro hacia una orilla que raras veces se contempla con la necesaria atención.

Alfredo Saldaña
asaldana@unizar.es
Departamento de Lingüística General e Hispánica
Universidad de Zaragoza
Pedro Cerbuna 12
50009 Zaragoza
ESPAÑA / SPAIN

Referencias bibliográficas

AA. VV. 1993. *Veintidós poetas europeos*, Madrid, Ediciones de la Torre.

Bigot, C. Le, ed. 2003. *Les polyphonies poétiques. Formes et territoires de la poésie contemporaine en langues romanes*. Rennes: Presses Universitaires de Rennes.

Bigot, C. Le, ed. 2007. *À quoi bon la poésie, aujourd'hui?*. Rennes: Presses Universitaires de Rennes.

Dietz, B. 1984. La poesía inglesa de los últimos veinte años: una visión sesgada. – *Cuadernos de Investigación Filológica*, X, 1 y 2, 3–16.

Friedrich, H. 1974. *La estructura de la lírica moderna*. Trad. de J. Petit. Barcelona: Seix Barral.

García, E. 2005. *Una poética del límite*. Valencia: Pre-Textos.

Milán, E. 2004. *Resistir. Insistencias sobre el presente poético*. México D. F.: FCE.

Prufer, K., Miller, W. 2008. *New European Poets*. Minneapolis: Graywolf Press.

Rico, F., y R. Lentini. 2009. *Mil años de poesía europea*. Barcelona: Backlist.

Riquer, M. de, Valverde, J. M.ª.1991. *Historia de la literatura universal*. Barcelona: Planeta.

Saldaña, A. 1997. *Modernidad y posmodernidad. Filosofía de la cultura y teoría estética*. Valencia: Episteme.

Saldaña, A. 2004. Posmodernidad, Historia, Literatura. – L. Romero Tobar, ed., *Historia literaria/Historia de la literatura*. Zaragoza: PUZ, 87–98.

Saldaña, A. 2008. *Un lugar en construcción. Crítica y cultura en la posmodernidad*. Zaragoza: Ediciones de la Librería Cálamo.

Saldaña, A. 2013. *La huella en el margen. Literatura y pensamiento crítico*. Zaragoza: Mira Editores.

Talens, J. 1989a. La coartada metapoética. – *Ínsula*, 512–513, 55–57.

Talens, J. 1989b. *De la publicidad como fuente historiográfica. La generación poética española de 1970*. Valencia: Episteme.

Talens, J. 1994. *Escritura contra simulacro*. Valencia: Episteme.

Talvet, J. 2010. *Del sueño, de la nieve (Antología 2001–2009)*. Ed. bilingüe, trad. de A. Lázaro-Tinaut y el autor, Zaragoza: Olifante.

Uriz, F. J., ed. 1995. *101 poemas nórdicos*. Zaragoza: Casa del Traductor.

Neid lähtetõdemusi tuleb väikekultuuridele kohaldades täpsustada. Ühelt poolt ei saagi väikekultuurid teisiti olla kui avatud. Neil puudub füüsilis-poliitiline võime luua keskusi, mis end sel määral välja puhastaksid, et piiri ja perifeeria – suhtluse põlisala – maha salgaksid või täieliku ühekõne kontrollile allutaksid. Väikekultuurid moodustavad tavaliselt ise enam-vähem tervikuna piiriala või perifeeria. Nende katsed tõeliste keskustena esineda kukuvad välja groteskina. Avatus on nende loomulik seisund. Kui väljastpoolt tuleb tõukeid nende avatust kuidagi teisiti korraldada, sellele kindlam suund anda, asetab see väikekultuurid sedamaid erilise haavatavuse seisundisse. Võimsate füüsilis-majanduslike hoobadega varustatud suurtest kultuuriruumidest juhitav akulturatsioon ähvardab väikekultuurid hoopistükkis alla neelata.

Jüri Talvet,
„Maailmakirjanduse kodustamise küsimusi"

When adapting these postulates to small cultures, a number of peculiarities should be taken into account. In the first place, small cultures cannot avoid openness. They do not possess a physical-political capacity to create such "purified" and "sanctified" centres that could deny their border and periphery – the most primeval territories of intercourse – or submit them to total monologues. Small cultures usually embody themselves, in their entirety, a border or a periphery. The attempts of their centres to become established as authentic power centres generally tend to look grotesque. Openness, instead, is their natural state. As soon as from outside pressure is exerted to organize their openness in a different way – to give it a "more determined" direction – small cultures become especially vulnerable. Acculturation directed from big cultural spaces, possessors of powerful physical and economical catapults, perpetually menaces to swallow up small cultures and, thus, to violate cultural ecology the world really desperately needs for its survival in a larger perspective.

Jüri Talvet,
"The Reception of World Literature in Estonia.
Some Preliminary Remarks"

INTERLITTERARIA 2015, SUPPL. 1: 130–147

Die Aneignung der Weltliteratur in Tartu[1]

LIINA LUKAS

Abstract. ***Taming World Literature in Tartu.*** A small literature – a literature with a small circle of authors and readers – has to deal with inevitable problems arising from its limited visibility and spread, but its advantage is that it cannot escape the existence of others, as the Estonian thinker and poet Uku Masing has claimed, aptly identifying the openness of a small culture. Big literatures, while pretending to universality, could allow themselves a certain amount of self-sufficiency, whereas small cultures can only be open to others, as Jüri Talvet has said. A small literature constantly defines its aesthetic goals and cultural responsibilities as based on a larger tradition, constructing for itself a world literature as part of its own literary tradition. It is essential for an aesthetic renewal of every culture, but particularly a small culture.

There are certain historical reasons for an active domestication of World Literature by Estonian literature. These lead us to the particular multilingual character of the historical cultural space of the Baltics. Estonian literary culture was formed in an intense interaction with other cultures, languages and mentalities – Baltic-German, Russian, Swedish, Finnish. Estonian written culture was born in other languages, developed as translative and, achieving its independence, draws on forms and motifs by written and spoken culture of other languages. As a result a large part of Estonian literature is of foreign origin and, *per contra*, texts from other cultures are so inherent that it becomes impossible and meaningless to draw boundaries between what is its own and what foreign. Instead of the search for originality and authenticity, what becomes more interesting is to ask how and for what purpose these exact cultural elements, at this exact point in time, have been bounded and synthesised into a meaningful functional whole.

Of course, we cannot overlook the colonial nature of this historically developed cultural exchange model. It is interesting to ask how much the historical (colonial) model of intercultural relations influenced the dialog with other literatures in the postcolonial period. In that World Literature had a central role to play: it functioned as a constructor of a postcolonial identity. It is characteristic to small cultures that remained under the domination of central cultures for a long period of time. As such, World Literature is a pedagogical project that takes care of the Weltbildung, as Goethe already found.

[1] Der Beitrag ist im Rahmen des institutionellen Forschungsprojektes „Estnische Literatur im Paradigma der vergleichenden Literaturwissenschaft“ (IUT 20-1) entstanden.

DOI: http://dx.doi.org/10.12697/IL.2015.S1.11

In the present article the notion of World Literature and the historical conditions of it – as an object of the comparative literary studies – will be explained using the example of Estonian literature. In order to do so, the excursus to the history of comparative literary studies at the University of Tartu will be taken, at which location the subject of comparative literature was practiced much earlier than Estonian literature was studied or appeared on the horizon of world literature. Thereby the 'home' (or 'homelessness') of comparative literary history and its re-positionings through time will be observed. Having roots in the studies of rhetoric and poetics in the Academia Gustaviana founded in 1632, comparative literary history in the German-language Kaiserliche Universität zu Dorpat (re-established in 1802) was initially a topic for professors of classical philology, while shortly after moving under the lectureship of German language and then, during the period of Russification, to the department of Russian language and literature. Beginning in 1904, comparative literature found its place in the chairs of Latvian and Estonian, where it developed as a modern disciple in the Estonian-language University of Tartu at the time of prof. Gustav Suits in the 1920s. The Soviet period formally maintained the World Literature environment of the Estonian literary canon under the label of 'foreign literature', but the notion of foreign literature narrowed, being limited to the established literary canon of the West, and even that selectively through those whom the Marxist ideology considered 'progressive'. 'Foreign literature', but mainly its relationship with Estonian literature was under ideological pressure to the extent that it was more rational to deal with it as a closed phenomenon boiling in its own juices. At the same time Russian literature was pushed to the fore. Its influence and role in the development of Estonian literature had to be emphasised. However, it was precisely Russian philology where Tartu literary studies was given an impulse, which gave the impetus to several disciples in Tartu as well as elsewhere, while also creating a completely new field – semiotics. The theory of periphery as an area, where semiotic processes accelerate, and the creative and dialogical function of the borders developed in Tartu by Juri Lotman, explains a great deal about the history of Comparative Literature in Tartu: the peripheral location of Tartu, its changing identity turns out to be the crossroad and meeting point of diverse cultures. This has facilitated the comparative approach of cultures and sees the only possible methodology of literary studies in comparison. At the periphery the perception of borders sharpens, and this exactly is the field of Comparative Literature. The understanding of borders also allows us to find a compromise – or rather work allocation – between World Literature and Comparative Literature. One has education as its core, the other science, but both together take care of the Weltbildung – as it seems from Tartu.

Keywords: World Literature, Comparative Literature, small literatures, Estonian literature, literary studies at the University of Tartu

I Die *Weltliteratur* als Bestandteil kleiner Literatur

Der unvermeidliche Nachteil der kleinen Literaturen[2] ist ihre begrenzte Verbreitung und geringe Wahrnehmbarkeit derselben. Aber im Gegensatz zu den großen und dominanten Literaturen können sie „an der Existenz der Anderen nicht vorbeikommen", wie der estnische Dichter und Theologe Uku Masing es mal formuliert hat (Masing 1989: 144). Die großen, dem „literarischen Meridian von Greenwich" (Casanova 2004: 4) nahe liegenden Literaturen, verschreiben sich – ohne es zu merken – der Universalität und Selbstgenügsamkeit. „Die kleinen Kulturen können nicht anders, als offen zu sein. Die Offenheit ist ihr natürlicher Zustand"[3], so Jüri Talvet (Talvet 2005a). Eine kleine Literatur bestimmt ihre ästhetischen Aufgaben, indem sie sich an eine weiterreichende Tradition anlehnt. Sie konstruiert sich eine „Weltliteratur", die sie als einen Teil ihrer eigenen literarischen Tradition betrachtet. So gewährleistet sie sich eine „Verdichtung der geistigen Atmosphäre" (Oras 2003a: 31), die nötig ist für ihre ästhetische Erneuerung. Nach einer essentialistischen Kulturauffassung könnte solch eine Art „kultureller Kreditnahme" als Fremdeinfluss oder sogar „Selbstkolonisierung" erscheinen. Geht man hingegen von einem dynamischen Kulturbegriff aus, so „findet eine Kultur den sichersten Garant ihrer Lebenskraft im Dialog mit anderen Kulturen, ja mit der Weltliteratur im weitesten Sinne" (Talvet 2005a).

Nachgegangen wird im Folgenden dem Begriff der Weltliteratur (als einer Konstruktion des (meta-)literarischen Kommunikationsprozesses) einer kleinen Literatur am Beispiel der estnischen Literatur; dabei werden die historischen Bedingungen für diesen Terminus technicus der vergleichenden Literaturwissenschaft Tartus erläutert.

Die estnische Literatur – mit ihren knapp eine Million potentiellen Lesern ist sie eine der kleinsten unter den europäischen Literaturen – hat in ihrer Aneignung der Weltliteratur eine lange Tradition, die auf ihrem multilingualen Entstehungskontext gründet. Estnische Literatur entstand und entwickelte

[2] Den Begriff der „kleinen Literatur" wird hier nicht im Sinne der *littérature mineure* verwendet, wie ihn von Gilles Deleuze und Félix Guattari (Deleuze-Guattari 1975) zur Charakterisierung der spezifischen Sprachsituation von Franz Kafka konzipiert wurde – als Literatur in einer großen, aber „deterritorialisierten" Sprache wie Prager Deutsch –, aber auch nicht im Sinne von Pascale Casanova als eine dominierte, unterpriviligierte oder benachteiligte Literatur (Casanova 2007: 181), sondern in einem wertneutralen Sinne als die Literatur einer kleinen Sprache, eine Literatur mit kleiner Autor- und Leserschaft.

[3] Alle Zitaten sind von der Autorin des Artikels ins Deutsche übersetzt worden.

sich im intensiven Kontakt mit anderen Kulturen und Sprachen – mit dem Deutschbaltischen, Russischen, Schwedischen als Kolonialkulturen, sowie dem Finnischen als einem (postkolonialen?) kulturell verwandtem und geographisch nahem Wahlvorbild. Estnische literarische Kultur entstand anderssprachig (*unestnisch*, um ein Antonym zur geläufigen kolonialen Benennung *undeutsch* zu verwenden). Sie entwickelte sich in Übersetzungen und Adaptionen der dominierenden Literaturen bis sie – sich dabei auf die weltliterarische Praxis stützend – die estnischsprachige mündliche Überlieferung entdeckte, die ihrerseits nicht authentisch war, sondern ihre Formen und Motive aus den anderssprachigen schriftlichen und mündlichen Kulturen schöpfte. So ist die estnische Literatur in hohem Maße fremden Ursprungs und umgekehrt – einige fremde Texte erscheinen so eigen, dass die Grenzziehung zwischen dem Eigenen und dem Fremden unmöglich und sinnlos wird. Möchte man sich die Mühe geben, „jenen Einfluss in Estland gründlicher zu analysieren, der uns schon so nahe getreten ist, dass wir ihn wegen der Nähe gar nicht mehr sehen können – so wäre dies der deutsche Einfluss. Er ist wirklich grösser als wir es uns vorstellen können. Vieles in diesem Rindenmoos ist mit dem Baum zusammengewachsen, angeeignet worden", schrieb der estnische Dichter Jaan Oks im Jahre 1909 über den deutschen Einfluss auf die estnische Literatur. (Oks 2004: 251).

Interessanter als die Suche nach der Originalität oder Authentizität, ist die Frage, aus welchem Grund, mit welchem Ziel und weshalb zu dieser oder jener Zeit bestimmte kulturelle Elemente ausgewählt und neu zu einem sinnvollen funktionalen Ganzen zusammengesetzt worden sind. Interessanter als der Ursprung der einzelnen Elemente erweist sich ihre Synthese.

Freilich darf man den kolonialen Charakter des historischen Modell der Kulturvermittlung zwischen den großen und den kleinen Kulturen in Europa nicht übersehen: Postkoloniale Theorien haben Werkzeuge für die Analyse der Abwehr- oder Adaptionsstrategien, die dominierte Kulturen in diesem Vermittlungsprozess entwickelt haben, zur Verfügung gestellt. Es gilt zu prüfen, ob es das „eingeübte" (koloniale) historische Modell des interkulturellen Verhältnisses im Baltikum in der postkolonialen Periode ermöglichte, offene Kulturtransfermodelle aufzubauen. Dass der „Weltliteratur" eine Schlüsselrolle bei der Bildung der postkolonialen Identität der kleinen Literaturen zukommt, ist mehrfach betont worden; z.B. schrieb der estnische Literaturkritiker und Übersetzer Ants Oras im Jahre 1937: "Die Tschechen gestehen, dass ihre geistige Selbständigkeit erst dann erreicht wurde, als das gewaltige Werk von Jaroslav Vrchlický sie mittels der Meisterwerke der Weltliteratur von der deutschen geistigen Hegemonie befreite." (Oras 2003c: 95). Und "wie die Tschechen von der deutschen, so bemühen sich die Finnen, sich von der schwedischen Vormundschaft zu befreien, und auch dort ist das Mittel, das am meisten Aufmerksamkeit und die meisten Enthusiasten hierfür gefunden hat, das Übersetzen der Weltliteratur" (Oras 2003b: 60).

Mit einem vergleichbaren selbstbewussten Konstruktivismus erklärte die junge Generation der estnischen Künstler und Dichter am Anfang des 20. Jahrhunderts: "Das, was unsere eigene Literaturgeschichte schuldig bleibt, soll die Historie der Weltliteratur bezahlen" (Tuglas 1912: 100). Die Umorientierung in den kulturellen Vorbildern war leichter zu verkünden als zu verwirklichen. In der angeeigneten Weltliteratur herrschten immer noch die Übersetzungen aus der deutschen Literatur vor. Dass die Befreiung der estnischen Kultur „von der germanischen Seelenhaltung" (und damit vom kulturellen Kolonialverhältnis) mit Blick nach Paris verlief, erstaunt wenig: "Man hatte sich daran gewöhnt, die Worte „Paris" und „Kultur" gleichzusetzen. " (Oras 2003c: 90) Außerdem war das Französische in den Gymnasien des russischen Zarenreiches ein Pflichtfach, während z.B. das Englische in den Gymnasialcurricula selten einen Platz hatte. Außer Paris schöpfte man neue Impulse aus der skandinavischen, finnischen und angloamerikanischen Literatur. Tatsächlich brachten die Erweiterung des kulturellen Horizonts und die Aufgeschlossenheit eine neue literarische Qualität mit sich und regten Werke an, die bis heute den Kernbestand des estnischen Literaturkanons ausmachen. Einige hätten ihren Platz sogar im Kanon der Weltliteratur verdient, da der Kredit, den man aufgenommen hatte, mit Zinsen zurückzuzahlen war. Wenn sie dort nicht zu finden sind, liegt der Grund nicht im apriorischen sekundären, anachronistischen oder nationalen Charakter der kleinen Literatur (Casanova 2007: 181–189), sondern in den ungleichen Machtverhältnissen, die es den Autoren der kleinen Sprachen schwer machen, sich auf der literarischen „Greenwich Mean Time" zu etablieren. Die großen Literaturmärkte sind zu überfüllt, um der Weltliteratur genügend Platz zu geben, besonders wenn diese keine sensationelle, politische oder exotische Anziehungskraft hat. Die Weltliteratur ist keine universelle Größe, sowie auch unser Begriff der Welt von unserem Standpunkt abhängt. So sei an dieser Stelle der Nullmeridian auf Tartu gelegt.

II *Weltliteratur* als *Weltbildung*

„... aber es ist gut, daß Sie sich nach und nach mit allem In- und Ausländischen bekannt machen, um zu sehen, wo denn eigentlich eine höhere Weltbildung, wie sie der Dichter bedarf, zu holen ist.«
(Goethe an Eckermann, 1828. Eckermann 1836: 15)

Eine höhere Weltbildung – „die Befruchtung der Geistigkeit mit allen großen Leistungen der Geistesarbeit der Vergangenheit und Gegenwart“ (Oras 2003c: 94) – so lautete das Argument, mit dem hundert Jahre später in Estland die Vermittlung der Weltliteratur gefordert und gerechtfertigt wurde.

Die Weltliteratur hatte hier – wie bei Goethe – eine pädagogische Aufgabe zu erfüllen; sie war ein Mittel zur höheren Weltbildung, die sowohl als eine Selbstbildung mit Hilfe der Kulturgüter der Welt als auch eine aktive Weltbildung verstanden wurde. Bei Goethe noch elitär gedacht („wie sie der Dichter bedarf“!), hat die Weltbildung bei Oras einen volksaufklärerischen Zweck: “Estnischsprachige Weltliteratur ist nicht für Fachleute, – der Spezialist muss schon *eo ipso* mehr als eine Sprache ausreichend beherrschen. Unser Traum und Ziel kann es nur sein, dem Gebildeten im weitesten Sinne eine Lebensatmosphäre auch dann zu gewährleisten, wenn er außer dem Estnischen keine andere Sprache in dem Maße beherrscht, um feinere Stilnuancen genießen zu können.... Geboten wäre es, dass ihm anhand der in seiner eigenen Sprache vorhandenen Literatur möglich wäre, sich in allen wesentlichen Richtungen bis zu einer befriedigenden Grenze zu einem reifen und auf allem nichtspezifischen Gebiet orientierungsfähigen Intellektuellen zu bilden.“ (Oras 2003a: 35).

Es gibt noch ein Unterschied zwischen den Weltbildungszielen von Goethe und Oras. Goethe legte auf die Sprache, durch die die Weltbildung vermittelt sein soll, kein so entscheidendes Gewicht. Er selbst konnte gut Latein und Französisch, etwas Altgriechisch und Hebräisch, befriedigend Italienisch, hatte Grundkenntnisse im Englischen. Sein Interesse für die Weltliteratur war damit kaum befriedigt. Asiatische und slawische Literaturen lernte er mittels Übersetzungen kennen. Oras dagegen betont die Bedeutung der Aneignung der Weltliteratur in der eigenen Sprache und damit das Existenzrecht der literarischen Übersetzung: „Einer kleinen Nation erweist sich das Problem der übersetzten Literatur als eine der wesentlichsten Fragen ihres geistigen Lebens – wesentlicher als für eine große Nation, und um so wesentlicher, je weniger Möglichkeiten die betreffende Nation gehabt hatte, selbständig etwas zu schaffen”

(Oras 2003a: 31). Festzuhalten ist, wie eng die Kolonialverhältnisse (geistige Unmündigkeit der Nation) mit dem Problem der literarischen Übersetzung verbunden sind.

Die estnische literarische Kultur nahm ihren Anfang in der Übersetzung. Sie entstand als Übersetzung bzw. Adaption der Weltliteratur. Für die kleinen Kulturen ist das Übersetzen alltägliches Geschäft, unabdingbar, um Texte anderer Kulturen und Sprachen zu decodieren und gleichsam sich selbst der Welt verständlich zu machen. Die Grenzen der kleinen Kultur sind immer nahe, alltäglich tastbar. Der ständige Dialog mit der Welt (und der Weltliteratur) beginnt schon diesseits der Grenzen.

So ist es verständlich, dass estnische Schullehrpläne eine weltliterarische Dimension haben: Einen bedeutenden Teil vom Schulkanon bilden die literarischen Übersetzungen. In der Übersetzung wird die Welt zugänglich.

Die Weltliteratur als übersetzte Literatur ist das pädagogische Projekt zur Weltbildung. Wenn Jüri Talvet als Professor für Weltliteratur in Tartu für diesen Begriff als Bezeichnung der akademischen Disziplin steht, will er in der vergleichenden Literaturforschung diese Weltbildung behalten, bevor man den engeren Pfad der Vertiefung geht. Die Aufgabe der Literaturforschung lautet: Darzulegen, was in der Übersetzung verschwunden und was gewonnen ist.

III Vergleichende Literaturforschung als eine akademische Disziplin an der Universität Tartu

An der Universität Tartu pflegte man vergleichende Literaturbetrachung schon lange bevor die estnische Literatur als Forschungsobjekt im Horizont der Weltliteratur auftauchte. Die Geschichte der vergleichenden Poetik in Tartu ist bis zur Zeit der Universitätsgründung (1632) vom schwedischen König Gustav II. Adolf zurückzuverfolgen. So wie an den damaligen Universitäten üblich, gab es auch an der Academia Dorpatensis (Academia Gustaviana) eine Professur für Poetik. Der bedeutendste Inhaber dieser Professur, Laurentius Ludenius (1592–1654), stützte sich auf die Poetik von Horatius (Viiding 2002: 24), bei der es sich um den Vergleich der griechischen und römischen Dichtkunst handelte. Die Dichtkunst der Griechen war die Messlatte für die römische Literatur. Die antiken Vorbilder stellten sich im damaligen Poetikunterricht aber auch dem Vergleich mit den gegenwärtigen, humanistischen oder volkssprachlichen Dichtern, besonders unter der Wirkung der poetischen Prinzipien von Martin Opitz, die sowohl in Tartu als auch in Tallinn in den 1630er Jahren Fuß fassten (vor allem durch die Vermittlung des gekrönten Poeten Paul Fleming, der die Jahren 1635/36 und 1639 in Tallinn verbrachte).

Erst vor der Erhabenheit der christlichen Poesie verliert das antike Vorbild seine absolute Gültigkeit, wie es in der Gratulation „Poeseos laus, oratione augurali“ (1671) von Johann Hörnick (1621–1686) zum Ausdruck kommt: “Lasst uns David, den glücklichsten unter den Königen und Sänger sehen. Welcher Gläubige bewahrt nicht seine erhabenen Psalme, gefüllt mit Seufzern und Klagen, mit Ermunterungen und Ermahnungen, mit Glückwünschen und Dankesreden, mit Weissagungen und schließlich auch mit seltsamen Geheimnissen, in den tiefsten Truhen seines Herzens - noch besser verwahrt als jene Werke, die sich in der Truhe des Alexanders befanden? Wer würde diese gegen tausende von Versen Hesiods, Pindars, Marods, Ovids austauschen? Wer von den Griechen, wer von den Römer hat Poetischeres vom Hohenlied seines weisen Sohnes gegeben, obwohl viele sich Mühe geben, um Liebesdichtung zu schaffen?“ (Hörninck 1671[4])

Weiter zeigt Hörnick, warum das Studium der heidnischen Poeten zur Erwerbung der Weltkenntnisse und im Streben nach Tugend doch nützlich ist.

Als im Jahre 1802 die Kaiserliche Universität zu Dorpat (als einzige deutschsprachige Universität im Russischen Imperium, zu dem Estland und Livland seit 1710 gehörten) eröffnet wurde, begnügte sich der dortige Literaturunterricht nicht mehr mit der klassischen Antike, obwohl eben zu diesem Zeitpunkt sich die klassische Philologie als selbständige Disziplin etablierte und geradenwegs aus ihrer Geburtsstätte Halle nach Tartu gekommen war. Einer der ersten, langwierigen und angesehenen Professoren der neugegründeten Universität war Karl Morgenstern (1770–1852), der in Halle unter der Betreuung von Friedrich August Wolf studiert hatte und im Jahre 1802 als Professor für Beredsamkeit und klassische Philologie, Ästhetik und Literaturgeschichte nach Tartu kam. 35 Jahren lang (bis 1832) unterrichtete Morgenstern neben der klassischen Philologie, Ästhetik, Eloquenz und Kunstgeschichte auch allgemeine Literaturgeschichte, indem er vergleichend griechische, römische, hebräische, jüdische sowie christliche Literatur behandelte. Darüber hinaus hielt Morgenstern Vorlesungen über Gegenwartsliteratur, was im damaligen Universitätsunterricht alles andere als selbstverständlich war. In seinen Vorlesungen (z.B. „Über den Geist und Zusammenhang einer Reihe philosophischen Romane“, 1810,

---

4 „Davidem, Regum Vatumque augustissimum, intuemini. Qvis piorum sublimes psalmos ejus, suspiriis, suppliciis, exhortationibus, comminationibus, gratulationibus, gratiarum actionibus, vaticiniis denique ac mysteriis abstrusissimis refertissimos, non in intimo potius cordis scrinio, qvam illa Alexandri cistella repositos habet? Qvis mille Hesiodis, Pindaris, Maronibus, Ovidiis commutaverit? Jam illo, sapientissimi Filii, Cantico canticorum qvis e Graecis, e Latinis (licet plerorumque opera in confingendis erasticis frivole occupetur) qvis tamen dedit poietikoteron?” Ich bedanke mich bei Kristi Viiding für den Hinweis.

1811, 1812; „Über das Wesen des Bildungsroman“, 1819, „Zur Geschichte des Bildungsroman“, 1820) behandelte Morgenstern die Geschichte des europäischen Romans; ausgehend von einer vergleichenden Perspektive, entwickelte er, anhand modernen Romane, vor allem mit Bezug auf Goethes „Wilhelm Meisters Lehrjahre“, seine Romantheorie – Theorie des Bildungsromans. Diese stellte er in den örtlichen literarischen Magazinen vor, z.B. in der von ihm gegründeten, ersten Tartuer literatur- und kunstkritischen *Zeitschrift Dörptsche Beiträge für Freunde der Philosophie, Litteratur und Kunst* (1813–1821) (Lukas 2015). Wie heute, war es auch damals schwierig, außerhalb der kulturellen Zentren ausgearbeitete wissenschaftliche Erkenntnisse in Umlauf zu bringen, und so aktualisierte erst der Berliner Gelehrte Wilhelm Dilthey den Begriff im Jahre 1906 (in seinem Buch „Das Erlebnis und die Dichtung“, Dilthey 2005: 253ff.). Seitdem hat der Begriff in der Romantheorie Konjunktur (siehe Moretti, Kontje, Minden, Jeffers, Mayer, Selbmann, Castle, Summerfield/Downward u.a)

Obwohl der Lehrstuhl für klassische Philologie auch weiterhin als „Exzellenzzentrum“ der allgemeinen Literaturgeschichte fungierte – von 1831 bis 1861 bekleidete Christian Friedrich Neue (1799–1886) diese Professur (Lehrstuhl für Literaturgeschichte, altklassische Philologie und Pädagogik), indem er neben der antiken Literatur auch Literaturgeschichte des Mittelalters und der Neuzeit vortrug (Anzeige der Vorlesungen 1852: 8) – übernahm das Lektorat für deutsche Sprache immer deutlicher die Verantwortung für die neuere Literatur.

Dem Vorbild von Morgenstern folgten Carl Eduard Raupach (1793–1882) und Victor Hehn (1813–1890) – beide hiesiger Herkunft und Zöglinge der Universität Tartu, beide Schüler von Morgenstern. Raupach, der aus dem nordestnischen Haapsalu stammte, unterrichtete in den Jahren 1820–1846 in Tartu italienische und deutsche Philologie. Seinen literarischen Interessen nachgehend hielt er – wie sein Lehrer – Vorlesungen über die moderne deutsche Literatur. Morgenstern's Nachfolger war er auch als Beförderer des örtlichen literarischen Lebens und Herausgeber der literarischen Magazinen (*Inländisches Museum*, 1820–1821, *Neues Museum der teutschen Provinzen Russlands*, 1824–25). Damit intendierte er, „etwas zu einem lebhafteren litterärischen Verkehr und Umfang unter den Gebildeten unseres Vaterlandes beizutragen“ (Raupach 1820: III). Dass dies gelang, zeigt die literarische Neigung vieler Professoren und Lektoren der Universität Dorpat: um den Deutsch-Lektor und Bibliothekar Carl Friedrich Ludwig Petersen (1775–1822) bildete sich der literarische Kreis *Winkel-Clubb*. Petersen sowie sein kurzfristiger Nachfolger August Heinrich Weyrauch (1788–1865) waren mehr Dichter als Philologen. Der Rektor der Universität, Friedrich Eberhard Rambach (1767–1826), verfasste Schauspiele (einige zusammen mit seinem Schüler Ludwig Tieck) und Schauerromane. Der Professor für Geographie und Statistikwissenschaften Karl Ludwig Blum (1796–1869) ist als Herausgeber des

Dramas „Der verwundete Bräutigam" von Jakob Michael Reinhold Lenz in der Literaturgeschichte eingegangen (Lenz 1845).

Im Jahre 1846 übernahm der aus Tartu gebürtige Viktor Hehn von Raupach die Lektorenstelle der deutschen Sprache, die er bis zu seiner Verhaftung und Verbannung nach Tula aus politischen Gründen im Jahre 1851 bekleidete. Es war die bedrückende Ära von Nikolai des I, die auch den Dorpater Freisinn gleichzuschalten versuchte. Hehn war zweifelsohne der begabteste und bekannteste Literaturwissenschaftler der deutschsprachigen Dorpater Universität, der in seiner Lehrtätigkeit als Lektor der deutschen Sprache und Literatur sich nicht nur mit einem philologischen Ansatz im engeren Sinne zufrieden gab, sondern moderne kulturwissenschaftliche Forschungsmethoden ausarbeitete: seine Arbeiten wie z.B. „Ueber die Physiognomie der italienischen Landschaft" (1844), „Das Salz. Eine kulturhistorische Studie" (1873), der Essay „Der Humanismus" (1866), vor allem aber *„Kulturpflanzen und Hausthiere in ihrem Übergang aus Asien nach Griechenland und Italien, sowie das übrige Europa. Historisch-linguistische Skizzen"* (1870) erscheinen heute überraschend aktuell wegen seines komparatistisch-kulturhistorischen Ansatzes, wegen seiner Absicht, das Zusammenwirken von Klima, Landschaft, Flora und Fauna und dem menschlichen Tun interdisziplinär zu erforschen. In seinen Dorpater Vorlesungen behandelte er auch die gegenwärtige deutsche Literatur: Seine posthum erschienenen Abhandlungen über Goethe (z.B. „Über Goethes Gedichte", 1911) haben in der Goethe-Forschung ihre Spuren hinterlassen.

Anschaulich für die komparatistische Perspektive der Dorpater Literaturwissenschaft ist der vom Dorpater Dozenten Johann Heinrich Neukirch (1803–1870) im Jahre 1853 in Kiew herausgegebene „Dichterkanon", dessen Untertitel die Ambition seines Verfassers gut ausdrückt: „Ein Versuch, die vollendetsten Werke der Dichtkunst aller Zeiten und Nationen auszuzeichnen nebst gedrängter Vorbereitung auf das Lesen der aufgeführten Schriften und Angabe der gewandtesten deutschen Uebersetzungen." (Neukirch 1853). Die über 500-seitige Liste der „vollendetsten Werke" der Weltliteratur umfasst chinesische, indische, persische, hebräische, arabische, griechische, römische, italienische, spanische, portugiesische, französische, englische, gälische, deutsche, niederländische, neugriechische, dänische, schwedische und russische Literatur samt der Angaben zu ihren Autoren. „Als Vorrede und Einleitung" wird eine Novelle („Ein Abend aus einem harmlosen Leben") gedruckt, die, exakt datiert (am 19. Dezember 1849 nach fünf Uhr abends) in einem Haus unfern vom berühmten Universitätsgebäude von Kiew spielt. In dieser 68 Seiten währenden Salonkonversation wird über das Wesen und Nutzen der Dichtkunst gesprochen und das Studium der Weltliteratur wie folgt gerechtfertigt: „Wollte man sich auf das Lesen der poetischen Literatur nur seiner Nation beschränken, so wäre das gerade so, wie wenn man nach der Kenntnis der Geographie und Geschichte nur seines Landes trachte. [...] Denn indem jemand eine einzelne Litteratur besonders durchforscht, ist es natürlich, dass das Vorzügliche, welches sich in denselben findet, in grösserer Klarheit vor seine Seele tritt, als alles das, was ausserhalb der Grenzen jener Litteratur liegt. Das klare Bewusstsein von den Vorzügen der einen Litteratur und die dunklere Vorstellung von den Vorzügen der übrigen Litteraturen kann aber wiederum Ursache sein, dass er die erstere überschätzt und zugleich die letzteren unter ihrem Werthe anschlägt." (Neukirch 1853: 53, 17).

Die Weltliteratur ist nach Neukirch der beste Weg zur Weltbildung, denn „Der Wert der Summe der Kenntnisse, die man sich aus den Dichtern anzueignen vermag, lässt sich nicht hoch genug anschlagen, indem jene ein durch kein Andres zu ersetzendes Mittel sind, zu einer allseitigen Bildung und dadurch zu einer immer grösseren geistigen Freiheit zu gelangen" (Neukirch 1853: 40).

Eben dieses Streben sowie einige unerwünschte Namen in der Liste wie George Sand oder Karl Gutzkow haben dem Verfasser einen strengen Verweis von der Seite des Ministeriums mitgebracht. Eine größere geistige Freiheit war kein geduldetes Ziel im Russischen Imperium unter Nikolai I.

Mit der Thronfolge änderten sich die Zustände zugunsten der Literaturwissenschaft. Im Jahre 1863 tritt eine neue Universitätsordnung in Kraft, die in allen Universitäten des Imperiums Lehrstühle für allgemeine Literaturgeschichte vorsah. Der im Jahre 1865 gegründete Lehrstuhl für deutsche und vergleichende Sprachwissenschaft, geleitet bis 1899 von Professor Leo Meyer (1830–1910), konzentrierte sich auf die Sprachwissenschaft, hatte aber auch altindische, griechische und deutsche Literatur im Vorlesungsprogramm. Der langjährige Lektor für deutsche und allgemeine Literatur, der Dozent Woldemar Masing (1836–1923), las als Kenner der italienischen und spanischen Literatur neben der deutschen Literatur auch vergleichende Literaturgeschichte und allgemeine Literaturwissenschaft. Seine Dissertation behandelte die Metrik („Über Ursprung und Verbreitung des Reimes", Dorpat 1866). Außerdem ergänzten auch andere Lehrkräfte den Literaturunterricht, z.B. Wolfgang Schlüter (1848–1919), Direktor der Universitätsbibliothek und Präsident der Gelehrten Estnischen Gesellschaft (1899–1912), der seit 1893 Vorlesungen über Mediävistik hielt[5], Wilhelm Hörschelmann (1849–1895), Professor der klassischen Philologie, der neben der Antikliteraturen und seinem Lieblingsfach Metrik auch Vorlesungen über Goethe im Lehrplan hatte, oder

---

[5] Über das Lied der Nibelungen, den „armen Heinrich" von Hartmann von Aue, über die literarischen Denkmäle aus dem Baltikum usw. (Siehe: *Biografičeskij Slovar''* 1903: 584; Lukas 2003).

Leopold von Schroeder (1851–1920), Dozent für Sanskrit und Indologie, der in seinen Abhandlungen der vergleichenden Religionsgeschichte den Begriff der Weltliteratur aus der estnischen Mythologie bis zur Geisteswelt der Indien ausweitete.[6]

Das Jahr 1893 markierte das Ende der deutschsprachigen Universität in Tartu. Die *Kaiserliche Universität Dorpat* wird in Императорский Юрьевский университет (*Imperatorskij Jur'evskij Universitet*) umbenannt. Da viele deutsche Professoren die Universität verlassen mussten und die Abschluss- und Promotionsarbeiten über deutsche Sprache und Literatur abgewiesen wurden, verlagerte sich der Schwerpunkt der allgemeinen Literaturwissenschaft in den Lehrstuhl für russische Sprache und Literatur: Den Lehrstuhl hierfür gab es an der deutschsprachigen Universität von Anfang an und er war meistens mit namhaften Slawisten besetzt. Für die dortigen Vorlesungen und die russische Literatur interessierten sich nicht nur Studenten der Slawistik. Der erste Professor für russische Literatur, Gregori Glinka (1776–1818), hielt seine Vorlesungen „Sur la littérature russe" der allgemeinen Verständlichkeit wegen zuerst sogar auf Französisch. In den 1890er Jahren las Jevgeni Bobrov (1867–1933) allgemeine Literaturwissenschaft. Mehrere Tartuer Slawisten hatten einen komparatistischen Blickwinkel schon aufgrund ihres akademischen Werdegangs: Andrei Kaissarov (1782–1813) hat in Göttingen als Slawist, Pavel Viskovatov (1842–1905) in Leipzig als Germanist promoviert. Viskovatov, von 1873 bis 1895 Professor für russische Sprache und Literatur in Tartu, spielte eine wichtige Rolle beim deutsch-russischen Kulturtransfer: als Lermotov-Forscher trug er mit seiner Abhandlung über Goethe's "Faust" (Viskovatov 1895) zur Vermittlung der deutschen Literatur in Russland bei, während seine Geschichte der russischen Literatur (Wiskowatov 1881) für die deutschsprachige Öffentlichkeit gedacht war.

Ein Zeichen von einer neuen kulturellen Dominanzverschiebung ist die Tatsache zu betrachten, dass seit 1904 die allgemeine Literaturgeschichte nicht mehr vom Lehrstuhl für Russisch oder Deutsch, sondern von jenem für Lettisch gelesen wird (Anzeige der Vorlesungen 1904: 10): der Lektor für Lettisch Jēkabs Lautenbahs (1847–1928) wurde im Jahre 1918 Dozent für allgemeine Literaturgeschichte. Seine Vorlesungen umfassen deutsche, französische, englische, italienische und spanische Literatur.

Estnische Sprache war ein Lehr- und Forschungsobjekt der Universität Tartu schon seit 1804, als Friedrich David Lenz (1745–1809), der Bruder von Jakob Michael Reinhold Lenz hier der erste Lektor für Estnisch wurde. Anfangs kam der Estnischunterricht vor allem den Bedürfnisse der zukünftigen Pastoren entgegen,

---

[6] Siehe auch Rosenberg 1931; *Biografičeskij Slovar"* 1903.

wurde aber eine immer ernster zu nehmende akademische Disziplin, die neben der wissenschaftlichen Beschäftigung mit der Sprache bald auch das Studium der estnischen Folklore und Mythologie mit einschloss. Im Jahre 1841 las der Professor für klassische Philologie Ludwig Preller (1809–1861) über das finnische Epos Kalewala, worüber man in der Gelehrten Estnischen Gesellschaft intensiv diskutierte. Diese Diskussion war auch anregend für die estnische Sagenforschung.

Estnische Sprache, Volksdichtung und Mythologie gehörten zunächst zum wissenschaftlichen Forschungsgebiet der Dorpater Germanisten (z.B. Leo Meyer (1830–1910), Wolfgang Schlüter (1848–1919))[7], bis sodann mit Dietrich Heinrich Jürgenson (1804–1841) der ersten gebürtigen Esten das Lektorat für das Estnische übernahm. In seinen Vorlesungen behandelte er auch die „Poesien der Ehsten" (Anzeige der Vorlesungen 1840: 12). Von Jürgenson stammt die erste systematische Darstellung der estnischen Literaturgeschichte, eine deutschsprachige „Kurze Geschichte der ehstnischen Literatur" (Jürgenson 1841), in der er eine philologisch-bibliographisch-kulturgeschichtliche Methode ausarbeitete, womit er den Grundstein für die weitere estnische Literaturgeschichtsschreibung legte. Eine umfassendere Geschichte der estnischen Literatur (auf Estnisch) verfasste der erste promovierte estnische Philologe[8] Karl August Hermann (1847–1928, Hermann 1898) während seines Lektorenamtes in Tartu (1889–1908). Seine Studien zur Literatur sind komparatistisch angelegt und behandeln die deutschen und russischen Einflüsse auf die estnische Literatur. (Hermann 1899, 1904, 1905)

In der Geburtsstunde der estnischsprachigen Universität 1919 wurde der Lehrstuhl für estnische und allgemeine Literatur gegründet, den seit 1922 der Dichter und Philologe Gustav Suits (1883–1956) – von 1924 bis 1944 als Professor – innehatte. Er war Schüler von Georg Brandes und bewunderte dessen „unvergleichliche literaturhistorische Reichweite" (Suits 2002: 347). In seinem Literaturunterricht ging Suits von einer historisch-vergleichenden Perspektive aus und bettete estnische Literatur in einen weiteren Kontext ein. Parallel zu der estnischen Literatur behandelte er Fragen der allgemeinen Literaturwissenschaft und Methodologie und die Geschichte der Weltliteratur, worüber er sowohl Überblicksvorlesungen hielt (z.B. über die Autoren des Vormärz, die Geschichte der Skandinavischen und Niederländischen Literatur, die neuere flämische und niederländische Literatur, die Entwicklung der deutschbaltischen und estnischen Literatur in der I Hälfte des 19. Jahrhunderts usw.) sowie Themen- bzw.

7 Siehe Meyer 1877, 1890, 1891, 1892; Schlüter 1882.

8 Hermann promovierte in Leipzig in der vergleichenden Sprachwissenschaft. Seine Dissertation behandelt den Stufenwechsel der estnischen Sprache.

Autorenseminare (zu Shakespeare's Hamlet, zu Voltaire's, Candide, zu Romain Rolland, Anatole France, Strindberg usw) anbot. Eine komparatistische Vorgehensweise wurde in Tartu zum Standard und dadurch gewährleistet, dass von einem Lektor der estnischen Literatur gute Kenntnisse der Weltliteratur vorausgesetzt wurden. Der Begriff der Weltliteratur damaliger Literaturlektoren (August Annist, Johannes Semper, aber auch Fremdphilologen wie Rudolf Gutmann) war im Vergleich zu ihren Nachfolgen umfassender und beinhaltete neben dem Kanon der westeuropäischen Literatur auch die Literaturen der Nachbarsländern (lettische, litauische, finnische, ost- und mitteleuropäische Literaturen).

Die Sowjetzeit behielt zwar formal das weltliterarische Umfeld der estnischen Literatur unter dem Schild der „Fremdliteratur", diese wurde jedoch enger als früher begriffen - als ein etablierter Kanon der westlichen Literatur. Eine normale literarische Kommunikation war unterbunden, aber man versuchte zumindest den Kern davon zu vermitteln, der im Sieb der marxistisch-leninistischen Ideologie erhalten geblieben war. Die Beziehungen der estnischen Literatur und dieser "Fremdliteratur" zu behandeln war ideologisch belastet. Die russische Literatur wurde in den Vordergrund gerückt, ihre Wirkung und Rolle bei der Entwicklung der estnischen Literatur wurde hervorgehoben. Um den ideologischen Vorschriften zu entgehen, war es zweckmäßiger, die estnische Literatur als eine geschlossene Einheit, in ihrer eigenen Entwicklung zu erfassen.

Und doch kam ein entscheidender Anstoß in die Tartuer Literaturwissenschaft eben von der Seite der russischen Philologie, der mehrere Disziplinen anregte und eine ganz neue Ausrichtung – die Tartuer Semiotik – ins Leben rief. Der relativ liberale Geist der Tartuer Universität lockte Juri Lotman im Jahre 1956 nach Tartu. Er wurde hier zuerst Lehrstuhlinhaber, dann Professor für russische Literatur. Nur eine komparatistische Vogelperspektive und ausgezeichnete Kenntnisse der Weltliteratur konnten ihn zu jener Abstraktionsstufe bringen, die eine semiotische Beschreibung und Typologisierung nicht nur der Literatur, sondern der ganzen Kultur ermöglichte.

In Tartu entwickelte Lotman seine Theorie von der Peripherie als einem Gebiet, wo sich die semiotischen Prozesse beschleunigen, sowie die Idee von der dialogischen/vermittelnden, deutenden/schöpferischen Funktion der Grenzen. Er war überzeugt, dass keine Kultur/bzw. Literatur sich aus sich selbst entwickeln kann, sondern allein im Dialog, im lebendigen Kontakt, in der Auseinandersetzung mit anderen denkbar ist. Die offene Grenze ist nach Lotman ein Ort des Übersetzens, ein Deutungsmechanismus, der mit einem aktiven Dialog erfüllt ist. Die Kultur bekommt ihre Bedeutung an der Grenze, oder sogar von jenseits der Grenze. Die Identität ist die Beziehung zum Anderen, sie ist ein Grenzphänomen, verbunden mit Grenzziehung und Grenzüberschreitung in einer dialogischen Situation.

So gedeutet, stellt sich die Geschichte der vergleichenden Literaturwissenschaft in Tartu in einem neuen Licht dar. Die „periphere" Lage erweist sich als ein Kreuzungs- und Begegnungsort verschiedenen Sprachen und Kulturen, der eine vergleichende Betrachtung begünstigt und fördert. In der Peripherie verschärft sich das Grenzbewusstsein, und das ist eben der Ansatzpunkt der vergleichenden Literaturwissenschaft – "Begegnung und Beziehung zu befürworten – zwischen den Texten, Kulturen, Disziplinen" (Saussy 2006: 23–24) und zugleich die Unvergleichbarkeit und Unübersetzbarkeit („untranslatability", siehe Apter 4) der literarischen Texte anzuerkennen.

Das Grenzbewusstsein ermöglicht eine Versöhnung, oder besser gesagt, eine Arbeitsteilung zwischen der vergleichenden Literaturwissenschaft und der Weltliteratur. Während die eine ihren Schwerpunkt in der Bildung, die andere in der Wissenschaft sieht, kümmern sich beide gemeinsam um die Weltbildung. Um die Weltbildung, so wie sie in Tartu erscheint.

Liina Lukas
liina.lukas@ut.ee
Kultuuriteaduste ja kunstide instituut
Tartu Ülikool
Ülikooli 16
51003 Tartu
EESTI / ESTONIA

Literatur

Anzeige der Vorlesungen, welche auf der Kayserlichen Akademie zu Dorpat ... gehalten werden. Dorpat: Mattiesen, 1802–1918.

Apter, E. 2013. *Against world literature. On the politics of untranslatability.* London-New York: Verso.

Biografičeskij Slovar" professorov" i prepodavatelej Jur'evskago, byvšago Derpt'skago universiteta (1802–1902). II. Pod red. G. V. Levickogo. Jur'ev", 1903. = *Биографический Словарь профессоровъ и преподавателей Юрьевскаго, бывшаго Дерптьскаго университета (1802–1902). II.* Под ред. Г. В. Левицкого. Юрьевъ, 1903.

Casanova, P. 2007. *The World Republique of Letters.* London: Harward University Press (Orig.: *La République mondiale des lettres*, Paris: Seuil, 1999)

Deleuze, G., Guattari, F. 1975. *Kafka: Pour une littérature mineure.* Paris: Les éditions de Minuit.

Dilthey, W. 2005. *Das Erlebnis und die Dichtung. Lessing. Goethe. Novalis. Hölderlin. Gesammelte Schriften Bd. XXVI.* Göttingen: Vandenhoeck&Ruprecht.

Eckermann, J. P. 1836. Gespräche mit Goethe in den letzten Jahren seines Lebens. 1823–1832. Bd. II. Leipzig: Brockhaus.

Hermann, K.A. 1898. *Eesti kirjanduse ajalugu esimesest algusest meie ajani*. Jurjev: K. A. Hermann.

Hermann, K. A. 1899. Puškin v èstskoj literature. Reč', proiz. v toržestv. Sobranii imperat. Jur'evsk. un-ta. 26.V 1899. = Херманн, К. А. 1899. Пушкин в эстской литературе. Речь, произ. в торжеств. Собрании императ. Юрьевск. ун-та. 26.V 1899. – *Acta et Commentationes Universitatis Tartuensis*, 5, 104–107.

Hermann, K. A. 1904. Гogol' v èstskoj literature. = Херманн, К. А. 1904. Гоголь в эстской литературе. – *Acta et Commentationes Universitatis Tartuensis*, 1904, 5, 120–123.

Hermann, K.A. 1905. Schiller in der estnischen Literatur. – *Sitzungsberichte der Gelehrten Estnischen Gesellschaft*, 39–44.

Hörnick, [J. 1671]. *Poeseos laus, oratione augurali, in Gymnasio Revaliensi, delibata Cal[endis] Maji, A[nno] M. DC. LXXI*. Revaliae: Adolphus Simon, C4.

Jürgenson, D.H. 1843. Kurze Geschichte der ehstnischen Literatur. Aus dem Nachlasse des Seminarinspektors Jürgenson. I, II. – *Verhandlungen der gelehrten Estnischen Gesellschaft zu Dorpat*. Bd. 1, H. 2, Dorpat: in Commission bei Fr. Severin (Leipzig : in Commission bei E. F. Köhler), 1843, 40–52; Bd. 1, H. 3, Dorpat: in Commission bei E. J. Karow (Leipzig : in Commission bei C. F. Köhler), 1844, 61–73.

Bakhtin, M. 2002. The Bildungsroman and Its Significance in the History of Realism. – M. Bakhtin, *Speech Genres & Other Late Essays*. Austin: University of Texas Press: 10–59.

Castle, G. 2006. *Reading the Modernist Bildungsroman*. Gainesville: University Press of Florida

Jeffers, T. L. 2005. *Apprenticeships: the Bildungsroman from Goethe to Santayana*. Gordonsville: Palgrave Macmillan.

Kontje, T. C. 1993. *The German Bildungsroman: History of a National Genre*. Columbia: Camden House.

Lenz, J. M. R. 1845. *Der verwunderte Bräutigam / von Jacob Michael Reinhold Lenz; im Manuscript aufgefunden und herausgegeben von K. L. Blum*. Berlin: Duncker & Humblot.

Lukas, L. 2003. Germanistik in Tartu in der Wendezeit – von der Inlands- zur Auslandsgermanistik. – *Germanistik in Tartu/Dorpat. Rückblick auf 200 Jahre*. Hg. v. Siret Rutiku, René Kegelmann. Tartu: Tartu Ülikool, 106–112.

Lukas, L. 2015. *Bildungsroman* – veel üks Tartu lisandus romaaniteooriasse. – *Methis. Studia humaniora Estonica*, 15, 188–193.

Masing, U. 1989 [1940]. Kiriku ülesanne kultuurimandumisel. – *Akadeemia*, 1, 144–150.

Mayer, G. 1992. *Der deutsche Bildungsroman: von der Aufklärung bis zur Gegenwart*. Stuttgart: Metzler.

Minden, M. 2010. *The German Bildungsroman: Incest and inheritance*. Cambridge: Cambridge University Press.

Moretti, F. 2000. *The way of the world. The Bildungsroman in the European Culture*. London: Verso.

Morgenstern, K. 1817. Über den Geist und Zusammenhang einer Reihe philosophischen Romane. – *Dörptsche Beyträge für Freunde der Philosophie, Literatur und Kunst III*, 180–205.

Morgenstern, K. 1820. Über das Wesen des Bildungromans. – *Inländisches Museum*, 1/2, 46–61; 1/3, 13–27.

Morgenstern, K. 1824. Zur Geschichte des Bildungsromans. – *Neues Museum der teutschen Provinzen Russlands*, 1/1, 1–46.

Neukirch, J. H. 1853. *Dichterkanon : Ein Versuch, die vollendetsten Werke der Dichtkunst aller Zeiten und Nationen auszuzeichnen nebst gedrängter Vorbereitung auf das Lesen der aufgeführten Schriften und Angabe der gewandtesten deutschen Uebersetzungen.* Kiew: Universitätsdruckerei.

Meyer, L. 1877. Über einige ältere estnische Volkslieder und ein finnisches Lied bei Goethe. – *Verhandlungen der gelehrten Estnischen Gesellschaft*, IV Heft. Dorpat: Laakmann, 33–46.

Meyer, L. 1890. *Ueber das älteste bekannte estnische Gedicht: Vortrag gehalten in der Jahresversammlung der Gelehrten Estnischen Gesellschaft am 18. Januar 1890.* Dorpat: Mattiesen.

Meyer, L. 1891. *Ueber die ältesten Denkmäler der Estnischen Sprache: Vortrag gehalten in der Jahresversammlung der Gelehrten Estnischen Gesellschaft am 18. Januar 1891.* Dorpat: Mattiesen.

Oks, J. 2004. *Kriitilised tundmused*. – J. Oks, *Orjapojad*. Tartu: Ilmamaa, 225–253, 251.

Oras, A. 2003a [1931]. Mõtteid tõlkekirjanduse puhul. – A. Oras, *Luulekool I*. Tartu: Ilmamaa, 31–40.

Oras, A. 2003b. Märkmeid kultuurist maailmakirjandusest ja meist. – A. Oras, *Luulekool I*. Tartu: Ilmamaa, 57–61.

Oras, A. 2003c. Maailmakirjanduse tutvustamine ja Eesti Kirjanduse Selts. – A. Oras, *Luulekool I*. Tartu: Ilmamaa, 94–97.

Raupach, C. E. 1820. Ankündigung des inländischen Museums. – *Inländisches Museum. Bd. I.* Dorpat: Schünmann, III–IX.

Rosenberg, A. 1931. *Literaturwissenschaft und Literaturforschung an der ehemaligen Universität Dorpat. Ein historischer Überblick.* Dorpat.

Schlüter, W. 1882. *Ein estnischer Zauberspruch.* Dorpat: Mattiesen.

Suits, G. 2002 [1927]. Georg Brandest mälestades. – G. Suits, *Vabaduse väraval*. Koost. P. Olesk, H. Runnel. Tartu: Ilmamaa, 336–347.

Talvet, J. 2005a. Maailmakirjanduse kodustamise küsimusi. – *Keel ja Kirjandus*, 6, 433–441.

Talvet, J. 2005b. *A Call for Cultural Symbiosis*. Toronto: Guernica.

Tuglas, F. 1912. Kirjanduslik stiil. – *Noor-Eesti IV*. [Tartu]: Noor-Eesti, 23–100.

Saussy, H. 2006. *Comparative Literature in an Age of Globalization*. Baltimore: JHU Press.

Selbmann, R. 1984. *Der deutsche Bildungsroman*. Stuttgart: Metzler.

Summerfield, G., Downward, L. 2009. *New Perspectives on the European Bildungsroman*. London-New York: Continuum.

Viiding, K. 2002. *Die Dichtung neulateinischer propemptika an der Academia Gustaviana (Dorpatensis) in den Jahren 1632–1656*. Tartu: Tartu University Press.

Wiskowatow, P. 1881. *Geschichte der russischen Literatur in gedrängter Übersicht: ein Leitfaden nebst bibliographischen Notizen mit besonderer Berücksichtigung der neueren Literatur.* Dorpat–Fellin. (Zweite Auflage 1884.)

Viskovatov, P. 1895. *O „Fayst''" Gete.* Sankt-Petersburg: Obŝestvennaja Pol'za. = Висковатов, П. 1895. *О „Фаустъ" Гете.* Санкт-Петерсбург: Общественная Польза.

In the Background of the 'Alphabet War': Slovenian-Czech Interliterary Relations and World Literature[1]

MARKO JUVAN

Abstract. In the context of the 1833 language controversy (the Slovenian Alphabet War), Slovenian literary historian and philologist Matija Čop commented at length on the review of the poetry almanac Krajnska čbelica that had been published in 1832 in Prague by František L. Čelakovský. Čelakovský's defense of France Prešeren's poetry (containing sample translations) was used by Čop as a foreign argument supporting his Romantic and cosmopolitan cultural program. This article examines these metadiscursive frames to point out the symptoms of interliterariness through which, in the Austrian Empire, three types of literary system were being established concurrently: systems of national literatures, Slavic literary centrism, and world literature (including geo-cultural differences between centres, subcentres, and peripheries).

Keywords: national revival, world literature, interliterariness, Slavic centrism, literary review, translation, Slovenian-Czech literary contacts

The 'Slovenian Alphabet War' was just one of the symptoms of the fetishisation of language in European cultural nationalism.[2] The literary conflict over language was triggered in 1833 by Matija Čop in the supplement to *Laibacher Zeitung* entitled *Illyrisches Blatt* (IB) with a commentary on the publication of a review of the poetry almanac *Krajnska čbelica* (KČ; 'Carniolan Bee') that had been written in 1832 for *Časopis českého Museum* (ČČM) by František Ladislav Čelakovský. In the controversy over the reformed writing system known as the Metelko alphabet (*metelčica* in Slovene), which in the view of Jernej Kopitar contributed towards bridging the differences among Slavs using the Latin alphabet, a clash broke out between two differing strategies for Slovenian national revival due to the ideology of language as a pillar of national identity; this clash also became

[1] Translated by Jean McCollister.

[2] Similar clashes over grammar also occurred among the Czechs, for example between the supporters and opponents of the Old Brethren orthography around 1815 (Vodička 1960: 127–131).

DOI: http://dx.doi.org/10.12697/IL.2015.S1.12

international in scope.[3] The Enlightenment and pre-Romantic ideas of Kopitar's circle relied on gradual philological-educational activities among the domestic peasantry (Kopitar, following Herder, saw the social-cultural foundation of the nation in the peasantry), while Čop along with Prešeren argued for a bolder, albeit unrealistic "culture planning" (Even-Zohar 2008) in the spirit of Romantic aesthetics and cosmopolitanism. In the background of the so-called Alphabet War the emerging Slovenian literary field, through criticism and translation – as the nodes of international cultural traffic –, began to integrate into the world literary system and the Slavic interliterary community.

Časopis českého Museum ('The Journal of the Bohemian Museum'), which under the editorship of Palacký was the central medium for Czech national revival, attempted to demonstrate that domestic culture was equal to that of the great nations of Europe (Vodička 1960: 125–129, 149–150, 161; Vinkler 2006: 245–248). Proving their worth in the literary field was all the more important for Czechs, since literature for them also compensated for the missing attributes of national sovereignty (Vodička 1960: 13). The path to European validation was paved for the Czechs in *ČČM* by the field of Slavic languages and literature and the Slavic idea, which offset the sense of being politically weaker and surrounded by a sea of Germans in Austria with an emboldening feeling of being connected with millions of Slavs. This idea was expressed in different images: from speculation about a Slavic soul and Russophilism through conceptions of a unified Slavic nation to 'Slavic reciprocity', i.e. cooperation through translations, book reviews, exchanges of books, social networks or common political initiatives (cf. Vodička 1960: 137–139; Pospíšil 2005). Since Slovenes were also of interest to *ČČM* from the standpoint of reciprocity,[4] Čelakovský printed a review of three volumes of the Slovenian poetry almanac from 1830–32 in this journal (Čelakovský 1832; Čop 1833: 22–24; 1983: 110–115). In light of the later Alphabet War it is paradoxical that the person responsible for the mentioned review of *Čbelica* happened to be the Viennese linguist Jernej Kopitar, who introduced *KČ* to Čelakovský and to Palacký, who encouraged Čelakovský as editor of *ČČM* to publish a review (Kvapil 1984: 280; Vinkler 2006: 216–218). Čelakovský was well suited to this task since he had been dealing with Slovene language and Slovenian folk poetry

---

3 For more cf. Prijatelj 1935: 142–149; Legiša 1959: 83–89; Paternu 1976: 232–242; Kos 1979: 144–177; Pogačnik 2002.

4 Pavel Josef Šafařík also published in *ČČM* among translations from other Slavic literatures and critical and historical essays on them. In 1833 he meticulously elaborated on Slovenian literature after 1820 ("literatura vindických Slovenův") in his *Survey of recent literature by Illyrian Slavs* and in the introduction shed light on its previous historical development (ČČM 7/2: 164–181).

since about 1820; three poems in modern translation had been included in his *Slovanské národní písně* ('Slavic Folk Songs'; 1822, 1825), the first international anthology of this kind (Závodský 1982: 160; Kvapil 1984: 278–279).

Although Čelakovský's review of 'Carniolan literature' is favourable in tone, and he sees in young literary enthusiasts the promise of a national revival, he is harsh and patronising in his judgment of the aesthetics of the almanac, viewing the efforts of what he clearly considers a backward periphery from the perspective of an observer from the artistically more developed capital that aspired to become the centre of Slavism. While he does attribute a ground-breaking significance to *Čbelica* in the Slovenian environment, at the same time he characterises it as artistically weak and a belated repetition of Czech "Puchmajerians" (Čop 1983: 111).[5] Referring to Šafařík's *Geschichte der slawischen Sprache und Literatur nach allen Mundarten,* he ironically considers that Slovenian literature before *KČ* effectively did not exist (with the exception of a glut of grammars): "So, even if one can count the whole of their literature on the fingers of one hand – who cares! – Slovenes have a fat dozen grammars and thus a glut of reading that enriches the heart and spirit!" (Čop 1983: 112) Of the dactylic and amphibrach meters so popular in *KČ*, he writes unreservedly that the "crowing [...] poetry meters borrowed from Austrian and German Styrian poems [...] make one sick" (Čop 1983: 111).

However, for Čelakovský all this is the background upon which he elevates the writings of France Prešeren, whose "excellent works impart a special value to *Krajnska čbelica*" (Čop 1983: 111). The ironic and patronising tone is replaced by admiration, and as an authority on Slavic languages and literature he argues that Prešeren's significance transcends provincial borders: "This young poet [...] truly deserves an honorable reception in the ranks of Slavic poets [...]." (111). In his texts he perceives the values that have been disseminated across Europe through aesthetic discourse since the 18th century (cf. Casanova 1999). The Czech critic characterises Prešeren with qualities similar to those we find in Jungmann's ideas regarding the classical "in literature generally and especially in Czech literature" (Jungmann 1827): Prešeren's "literary treasures" are of different genres, he expresses himself skilfully, his ideas are harmonious, his verses flowing, his diction concise and "authentically Slovene" (Čelakovský in Čop 1983: 111–112). To illustrate these qualities Čelakovský publishes his translations of four poems by Prešeren, adds Prešeren's satirical sonnet *Črkarska*

[5] Czech original in *ČČM*: Čelakovský 1832: 444. Citing of the original in *ČČM* is henceforth followed by quotes from the Slovenian translation by Janko Moder (Čop 1983) of Čop's *Discacciamenta* (Čop 1833).

pravda in the Slovene original, and uses it to illuminate the Czech situation (Čelakovský 1832: 446–450).

To this satirical sonnet on the alphabet controversy he attaches a critique of the new Slovenian writing system called *metelčica* (his arguments were later developed further by Čop in the debate with Kopitar's supporters), and proposes as a solution the Czech-Polish method of diacritics, arguing that a common alphabet would facilitate mutual intelligibility among the Slavic languages. The idea of Slavic reciprocity moves from criticism of the alphabet to the desire "that Slovenes engage more in translation from other Slavic languages than from other languages so that their language will not be so easily led astray" (Čop 1983: 114), concluding with the advice that Slovenes adhere to Czech quantitative metrics instead of "being guided by the German mode" (Čop 1983: 114). With this suggestion Čelakovský attempts to remove Slovenes from German influence and bring them closer to the Czech example and Slavic "interliterary centrism" (cf. Ďurišin 1992: 170–174; 1995: 11–19, 48–51). The spirit of Slavic centrism ultimately also branches from his rhetorical encouragement of circles of Carniolan literary revivalists: "Do not complain about the small number of your readers; your grateful compatriots are your nearest public [...]. Your next public is – what a lofty idea! – the 60 million and more Slavs who look with favor on your zeal [...]." (Čop 1983: 115)

Čelakovský sent his review of *KČ* to Prešeren in a letter dated 24 December 1832, and in a letter to Palacký on 14 January1833 Čop characterised it as "water for our mill" that should be "brought to the attention of *our* public" (Čop 1986: 239–240). He therefore gave it to a Czech in Ljubljana to be translated into German, corrected the translation, sent it to the author for review and, adding his introduction, printed it under the title of *Krainische Literatur* in *Illyrisches Blatt* on 9 February 1833, and published his comments and follow-up notes in two instalments from 16 to 23 February (Berkopec 1961/62: 231–232). These sparked the notorious philosophical, aesthetic, and cultural–political controversy with the camp of Metelko supporters (including Burger and Kopitar), which Čop reprinted in 1833 along with Čelakovský's critique under the title *Nuovo discacciamento di lettere inutili, Das ist: Slowenischer ABC-Krieg* (Berkopec 1961/62: 236).

Čop's metatext frames Čelakovský's text with his own intent and he comments on it to this effect. Čop also expresses his views on Slovenian literature using words borrowed from the Czech critic, but in the course of the polemic with Metelko and Kopitar he develops his own independent views. The translation of the review is itself a metatext evaluating the almanac *KČ*, and a framework for the four translations of Prešeren. The review in *ČČM* transmits these translations from the original literary system to the Czech, while the German translation of the Czech review informs readers in Carniola who are interested in Slovenian literature of how a high profile foreign author views their literary life. The outlined interliterary mirroring and framing are placed into processes of forming world literature, national literatures, and interliterary communities.

In particular, the age of world literature as explained by Goethe since 1827 was established through international intellectual exchange, intensive translation and reviewing of texts, a thriving cross-border cultural trade, and the participation of European literati in cosmopolitan networks (Juvan 2012a: 82–125). Goethe read British, French, and Italian cultural journals and reflected on foreign literature in his periodical *Kunst und Altertum*. The origins of the international linking of publications in the Slavic space can also be seen in the connection described among texts from *KČ, ČČM* and *IB*: in this instance, a reciprocal reflecting upon literatures and the active presence of texts outside the area of their mother tongues, which are two main features of world literature, was realised through a node of reviews and translations (Damrosch 2003: 4, 15). Čelakovský recognised Prešeren as an artist who transcended his native space even before Slovenes did (Závodský 1982: 594). His review and translation were acts of "consecration" (Casanova 1999: 179–226) that opened up a path for Prešeren to enter into international circulation and established him as being among the best Slavic poets. The reception by Czech reviewers, translators, and in part also artists opened up Prešeren's lengthy path into world literature, though up until the present day he has remained more at the margins, even in the Czech Republic.[6]

The emerging world literary system was initially created by cosmopolitan artists and intellectuals of the 'literary republic'. The correspondence between Zois, Kopitar, and Dobrovský bears witness to the fact that Slovenian and Czech intellectuals were networking as early as at the turn of the 18th to the 19th century. While each pursued his own aims, they shared the common aspiration of becoming equal members of European literary exchange, in part by forming interliterary communities. For instance, Čelakovský sent Goethe a translation of a selection from his collection *Ohlas písní ruských* ('Echoes of Russian Songs', 1829), with which he was "entirely in accordance with the tendencies of European literary development that Goethe at the same time theoretically formulated and proved with his conception of 'world literature'" (Dvořák 1960: 292–297). Czech and Slovenian writers strove to improve themselves linguistically and artistically according to the imagined standards of achievement represented by the aesthetically developed literature of the West (cf. Vodička 1960: 8, 128–129;

[6] Although Vinkler enthusiastically claims that Čelakovský "permanently engraved [Prešeren] into Czech cultural consciousness" (2006: 214–215, 244), Prešeren's work despite numerous translations in the 19th and 20th centuries did not penetrate the broader public since it was not part of the canon used in Czech schools.

Vinkler 2006: 244–248). The standards were embodied for them not only by the giants of the Western literary canon (whose role is emphasised by Casanova), but also by Slavic writers, for example Mickiewicz and Pushkin.

Goethe saw in the age of world literature an opportunity for the international affirmation of nations that had not yet achieved the prestige of English or French literature (Juvan 2012a: 86–88, 119). The works of smaller and non-European cultures, among them Slavic, were attracting interest; Goethe was enthusiastic about *Hasanaginica*. The emerging international literary space made it possible for any national literature to be observed from an outside perspective and be judged according to aesthetic standards that were apparently general in Europe. Foreign critics became the arbiters of the internal literary disputes of particular nations. Goethe, for example, followed the debates among the Italian neoclassicists (Strich 1949: 23–24). Čelakovský also accumulated symbolic capital during the time that he intervened in the Slovenian literary situation: he was a leading Czech author recognised throughout the Slavic world, Goethe's correspondent, and an authority to whom John Bowring dedicated his *Cheskian Anthology* (Bowring 1832: vii–viii). Čop regarded the translation of Čelakovský in *IB* among Carniolan readers as an external reflection and argument by a foreign authority. By referencing an international environment he harnessed him to internal cultural policy and his plans: "'*An outside opinion, neither elicited nor agreed on*' (to use *Goethe's* expression) already in general has an advantage since it is free of tension; this is all the more important since its author, František Ladislav Čelakovský, is not only *one of the most outstanding of currently living Czech* writers, but he has also, based on his collection and translations of folk poetry from all Slavic nations [...], shown himself to be an authoritative *connoisseur of all Slavic languages*." (Čop 1983: 110; emphases added).

The mirror that the foreign reviewer placed in front of Slovenes through metatextual and translation reflection was an additional incentive for Čop to locate domestic literary production in the coordinates of the European space and the criteria that presupposed the internationality of the literary aesthetic sphere. The expression *Weltliteratur* for Goethe meant a literary circulation that renews every national literature and enables its reflection in other literatures through foreign encouragement. His ideal of a 'classical national author', who objectivises himself through intertextual connections to ancient, early modern, contemporary and non-European literary repertoires, was close to the Romantic literary cosmopolitanism that the brothers Friedrich and August Wilhelm Schlegel cultivated in their aesthetic–philosophical, critical, literary and translation works. The brothers tried to elevate German literature, which seemed to them – similarly as to Goethe – to lag behind and aesthetically less developed, by connecting it to Romance forms and bringing it closer to the great traditions of the world, for example, the Indian. During the years that Goethe was introducing the concept of world literature into European intellectual discourse, Čop and Prešeren were introducing the cultural transfer of Schlegelian Romantic cosmopolitanism with a similar intent: to ground Slovenian literature, embedded in the national movement, in the universality of aesthetic humanism and the repertoires of European literary traditions from the ancient to the Romantic (Juvan 2012a: 250–277; 2012b). This kind of universalism, which Čop and Prešeren adopted for cultivating the young literature, was through the defence of Prešeren supported from outside by Čelakovský, although he adhered to a different, more folklorised aesthetics; Jungmann's program of Czech national classics also differed from the concept of Čop and Prešeren.[7] Regardless of such differences, Čop framed Čelakovský in such a way that his voice came across as complete support for the cosmopolitan and erudite aesthetic canons of Prešeren's poetry intended for intellectuals. Using Čelakovský, Čop compared the domestic literary and cultural situation with other literatures of Europe (in particular with Slavic ones), focusing on the question of literary language:

> Language is able to acquire the appropriate civilizational stature only by means of being gradually introduced into these circles [=higher circles of life and science as a communicational tool]. This stature up until now has been lacking in the Carniolan-Slovenian language to a greater extent than in any other *Slavic language* (with the possible exceptions of *Sorbian* or *Luzatian Slovak*). [...] Our writers can best learn what the *Slavic* literary style is from the writings of those *Slavs* who already have a rich literature; only we must not immediately proclaim everything in it as unacceptable *Germanisms, Gallicisms* and so on when these are artistic expressions common to all *European literatures* or a *general European* phrase dictated by common usage and culture. (Čop 1983: 170–171; emphases added)

The emergence of a world literary space made it additionally possible for Čop to present a comparative context of Prešeren's poetics, quite different from the usual Carniolan familiarity and typification, to a domestic readership through external reflection. He highlights Prešeren's cosmopolitan citationality and the semantisation of foreign poetic forms. By highlighting international repertoires

7 Jungmann recommended a somewhat different strategy to Czechs compared to Čop's for Slovenes: following the examples of ancient classics and the most accomplished works of early modern European literatures, national classics must mature from folk tradition. For him one isolated genius is not sufficient; there must be a pleiad of authors. Literature must achieve a complete segmentation of genres, linguistic perfection and harmony, and be rooted not only among the educated classes but among all social strata – only in this way can it become a "comprehensive national literature" (Jungmann 1841: 176–185; cf. Vinkler 2006: 247–248).

and by means of comparisons, he provides a basis for the Slovene-Carniolan adoption of aesthetic universalism and defends

> *Italian* and *Spanish* forms that [Prešeren] uses and that must not be any less familiar to educated readers because they are also frequently used by *German* poets, especially more recent ones. [...] The Carniolan poet can thus more freely choose metric forms since in fact we do not have any national ones (such as those that the *Serbs* have, for example). So why should he not select those which are generally recognized as the most beautiful among recent ones (leaving aside *ancient* ones), namely, *Southern European*, and especially neighboring *Italian*, which are painstakingly copied even by those peoples, for example the *Germans, English,* and others, whose languages have more difficulty adapting to these forms than Carniolan does? Moreover, these forms are already in wide use by *other Slavs*. (118; emphases added)

Čop concludes his comments on the review by Čelakovský with a concise literary revival program that proclaims poetry as the most suitable genre by means of which Slovenes can join the civilised nations without having to first fully develop their media and differentiated public discourse: "Although [...] due to circumstances it is scarcely possible to imagine the cultivation of true sciences in our provincial language, there is nothing to prevent our poets from competing successfully with the poets of other Slavic peoples." (122)

The international aesthetic competition that Čop hinted at delineated the space of world literature that took shape parallel with the establishment of national literatures (Casanova 1999: 55–67).[8] Literatures did indeed build their identity comparatively, not merely in a competitive way and in relation to western literatures, as emphasised by Casanova, but in diverse mutual relations and with a view towards nearby or similar literary systems, semi-peripheries or regional centres. Literatures in the world system in general are distinguished by traditional prestige or linguistic or political influence, and therefore occupy central or peripheral positions (Casanova 1999; Moretti 2000), as well as positions of "sub-centers" (Thomsen 2008: 35–39). With Čop and Prešeren Slovenian poetry was set upon the imagined background of European classics, while through Čelakovský it entered into an alliance with the more powerful Czech literature. However, in relation to the Western core and the German semi-periphery, Czech literature was

[8] World literature throughout the 19th century by analogy with the contemporaneous formation of the interstate world system was regarded by most as an exchange between national literatures, or rather as a selection of the best that national literatures – as the main, if not only, units of the world space – contribute to the timeless treasure trove of "general humanity" (Juvan 2012a: 153–160).

in a similar position to that of Slovenian, and likewise functioned as the foundation for a "non-state" nation (Vodička 1960: 125–137). Allies from the Slovenian and Czech literary fields in fact embraced two transnational ideologies: a Romantic conception of literature as an aesthetically autonomous sphere and a belief in cultural nationalism that artistic literature and a cultured language are proof of the international validation of a nation.

Goethe saw a fragmented Germany as the periphery of the West; however, the German semi-periphery including Austria's Vienna was stronger than the Czech capital. Czech literature in the 19th century strengthened its role of a regional sub-centre producing models that the Slovenes also increasingly followed. In the ideology of national revival among Slovenes and Czechs, German identity was regarded as a dominating opponent mingled among the domestic language community, one that could only be parried by an alliance among weaker nations. But differences also emerged among the weaker. They can be observed in the patronising attitude of Čelakovský towards the younger and aesthetically less developed Slovenian literature, with its poorer differentiation of genres and inadequate media and institutional infrastructure. While Čop relied on the international stature of Čelakovský, he also countered him as a representative of the more powerful centre in order to assert the particularity of Slovenian culture.

During the Alphabet War it was shown not least of all that Slovenian literary culture found itself at the intersection of the areas of influence of Vienna and Prague, two regional centres that competed in the Habsburg state for the position of primary centre for Slavic studies and Slavic identity. Kopitar, who strove to take on the role of "patriarch of Slavic languages and literature" from Dobrovský and preserve Vienna as the centre of Slavism, had difficulty tolerating the growing strength of Slavic studies in Prague and the meddling of Czechs in internal Carniolan-Slovenian affairs, since this was supposed to be his domain (cf. Vinkler 2006: 232–234). In his pamphlet, in which he intervened in the disputes between Čop and the domestic proponents of Metelko, he therefore aimed barbs at Čelakovský as an overpraised "Czech patron" and at Palacký, who also ridiculed the plethora of grammars in Slovenia (Kopitar 1973: 52–54, 59).

The Slovenian–Czech interliterariness in the case of Čelakovský and Čop is imbued with the Slavism of "Slavic reciprocity", which in central and southeastern Europe legitimised the formation of interliterary communities as interfaces between national literatures and world literature (cf. Ďurišin 1984: 273–299; Zelenka 2002: 59–97). That through "Slavic reciprocity" a regional subsystem was built ideologically in which nations of (semi)peripheral central and southeastern Europe could play a more visible role can also be inferred in the words of Čelakovský, who promises Slovenian revivalists a public of "sixty and more million Slavs". However, in the central current of Slovenian literature it was Čop and Prešeren who instilled a national-autonomistic tendency and resistance to closer ties with Slavs. In so doing Slovenian literature did protect its identity, but it also probably hindered its entry into world literature.

Marko Juvan
marko.juvan@zrc-sazu.si
Inštitut za slovensko literaturo in literarne vede
ZRC SAZU
Novi trg 2
SI-1000 Ljubljana
SLOVENIJA / SLOVENIA

References

Berkopec, O. 1961/62. Doneski k literarnim stikom Prešerna in Čopa s Fr. Čelakovskim in Fr. Palackim. – *Slavistična revija*, 13/1–4, 225–240.

Bowring, J. 1832. *Cheskian Anthology: Being a History of the Poetical Literature of Bohemia with Translated Specimens*. London: Hunter.

Casanova, P. 1999. *La République mondiale des Lettres*. Paris: Ed. du Seuil.

Casanova, P. 2011. Combative Literatures. – *New Left Review*, 72, 123–134.

Čelakovský, F. L. 1832. Krajinská literatura. – *Časopis českého Museum*, 6/4, 443–454.

Čop, M. 1833. *Nuovo discacciamento di lettere inutili, Das ist: Slowenischer ABC-Krieg. Eine Beilage zum Illyr. Blatt*. Laibach: Kleinmayr.

Čop, M. 1983. *Pisma in spisi*. Ed. Janko Kos, trans. Janko Moder. Ljubljana: Mladinska knjiga.

Čop, M. 1986. *Pisma Matija Čopa*. 1. Eds Anton Slodnjak and Janko Kos. Ljubljana: SAZU.

Damrosch, D. 2003. *What Is World Literature?* Princeton, N. J.: Princeton Univeristy Press.

Ďurišin, D. 1984. *Theory of literary comparatistics*. Bratislava: Veda.

Ďurišin, D. 1992. *Čo je svetová literatúra?* Bratislava: Vydavatel'stvo Obzor.

Ďurišin, D. 1995. *Théorie du processus interlittéraire I*. Bratislava: SAV.

Dvořák, K. 1960. František Ladislav Čelakovský (*1799–1852). – *Dějiny České literatury II: Literatura národního obrození*. Ed. Felix Vodička. Praha: Nakladatelství Československé akademie věd, 282–306.

Even-Zohar, I. 2008. Culture Planning, Cohesion, and the Making and Maintenance of Entities. – A. Pym, M. Shlesinger, D. Simeoni, eds., *Beyond Descriptive Translation Studies: Investigations in Homage to Gideon Toury*. Amsterdam and Philadelphia: John Benjamins, 277–292.

Jungmann, J. 1827. O klasičnosti v literatuře vůbec a zvláště české. – *Časopis Společnosti vlastenského museum v Čechách*, 1/1, 29–39.

Jungmann, J. 1841. *Sebrané drobne spisy: veršom i prozou*. Praga: W komissí Kronbergra a Řivnáče.

Juvan, M. 2012a. *Prešernovska struktura in svetovni literarni sistem*. Ljubljana: LUD Literatura.

Juvan, M. 2012b. World Literature in Carniola: Transfer of Romantic Cosmopolitanism and the Making of National Literature. – *Interlitteraria*, 17, 27–49.

Kopitar, J. 1973. Beseda o ljubljanski abecedni vojski: Iz pisma z Dunaja gospodu M***. – J. Kopitar, M. Čop, *Izbrano delo*. Ljubljana: Mladinska knjiga. Ed. Janko Kos, trans. Janko Moder, 52–66.

Kos, J. 1979. *Matija Čop*. Ljubljana: Partizanska knjiga.

Kvapil, M. 1984. F. L. Čelakovský a Slovinci. – *Slavia*, 53/3–4, 278–285.

Legiša, L. 1959. Romantika. – L. Legiša, A. Slodnjak, *Zgodovina slovenskega slovstva II: Romantika in realizem I*. Ljubljana: Slovenska matica, 5–176.

Ludvik, D. 1949. Ozadje Prešernovega pisma Čelakovskemu iz leta 1836. – *Slavistična revija*, 2/1–2, 141–151.

Moretti, F. 2000. Conjectures on World Literature. – *New Left Review*, 1: 54–68.

Paternu, B. 1976. *France Prešeren in njegovo pesniško delo*. Vol. 1. Ljubljana: Mladinska knjiga.

Pogačnik, J. 2002. Prešeren – Čop – Kopitar. – *France Prešeren – kultura – Evropa*. Ed. Jože Faganel and Darko Dolinar. Ljubljana: Založba ZRC, ZRC SAZU, 225–239.

Pospíšil, I. 2005. Problem slavizmov in njegov kontekst. Trans. Bojana Maltarić. – *Primerjalna književnost*, 28/2, 17–31.

Prijatelj, I. 1935. *Duševni profili slovenskih preporoditeljev*. Za šestdesetletnico izdali Prijateljevi učenci. Ljubljana: s. n. [Tiskarna Merkur].

Strich, F. 1949. *Goethe and World Literature*. London: Routledge & Kegan Paul Ltd.

Šafařik, P. J. 1826. *Geschichte der slawischen Sprache und Literatur nach allen Mundarten*. Ofen: Kön. Ung. Universitäts Schriften.

Šafařik, P. J. 1833. Přehled nejnovější literatury illyrských Slovenův: Literatura vindických Slovenův. *Časopis českého Museum*, 7/2, 164–181.

Thomsen, M. R. 2008. *Mapping World Literature: International Canonization and Transnational Literatures*. New York: Continuum.

Vinkler, J. 2006. *Posnemovalci, zavezniki in tekmeci: Češko-slovenski in slovensko-češki kulturni stiki v 19. stoletju*. Koper: Annales.

Vodička, F. 1960. *Dějiny České literatury II: Literatura národního obrození*. Ed. Felix Vodička. Praha: Nakladatelství Československé akademie věd.

Závodský, A. 1982. *František Ladislav Čelakovský*. Praha: Melenatrich.

Zelenka, M. 2002. *Literární věda a slavistika*. Praha: Academia.

The Periodical as a Strategy of Recognition for Small Literatures

JEANNE E. GLESENER

Abstract. This article addresses the topic of the visibility of small literatures in a world literature context. A brief outline of the discourse on smallness allows us to see how this topic has been assessed and handled by small literatures. In a second step, the paper investigates the initiatives taken to promote the circulation of the literary production of small literatures. The focus is on the role of the multilingual periodical with a transnational outlook. The main example, taken from the Luxembourg context, concerns the interculturally conceived bilingual periodical Floréal, published from 1907 to 1908. The article will argue that, despite its ephemeral existence, this periodical counts as one of the earliest attempts to promote Luxembourg literatures in French and German in a World Literature context.

Keywords: small literature, world literature, Luxembourg literatures, periodical, literary field, strategies of recognition, discourse on smallness

In 1977, György Gera, Hungarian *homme de lettres*, writer, translator and chief editor of the trilingual periodical *Le Livre hongrois*, did a survey of roughly one hundred writers, poets and editors from all over the world asking their opinion on the possibility of promoting the literatures of lesser known languages. In his invitation letter, Gera quotes Valéry Larbaud's famous statement of 1927 in which the French poet and writer deplores the general ignorance, in France, of literatures in smaller languages and advocates that specialists, translators and literature enthusiasts give them more attention (Boldizsár 1979: V). Among the many responses to the survey, that of Vercors, author of the classic *Le Silence de la mer* (1942), stands out in that he tries to explain the apparent 'imperialism' of major literatures in the world literature context:

> Personnellement, je ne crois pas du tout à une sorte de mépris inconscient des grands pays pour les petits. La théorie 'à grand pays grande littérature' n'est pas seulement simpliste, elle est raciste et, encore plus, absurde. La preuve en est que nombre des œuvres majeures dont l'existence a influencée la pensée humaine provient de ces petits pays : tchèques (Kafka), hongroises (Petöfi), danoises (Kierkegaard), norvégiennes (Ibsen), etc. Et de seulement citer ces quelques auteurs montre que lorsque une œuvre atteint une certaine hauteur,

DOI: http://dx.doi.org/10.12697/IL.2015.S1.13

> il n'est pas de frontières ni de langues qui tiennent. Ce qui franchit mal les barrières, c'est ce qu'on pourrait appeler la seconde littérature, les œuvres encore de très bonne qualité mais, disons, dont l'influence sur la pensée mondiale est moins visible. Comme si, en face d'œuvres ni plus ni moins bonnes mais écrites en langue de grande circulation, elle ne 'faisait pas le poids', comme on dit. D'où l'impression d'une sorte d'impérialisme des littératures de grands pays aux dépens des petits. (Ibid. 85)

By insisting that it is language rather than quality that enables a work to travel beyond its context of origin, Vercors maintains that works written in major languages travel more easily than those of the same quality written in a lesser known language. The impression that there is an imperialism of major literatures over small ones derives, so Vercors contends, from this disequilibrium in the dissemination of literatures.

Of course, the idea of a link between major/small languages and the dissemination of literature had already been addressed in peripheral world literature areas since the late nineteenth century by such eminent world literature scholars as the Hungarian Hugo von Meltzl (1846–1908) and the Dane Georg Brandes (1842–1927), as we shall see further below. Whether the 'imperialism' of major literatures can be considered merely an impression, however, is questionable especially with regard to past and recent world literature scholarship. The terminology may have changed as contemporary theory draws on models from the world economic system but the dominance of the great central powers over peripheral areas of world literature is far from being a thing of the past. If, in the nineteenth and for most of the twentieth century, European scholars tended to see "world literature as radiating outward from metropolitan centers toward relatively passive provincial recipients" (Damrosch 2006a: 214), contemporary scholarship proceeds in much the same way, as Theo D'haen notes: "The theories of [Pascale] Casanova and [Franco] Moretti, in their 'irradiation' or 'diffusionist' perspective centred upon Paris, or Paris and London, cast Europe's minor literatures as purely re-active in relation to the 'centre' or 'centres' of Europe. [...] If anything, this has led to an ever growing marginalization, or perhaps we should say 'peripheralisation,' of Europe's minor literatures" (D'haen 2012: 153). Since Gera's survey and despite the new approaches and theories developed to account for the global scope of world literature today, the problems surrounding the visibility of small literatures in the world literature system have lost none of their significance.

Rather than appraising the contemporary situation however, this paper will look at how the topic of visibility was handled by small European literatures in the nineteenth and the beginning of the twentieth century.

When addressing the peripherality of small literatures, it is worthwhile to venture beyond the dominance discourse of the centre(s) and to confront it with the discourse of smallness developed, over time, by small literatures themselves. The discourse is not only highly revealing of their inner trials and tribulations but it also informs us on the attempts to promote their production abroad. As we shall see, the rather negative tenor of the discourse stands in stark contrast to the energetic and dynamic spirit of the editorship of periodicals and journals.

Some of the new vistas on world literature put forth in recent decades enable us to consider the activity of smaller literary fields in terms other than passiveness and to reevaluate the attempts made to enhance the international visibility of their production. And since, according to David Damrosch, world literature can be understood as a "mode of circulation and reading [...] as applicable to individual works as to bodies of material" (Damrosch 2003: 5), this raises interesting perspectives on the function attributed to transnational multilingual periodicals or journals towards the end of the nineteenth and the beginning of the twentieth century. Given that, at that time, small literary fields often still lacked a well-established publishing sector, periodicals and journals became an important platform for publication. Moreover, if their outlook was international from the start, they turned out to be an effective medium for works to "circulate beyond their culture of origin" and consequently to reach "beyond [their] home base" (ibid. 4).

In the following, I propose a summary outline of the discourse on smallness in peripheral European literatures by paying special attention to the determining role of such aspects as space, age and language. This outline will provide the necessary background to showcase the role attributed to the periodical in a small literary field, as will be briefly shown by the reference to Hugo von Meltzl's *Acta Comparationis Litterarum Universarum*. My main example, taken from the Luxembourg context, concerns the interculturally conceived bilingual periodical *Floréal*, published from 1907 to 1908. I will argue that, despite its ephemeral existence, it counts as one of the earliest attempts to promote Luxembourg literatures in French and German in a world literature context.

The discourse on smallness: an outline

The discourse on smallness is multifaceted and reflects on such various topics as belatedness, lack of visibility, fear of provincialism, etc. Furthermore, if it is concerned on the one hand with interrogating the condition of smallness it grapples, on the other, with literature being denied a cosmopolitan dimension from the central powers that be.

With regard to the condition of smallness, it is important to understand to what extent it is shaped by the belief that small literatures lack both the momentum and the space to reverberate beyond their context of origin. Territory and location often occupy centre stage in the discourse. Unlike Vercors, who dismisses the assumption that a large country necessarily produces a major literature ("à grand pays grande littérature"), small literatures do subscribe to the notion that the small size of a country inevitably limits the capacity of its literature to reverberate across borders. Rather than being understood as a dissemination problem though, this limited international visibility was often interpreted as a sign that the production was lacking in literary qualities. When addressed by the discourse, this issue of the perceived interdependence of space and creative impulse or genius is usually also linked to small literatures' passiveness and reactiveness, as can be seen for instance in the following statement by the Luxembourg author and critic Mars Klein: "Ein kleiner Raum agiert nicht. Er reagiert. Reagiert auf die in grossen Räumen formulierten Ideologien und die daraus abgeleiteten (diktierten oder angebotenen) geopolitischen und kulturpolitischen Konditionen" (Klein 1988: 2). Klein mainly stresses the orientation offered to small literary cultures by the dominance of major ones, but there is also an indirect hint at the universalist perspective on literary norms imposed by major literatures. The latter tend to see themselves as 'prototypes', reducing those literatures that do not conform to their standard to mere imitators or epigones of the 'original' (Jusdanis 1990: 14).

The Francophone Swiss writer Charles-Ferdinand Ramuz's use of the aquamarine metaphor lays bare the conviction that the effect small literatures can ever aspire to is to produce insignificant ripples on the ocean of world literature:

> Un petit pays est-il condamné par sa petitesse même à ne pas connaître la grandeur? Les petits pays ont une activité qui est à leur taille, c'est-à-dire une petite activité. Et les pensées ne tardent pas, elles-mêmes (eussent-elles à l'origine des dimensions différentes), à se proportionner, étant causes, à leurs effets, qui ne peuvent être grands. C'est ainsi que les vagues sur le Pacifique prennent singulièrement plus d'ampleur que sur la Méditerranée. (Ramuz 1979: 33)

Ramuz's statement conveys the impression that the exiguity of the space of a small literature acts as a natural barrier to enter the world beyond its constricted confines. Even before world literature was expressly discussed in terms of geopolitical power relations[1] (Hroch 2000: 9), small literatures have been aware of the asymmetrical power distribution between the centres and the peripheries. Because the dissemination across the border was limited, given the lack of a strong

1 Admittedly, this has been the case ever since Goethe introduced the term of 'Weltliteratur' in 1827 which built on the recognition of the birth of a 'Weltmarkt' of literature. (Pizer 2000: 214).

institutional and developed editorial apparatus, interliterary communication was perceived as an asymmetrical exchange in which major literatures entered the space of small ones whereas the reverse was rather an exceptional occurrence.

Apart from space, the age of a literary culture is deemed equally relevant. Indeed, the fear of belatedness harks back to the late rise of the small nation states after the Vienna Congress of 1815 and the subsequent 'delay' in the emergence of their literature. In those nations that correspond to Miroslav Hroch's pattern of 'nations without history' (Hroch 2000: 9), the development of national movements, characterised by philological, scholarly and literary activities, occurs when in most major literatures, the process of nation-building is already completed[2]. Furthermore, the recognition of a literature's existence depends on whether or not it is considered modern, a condition determined by the age of a literature. "La loi temporelle de l'univers littéraire", writes Pascale Casanova, "peut s'énoncer ainsi: il faut être ancien pour avoir quelque chance d'être moderne ou de décréter la modernité. Il faut avoir un long passé national pour prétendre à l'existence littéraire pleinement reconnue dans le présent" (Casanova 1999: 129). Deprived of noble lineage and missing the necessary ancestry (read tradition), the conviction of belatedness is deeply ingrained in the discourse on smallness, as illustrated by the following statement by the Luxembourg essayist Corina Mersch: "Une culture mineure livre, pendant des siècles, une bataille perdue d'avance, car même ses avant-gardes arrivent trop tard, lorsque tout a été déjà dit : les 'têtes de série' doivent intervenir dans une partie où les jeux sont faits, les vedettes doivent assister à un spectacle où les fauteuils d'orchestre sont réservés, etc." (Mersch 1999: 38).

But the asynchronicity underlying the development of small and major literatures (Kundera 1993: 230) is seldom given consideration when the topic of belatedness is discussed. As a consequence, the late rise of small literatures and their engagement in the nation building process resulted in their being perceived as focusing on national issues mainly.

---

[2] Jacques Le Riders' description of the belatedness of the nations and literatures of Central Europe is also valid for small nations and literatures in Western Europe: "'Retardés' du fait de leur assujettissement à des grands ensembles impériaux (allemande, habsbourgeois, russe, ottoman), ces pays n'accèdent à l'unité nationale ou au sentiment d'appartenance nationale qu'au XIXe siècle. 'Retardé' signifie souvent 'interrompu' : la prise de conscience nationale au XIXe siècle cherche alors à renouer avec une époque antérieure – plus ou moins légendaire – d'indépendance et de puissance. Cette prise de conscience nationale passe par la redécouverte et la codification, voire l'invention, d'une tradition culturelle et d'une identité linguistique" (Le Rider 1998: 24).

> Dissimulées derrières leurs langues inaccessibles, les petites nations européennes (leur vie, leur histoire, leur culture) sont très mal connues ; on pense, tout naturellement, que là réside le handicap principal pour la reconnaissance internationale de leur art. Or, c'est le contraire : cet art est handicapé parce que tout le monde (la critique, l'historiographie, les compatriotes comme les étrangers) le colle sur la grande photo de famille nationale et ne le laisse pas sortir de là. (Ibid. 231)

In this assessment, Milan Kundera contests the almost axiomatic gesture of both the agents and the observers of small literatures which consists of denying them the capacity to achieve 'literary worldliness' (Damrosch 2011: 307) or to have an impact on the wider literary world on the grounds that their concerns can only ever stretch to those of the nation-state. The ascription of purely 'national' and by extension political concerns to small literatures has been perpetuated ever since the centre decreed this to be the case, such as when Gilles Deleuze and Félix Guattari contend in their model of minor literatures that "Le second caractère des littératures mineures, c'est que tout y est politique" (Deleuze, Guattari: 1975: 30). Statements such as these, proclaimed from such an authoritative position as that enjoyed by Deleuze, inevitably influence the discourse on small literatures. Quite apart from the fact that this view participates in their politicisation, it also proceeds to an unwarranted restriction of their thematic and aesthetic scope[3].

As already mentioned, there is the issue of the literary language to be considered. Whereas Kundera talks of the inaccessibility of smaller languages, Georg Brandes, writing at the end of nineteenth century, highlights the latters' lack of prestige and leverage, when he maintains: "But whoever writes in Finnish, Hungarian, Swedish, Danish, Dutch, Greek or the like is obviously poorly placed in the universal struggle for fame. In this competition he lacks the major weapon, a language – which is, for a writer, almost everything" (Brandes [1899] 2009: 63). 'Worse' still than writing in a language deprived of symbolic capital is writing in several literary languages. The geocultural location of small literatures on cultural and linguistic cross-roads or their history of domination by foreign/ neighbouring nations[4] often led to the coexistence of several languages in their literary cultures which, more often than not, gave rise to a history of power struggle of societal and literary multilingualism, a struggle in which not all of the languages possessed the same prestige. Add to that the Goethean dictum, paraphrased by Brandes in his 1899 essay "*Weltliteratur*", that "it is impossible to write anything of artistic value in a language other than one's own. On that, everyone agrees"

---

3 For deconstructions of the Deleuzian model, see Casanova 1997 and Gauvin 2003.

4 See Hroch 2000 and Cornis-Pope, Neubauer 2004.

(ibid.), small multilingual literatures were once again at a disadvantage as they fell short of conforming to the authoritative monolingual norm of major world literatures. As Yasemin Yildiz has argued in her seminal work *Beyond the Mother Tongue: The Postmonolingual Condition* (2012), the emergence of the paradigm of monolingualism and the subsequent consecration of writing in the mother tongue in the eighteenth and nineteenth centuries resulted in "a disavowal of the possibility of writing in nonnative languages or in multiple languages at the same time" (Yildiz 2012: 9).

All these aspects contributed greatly to the limited visibility of small literatures in the world republic of letters. However, as stipulated above, the literary periodical turned out to be a valuable strategy for their international recognition. In his research on Belgian periodicals, Paul Aron has demonstrated their key function in a literary field whose institutionalisation is still in process. Here, they tend to take on a leading role in the legitimation process, especially if the editorial apparatus of a literary field is underdeveloped or experiencing structural problems (Aron 1997: 110).

Moreover, in a spatial perspective, the periodical with an international outlook was in fact a useful tool to overcome the impediment of territorial exiguity. As Karen Vandemeulebroucke has shown, the nature of the periodical is such that it can act as a (trans)-national space (Vandemeulebroucke 2008: 116): while remaining locally anchored, it crosses borders both literally, by circulating internationally, and metaphorically, by admitting foreign literature into its pages (ibid. 119). Conceived of as a meeting place for authors of various national provenances, the periodical is also instrumental in claiming literature's autonomy from national ideology while at the same time helping those authors associated with it to delineate a distinct literary identity. Again, this is particularly important in a context lacking literary institutions and where the literary activity is still in search of recognition and legitimation.

The *Acta Comparationis Litterarum Universarum*

The most prominent initiative representative of the strategy of recognition outlined above is undoubtedly the *Acta Comparationis Litterarum Universarum*. This very first journal of comparative literature, edited from 1877 to 1888 by the Hungarian comparatist Hugo von Meltzl in Cluj, has entered the annals of comparative literature history as one of the earliest attempts to revive Goethe's idea of *Weltliteratur* and, as indicated by its title, to extend it to a truly global scale. At the same time, it was also set on promoting peripheral Hungarian literature in a world literature context.

Of Transylvanian origin, the polyglot Meltzl (1846–1908) teamed up with the last Hungarian polyhistor Samuel Brassai (1800–1897), co-editor of the journal until 1883. The journal, which released around one hundred issues, comprised essays, reviews, overviews on contemporary world literature, polyglot accounts on the Hungarian poet Petöfi, Schopenhaueriana, discussions on the nascent discipline of comparative literature, etc. (Berczik 1978: 92–93) The editorial decision to print the journal's title in no less than ten languages clearly shows how much store the editors set in polyglottism, which is also reflected in the international set-up of the editorial board which included members from Hungary, Germany, England, France, Italy, Switzerland, Holland, Portugal, Iceland, Sweden, Poland, the USA, Turkey, India, Egypt and Australia.

The driving force behind the journal, indeed its fundamental idea, was "the reform of literary history, a reform long awaited and long overdue which is possible only through an extensive application of the comparative principle" (Meltzl [1877] 2009: 42). The editors sought to enhance the principles of the nascent discipline of comparative literature, which they saw as the only efficient way to emancipate Goethe's cosmopolitan conception of *Weltliteratur* from the service of narrow nationalistic concerns it had been reduced to by literary history (Damrosch 2008: 48). It is undoubtedly for this reason that, in his statement of intent, Meltzl put so much stress on the autonomy of literature and the distancing from ideology: "Es gibt kein sichereres Kennzeichen wahrer höherer Bildung als Vermeidung aller patriotischen sowie auch übrigen confessionellen, namentlich religiösen Ausbrüchen im Leben [...]. Wir Culturmenschen, zunächst Bürger einer grösseren Gemeinde sind mehr als Glieder des durch farbige Schlagbäume begrenzten Vaterlandes [...]" (Berczik 1978: 93)

The aims pursued by Meltzl were manifold. Intended as "a meeting place of authors, translators and philosophers of all nations" (Meltzl [1877] 2009: 43), the journal endeavoured to overcome the nationalism of the great European powers by widening the field of world literature to include masterpieces of other cultures and especially by representing literatures of smaller countries (Damrosch 2006b: 102).

Meltzl was also acutely aware of the consequences the power struggle between Europe's major literatures was having on the visibility of smaller literatures and saw in comparative literature a valid tool to introduce the latter into a larger international context: "Our secret motto is: nationality as individuality of a people should be regarded as sacred and inviolable. Therefore, a people, be it ever so insignificant politically, is and will remain, from the standpoint of comparative literature, as important as the largest nation. The most unsophisticated language may offer us most precious and informative subjects for comparative philology" (Meltzl [1877] 2009: 45). The equality of the world's literatures heralded here is realised by the inclusion of essays and folksongs in Armenian, Gaelic, Aztec, Japanese and Chinese for instance, which where juxtaposed with texts in major world languages.

Hungary's cultural, linguistic and institutional borderland position was undoubtedly decisive in defining the scope of the project. While Meltzl's championing of comparative literature and the way he epitomised Goethe's concept of *Weltliteratur* have been often commented upon, his agenda for the promotion of Hungarian literature is generally less at the forefront.

However, and this is perhaps the most important point with regard to our present concern, despite the world literature focus, Meltzl was determined to make his project directly relevant to his home ground, as Arpad Berczik underlines:

> Der Redakteur wollte mit seiner Zeitschrift zwei literarische Aufgaben bewältigen: einerseits war er im letzten Viertel des 19. Jahrhunderts, also zur Zeit der literarischen Einengung Ungarns um die Hebung des Niveaus des heimischen Schrifttums durch Bekanntmachen der ausländischen Literaturen und um die Erweiterung des Horizonts seiner Landsleute bemüht, andererseits wünschte er die ungarische Literatur durch den – seiner Meinung nach – bisher einzigen weltliterarisch würdigen magyarischen Dichter Petöfi in die Weltliteratur einzuführen. (Berczik 1978: 92)

Thus, while the international circulation of the journal was intended to promote the international reception of Hungarian literature, the national circulation was supposed to provide local writers with new creative impulses, an aspect that, as we will see later on, is also at the forefront of *Floréal*.

Floréal in a world literature perspective

It may seem preposterous to compare the short-lived literary journal *Floréal*, which barely existed for a year and only involved twelve issues, with the global scope of Meltzl's *ACTA*. Indeed, *Floréal*'s scope was much more modest and its world literature dimension is only indirectly hinted at. Nevertheless, despite its ephemeral existence, it counts as one of the defining instances in Luxembourg's cultural history of the first half of the twentieth century, not least because it acts as a kind of prequel to the construction of Luxembourg's hybrid identity at a time when, in European cultural discourses, cultural and linguistic purity were heralded as the cornerstones of national identity. More importantly, it signals the decisive moment consisting of the open recognition of the importance of writing in non-native languages (here German and French) in a literary field that has been grappling to come to terms with its multilingual situation.

As was the case elsewhere, in the nineteenth century literary activity in Luxembourg focused on literature written in the mother tongue, *Lëtzebuergesch*, linguistically defined as a Moselle Franconian dialect. Lacking prestige in the trilingual set-up of the country, intellectuals and writers sought to explore its literary potential and to develop it into a literary language in its own right. At that time, Luxembourg, whether on the political or cultural level, was, as an entity created by the European superpowers in 1839, in quest of international recognition. All efforts were therefore dedicated to the task of conferring legitimacy to the nation and, as is characteristic for the century of nationalities, literature and language were conscripted to participate in this process. It goes without saying that the French and German literary languages were somewhat sidelined in this process.

The beginning of the 20th century coincides with a decisive shift in the approach and the perception of literary production in different languages in Luxembourg. While on the one hand, it marks the consecration of the great poets of the previous century Michel Lentz (1820–1893), Edmond de La Fontaine (1823–1891) and Michel Rodange (1827–1876), who had provided the mother tongue with its literary credentials, on the other, leading intellectuals turned their back on Luxembourgish (Tockert 1948: 251). The seed for the recognition of Luxembourg literature as a trilingual literature was sown, although literature in *Lëtzebuergesch* was much less in the limelight as was hitherto the case. In any case, the reorientation signals a more open embrace of linguistic multiplicity which went hand in hand with the pronounced aspiration for close literary exchange and contacts with the neighbouring literatures and the creation of the bilingual French-German *Floréal* bears testimony to this new transnational outlook.

As a publishing venture, *Floréal* needs to be seen in context and its emergence is in itself revealing of the state of the literary field at the time. As Germaine Goetzinger has noted, the periodical arose out of the tradition of the literary salons, cenacles and coffee house culture rather than from a professional cultural journalism initiative (Goetzinger 1985: 57). In his memoirs, Marcel Noppeney, one of the co-editors, fondly remembers the lively evening in the *Café du commerce*, located in the heart of Luxembourg City, where *Floréal* was conceived in early February 1907 (Noppeney 1957). Marcel Trébitsch has underlined the role of the structures of productive sociability, such as schools, movements, periodicals, cafés and salons, that, next to the more regulated and professional instances, determine the activity and the dynamic in a literary field[5]. In 1900, Luxembourg barely had a literary field to speak of: the publishing sector was

[5] Quoted in Aron 1997: 109.

almost non-existent, the literary scene was small and lacking in contours, there was virtually no literary criticism and there was no university either.

Given the institutional bareness of its contextual background, *Floréal* counts among the earliest definitive initiatives towards the establishment of the literary field. It is also for this reason that, as we shall see, it counts as a space where literary identity could be fostered.

Floréal was the brainchild of the Francophone writer Marcel Noppeney (1877–1966) and the Germanophone writers Frantz Clément (1882–1942) and Eugène Forman (1878–1955). From the outset, the idea was that the periodical should pay tribute to Luxembourg's polyglottism on the one hand and highlight its cultural mixity on the other. As noted above, at the turn of the century, leading writers turned their back on writing in Luxembourgish and adopted French and/or German as their literary languages, thereby contributing to the rise of Luxembourgish literatures in French and German.

This language reversal is clearly marked by the editorial decision to invite German, French and Belgian literatures into the pages of *Floréal*. In this sense, just like the *ACTA*, *Floréal* became a meeting place for authors from different countries. *Floréal* counted among its contributors not only leading Luxembourgish writers in German, such as Frantz Clément, Eugène Forman, Batty Weber (1860–1940) and Nikolaus Welter (1871–1951), and in French, such as Joseph Hansen (1874–1952), Marcel Noppeney, Paul Palgen (1883–1966) and Nicolas Ries (1876–1941), but also had an impressive array of international collaborators. Thus, Germany was represented by Richard Dehmel (1863–1920) and Johannes Schlaf (1862–1941), Belgium by Émile Verhaeren (1855–1916), and France by Henri Albert (1869–1921), Achille Ségard (1872–1936) and Paul Lévy (1886–1959). The texts, printed in the original languages, were generically very diverse and included poems, novellas, novel fragments, critical and linguistic essays, reviews, aphorisms, etc.

In the statement of intent for the first issue, Noppeney and Clément explicitly subscribe to the autonomy of literature when they write that "Der *Floréal* ist unabhängig und unparteiisch, keiner Konfession, keiner Fraktion, keiner Clique dienstbar. Er besteht ohne Geheimfonds und ohne Nebenregierung" ([Clément] 1907: 5). The independence from political, ideological and confessional matters is underlined in the title in the two languages which reads *Revue libre d'art et de littérature – Freie Rundschau für Kunst & Litteratur*. Furthermore, the editors dispensed with national borders of literatures and, rather than using such categories as 'International Literature' or 'Foreign Literature', the contributions by the Belgian, French and German authors stand alongside those of their Luxembourgish colleagues. In addition, the editors seem to have thought in terms of language areas rather than national literature areas as the columns 'Deutsche Litteratur' and 'Revue critique' featured overviews of recent publications of literature in Germany, Austria and Switzerland for the first and Belgium, France and Switzerland for the second.

Floréal was intent on showcasing Luxembourg's cultural *métissage* or, to use the term proposed by the editors, its *Mischkultur*. *Mischkultur* is not only programmatic of the periodical's agenda of international collaboration but is self-consciously claimed as the identity concept of Luxembourg. The first volume is prefaced by two introductions, one in French and one in German and these two independent texts clearly announce the aim the periodical set itself. The introduction in German delineates the concept of *Mischkultur*:

> Die Gründer des Floréal sind der Ansicht, dass sich in unserem Lande eine ganz eigenartige Mischkultur in eigenartiger Weise äussern kann, und sie wollen in ihrer Zeitschrift diesen Äusserungen und dem Streben nach Äusserung ein Zentrum leihen. Unsere Monatsschrift ist zweisprachig. Zu begründen haben wir das kaum. Wir schulden zwei Völkern unser Hirn und sind stets zwei Völkern für ihre Anregungen dankbar. (Ibid.)

Both bilingualism and the influence of the French and German cultural and literary worlds on the local production are thus clearly highlighted. The inclusion of literature from Belgium, France and Germany was seen as an attempt to build closer relationships with the European cultural centres (ibid.: 6). Furthermore and not unlike the case of Meltzl's *ACTA*, the editors pursued a pedagogical goal as international literature was counted on to inspire local writers and to stimulate their creative impulse: "Der *Floréal* betrachtet es als eine seiner wichtigsten Aufgaben, die Luxemburger zur Ehrfurcht vor jeder freien und starken künstlerischen Produktion miterziehen zu helfen" (ibid. 5–6).

As a platform and international meeting place for authors and literatures, *Floréal* acted as a liminal space in-between cultures as it was understood as a threshold from whence intercultural transfer processes might proceed but were also already realised, or so it was implied, in the Luxembourg production, which drew its inspiration from the Belgian, French and German areas of influence.

However, it is in the introduction in French, penned by Marcel Noppeney, that the world literature perspective, albeit not explicitly voiced, makes itself felt. Noppeney defines the object of the journal as the endeavour to decompartmentalise Luxembourg literatures by taking them out of their national isolation in order to put them into a network of international exchange. When he talks of the "tentative de double décentralisation littéraire" ([Noppeney] 1907:

3), it is evident that *Floréal* was not only set on promoting exchange between the four countries involved. It was also designed to present an international readership with the "possibilité de se rendre compte de la place que le Luxembourg peut prétendre occuper en littérature" (ibid.). Incidentally, Meltzl offers an almost identical statement when he writes "[dass] der Deutsche und sonstige Europäer und Ausländer allererst aus unserem Journal ein treues Bild von der ungarischen Literatur par excellence erhalten wird" (Berczik 1978: 94).

What is important to underline here is the attempt to put an end to the isolation of both Luxembourg literature and Luxembourg writers. Moreover, the lack of public interest in local literary matters lent some urgency to the question of literary identity. As such, *Floréal* did more than provide authors with a platform where they felt they could belong. It also became a space where literary identity could be fostered. "In *Floréal*", writes Goetzinger, "haben sich in einer Art Notgemeinschaft [...] und auf schmaler Basis Autoren zusammengefunden, die in der luxemburgischen Gesellschaft keinen Ort fanden, der ihrem Selbstwertgefühl entsprochen hätte. Das Bestreben, den Luxemburgern literarische Kultur zu vermitteln, und die Überzeugung, dazu befähigt zu sein, hat sie zusammengeführt. Öffnung nach aussen vollzieht sich in Wechselwirkung mit dem Gewinn an Identität nach innen" (Goetzinger 1985: 61).

The adoption of French and German as literary languages is ultimately to be understood not only as a more open embrace of multilingualism and multilingual writing practices – a practice that, as noted above, was not universally accepted – but more importantly, as the desire to seek and cultivate international literary exchange. It is this same desire that lies at the heart of Goethe's notion of *Weltliteratur*: to transcend national parochialism through cosmopolitan cultural exchange (Juvan 2011: 74). Writing in German and in French rather than in Luxembourgish – the lowly *Mundart* – guaranteed a move away from parochialism. Because of the language's role in the nation-building process in the previous century, writers, through linguistic border-crossing, could avoid inscription in a national context only. Writing in French and German literally opened worlds, with regard both to international dissemination and a closer link to literary traditions other than one's own. And it should be noted that most of the Luxembourgish collaborators did become published authors in France and Germany and regular correspondents to French and German literary magazines and journals[6]. This transnational literary activity initiated by *Floréal* was going to be instrumental in establishing Luxembourg's intellectuals' self-perception

[6] See www.autorenlexikon.lu.

as mediators between Germany and France, an identity paradigm that subsisted until as late as the 1970s (Conter 2007).

Goethe's conception of world literature builds on the idea that it is a network of practices, media and institutions that enables the transnational circulation of texts, concepts, ideas, etc. Consequently multilingual transnationally conceived journals such as the *ACTA* and *Floréal* constitute highly valuable tools for literary dissemination and count as an important medium for supporting the international circulation of texts from small and peripheral literatures. It is in this respect that we can apprehend them as an indispensable tool in their struggle for wider recognition. The fact that in the two journals the local literatures were embedded among major ones was intended to prove the fact that, despite the anxieties and views generally voiced in the discourse on smallness, they had a legitimate place amidst the world's major literatures.

Jeanne E. Glesener
jeanne.glesener@uni.lu
Institut de langue et de littératures luxembourgeoises
Université du Luxembourg
FLSHASE UR-IPSE
Route de Diekirch (B.P. 2)
L-7201 Walferdange
LUXEMBOURG

References

Aron, P. 1997. Les Revues littéraires: média privilégié de l'identité culturelle? – P. Gorceix, ed., *L'identité culturelle de la Belgique et de la Suisse francophones*. Actes du colloque international de Soleure (juin 1993), Paris: Honoré Champion, 109–120. http://www.autorenlexikon.lu

Berczik, A. 1978. Hugo von Meltzl. – *Német Filológiai Tanulmányok*, XII, 87–100.

Boldizsár, I. 1979. Introduction. – I. Boldizsár, ed., *Petits pays, grandes littératures? Small countries, great literatures? Une enquête international du Livre Hongrois*. Budapest : L'Union des éditeurs et distributeurs de livres hongrois, V–VIII.

Brandes, G. [1899] 2009. World Literature. – D. Damrosch, N. Melas, M. Buthelezi, eds., *The Princeton Sourcebook in Comparative Literature. From the European Enlightenment to the Global Present*. Princeton and Oxford: Princeton University Press, 61–66.

Casanova, P. 1997. Nouvelles considérations sur les littératures dites mineures. – *Littératures classiques*, 31, 233–247.

[Clément, F.] 1907. Ein Geleitwort zu 'Floréal'. – *Floréal. Revue libre d'art et de littérature. Freie Rundschau für Kunst & Litteratur*, 1, 5–6.

Conter, C. D. 2007. Mischkultur. – S. Kmec, B. Majerus, M. Margue, P. Péporté, eds., *Lieux de mémoire au Luxembourg. Erinnerungsorte in Luxemburg.* Luxembourg: Saint-Paul, 23–28.

Cornis-Pope, M., Neubauer, J. 2004. *History of the Literary Cultures of East-Central Europe. Junctures and Disjunctures in the 19th and 20th Centuries. Volume IV: Types and Stereotypes,* Coll. A History of Literature in European Languages. Amsterdam and Philadelphia: John Benjamins Publihsing Company.

D'haen, T. 2012. *The Routledge Concise History of World Literature.* London and New York: Routledge.

Damrosch, D. 2003. *What is world literature?* Princeton: Princeton University Press.

Damrosch, D. 2006 a. Where is World Literature? – G. Lindberg-Wada, Ed., *Studying Transcultural Literary History.* New York: De Gruyter, 211–220.

Damrosch, D. 2006 b. Rebirth of a Discipline. – *Comparative Critical Studies,* 3 (1), 99–112.

Damrosch, D. 2008. Global Regionalism. – N. Bemong, M. Truwant, P. Vermeulen, Eds, *Re-Thinking Europe. Literature and (Trans)National Identity.* Amsterdam and New York: Rodopi, 47–59.

Damrosch, D. 2011. World Literature as an Alternative Discourse. – *Neohelicon,* 38, 307–317.

Deleuze, G., Guattari, F. 1975. *Kafka. Pour une littérature mineure.* Paris: Les Éditions de Minuit.

Fehlen, F. 2013. Sprache(n) und Nationalbewusstsein. Die Sprachenfrage im Spiegel der ersten zehn Jahrgänge des Escher Tageblattes. – D. Scuto, P. Lesch, Y. Steichen, eds., *Un journal dans son siècle: Tageblatt (1913–2013).* Esch-sur-Alzette: Le Phare, 52–69.

Gauvin, L. 2003. Autour du concept de littérature mineure. Variations sur un thème majeur. – J-P. Bertrand, L. Gauvin, eds., *Littératures mineures en langue majeure. Québec / Wallonie-Bruxelles.* Bruxelles and Montréal: Presses Interuniversitaires Européennes Peter Lang – Les Presses de l'Université de Montréal, 19–40.

Goetzinger, G. 1985. Floréal: Eine Fallstudie zur literarischen Öffentlichkeit in Luxemburg. – *Clierwer Literaturdeeg 1985. D'Texter – Les Exposés – Die Referate.* Luxembourg: Ministère des Affaires Culturelles, 56–63.

Hroch, M. 2000. *Social Preconditions of National Revival in Europe. A Comparative Analysis of the Social Composition of Patriotic Groups among the Smaller European Nations.* New York: Columbia University Press.

Jusdanis, G. 1990. The Importance of Being Minor. – *Journal of Modern Greek Studies,* 8, 5–33.

Juvan, M. 2011. World Literature(s) and Peripheries. – M. Juvan, *Literary Studies in Reconstruction. An Introduction to Literature.* Frankfurt am Main: Peter Lang, 73–89.

Klein, M. 1988. Schreiben in Luxemburg. Skizze zum Problem der literarischen Dreisprachigkeit. – *d'Letzebuerger Land,* 47, supplément à l'édition du *Letzebuerger Land,* 1–7.

Kundera, M. 1993. *Les Testaments trahis.* Paris: Gallimard.

Le Rider, J. 1998. Pour une histoire interculturelle de la production littéraire de langue allemande en Europe Centrale. – J. Le Rider, F. Rinner, Eds, *Les littératures de langue allemande en Europe Centrale. Des Lumières à nos jours.* Paris: PUF, 21–49.

Mersch, C. 1999. *Un miroir aux alouettes. Petit dictionnaire de la pensée nomade.* Echternach : Éditions Phi-Centre national de littérature.

Meltzl, H. von. [1877] 2009. Present Tasks of Comparative Literature. – D. Damrosch, N. Melas, M. Buthelezi, eds., *The Princeton Sourcebook in Comparative Literature. From the European Enlightenment to the Global Present.* Princeton and Oxford: Princeton University Press, 41–50.

[Noppeney, M]. 1907. Pour servir d'introduction. – *Floréal, Revue libre d'art et de littérature. Freie Rundschau für Kunst & Litteratur,* 1, 3–4.

Noppeney, M. 1957. *Si* Floréal *m'était conté … Histoire d'un cinquantenaire (fragments de mes mémoires).* Luxembourg: Editions S.E.L.F.

Pizer, J. 2000. Goethe's 'World Literature' Paradigm and Contemporary Cultural Globalization. – *Comparative Literature,* 52, 213–227.

Ramuz, C.-F. 1979. *La pensée remonte les fleuves.* Paris: Plon.

Tockert, J. 1948. Unsere Literatur um die Jahrhundertwende. – *Les Cahiers luxembourgeois,* 4, 247–255.

Vandemeulebroucke, K. 2008. The Periodical as a (Trans-)national Space : Nineteenth-Century Literary Periodicals in Belgium. – K.-M. Simonsen, J. Stougaard-Nielsen, eds., *World Literature, World Culture.* Aarhus: Aarhus University Press, 116–132.

Yildiz, Y. 2012. *Beyond the Mother Tongue. The Postmonolingual condition.* New York: Fordham University Press.

Kirjandus on peaaegu piiritult mitmekülgne vaimuala, mis pole käsitatav pelgalt kauniskunstina, poeetilis-esteetilise elamuse looja ja vahendajana, vaid see on täitnud ühiskondades nii esmajärgulist religioosset-müütilist-kosmoloogilist, juriidilist, filosoofilis-semiootilist, eetilist, pedagoogilist, sotsiaalset ja sotsioloogilist, esteetilist, psühholoogilist, ajalooteaduslik-kroonikalist-asitõenduslikku, teaduslikteoreetilist, poliitilis-ideoloogilist funktsiooni, nagu ka olnud põhitegur loomulike keelte püsimises elava, areneva ja teiseneva korpusena. Pole imekspandav, kui mitmesugustes ummikseisudes, millesse maailm ikka ja jälle on sattunud, usutakse seletajate ja väljapääsu osutajate rollis pigem ülemaailmse tuntuse pälvinud kirjanikke kui poliitikuid või erialateadlasi.

Jüri Talvet,
„Maailmakirjanduse kodustamise küsimusi"

Literature is an almost boundless spiritual-intellectual field, which in different historical epochs has not been acknowledged exclusively as beaux arts, belles lettres *– a source and a means of poetical-aesthetical experience –, but has had a primary function in the religious, mythical, cosmological, juridical, philosophic-semiotic, ethical, pedagogical, sociological, psychological, historical-documental, scientific-theoretical and political-ideological conscience of societies. Literature is, thus, an interdisciplinary field* par excellence, *by its very nature. It does not have the "innocence" of some other arts. It has been under a special watch and scrutiny of ideological and moral censors of all times.*

Jüri Talvet,
"The Reception of World Literature in Estonia.
Some Preliminary Remarks"

Montaigne et l'amour de la sagesse

DOROTHEA SCHOLL

Montaigne and the love of wisdom. The *Essais* of Montaigne can be considered as expressions of love of wisdom in an existential sense. Montaigne tries to communicate his love of wisdom by contrasting it with human knowledge in all kinds of field – theology, philosophy, literature, rhetoric, pedagogy, medicine, astrology and occult sciences. This article examines Montaigne's attitude with reference to in front of science(s), knowledge and wisdom by a close reading of the *Essais* and by taking into account the Renaissance discussion of these topics. Montaigne subjects the whole system of knowledge in ancient and modern arts and sciences to a critical examination. In order to disturb the doxa, he uses paradox and creates a critical and satirical encyclopaedia of the different sciences and knowledges of mankind. By using irony and paradox, Montaigne approaches the satirical anti-pedantic literature of his time and finds the appropriate way to communicate his love of wisdom.

Keywords: coincidence of contraries, common places, docta ignorantia, knowledge, memoria, microcosm-macrocosm, paradox sciences, wisdom

Grau, teurer Freund ist alle Theorie,
Und grün des Lebens goldner Baum
Goethe

The Tree of Knowledge is not that of Life
Lord Byron

Die Nacktheit der Frau ist weiser als die Lehre des Philosophen
La nudité de la femme est plus sage que l'enseignement du philosophe
Max Ernst

DOI: http://dx.doi.org/10.12697/IL.2015.S1.14

Introduction

Dans son essai « What is Ethical Literary Criticism ? Some Reflections on the Lady Called *Filosofia* in Dante Alighieri and the Following », Jüri Talvet nous propose une approche intéressante de l'éthique dans la littérature mondiale. À la différence des approches qui reposent exclusivement sur des théories et appliquent ces théories à la littérature, la sienne s'inspire directement de la littérature et de sa réflexion sur l'éthique, à commencer par Dante, qu'il considère tant sous l'aspect théorique que sous l'aspect créateur. Cette approche permet non seulement de mieux cerner la corrélation entre l'éthique et l'esthétique, mais aussi de découvrir des aspects importants – négligés par la théorie éthique actuelle –, comme la question de l'amour de la sagesse, au sens étymologique et éthique du terme « philosophie ».

Comme chez Boethius dans *De consolatio philosophiae* et comme chez Christine de Pizan dans *Le chemin de longue vertu*, la philosophie apparaît chez Dante comme une figure allégorique féminine qui entre en dialogue avec l'être humain et l'aide à mieux comprendre l'existence et la condition humaine et à mieux vivre la vie. Elle est une médiatrice entre le monde et l'au-delà, entre l'imperfection humaine et le *summum bonum*.

Jüri Talvet souligne le fait qu'à partir de la Renaissance italienne, la « donna filosofia » devient de plus en plus humaine et commence « to appear ever more openly embodying love as well as love for wisdom in its essential sensuality, having her origin in the senses and sensitivity » (Talvet 2014 : 12), et que l'aspect dialogique de la philosophie « is quite contrary to such "knowing", cognition, of which the ultimate goal is domination, possession, and subjugation, if not annihilation of the "other" – a monologue of which the vehicle is knowledge deprived of love » (Talvet 2014 : 13).

Les observations de Jüri Talvet nous ouvrent la possibilité d'approfondir l'éthique et l'esthétique de la littérature en portant justement notre attention sur l'aspect de l'amour de la sagesse en fonction de l'amour de soi-même et de l'Autre. Un auteur comme Montaigne se prête à merveille à un examen dans cette perspective nouvelle, d'autant plus que l'aspect de l'altérité est négligé dans les études qui s'intéressent surtout à la conception du « Moi » chez Montaigne et qui ne semblent pas tenir compte du fait que ce « Moi » se conçoit toujours en relation avec les autres – les Anciens, les personnes mortes ou vivantes, la famille, les domestiques, le roi, les savants, les lecteurs contemporains et la postérité.

Le « Moi » de Montaigne est un don à « l'Autre », et cette ouverture généreuse vers l'Autre par la sympathie, l'empathie, la compassion et la communication explique la familiarité que la plupart des lecteurs éprouvent à la lecture des *Essais* et d'autres textes de Montaigne. La « Société des Amis de Montaigne » ou les

Ten Letters to Montaigne (sous presse) de Jüri Talvet en témoignent (cf. aussi Talvet 2011 : 191–203). L'introspection de Montaigne n'est pas narcissique et elle n'est pas un but absolu, mais c'est par l'introspection que Montaigne arrive à la compréhension de l'Autre, car « Chaque homme porte en soi la forme entiere de l'humaine condition » (Montaigne 1962, III, II : 782).

Philosophie folâtre et plaidoyer pour une science gaie

« Il n'est desir plus naturel que le desir de connoissance », nous dit Montaigne dès la première phrase de son essai *De l'expérience* (III, XIII : 1041). « Nous essayons tous les moyens qui nous y peuvent mener », continue-t-il. Un de ces moyens, c'est l'essai, genre digressif et libre créé et cultivé par Montaigne dans son désir de connaissance. Dans l'espace silencieux de sa bibliothèque, l'essai est pour Montaigne le pendant du voyage et de la promenade dans le monde, et il a souvent recours à la métaphore du voyage et de la promenade pour exprimer la dynamique et l'incohérence capricieuse de son écriture : « il faut que j'aille de la plume comme des pieds » (III, IX : 969). L'essai permet à Montaigne de réunir les moyens de recherche de la connaissance : la réflexion, l'écriture, le voyage et l'expérience, la conversation en société et la lecture.

Au moyen de l'essai, Montaigne repense le savoir ou la sagesse des Anciens et des Modernes à travers son propre tempérament et à la lumière de son expérience. Et il constate qu'entre science et expérience il y a un gouffre incommensurable, et que les préceptes exigeants de la philosophie morale ne correspondent pas à la nature humaine et aux besoins de l'être humain.

> [...] la meilleure part des sciences qui sont en usage est hors de nostre usage [...] (I, XXVI : 158)

> A quoy faire ces pointes eslevées de la philosophie sur lesquelles aucun estre humain ne se peut rasseoir, et ces regles qui excedent nostre courage et nostre force ? (III, IX : 967)

Aux yeux de Montaigne, la philosophie est méconnue par ceux qui la transforment en un instrument de domination et qui la travestissent en une figure terrible et angoissante qui, au lieu de provoquer l'amour de la sagesse, suscite l'aversion et la peur.

> Je croy que ces ergotismes en sont cause, qui ont saisi ses avenues. On a grand tort de la peindre inaccessible aux enfans, et d'un visage renfroigné, sourcilleux

> et terrible. Qui me l'a masquée de ce faux visage, pasle et hideux ? Il n'est rien de plus gay, plus gaillard, plus enjoué, et à peu que je ne dise folastre. Elle ne nous presche que feste et bon temps. (I, XXVI : 159–160)

Bien longtemps avant Nietzsche qui l'apprécia beaucoup,[1] Montaigne plaide pour une science gaie et plaisante, une « philosophie folâtre » qui permet à l'homme de se libérer des contraintes autoritaires et doctrinales et de découvrir les bienfaits d'une convivialité agréable.

Élevé par des maîtres et des personnes qui ne lui parlaient qu'en latin et ennuyé par les sociétés savantes qui paraissent chercher et communiquer le savoir uniquement en vue de leur ambition et leur profit, fatigué aussi par les conventions et les contraintes des institutions scolaires et universitaires, Montaigne abandonne volontiers le langage savant de la théologie et de la science pour exprimer sa subjectivité.

> Qui sera en cherche de science, si la pesche où elle se loge : il n'est rien dequoy je face moins de profession. Ce sont icy mes fantasies, par lesquelles je ne tasche point à donner à connoistre les choses, mais moy [...]. (II, X : 387)

Cependant, se mêler d'écrire en français de *toutes* sortes de sujets ne va pas sans risques. Dans sa préface au Lecteur (1580), Montaigne, tout en prétendant se conformer aux bienséances, défend la liberté d'expression, et dans d'autres passages de caractère préfaciel, il se plaint d'être obligé de *masquer* son discours, de ne pas pouvoir dire tout : « [...] à l'adventure ay-je quelque obligation particuliere à ne dire qu'à demy, à dire confusément, à dire discordamment » (III, IX : 974). La confusion et la contradiction permettent de brouiller les pistes et de s'exprimer d'une manière décontractée, ce qui correspond à un ordre naturel du discours : « [...] et n'est par jugement que j'ay choisi cette sorte de parler scandaleux : c'est Nature qui l'a choisi pour moy » (III, V : 867).

Montaigne prend soin d'avertir ses lecteurs de ne pas considérer ses « fantaisies » et opinions – d'ailleurs changeantes – comme des doctrines ou des articles de foi :

[1] « Daß ein solcher Mensch geschrieben hat, dadurch ist wahrlich die Lust auf dieser Welt zu leben vermehrt worden. [...] Mit ihm würde ich es halten, wenn die Aufgabe gestellt wäre, es sich auf der Erde heimisch zu machen. » Nietzsche : 1976 : 211.

> Je propose les fantaisies humaines et miennes, simplement comme humaines fantaisies, et separement considerées, non comme arrestées et reglées par l'ordonnance celeste, incapables de doubte et d'altercation ; matiere d'opinion, non matiere de foy ; ce que je discours selon moy, non ce que je croy selon Dieu, comme les enfans proposent leurs essais ; instruisables, non instruisants ; d'une maniere laïque, non clericale, mais très-religieuse tousjours. (I, LVI : 308–309)

Malgré ces précautions, l'Église romaine, en 1676, mettra les *Essais* à l'index. Dès le début du XVIIe siècle, Montaigne est considéré comme un libertin dangereux, instable, subversif, impudique et corrupteur (cf. Millet 1995). En vain Marie de Gournay cherche-t-elle à défendre celui qu'elle appelle son « père adoptif »[2] contre ceux qu'elle appelle des « gros bonnets » (Gournay 1727 : 173), des pédants trop étroits pour comprendre et apprécier l'ampleur des matières traitées par Montaigne. Dans son apologie passionnée de Montaigne, cette fille, qui s'était éprise de Montaigne à la lecture des *Essais*,[3] distingue entre *la vraie et la fausse sagesse* dans l'attitude à l'égard des sciences. Pour elle, l'œuvre de Montaigne est « la quintessence de la vraye philosophie » (Gournay 1727 : 155) tandis que « Ces messieurs avec leurs belles animadversions ont volontiers cueilly l'une des branches de cette ignorance doctorale, laquelle mon père nous advertit en quelque lieu, que la science faict & engendre [...] » (Gournay 1727 :178).

L'ignorance doctorale

En effet, cette « ignorance doctorale », engendrée par la science, est un topos qui revient souvent dans les *Essais*. Elle est le contraire de la *docte ignorance*. Montaigne – qui se moque un peu du culte presque religieux que son père bien-aimé avait porté aux sciences et aux savants de toutes les disciplines – renverse l'ordre des valeurs en nous apprenant que *la science mène à l'ignorance*. Et il nous offre une explication :

---

2 « Lecteur, ayant à desirer de t'estre agreable, je me pare du beau titre de ceste alliance, puisque je n'ay point d'autre ornement : & n'ay pas tort de ne vouloir appeler que du nom paternel, celuy duquel tout ce que je puis avoir de bon en l'ame est issu. L'autre qui me mit au monde, & que mon desastre m'arracha dez l'enfance, tresbon pere, orné de vertus, & habile homme, auroit moins de jalousie de se voir un second, qu'il n'auroit de gloire de s'en voir un tel. » Gournay 1727 : 143.

3 « Je ne regarde plus qu'elle au monde. [...] Le jugement qu'elle fit des premiers *Essais*, et femme, et en ce siecle, et si jeune, et seule en son quartier, et la vehemence fameuse dont elle m'ayma et me desira long temps sur la seule estime qu'elle en print de moy, avant m'avoir veu, c'est un accident de très-digne consideration. » Montaigne 1962, II, XVII : 646.

> Les sciences traictent les choses trop finement, d'une mode trop artificielle et differente à la commune et naturelle. Mon page faict l'amour et l'entend. Lisez luy Leon Hébreu et Ficin : on parle de luy, de ses pensées et de ses actions, et si, il n'y entend rien. (III, V : 852)

Le page, expert en amour, ne comprend plus rien lorsqu'on le confronte aux théories abstraites de l'époque sur l'amour. Ces théories, même si elles expriment la vérité sur les sentiments et le comportement de l'amoureux, lui sont incompréhensibles. La science éloigne de la vie immédiate. De même, les commentaires savants travestissent aussi les auteurs et éloignent non seulement de la source originale, mais déforment cette source et empêchent un accès naturel et immédiat :

> Je ne recognois pas chez Aristote la plus part de mes mouvemens ordinaires ; on les a couverts et revestus d'une autre robbe pour l'usage de l'eschole. (III, V : 852)

L'eau de la source est ternie, sinon tarie. Les commentaires savants faussent ou singent la pensée des Anciens, surévaluée à tel point que l'autonomie, l'originalité et la créativité de l'individu semblent en voie de disparition : « nous ne faisons que nous entregloser » (III, XIII : 1045).

> Nous sçavons dire : « Cicero dit ainsi ; voilà les mœurs de Platon ; ce sont mots mesmes d'Aristote. » Mais nous, que disons nous nous mesmes ? que jugeons nous ? que faisons nous ? Autant en diroit bien un perroquet. (I, XXV : 136)

La science peut aliéner l'homme de la vie, et Montaigne se moque avec joie de ceux qui ont perdu la faculté d'appeler les choses par leur nom ou qui ont besoin de théories sophistiquées pour exprimer les choses simples :

> J'en cognoy à qui, quand je demande ce qu'il sçait, il me demande un livre pour me le montrer ; et n'oseroit me dire qu'il a le derriere galeux, s'il ne va sur le champ estudier en son lexicon, que c'est que galeux, et que c'est que derriere. (I, XXV : 136)

Cette aliénation par le savoir et par la science, ce divorce entre théorie et pratique, peuvent être anéantis uniquement lorsque le savoir est intériorisé et assimilé :

> [...] Que nous sert-il d'avoir la panse pleine de viande, si elle ne se digere ? si elle ne se transforme en nous ? si elle ne nous augmente et nous fortifie ? (I, XXV : 136)

Dès que le savoir est incorporé et digéré, il devient consubstantiel et porte bénéfice à la santé morale et intellectuelle. Montaigne se sert également de la métaphore de l'abeille – répandue à l'époque aussi chez les poètes de la Pléiade – pour rendre compréhensible le passage de l'inspiration à la création :

> Les abeilles pillotent deça delà les fleurs, mais elles en font après le miel, qui est tout leur ; ce n'est plus thin ny marjolaine [...]. (I, XXVI : 150–151)

Pour réconcilier la science et la vie et inciter à l'amour de la sagesse, il utilise aussi des métaphores suggestives tirées du langage amoureux : au lieu de battre les enfants et d'en faire « des asnes chargez de livres », il vaut mieux « d'allécher l'appétit et l'affection [...], il ne faut pas seulement loger [la science] chez soy, il la faut espouser » (I, XXVI : 177). La sagesse de Montaigne « has everything to do with how we ought to live : self-knowledge leads to self-acceptance, accurate self-expectations, and goodness toward the self and others » (Bloom 2004 : 148).

Montaigne blâme l'abstraction et la stérilité de la théorie, c'est pourquoi il l'investit d'images corporelles et organiques, voire érotiques, pour rendre la philosophie attirante et aimable – à l'instar de la littérature de la sagesse dans l'Ancien Testament, où la sagesse est personnifiée comme une fille sereine qui joue devant Dieu (*Proverbes* 8, 30). La poétique de Montaigne a été qualifiée de « véritable érotique [...] comme sa sagesse » (Demers 1973 : 321). L'amour de la sagesse comprend l'homme dans sa totalité ; tandis que la science peut conduire à l' « ignorance doctorale », qui se fait une fausse idée de l'homme dans sa condition naturelle. La sagesse peut certes être trouvée dans la littérature mondiale (cf. Bloom 2004), et Montaigne y cherche et y trouve des exemples propres à confirmer sa thèse d'une aliénation de la sagesse autonome par l'hypocrisie des savants, qui utilisent leur savoir pour donner des préceptes aux autres dont ils tirent profit :

> Antisthenes permet au sage d'aimer et faire à sa mode ce qu'il trouve estre opportun, sans s'attendre aux loix ; d'autant qu'il a meilleur advis qu'elles, et plus de cognoissance de la vertu. (III, IX : 968)

Savoir et sagesse en question

Dans son essai *Du Pédantisme*, Montaigne distingue entre savoir et sagesse.

> Quand bien nous pourrions estre sçavans du sçavoir d'autruy, au moins sages ne pouvons estre que de nostre propre sagesse. (I, XXV : 137)

Le savoir nous vient des autres, la sagesse nous vient de nous-mêmes, de notre expérience personnelle. Mais on ne devient pas forcément sage en vieillissant, car l'esprit humain n'est pas perfectible à l'infini, et chaque âge a sa force et ses faiblesses, de sorte que du point de vue éthique, il reste un point d'interrogation :

> [...] mon entendement ne va pas toujours en avant, il va à reculons aussi. [...] Nous nous corrigeons aussi sottement souvent comme nous corrigeons les autres. Mes premieres publications furent l'an mille cinq cens quatre vingts. Depuis d'un long traict de temps je suis envieilli, mais assagi je ne le suis pas d'un pouce. Moy à cette heure et moy tantost, sommes bien deux ; mais, quand meilleur ? (III, IX : 941)

Ainsi, Montaigne ne questionne pas seulement le savoir et la sagesse des autres, mais aussi son propre savoir et sa propre sagesse, et il l'exprime par sa devise : « Que sais-je ? » Ce point d'interrogation préserve contre toute arrogance intellectuelle : « Et n'est enfant des classes moyennes qui ne se puisse dire plus sçavant que moy, qui n'ay seulement pas dequoy l'examiner sur sa premiere leçon, au moins selon icelle » (I, XXVI : 144).

Docta ignorantia

> [...] ma maistresse forme [...] est l'ignorance. (I, L : 290)

> L'ignorance qui se sçait, qui se juge et qui se condamne, ce n'est pas une entiere ignorance : pour l'estre, il faut qu'elle s'ignore elle-mesme. (II, XII : 482)

L'homme, nous répète Montaigne, n'a ni le privilège d'être savant, ni celui d'être sage. « Si l'homme estoit sage, il prenderoit le vray pris de chaque chose selon qu'elle seroit la plus utile et propre à sa vie » (II, XII : 467). L'ignorance doctorale est le contraire de la *docte ignorance.* Il est assez étonnant de voir que l'influence de Nicolas de Cues – dont l'œuvre a été traduit tout au long du XVIe siècle – sur Montaigne n'a pas beaucoup retenu l'attention de la critique. Hans Blumenberg, qui a analysé l'idée de la *docte ignorance* chez plusieurs auteurs de la Renaissance, fait exception en rapprochant le Cusain de Montaigne. Selon Blumenberg, le concept de la *docta ignorantia* indique que l'individu commence à se libérer, à s'émanciper dans la mesure où l'expérience intérieure gagne en autonomie par rapport aux autorités.[4] Comme chez le Cusain, les idées de Montaigne sur

[4] Blumenberg 1989 : 58–67. Ajoutons que l'affirmation – et aussi l'affectation – de l'ignorance peut être considérée comme un topos de modestie et qu'elle est aussi une précaution à une époque où la liberté d'expression est menacée.

la *docte ignorance* remontent également à l'*Ecclésiaste*, à Socrate et à Pyrrhon, selon lequel il n'y a aucune vérité arrêtée.[5] Montaigne appelle Pyrrhon « celuy qui bastit de l'ignorance une si plaisante science » (II, XXIX : 683) et applique cette « plaisante science de l'ignorance » dans les *Essais*, en contrebalançant chaque jugement par un jugement contraire. L'importance de cette « plaisante science » pour Montaigne se manifeste dans l'emblème de la balance ainsi que dans la fameuse devise : « Que sais-je ? » et la formule *Ἐπέχω* – « Je suspends [mon jugement] ».[6] L'abstention de tout jugement arrêté est également un précepte biblique : « Ne jugez pas afin de ne pas être jugés, car vous serez jugés selon la mesure que vous-même appliquerez » (*Mt* 5, 38). Encore une fois, l'abstention du jugement préserve contre l'arrogance et la présomption : « C'est folie de rapporter le vray et le faux à nostre suffisance » (I, XXVII : 177–181), car les convictions et les croyances sont enfants des époques ; tout système de pensée peut s'écrouler, et se rappeler cette vérité universelle peut protéger contre la présomption et le dogmatisme scientifique et religieux.

> Que ne nous souvient-il combien nous sentons de contradiction en nostre jugement mesmes ? combien de choses nous servoyent hier d'articles de foy, qui nous sont fables aujourd'huy ? (I, XXVII : 181)

Ainsi, la sagesse authentique, comme le souligne Jean Starobinski, est celle qui reconnaît ses limites.

> L'un des pires défauts humains – la présomption, le "cuider" – consiste à se croire possesseur de la véritable image des choses et de la véritable figure de Dieu. Nous ne faisons alors que les forger à notre convenance. Nous construisons des simulacres. La sagesse authentique, elle, connaît des limites que l'esprit ne franchira jamais. (Starobinski 1993 : 159–160)

Une méthode de la science de l'ignorance : le paradoxe

Montaigne contrebalance les idées reçues et les lieux communs du savoir en contredisant la *doxa* par le paradoxe. Ainsi, la raison humaine n'est plus rationnelle,

---

5 Voir à ce sujet les travaux de Gierczynski 1967 et 1970 ; Baraz 1967 ; Russel 1975.

6 « On a trouvé dans les décombres du château de Montaigne un jeton en cuivre portant d'un côté les armes de Montaigne ceintes du collier de Saint-Michel, avec l'inscription *Michel seigneur de Montaigne*, et de l'autre une balance en équilibre avec la mention suivante : 42 (son âge), 1576 (l'année), *Ἐπέχω* "Je suspends [mon jugement]." » Maurice Rat, dans Montaigne 1962 :1593, n. 2.

mais chaotique et grotesque. Montaigne l'associe au rêve et à la confusion et va jusqu'à faire l'éloge de la folie :

> Nostre veillée est plus endormie que le dormir ; nostre sagesse, moins sage que la folie ; noz songes vallent mieux que noz discours. (II, XII : 551)

Au moyen du paradoxe, Montaigne renverse les idées établies par les sciences sur l'homme et le monde. Dans l'essai *De la ressemblance des enfans aux peres* (II, XXXVII), c'est la dissemblance qui est soulignée. Dans l'essai *De la vanité,* Montaigne affirme s'employer « à faire valoir la vanité mesme et l'asnerie » (III, IX : 974–975). Dans l'essai *Du Repentir,* il n'y a aucun repentir :

> Si j'avois à revivre, je revivrois comme j'ay vescu ; ny je ne pleins le passé, ny je ne crains l'advenir. (III, II : 794)

La philosophie se voit attaquée avec ses propres armes :

> [...] la Philosophie [...] a tant de visages et de variété, et a tant dict, que tous nos songes et resveries s'y trouvent. L'humaine phantaisie ne peut rien concevoir en bien et en mal qui n'y soit. *"Nihil tam absurde dici potest quod non dicatur ab aliquo philosophorum."* [*On ne peut rien dire de si absurde qui ne soit déjà dit par quelque philosophe.* Cicero, *De Divinatione,* II, 58)]. (II, XII : 528)

Quant à la philosophie morale, l'éthique, Montaigne – comme plus tard Jacques Esprit, La Rochefoucauld et Saint-Évremond –, dénonce la « fausseté des vertus humaines » et entreprend – par amour de la sagesse et avec joie – de *démasquer* les vertus, de sorte que non seulement celles-ci apparaissent comme des vices déguisées, mais que les vices deviennent des vertus déguisées :

> [...] Quoy qu'ils dient, en la vertu mesme, le dernier but de nostre visée, c'est la volupté. Il me plaist de battre leurs oreilles de ce mot qui leur est si fort à contrecœur. (I, XX : 80)
>
> La volupté est qualité peu ambitieuse : elle s'estime assez riche de soy sans y mesler le pris de la reputation, et s'ayme mieux à l'ombre. (III, V : 820)

Ainsi, toute la classification des vices et des vertus dans les sciences est ébranlée par l'amour de la sagesse. Les vices cachent des vertus et *vice versa.*

> Je voy que plusieurs vertus, comme la chasteté, sobrieté et temperance, peuvent arriver à nous par defaillance corporelle. (II, XI : 405)

En se jouant du savoir pédantesque,[7] Montaigne s'éloigne du discours sérieux et s'approche de la littérature des éloges paradoxaux dans la lignée d'Érasme (*Moriae encomium*, 1511) et d'Ortensio Lando (*Paradossi cioè, sententie fuora del commun parere*), traduits par Charles Estienne en 1553. En même temps, il fait observer qu'à la différence des plantes qui « s'estouffent de trop d'humeur » et des « lampes de trop d'huile [...], nostre ame s'eslargit d'autant plus qu'elle se remplit » (I, XXV : 133) et suppose que la véritable sagesse consiste dans un juste milieu entre la réflexion théorique et l'action pratique (*ibid.*).

La crise du savoir et des sciences : Agrippa et Montaigne

Toute la littérature cultivant la satire des pédants et le paradoxe à l'époque de Montaigne semble indiquer une crise du savoir et du statut des sciences et des autorités en général. Elle est l'expression de l'énorme prestige de l'érudition et elle en annonce le déclin. D'un côté, le paradoxe permet de se distancer des autorités ; de l'autre côté, il permet également de se sauver. Vers la fin du XVIe siècle, la recherche scientifique devient de plus en plus dangereuse, les cas de Giordano Bruno et de Galilée en témoignent ; on risque d'être traîné devant le tribunal de l'Inquisition – et le discours ambigu et paradoxal devient un moyen d'échapper à la censure.

Contredire les lieux communs du savoir établi, c'est également le procédé d'Agrippa de Nettesheim. Montaigne a pu connaître les écrits de Corneille Agrippa, qui avait publié en 1530 *De incertitudine et vanitate omnium scientiarum et artium atque excellentia verbi Dei declamatio invectiva*. Dans ce texte, écrit cinquante ans avant la première édition des *Essais* et plus de deux siècles avant le *Discours sur les sciences et les arts* de Jean-Jacques Rousseau, on trouve l'idée que la science est à l'origine de la corruption du genre humain (Agrippa 1993 : 20). Les sciences et les arts y sont soumis à l'examen et considérés comme incertains et vains, comme l'indique déjà le titre. Selon Agrippa, la curiosité de savoir a causé le péché originel

---

7 On peut rapprocher Montaigne du courant satirique de la littérature écrite contre les pédants (p. ex. Rabelais, Giordano Bruno, Della Casa, Giovan Battista Pino, Francesco Belo, Lomazzo). Montaigne connaissait les comédies italiennes avec leurs pédants (cf. I, XXV : 132). Au début du chapitre « Du Pedantisme », il cite Du Bellay : « Mais je hay par sur tout un sçavoir pedantesque » (I, XXV : 132) et Rabelais : « *magis magnos clericos non sunt magnos sapientes* » [Les plus grands clercs ne sont pas les plus sages] (I, XXV : 132 ; cf. 1460).

et a introduit tous les maux du monde (Agrippa 1993 : 20). « Tous les sages sont des fous », dit Agrippa (1993 : 257). « Rien ne savoir est la vie la plus heureuse » (Agrippa 1993 : 9), et le Christ n'a pas choisi des Savants pour répandre la vérité dans le monde, mais des gens simples, sans formation, des ignorants et des ânes (Agrippa 1993 : 258). Dans le dernier chapitre, Agrippa fait l'éloge de l'âne et le présente comme un animal profondément religieux dans sa sainte simplicité.[8]

Montaigne, qui se réfère aussi à l'idéal biblique de la simplicité (cf. II, XII : 477), a lui aussi recours à l'histoire du péché originel pour s'attaquer à la science. Mais la perspective de Montaigne est beaucoup plus nuancée. Aux yeux de Montaigne, ce ne sont pas les sciences en elles-mêmes qui sont vaines, mais c'est la prétention de savoir.

> [...] la premiere tentation qui vint à l'humaine nature de la part du diable, sa premiere poison, s'insinua en nous par les promesses qu'il nous fist de science et de cognoissance : "*Eritis sicut dii, scientes bonum et malum.*" Et les Sereines, pour piper Ulisse, en Homere, et l'attirer en leurs dangereux et ruineux laqs, lui offrent en don la science. La peste de l'homme, c'est l'opinion de sçavoir. Voilà pourquoy l'ignorance nous est tant recommandée par nostre religion comme piece propre à la creance et à l'obéissance. (II, XII : 467–468)

L'homme n'est pas le couronnement de la création, et on ne sait même pas s'il est supérieur aux animaux.

> [...] Comment cognoit il, par l'effort de son intelligence, les branles internes et secrets des animaux ? par quelle comparaison d'eux à nous conclud il la bestise qu'il leur attribue ? Quand je me jouë à ma chatte, qui sçait si elle passe son temps de moy plus que je ne fay d'elle ? (II, XII : 429–430)

> Nous ne sommes ny au dessus, ny au dessoubs du reste : tout ce qui est sous le Ciel, dit le sage [l'*Ecclésiaste*], court une loy et fortune pareille [...]. (II, XII : 436)

L'homme n'est pas supérieur aux animaux, le monde n'est pas à son service, il doit accepter la différence radicale et même la *coïncidence des contraires* :

> Il faut apprendre à souffrir ce qu'on ne peut eviter. Nostre vie est composée, comme l'armonie du monde, de choses contraires, aussi de divers tons, douz et

[8] Cette *asinitas* sera raillée par Giordano Bruno dans *Cabala del cavallo pegaseo* et *De gl'heroici furori*. Cf. Couliano 1984 : 262–263.

> aspres, aigus et plats, mols et graves. Le musicien qui n'en aymeroit que les uns, que voudroit-il dire ? Il faut qu'il s'en sçache servir en commun et les mesler. Et nous aussi, les biens et les maux, qui sont consubstantiels à nostre vie. Nostre estre ne peut sans ce meslange, et y est l'une bande non moins necessaire que l'autre. (III, XIII : 1068)

Qui suis-je ? Que sais-je ?

Pour ramener l'homme à la condition humaine, Montaigne cite avec plaisir et raillerie des exemples qui dévoilent la contradiction entre les discours et les actions des savants et présente les philosophes dans ce qu'ils ont d'humain et de trop humain :

> Je ne sçay quels livres, disoit la courtisane Lays, quelle sapience, quelle philosophie, mais ces gens là battent aussi souvant à ma porte que aucuns autres. (III, IX : 968)

> Je sçay bon gré à la garse Milesienne qui, voyant le philosophe Thales s'amuser continuellement à la contemplation de la voute celeste et tenir tousjours les yeux eslevez contremont, luy mit en son passage quelque chose à le faire broncher, pour l'advertir qu'il seroit temps d'amuser son pensement aux choses qui estoient dans les nues, quand il auroit prouveu à celles qui estoient à ses pieds. Elle luy conseilloit certes bien de regarder plustost à soy qu'au ciel. (II, XII : 519)

Regarder à soy, c'est ce qui mène à la connaissance du monde. Se connaître, c'est connaître le monde.[9] Une des 57 sentences peintes sur les bois des poutres du plafond, dans la bibliothèque de Montaigne, exprime l'idée d'un rapport entre microcosme et macrocosme[10] d'une manière encore plus claire :

> Orbis mangnæ vel parvæ earum rerum quas Deus tam multas fecit notitia in nobis est. *Eccl.* [Du grand et du petit monde des choses que Dieu a faites en si grand nombre, la notion est en nous]. (Montaigne 1962 : 1420)

Cependant, là encore, le savoir est mis en question : même si se connaître est la science suprême, c'est une entreprise aussi difficile que d'atteindre à la

9 Sur l'idée de l'auto-connaissance depuis Zoroastre et sa réception chez Montaigne, cf. Levi 1964 : 52–53.

10 Sur la tradition philosophique de cette idée, cf. Couliano 1984 : 160–162.

connaissance de Dieu. L'homme est un monstre, un prodige impénétrable, impossible à déchiffrer :

> Je n'ay veu monstre et miracle au monde plus exprès que moy-mesme. On s'apprivoise à toute estrangeté par l'usage et le temps ; mais plus je me hante et me connois, plus ma difformité m'estonne, moins je m'entens en moy. (III, XI : 1006)

L'homme n'est pas capable de se connaître et de connaître le sens des signes qui l'entourent.

> Ce que nous appellons monstres ne le sont pas à Dieu, qui voit en l'immensité de son ouvrage l'infinité des formes qu'il y a comprinses ; et est à croire que cette figure qui nous estonne, se rapporte et tient à quelque autre figure de mesme genre inconnu à l'homme. De sa toute sagesse il ne part rien que bon et commun et reglé ; mais nous n'en voyons pas l'assortiment et la relation. (II, XXX : 691)

Même si une *analogia entis* est présupposée, l'homme ne sait pas la déchiffrer, et ni le livre de la nature, ni la révélation des livres saints, ni les sciences occultes ou la divination ne peuvent accéder à un savoir qui justifierait la supériorité d'un homme ou d'une religion.[11]

Étant donné que les sciences sont une accumulation d'un savoir souvent erroné et plein de préjugés, l'homme doit vider sa mémoire pour arriver à la docte ignorance. « De vuyder et desmunir la memoire, est ce pas le vray et propre chemin à l'ignorance ? » (II, XII : 474) Par là, Montaigne – qui affirme aussi à plusieurs reprises que la mémoire lui fait défaut – s'attaque à la culture de la

[11] « En récusant l'idée de la royauté de l'homme, en refusant par là un thème nécessaire à la pensée analogique, en rejetant toute croyance en une divination, Montaigne dérange profondément cette vision de l'homme et de la nature. La vérité, pour Montaigne, n'est plus une vérité dévoilée ; si l'homme du monde a sa raison, Dieu seul la connaît. Autrement dit, la science de l'homme n'est pas le reflet, aussi dégradé que l'on voudra, de la science de Dieu : il faut poser, par révérence pour Dieu, que ce que nous appelons monstre ne l'est pas pour lui, mais l'homme n'a aucun moyen de participer au savoir de celui de qui "ne part rien que de bon et commun et réglé". Il doit seulement se convaincre que, n'étant qu'un point dans l'univers, non un centre, et n'ayant aucun privilège spécial, il ne lui appartient pas de décider du possible et de l'impossible ; ce que Pascal a appelé la crédulité de Montaigne ne consiste pas à croire que tout est possible, mais à dénier à l'esprit humain la capacité de déterminer les conditions du possible et de l'impossible. » Céard 1996 : 493.

mémoire qui à l'époque de la Renaissance jouit d'un énorme prestige scientifique (cf. Bolzoni/Corsi 1992 ; Yates 1994 ; Bolzoni 1995).

Conclusion

Afin de pouvoir propager sa conviction de l'ignorance universelle en tant que moyen régulateur qui aide à respecter l'Autre et la religion de l'Autre, Montaigne, par amour de la sagesse, a besoin de révéler la problématique de tout savoir acquis et de remettre en cause ce savoir. Pour ce faire, il met ce prétendu savoir en scène, le donne en spectacle, en fait une matière grotesque et comique, et s'en moque.

> Nos folies ne me font pas rire, ce sont nos sapiences. (III, III : 801)

L'homme, dans le théâtre du monde mis en scène par un Dieu caché, est un personnage ridicule.

> [...] toy, qui embrasses l'univers ; tu es le scrutateur sans connoissance, le magistrat sans jurisdiction et, après tout, le badin de la farce. (III, IX : 980)

En accord avec l'idée issue de la théologie négative que Dieu est caché et que l'homme ne peut pas prétendre à la connaissance, Montaigne propose une encyclopédie négative du savoir de son époque en mettant en question la *doxa* au moyen du paradoxe. Le paradoxe est la forme qui reflète l'impénétrabilité du monde. Le paradoxe, c'est aussi l'arme contre le préjugé et le cliché, que ce soit le cliché dans la pensée du peuple ou le cliché dans la pensée des sociétés savantes.

> L'obstination et ardeur d'opinion est la plus seure preuve de bestise. (III, VIII : 913)

> On couche volontiers le sens des escris d'autrui à la faveur des opinions qu'on a prejugées en soi ; et un atheïste se flate à ramener tous autheurs à l'atheïsme, infectant de son propre venin la matiere innocente. (II, XII : 425)

Avant Francis Bacon, Flaubert et Ionesco, Montaigne réfléchit sur les préjugés, les idoles et les idées reçues, et soumet les sciences et le savoir à une mise en question et une critique des idéologies et des idoles. Se libérer des préjugés est difficile sinon impossible, car même la contradiction est vanité : le seul être qui aux yeux de Montaigne ne peut pas se contredire et ne pas être contredit, c'est Dieu.

Pourtant, afin de mettre en question le prétendu savoir et les préjugés humains, la contradiction est un mal nécessaire, et donnons, pour terminer, encore une fois la parole à Montaigne – dont l'agressivité émotionnelle et verbale s'explique uniquement par son altruisme et son amour de la sagesse.

> Le moyen que je prens pour rabatre leur frenaisie et qui me semble le plus propre, c'est de froisser et fouler aux pieds l'orgueil et humaine fierté ; de leur faire sentir l'inanité, la vanité et la deneantise de l'homme ; leur arracher des points les chetives armes de leur raison ; leur faire baisser la teste et mordre la terre soubs l'authorité et reverance de la majesté divine. C'est à elle seule qu'apartient la science et la sapience ; elle seule qui peut estimer de soy quelque chose, et à qui nous desrobons ce que nous nous contons et ce que nous nous prisons. [...] L'intelligence est en tous les Dieux, dict Platon, et en fort peu d'hommes. (II, XII, p. 426)

Dorothea Scholl
dscholl@romanistik.uni-kiel.de
Romanisches Seminar der Universität Kiel
Leibnizstr. 10
D-24098 Kiel
DEUTSCHLAND / GERMANY

Bibliographie

Agrippa von Nettesheim, H. C. 1993. *Über die Fragwürdigkeit, ja Nichtigkeit der Wissenschaften, Künste und Gewerbe* [*De incertitudine et vanitate scientiarum*, 1530]. Mit einem Nachwort hrsg. von Siegfried Wollgast. Übers. und mit Anm. vers. von Gerhard Güpner. Berlin : Akademie-Verlag.

Baraz, M. 1967. « Sur la notion d'inscience chez Montaigne », dans Coll., *De Ronsard à Breton. Hommages à Marcel Raymond*. Paris : Corti, 42–50.

Bloom, H. 2004. *Where Shall Wisdom Be Found ?* New York : Riverhead Books.

Blumenberg, H. 1989. *Die Lesbarkeit der Welt*. Frankfurt/Main : Suhrkamp.

Bolzoni, L. / Corsi, P. 1992. *La Cultura della Memoria*. Bologna : Il Mulino.

Bolzoni, L. 1995. *La stanza della memoria. Modelli letterari e iconografici nell'età della stampa*. Torino : Einaudi.

Céard, J. 1996. *La Nature et les prodiges. L'insolite au XVIe siècle*, Genève : Droz.

Couliano, I. P. 1984. *Éros et magie à la Renaissance – 1484*. Avec une préface de Mircea Eliade. Paris : Flammarion.

Demers, J. 1973. « La "sagesse" de Montaigne : une poétique », dans : *Études françaises*, vol. 9, n° 4, 303–321.

Gierczynski, Z. 1967. « La science de l'ignorance de Montaigne », dans *Roczniki Humanistyczne (Annales des lettres et sciences humaines)* XV, 3, 5–85.

Gierczynski, Z. 1970. *Le "Que sais-je ?" de Montaigne. Interprétation de l'"Apologie" de Raymond de Sebond*, Lublin : Annales des Lettres et Sciences humaines de l'Université catholique de Lublin, t. XVIII.

Gournay, M. 1727. « Préface sur les *Essais* de Michel, Seigneur de Montaigne, par sa fille d'alliance [1635] », dans *Essais de Michel de Montaigne*, éd. par Pierre Coste, t. V., La Haye : P. Gosse et J. Neaulme, 139–191.

Levi, A. 1964. *French Moralists: The Theory of Passions, 1585–1649*. Oxford : Clarendon.

Millet, O. 1995. *La première réception des* Essais *de Montaigne (1580–1640)*. Paris : Champion.

Montaigne, M. 1962. *Œuvres complètes*. Textes établis par Albert Thibaudet et Maurice Rat. Introduction et notes par Maurice Rat, Paris : Gallimard (Bibliothèque de la Pléiade).

Nietzsche, F. 1976. *Unzeitgemäße Betrachtungen [Drittes Stück. Schopenhauer als Erzieher», 1873–1876]*, Stuttgart : Kröner.

Russel, D. 1975. « On Montaigne's Device », dans *Studi Francesi* XIX, 84–88.

Starobinski, J. 1993. *Montaigne en mouvement*. Paris : Gallimard.

Talvet, J. 2011. « Can Philosophy Do Without Morals ? Creative Humanism in the European Renaissance and the Spanish Baroque », dans V. Kapp / D. Scholl, *Literatur und Moral*. Berlin : Duncker & Humblot, 191–203.

Talvet, J. 2014. « What is Ethical Literary Criticism ? Some Reflections on the Lady Called *Filosofia* in Dante Alighieri and the Following », dans *Interlitteraria* 19/1 : *National Literatures and Comparative Literary Research*, 7–21.

Yates, F. A. 1994. *Gedächtnis und Erinnern. Mnemonik von Aristoteles bis Shakespeare*. Berlin : Akademie Verlag.

Chinese Ibsenism: A Theoretical Reflection on Contestation and Reception[1]

KWOK-KAN TAM

Abstract. This article reviews how Ibsen has been received in China since the beginning of 1900s and the role Ibsen has played in the Chinese quest for a modern culture based on the concept of a person as an individual and a self. Cultural reinvention involving the state, society and the self is the process with which the Chinese has experimented alongside the reception of Ibsen. For this reason, the Chinese has always been interested in the implications of Ibsenism for the social revolution and for a redefinition of self-identity. When it is received together with other isms, such as Marxism and Feminism, Ibsenism is inevitably given new dimensions of interpretation that form a relation of contestation. Chinese Ibsenism is thus a process of reinvention and contestation among the diverse and even conflicting ideologies that take root in China's cultural transformation. As one of the sites of ideological contestations in modern China, the Chinese theatre is particularly noted for its experiments with new forms of Ibsen productions and new ways to reinterpret Ibsenism.

Keywords: Chinese Ibsenism, Marxism, Feminism, ideology, theatre, the self

The reception of Ibsen in China began in the early 1900s when the Chinese civilisation was at the historical juncture of transformation from a dynastic state to a modern democratic state and from the Confucian social–moral order to a modern republican culture. To the Chinese intellectuals of that time, to be modern meant to be Western, and to be anti Confucian meant to be freed from the bondage of family, clan and state. Hence, the reception of Ibsen in China has long been part of the Chinese pursuit of cultural change, at the heart of which is a reconceptualisation of the self when it is freed because it was Ibsen who brought up the concept of individualism.

Right from the beginning in the 1900s, Chinese critics, as exemplified by Lu Xun, considered Ibsen mainly a social thinker and his plays were vehicles

[1] The research carried out in this article was partially funded by a grant from the Research Grants Council of the Hong Kong Special Administrative Region, China (UGC/FDS16/H11/15).

DOI: http://dx.doi.org/10.12697/IL.2015.S1.15

to bring out messages of social revolution. Since then, Ibsen has remained the only Western dramatist who has continued to be so powerfully influential, both artistically and politically, in China ever since his initial reception in the 1900s. However, there have been various attempts to sinicise Ibsen and his ideas for adoption in the Chinese context. Chinese Ibsenism refers to such attempts that intend to make Ibsen's ideas more readily applicable to the social changes in China. Chinese Ibsenism, first expounded by the Americanised liberalist Hu Shi in 1918 and later reinterpreted by the socialists in the 1930s and 1950s, has undergone a process of localisation for almost a century. It has inherited from Bernard Shaw's Ibsenism in its emphasis on the social ideas in Ibsen's drama, but also deviated from it in that Chinese Ibsenists have tended to re-brand Ibsenism as a Chinese moral authority for debates over the socio-political dimensions of life.

However, Ibsen is much more than a philosopher. His ideas about women, society and religion are presented through his plays. Theoretical treatises on Ibsenism have to come to grips with the literary analysis of his plays and the advocacy of his iconoclastic ideas have to be presented through stage images. Staging *A Doll's House* presented a problem to the Chinese theatre at the beginning of the twentieth century, as China at that time did not have a theatre or performance style close to modern Western drama, which has dialogue as the main form of verbal interaction between the characters. Figuring a woman who claimed to have an individual self-identity, other than that as subordinate to men, was unfathomable to the Chinese actresses and audiences alike. But why did Ibsen, particularly his play *A Doll's House*, later become so popular in China and how come he could have achieved such an important role as the major Western source for the formation of modern Chinese drama?

Ibsen and Cultural Change in China

Ibsen was introduced to China when the nation was undergoing large-scale cultural, political and social turmoil as a result of the collapse of the traditional dynastic political system based on Confucian ideology, through which the traditional Chinese defined themselves as role-subjects within the network of state–family–self relations. It was in this state of ideological change with the Chinese self-identity at stake that Ibsen was considered a soul-healing remedy by the two Chinese thinkers and writers Lu Xun (1908) and Hu Shi (1918). Hence, right at the beginning the Chinese were deeply interested in what Ibsenism could offer to China, that is, in the ideological and social implications of his iconoclastic ideas, which the Chinese believed to be one of the possible remedies that could save China from its cultural and moral degradation. Ibsenism was one of the isms, amongst Darwinism, Marxism, Liberalism and Pragmatism, that were brought to China by the Western or Japanese-educated Chinese, many of whom aspired to be intellectual leaders of the new generation.

With so many isms brought from the West by the newly awakened intellectuals, China experimented with various paradigms in re-defining the self, particularly in contradistinction to traditional familial collectivism. Ibsen's idea of individualism exemplified in Nora's leaving home, abandoning her husband and her children, and most importantly shattering her old self in search of a new identity, provided a new model of self-definition for the Chinese, male and female alike. That a woman could have her own self was a new thing in China at the beginning of the twentieth century when womanhood was defined as an extension of man. A woman's aspirations had to be realised through the achievements made by her husband or son.

What *A Doll's House* has presented is not simply ideas of leaving things behind in an irresponsible manner and abandoning a life of financial certainty, but more importantly that a person's self can be re-invented and re-fashioned. The awakened Nora is an image of a woman who can have a self and whose identity is becoming something other than fixed, and is re-definable on the basis of personal choice. Such a new concept of the self liberated the Chinese of the early twentieth century from the prison house of Confucian discourse, in which the self had been regarded as a moral unit institutionalised in the social fabric of self–other relations (Tam 1997: 991–992; Tam 2006b: 295–298). The emergence of the new self in the image of Nora has been referred to as the "New Woman" in the cultural history of modern China. When the traditional dynastic political structure collapsed in China a hundred years ago, intellectuals found that China urgently needed to have a new linguistic means to express the new sensibility in life. The theatre became this new means of expression, and Nora its spokesperson.

Articulation of Social Messages

Leaving home meant to the Chinese in the early twentieth century, first of all, the acquisition of a new physical space for self-autonomy. Nora's abandoning the family became abandoning the parental family for the Chinese in period of the 1920s–1940s, which meant, furthermore, freeing oneself from familial bondage. Familial bondage is not one's choice, but building up one's social relations is. Fleeing from the family has another more significant level of meaning for the Chinese because building up one's social relations according to one's choice is a process of socialisation. When a new generation of Chinese in the 1920s–1940s was inspired by this idea of building up their social relations by abandoning the parental family, what occurred in China was a great social movement effecting a change in class structure with the emergence of numerous floating and wandering youths looking for shelter and organising themselves into factions. This change in social structure created a new social space for the young Chinese in which to experiment with different options of self-realisation. As portrayed in the many novels and short stories by modern Chinese writers such as Mao Dun and Zhang Tianyi, Nora had become a model of behaviour for the new woman. In Mao Dun's short story "Creation" (Chuangzao 1926) and novel *Rainbow* (Hong 1934), there is depiction of young women using Nora as a model in their search for a new self by fleeing home. Zhang Tianyi's story "After Leaving Home" (Chuzou yihou 1936) provides a full account of how it became a fad for a new generation of Chinese women to leave home to search for autonomy. Seen in this light, almost all the stage productions of Ibsen's major plays, including *A Doll's House* and *Ghosts*, performed the ideological function of inciting women to re-invent themselves by shattering the bondage of home and dependence on men. Ibsen's plays had in effect become scripts for social rebellion. They were instructing young people by providing agendas for leaving home. When thousands of young people left home as a result of response to Ibsen's call for independence, it become a social movement and a political event, not simply an individual's pursuit for freedom.

The emergence of a nationwide phenomenon of young Chinese women seeking autonomy in between the 1920s and 1940s can be attributed to the rising popularity of Ibsen, whose influence was propagated by his Chinese followers, particularly intellectuals such as Hu Shi. These intellectuals promoted Ibsenism as a new discourse of self-definition in an attempt to break away from the repression of social institutions. The Chinese reception of Ibsen, with a great emphasis on his ideas of iconoclasm, can thus be seen in the light of contemporary theories of language and gender performativity. As J. L. Austin has argued, language has a discursive function and can make people perform certain roles. Extending this theory to gender formation, Judith Butler points out that gender can be formed as a result of reiterated acting (Butler 1990). In the context of the global reception of Ibsen, such ideas of gender performativity are substantiated by Julie Holledge's study of how actresses from different cultures and ages have been influenced by Ibsen's Nora in their later choices in life (Holledge 2010). In other words, it is ideology that can effect change in people's identities through iterations of language. Ibsen's ideas of individualism, portrayed through the image of Nora, have served a great ideological function in transforming women's view of themselves in China in the last one hundred years.

The last scene when Nora stands up and confronts Helmer has been of particular interest to the Chinese critics and theatregoers since the 1920s, as the scene conveys several important notions of change in gender identity. Nora's confrontation with Helmer stands for, first of all, a reversal of power in which a woman assumes a new power position and asks Helmer to listen to her. This is the time a woman becomes a subject of her own, rather than that of a man. When Nora can speak to Helmer in a commanding voice, she not only asserts herself, but also has her 'own' voice, which is not Helmer's or her father's. This inner voice of the new woman is crucial to her self-definition. Whether leaving home to become independent or to join a social group, a woman does not have her own identity if she does not have this inner voice, this self-articulation. Seen in this way, almost all Chinese literary or theatrical portrayals of women since the 1910s are attempts to construct this inner voice of self-redefinition.

In almost all Chinese stage adaptations of *A Doll's House*, how the last scene should be presented has become not only an exercise in theatre techniques, but also a test of the director's critical strategy in how to present an awakened woman who needs to air her voice and assert a self and her new identity. In the history of the Chinese reception of Ibsen, the stage renderings of the play exhibit a close interplay between identity politics and the dominant discourses of Chinese theatre. Adaptations of *A Doll's House* betray the ideological changes behind the theatre styles that have taken place in China over the last century, namely Social Realism, Class Discourse, National Allegory and Postmodernist Experimentations.

Chinese Reinterpretations of Ibsenism

The emergence of the social realistic discourse in modern Chinese theatre was attributed to a special issue on Ibsen that appeared in the influential intellectual journal *New Youth* (Xin qingnian) in 1918. In this issue, Hu Shi wrote a long essay expounding on what Ibsenism was, in which he defined it as an artistic way of unravelling the evils hidden in social institutions. He specifically highlighted the artistic vision of Rubek discussed in Ibsen's *When We Dead Awaken* as a literary method derived from "social realism", as he said, "This is the Ibsen's method. The portrayal of the girl unstained by life is idealised literature, while that of people with the faces of beasts beneath the human masks is realistic literature. Ibsen's works and his philosophy can be summarized in the word of Realism" (Hu Shi 1918: 489). Instead of taking social realism to refer to a literary style, Hu Shi considered it an artistic means of presenting the evils in social reality and he further believed that realism in art and literature had a role to play in critiquing social reality.

For a quarter of a century from the 1920s, *A Doll's House* served as a model play for modern Chinese playwriting. Most Chinese dramatists and theatre practitioners relied on Hu Shi's idea of social realism as guiding principles in their creative work, as well as in stage productions. It was in this tradition that *A Doll's House* was first adapted for stage performance in Beijing (Peking) in May 1923. This performance was given by students at the Peking Normal College for Women, which emphasised the right of a woman to rebel against the patriarchal authority represented by Helmer. The audiences' responses to the play were mixed. Some found themselves unable to accept the final ending in which Nora confronts Helmer, while others pitied Nora for being ill-treated by Helmer. Presented on the stage was a woman who was resolute in her rebellion against the authority of her husband. Although considered by theatre critics as a faithful production, many audiences left the theatre halfway through the performance. The audiences, who were female student teachers, found it hard to accept a woman who borrows money without the husband's knowledge and endorsement. The rebellious Nora in confronting her husband and abandoning her children was equally unconvincing and unacceptable. Apparently *A Doll's House* was adapted into a Chinese melodrama to arouse emotions in audiences. It was reported in theatre reviews that some audiences wept when they saw Nora caught in her anxieties and fears.

When considered together with the famous speech Lu Xun made about *A Doll's House* in the Peking Normal College for Women in the same year, it is not difficult to understand why the performance was not well received. In his speech, Lu Xun advised students at the College to be cautious about the idea of leaving home in their pursuit of autonomy because Chinese society at that time was not ready for women's financial independence. Why would Lu Xun need to remind the female student teachers that they had to be mindful of the difficulties they would face if they decided to leave home for an autonomous life? Obviously there was a strong appeal for women to leave home in the 1920s to join the revolution or to rebel against the family. *A Doll's House* was performed during such a period of social turmoil in China for the purpose of presenting a revolutionary female figure. The social message of the production was clearly to address the hardships of women in China by making a comparison with Nora, as one of the critics said: "It is not only Nora who is suffering from her misery, all women are if they do not follow the example of Nora in rebelling against social oppression" (Fang Xin 1923: 4). As pointed out by many critics, one of the purposes of staging *A Doll's House* was to re-educate audiences (Tam 1984: 165–167) and to induce them to social actions.

Other adaptations of *A Doll's House* in China in the 1920s included a performance by the 26 Drama Society in 1924, given at the YWCA in Peking on 19 December 1924. The production again was meant to incite women to leave home and join the revolution. Helmer became a Chinese warlord in the adaptation and was presented as an oppressive male figure on the stage. Hence, Nora's confrontation with Helmer gave audiences the extra message that revolting against family oppression was inseparable from fighting against political repression. Staging *A Doll's House* in China was not just an exercise in the theatre, but more importantly a social and political phenomenon that was dominated by a social realist discourse. With *A Doll's House* being considered a social problem play, the discourse served the ideological function of resisting the traditional Confucian discourse of collectivism in which women were denied individual self-identity. The story of Wang Ping, a teacher who was fired by her school for having taken part in the performance of *A Doll's House* in Nanjing, is a good example to illustrate the fact that advocating the woman's right to leave home was a strategy to resist patriarchal as well as political repression in the 1920s and 1930s.[2]

Chinese Socialist Ibsenism

A new phase in the staging of *A Doll's House* occurred in the 1930s when issue of class became a new political discourse in the Chinese communists' advocacy for a new personal identity. In the 1930s, Shanghai gradually became the centre for stage experimentations with Ibsen's plays. Productions of *A Doll's House* in Shanghai were attempts to understand a woman who had class awareness. With the full text translated by Ouyang Yuqian and the gradual founding of a directorial system by Hong Shen,[3] it had now become much easier to control and thematise a production. The numerous productions of *A Doll's House* in Shanghai in 1934 and 1935 were meant to establish a model for presenting a class-conscious Nora. The year 1935 even marked the so-called "Year of Nora", in which there were many productions of *A Doll's House* in Shanghai as well as in other cities.

A notable phenomenon relating to the social debates of the 1920s and 1930s was the various experiments in the construction of not only a modern female figure who has a concept of self, but also a working class model of the female self. As the most oppressed in traditional society, women had very low status under the patriarchal authority of religion, family and state in traditional

2 For details of the incident, see Kwok-kan Tam 1984.

3 Hong Shen was the first Chinese person trained in George Baker's Drama Workshop at Harvard in the early 1920s and expressed his desire to become China's Ibsen when he returned to China. He is known to be the first person to set up a directorial system in China. For more details, please refer to Kwok-kan Tam 1984. In this thesis, there is a full chapter dealing with stage adaptations of Ibsen's drama in China up to the 1980s.

China. Reflecting the urgency of the need to extend freedom of education to Chinese women, many influential journals in the 1920s and 1930s devoted special issues to the discussion of the injustice done to women. In addition, more than ten magazines were dedicated to creating a new consciousness among Chinese women. The most famous of these were *Women's Bell* (Nüxing zong), *Women's Magazine* (Funü zazhi), *Women's Review* (Funü pinglun) and *Women's Life* (Funü shenghuo), in which there were articles on the evils of foot binding and inequality between sexes. These feminist journals were very important tools for Chinese women to learn what was happening to their counterparts in the West as there were many articles and translations of feminist literature, particularly the plays of Ibsen and Bernard Shaw.

Published in the Chinese journals in the 1920s and 1930s were innumerable articles and translations dealing with Ibsen and the theme of women's emancipation in his plays, such as Li Zhiye's "The Woman Issue in Ibsen's Plays" (Yibusheng xiju zhong de funü wenti), which appeared in *Women's Magazine* in December 1924, and Jin Zhonghua's "Women's Emancipation in Modern Times as Reflected in Literature" (Jinshi funü jiefnag yundong zai wenxue shang de fanying), which was published in the same journal in July 1931. In the midst of this feminist debate, Nora became a model of the new woman to the Chinese, whose qualities of individualism were de-emphasised in pursuit of a class-aware self. From the 1920s to the 1930s there was a gradual shift in social debates on women's rights from an interest in individualism to an interest in class consciousness. A public sphere debating on female emancipation was formed in Shanghai in the 1930s on the joint forces of newspaper, journals, magazine and the theatre.

In the new productions of *A Doll's House*, Nora was represented as a working-class woman awakened to her role in class struggle. The best known of these experiments was the production by the Shanghai Amateur Drama Society in June 1934, in which Lan Ping (stage name of Jiang Qing, who later went to Yan'an and married Mao Zedong) played the role of Nora. She claimed that she interpreted Nora as a newly awakened woman who left her family to join other women in the cause of changing the world. This production of *A Doll's House* presented a shocking event to the Shanghai audience in 1934. It was the spectacularly realistic effect that distinguished the production from all previous versions, which were in one way or another tinted by the colours of traditional operatic performance. In this production, Director Zhang Min for the first time introduced the Stanislavsky Method to the Chinese theatre. Zhao Dan, the actor who played Helmer, remembered how they were at first influenced by the concepts of class analysis practised and subjected the roles to critical examination. Role analysis brought about a repudiation of Helmer and he was thus "portrayed with the purpose of revealing his bourgeois nature".[4] The result was that the performance became a critique of Helmer and the class values he represented. Such an analysis, however, made the performance a mechanical illustration of Marxist class theory. Through practice, the actors and the director Zhang Min found that a good performance should be different from a political sermon. They began to study Stanislavsky and learned how to be immersed in their roles and finally overcame any mechanical and doctrinal interpretation of the play (Figure 1).

Marked by its realistic production style, the performance was meant to convey a socio-political message. The production team claimed that in Europe people had nearly forgotten the name Nora, for they had produced numerous Noras, not only on the stage but also in real life, and they even had greater and more individualistic personalities than Nora. In China, Nora was still an unusual name because there were not many real Noras. This was the reason why they hoped that their presentation of *A Doll's House* would serve as a reminder for Chinese women that they still lived in the age of Nora (Zhao Dan 1980: 27–28). The performance was regarded by the production team not as entertainment but as an educational experience for both the actors and the audience.

Ibsenism Beyond Socialism

Since its adoption in China, Ibsenism has undergone various stages of transformation. Ibsen was introduced to China in the 1910s when the nation was undergoing large-scale cultural, political and social turmoil. It was in this state of ideological change with Chinese self-identity at stake that Ibsenism became popularly known among the May 4th intellectuals as a soul healing remedy because of Ibsen's advocacy of individualism. The May 4th intellectual leader Hu Shi borrowed the major concepts of Ibsenism from Bernard Shaw, which were meant to be a critique of social hypocrisy in 19th-century British society. Hu Shi reinterpreted them for a battle of anti-hypocrisy and anti-Confucianism in China. Under Hu Shi's influence, early stage productions of Ibsen's works focused mainly on concepts of individualist self-identity, self-freedom, and anti-social hypocrisy.

With the rise of socialist ideas in China since the 1930s, class analysis began to be adopted as a method to interpret dramatic character's motives. Ibsenism was redefined as a class ideology that the Chinese Marxists saw as a way of

4 According to Zhao Dan (1980, p. 27), actors had to study Marxist theory of class and the Stanislavsky Method before they rehearsed A Doll's House.

redefining the self in relation to class and state at a time when China was politically divided in party politics and class politics and culturally caught in a crossroads between individualism and collectivism. Numerous versions of Ibsen's *A Doll's House* were staged for a new experimentation with the concept of class in the redefinition of an individual. This aspect of Ibsenism persisted into the 1960s with the individual characterised as a product of class consciousness. In this context, Ibsen's Nora and other characters were then seen in the new light of socialist characterisation.

Since the opening up of China in the 1980s, Ibsenism, however, has been given new interpretations. Experiments with gender and feminist ideas can be found in the latest stage productions of *A Doll's House*. Ibsen's other plays that deal with the concept of self and self-identity, such as *Peer Gynt, Ghosts* and *The Master Builder,* were added to the Chinese theatre repertoire and became new sites of contestation in representing complexities of the self with psychical depths. Chinese Ibsenisms are actually the result of contested ideologies involving complex relations between the self, gender, class, state, culture and stage representations. *Peer Gynt, An Enemy of the People, A Doll's House, Ghosts, The Lady from the Sea, Hedda Gabler, The Wild Duck* and *The Master Builder* have become sites of experimentation with contested ideologies (Figure 2).

Even today dramatists in China still experiment with various possibilities in (re)presenting Ibsen in postmodernist forms. Why has Ibsen, particularly his play *A Doll's House,* become so popular in China, and how has Ibsen achieved such an important status as one of the major Western sources for the reinvention of the modern Chinese self, particularly in terms of gender and social role? To answer these questions and more, Ibsenism, as exhibited in the Chinese stage adaptations, has to be re-examined in the light of performance discourse, which inevitably has to deal with cultural politics in the Chinese reception of foreign drama, the interaction between Western culture and Chinese politics, as well as how the theatre serves as a means to the construction of identity. It has to bring to light the performance discourse at work behind social framing in Chinese experiments with Ibsen, which are always audience targeted and purpose-designed with ideological underpinnings.

Figure 1. Lan Ping playing Nora with Zhao Dan playing Helmer in *A Doll's House,* Shanghai Amateur Drama Society, 1934.

Figure 2. A Doll's House, Beijing, 2010

Figure 3. An Enemy of the People, directed by in Zhaohua, Beijing, 2014

Since China's opening up in the 1980s, changes have occurred in almost all spheres of cultural production with Chinese Marxist class ideology being challenged by Western liberalism, and modern cultural practices by traditional aesthetic considerations. Various critical theories, such as neo-Marxism, psychoanalysis, post-structuralism, deconstruction and feminism have gained grounds in China's cultural arena, making cultural production as well as artistic practices much contested and multifarious. One of the sites of contestation can be found in theatre productions, particularly in the figuring of the self and gender. Having been revisited and reimagined beyond its previous function as state ideological apparatus, Ibsenism has now become a mode of inquiry problematising the self and its reinvention. New paradigms in Chinese Ibsenism, whether the experiment happens in Beijing or Shanghai, will have an impact in other parts of China, and vice versa. The recent productions and adaptations of *A Doll's House, The Wild Duck* and *Hedda Gabler* (Figure 3) are not only responses to the new experiments in China, but also attempts to explore a new theatre language in the representation of the Ibsenian character as psychic configurations of the self.

An examination of theatrical innovations in recent Chinese stage productions of Ibsen will shed light on artistic representations of the self in relation to gender, class, state, and the ethical categories present in social framing and cultural formation. It will arrive at a new understanding of the theorisation of dramatic characters. It will also provide analysis of ideological discourses at work behind stage representation in contemporary Chinese theatres and Chinese interpretations of Ibsen by contextualising them as an inseparable part of global Ibsenism. The new experiments can show theatre critics, practitioners and teachers how new paradigms in ideological positions can effect changes in art form.

Theoretical Reflections on Chinese Ibsenism

Because of the historical roles that Ibsen has played in the ideological formation of modern self-identity, numerous Chinese novelists and dramatists have come under his influence. These writers include Lu Xun, Hu Shi, Ba Jin, Mao Dun, Cao Yu and Eileen Chang. 'Revisioning' Ibsen in terms of his concepts of the self will clear the ground for contemporary Chinese culture to be placed in better perspective. In drama and literature, how to account for the relationship between critical interpretation and creativity is always an issue not easy to handle, particularly when historical and cultural issues come into play. Theoretical probing will thus provide reflections on how drama and literature can be considered in relation to history and cultural changes.

There is a need to situate the study of Chinese Ibsenism as contested ideologies in the context of social framing and self-fashioning, and as politics in the Chinese theatre culture. Such an approach will explore the ideological implications in recent Chinese stage productions of Henrik Ibsen, a 19th-century Norwegian playwright, particularly with reference to the reinvention of the post-socialist self in China, in order to arrive at an understanding of the interplay between aesthetics and politics.

As the father of modern drama, Ibsen has exerted a great impact upon the shaping of modernist culture, not only in the West, but also in the East, particularly in the construction of modern self-identity in Asia. Ibsen is ranked second to Shakespeare in terms of impact upon the formation of world culture. He is a global author, in the sense that he is taught in almost all cultures. His drama is considered by many practitioners as a necessary foundation for theatre training, for his plays are illustrative of many modern breakthroughs in dramatic form. From the perspectives of both art and ideology formation, Ibsen is a phenomenon in the creation of the modernist theatre and modernist culture.

In China, Ibsenism has been synonymous with the pursuit of modernity and the advocacy of individualism in self-identity. For almost a century, Ibsen's plays have served as models of dramaturgy for Chinese playwrights and theatre directors. Early theories of modern Chinese drama are derived from Ibsen's method in his problem plays. The three dominant discourses of modern Chinese theatre all find their roots in Ibsen's dramatic vision: (1) the critical realist discourse that dominated the Chinese theatre in the 1910s and 1920s originated from a sinicised view of Ibsenism; (2) the socialist discourse that emphasised class conflicts in theatre representation between the 1930s and 1970s is based on a Marxianised Ibsenism, and (3) the post-socialist discourse that emerged after the 1980s is indebted to (post)modernist representations of the self (Tam 1988).

In the field of Chinese Ibsen studies, there are two major approaches to dealing with Chinese Ibsenism. The first treats Chinese performances of Ibsen as 'intercultural theatre'. In this approach, the focus is placed on the theatrical form in Chinese adaptations of Ibsen, particularly on how traditional Chinese theatre arts can be appropriated for Ibsen performances. The second approach is marked by its critical prominence in dealing with the cultural and ideological issues in Ibsen's impact upon both the theatre and culture in China. While most existing scholarship in the first approach tends to be descriptive in such issues as cross-dressing in the Yue opera adaptation of Ibsen's *The Lady from the Sea,* the second approach – because of its critical nature – handles issues of ideological discourse behind the theatrical form and is thus able to explain the changes in form. The second approach is more revealing for the obvious reason that the Chinese interest in Ibsen does not lie simply in the dramatic form, but more importantly in the ideology embedded in its cultural revisioning – for example, in the Nora image from which the modern Chinese feminist identity takes its inspiration. Another reason why an ideology-focused critical approach is more appropriate for the study of Chinese Ibsenism is that the concept of 'intercultural theatre', as recent debates show, has created confusion in theatre criticism (Fischer-Lichte 2008). Moreover, such studies fail to identify and explain the relationship between the cultural politics and aesthetics behind theatrical experimentation.

A more fruitful approach to Chinese Ibsenism is to examine it in relation to Chinese stage adaptations from the 1980s to the present. Hence, there is the need to reconsider theatrical innovations in staging Ibsen as experiments with new conceptions of the theatre, embedded in which are the ideological underpinnings and discursive strategies that shape the debates on Chinese Ibsenism, as well as on post-socialist reconceptualisations of the self in relation to gender, class, state, and ethical categories in social framing and cultural formation, particularly with reference to Chinese-Western encounters.

Ibsenism emerged at the end of the 19th century long before philosophers, such as Sartre, proposed the problematisation of the self in drama. However, many of the issues that contemporary philosophical enquiries deal with have already been raised by Ibsen in his drama. Peer Gynt, Dr Stockmann, Nora, Mrs Alving and Solness are Ibsen's re-enactments of the self as an individual in psychosocial formation. It is through literature, drama in particular, that a new culture has swept through the world bringing new concepts of iconoclasm and individuality not only to the West, but also to Asia and other parts of the world. The term Ibsenism was coined by Bernard Shaw (1891) to invoke the individual's power to resist social hypocrisy. In China, Hu Shi (1918) expanded the basic concepts of Shaw's Ibsenism by extending them to a critique of traditional Chinese ethical categories, as exemplified in Confucianism. Hu's critique formed the foundation of a sinicised Ibsenism in the 1920s and 1930s. However, the mid-1930s saw in China the emergence of a new interpretation of Ibsenism – a Marxianised Ibsenism – that refers gender differences to class oppositions, and turns ideas of individualism into class collective ideology (Zhao Dan 1980). Ibsenism has seen various reinterpretations in China since the 1980s with the resurgence of (post)modernist renderings of the self in stage representations. Following the reinterpretations come certain attempts to incorporate feminism and psychoanalysis of gender into a revisioning of Ibsenism (Tam 1984, 1986a, 1986b, 1986c, 1986d, 1987a, 1988, 1990, 1992, 1993, 1994a, 1994b, 1995, 1998a, 1998b, 1998c, 2001, 2002, 2005, 2006b, 2007, 2008, 2012).

There is a need to study how the self, which is central to the tenets of Ibsenism, is reconceptualised in Chinese stage adaptations of Ibsen's drama in relation to gender, class, state, ethical categories in social framing and cultural formation, and particularly to issues in Chinese-Western encounters. Differences in stage performance and in conceptions of the self between China and the West turn such stage adaptations into processes of contestation between Chinese and Western cultural traditions. Chinese Ibsenism is both the Chinese desire to own Ibsen by sinicising and thus domesticating his ideas, and the result of contestation between the global and the local, as well as between the foreign and the domestic.

Kwo-kan Tam
kktam@ouhk.edu.hk
School of Arts & Social Sciences
Open University of Hong Kong
Homantin, Kowloon
Hong Kong SAR

References

Anonymous. 1956. *A Doll's House* in Shanghai 1934 (1934 nian 'Nuola' zai Shanghai). – *Beijing Daily* (Beijing ribao), 28.07, 3.

Anonymous. 1998. Chinese Version: *A Doll's House*. – *Beijing This Month*, April 1998 (http://www.google.com.hk/imgres?imgurl=http://www.cbw.com/btm/issue53/images/doll.jpg&imgrefurl=http://www.cbw.com/btm/issue53/doll.html&usg=__53a4GfUEVMOASmRYpcWK6LtOffc=&h=180&w=220&sz=19&hl=en&start=2&zoom=1&tbnid=fhMbI9m8Nu-LYM:&tbnh=88&tbnw=107&ei=48pyTsufB6mWiQfF1pihBg&prev=/search%3Fq%3DChinese%2Bversion%2B%2522A%2BDoll%2527s%2BHouse%2522%26hl%3Den%26sa%3DX%26tbm%3Disch%26prmd%3Divns&itbs=1). Accessed 16 September 2011.

Archer, W. 1944. *Play-making*. New York: Dodd, Mead & Company.

Brockett, O. G., Findlay, R. 1991. *Century of Innovation: A History of European and American Theatre and Drama Since the Late Nineteenth Century*. 2nd ed. Boston: Allyn and Bacon.

Cao Juren. 1963. The Second Time I Saw *A Doll's House* (Zai kan "Nuola"). – *New Comments on People and Events* (Ren shi xin yu). Hong Kong: Chunyi chbanshe, 271–272.

Connor, S. 1989. *Postmodernist Culture: An Introduction to Theories of the Contemporary*. Oxford: Blackwell.

Fang Xin. 1923. Kan liao "Nola' hou de lingshui ganxiang (Random Thoughts after Watching *A Doll's House*). – *Chenbao fukan* (Supplement to Chenbao), 12.05, 4.

Hu Shi. 1918. Yibusheng zhuyi. – *Xinqingnian* 4.6 (June), 489–507.

Jameson, F. 1981. *The Political Unconscious: Narrative as a Socially Symbolic Act*. New York: Cornell University Press.

Jameson, F. 1986. Third-World Literature in the Era of Multinational Capitalism. – *Social Text*, 15, 65–88.

Jiang Yuxia. 2010. Enter the Doll's House. – *Global Times*, 22 October, 17.

Jin Yaoji (King, A. Y. C.). 1996. On Modernization and Modernity: The Construction of a Modern Chinese Civilizational Order (Lun xiandaihua yu xiandaixing: Zhonggua xiandai wenming zhixu de jiangou). – *Peking University Journal*, 1, 1–26.

Kristeva, J. 1980. *Desire in Language*. Trans. by L. S. Roudiez. Oxford: Blackwell.

Li Jianwu. 1960. Dramatic Conflicts in Socialist Drama (Shehui zhuyi huaju de xiju congtu). Reprinted in *New Horizons in Drama* (Xiju xintian), Shanghai: Shanghai wenyi chubanshe, 1980, 55–60.

Lu Xun. 1981a [1908]. Moluo shili shuo (The power of *mara* poetry). – *Lu Xun quanji* (Complete works of Lu Xun), Vol. 1. Beijing: Renmin wenxue chubanshe, 63–115.

Lu Xun. 1981b [1908]. Wenhua pianzi lun (On cultural extremes). – *Lu Xun quanji* (Complete works of Lu Xun), Vol. 1. Beijing: Renmin wenxue chubanshe, 44–62.

Lu Xun. 1973 [1923]. Shangshi (Regret for the past). – *Panghuang* (Hestiation). Beijing: Renmin wenxue chubanshe, 114–137.

Mao Dun. 1926. Chuangzao (Creation). – *Mao Dun duan pian xiaoshuo xuan* (Short stories by Mao Dun), Vol. 1. Hong Kong: Yixin shudan, n.d, 17–34.

Mao Dun. 1934. *Hong* (Rainbow). Hong Kong: Lingnan chubanshe, n.d.

Oliver, H. 1992. The Relational Self. – L. S. Rouner, ed., *Selves, People and Persons: What Does It Mean to Be a Self?* Notre Dame: University of Notre Dame Press, 37–52.

Pellegini, N. 2010. A Chinese Doll's House. – *TimeOut Beijing*, October, 74 (www.timeout.com/beijing/ october 2010). Accessed 16 September 2011.

Qin Mei. 2010. Less Words but More to Say, a New Version of *A Doll's House*. – CRIEnglish.com (http://english.cri.cn/7146/2010/10/27/2001s601358.htm). Accessed 16 September 2011.

Tam, K. 1984. *Ibsen in China: Reception and Influence*. PhD thesis, University of Illinois at Urbana-Champaign.

Tam, K. 1986a. From Social Problem Play to Socialist Problem Play: Ibsen and Contemporary Chinese Dramaturgy. – *Journal of the Institute of Chinese Studies*, 17, 387–403.

Tam, K. 1986b. Ibsen and Modern Chinese Dramatists: Influences and Parallels. – *Modern Chinese Literature*, Vol. 2, No. 1 (Spring), 45–62.

Tam, K. 1986c. Marxism and Beyond: Contemporary Chinese Reception of Ibsen. – *Edda*, 3, 202–225.

Tam, K. 1986d. Issues in Reception Theory and Chinese-Western Comparative Literature. – *Tamkang Review*, Vol. 16, No. 4, 325–341.

Tam, K. 1987a. The Shanghai Performance of *A Doll's House* and the Mystery of Jiang Qing's Role in the Stage Production and in the Revolution: A Research Note and Review. – *Journal of Oriental Studies* 25.2, 197–201.

Tam, K. 1987b. 〈《玩偶之家》與中國20年代問題劇〉 "*Wan'ou zhi jia* yu Zhongguo 20 niandai wenti ju" (*A Doll's House* and the Chinese problem play in the 1920s). – Zhong Tinghu, ed., 《名家論學》 *Mingjia lunxue* (Scholars on scholarship). Shanghai: Fudan University Press, 260–269. Reprinted in 《中國話劇》 *Zhongguo huaju* (Chinese spoken drama), 1993, 7, 27–35.

Tam, K. 1988. 〈中國話劇的三種話語與劇壇創新〉 "Zhongguo huaju de sanzhong huayu yu jutan chuangxin" (Three discourses of modern Chinese drama and theatrical innovations). – Tian Benxiang 田本相 et al., eds., 華文戲薈*Huawen xihui* (Chinese drama and the stage). Beijing: Zhongguo xiju chubanshe, 58–61.

Tam, K. 1990. Iconoclasm as Ibsenism: Ibsen in the May Fourth Era. –M. Gálik, ed., *Interliterary and intraliterary Aspects of the May Fourth 1919 Movement in China*. Bratislava: Publishing House of the Slovak Academy of Sciences, 119–128.

Tam, K. 1992. Decoding Literary History: Cultural Transformation and the Chinese Reception of Ibsen. – *Tamkang Review*, 22.1–4 (Autumn 1991–Summer 1992), 263–286.

Tam, K. 1994a. Feminism and Ibsenism: Portrayals of a New Female Identity in Modern Chinese Literature. – M. Gálik, ed., *Chinese Literature and the European Context*. Bratislava: Institute of Asian and African Studies, the Slovak Academy of Sciences, 113–118.

Tam, K. 1994b. Ibsenism and Contemporary Chinese Dramatic Forms (Yibusheng xiju yu dangdai Zhongguo xiju lilun de xingshi 易卜生戲劇與當代中國戲劇理論的形式). – Chen Bingliang, ed., *Literature and the Performing Arts* (Wenxue yu biaoyan yishu 文學與表演藝術). Hong Kong: Department of Chinese, Lingnan College, 140–183.

Tam, K. 1995. Theatrical Innovations and Ideological Change in China in the 1980s. – V. Ooi, J. Lai, eds., *New Challenge: Form and Content of Contemporary Asian Theatre*. Hong Kong: Urban Council and International Association of Theatre Critics, 101–118.

Tam, K. 1997. Subjectivity, Modernity and the Chinese Problematic of the Self. – *Canadian Review of Comparative Literature*, Vol. 24, No. 4 (December 1997), 989–997.

Tam, K. 1998a. Ibsenism and Ideological Constructions of the 'New Woman' in Modern Chinese Fiction. – *Tamkang Review*, Vol. 29, No. 1 (Summer 1998), 95–105. Reprinted in P. Chen, W. C. Dilley, eds., *Feminism/Femininity in Chinese Literature*, Amsterdam & New York: Rodopi, 179–186.

Tam, K. 1998b. Postmodernist Performance in Contemporary Chinese and Japanese Theatre. – *Performing Arts International*, 3.1, 65–73.

Tam, K. 1998c = Tam, K., Yip, T. S. H. 1998. The Self in Transition: Moral Dilemma in Modern Chinese Drama. – R. Ames, W. Dissanayake, P. Kassulis, eds., *Self as Image in Asian Theory and Practice*. Albany: State University of New York Press, 200–216.

Tam, K. 1999. Subjectivity, Modernity, and the Chinese Problematic of the Self. – *Canadian Review of Comparative Literature*, 24.4 (September 1997), 989–997.

Tam, K. 2000. An Unfinished Project: Ibsen and the Construction of a Modern Chinese Consciousness. – *East-West Dialogue*, Vol. 4, No. 2 – Vol. 5, No. 1 (June), 113–145.

Tam, K. 2000.《主體建構政治與現代中國文學》*Zhuti jiangou zhengzhi yu dangdai Zhongguo wenxue* (The politics of subject construction in modern Chinese literature). Hong Kong: Oxford University Press.

Tam, K. 2001. *Ibsen in China 1908–1997: A Critical-Annotated Bibliography of Criticism, Translation and Performance*. Hong Kong: Chinese University Press.

Tam, K. 2002. The Politics of the Postmodern Theatre in China. – *Interlitteraria*, 7.1, 39–57.

Tam, K. 2005. Spatial Poetics of the Self and the Moral-Dramatic Structure in *A Doll's House*. – *Ibsen Studies*, Vol. 5, No. 2 (December), 180–197.

Tam, K. 2006a. Ibsenism and Feminist Awakenings among Early Modern Chinese Writers. – *Interlitteraria*, 11.1, 113–128.

Tam, K. 2006b. Ibsenism and the Modern Chinese Self. – *Monumenta Serica* (Germany), 54, 287–298.

Tam, K. 2007. Dramatic Voices of the Self: Ibsen's Ideological Intervention in the Chinese Quest for a Modern Female Identity. – F. Helland et al., eds., *The Living Ibsen* (*Acta Ibseniana V*). Oslo: Centre for Ibsen studies, University of Oslo, 347–351.

Tam, K. 2010. The Dialogic Self in *A Doll's House* and *The Wild Duck*. – K. Tam et al., eds., *Ibsen and the Modern Self*. Oslo: Centre for Ibsen Studies, University of Oslo; and Hong Kong: Open University of Hong Kong Press, 78–90.

Tam, K. 2012. Chineseness in Recreating Ibsen: *Peer Gynt* in China and Its Adaptations. – *Interlitteraria*, 17, 268–280.

Tam, K. et al., eds. 2010. *Ibsen and the Modern Self*. Oslo: Centre for Ibsen Studies, University of Oslo; and Hong Kong: Open University of Hong Kong Press.

Tan Peisheng. 1980. *On Dramaticity* (Lun xiju xing). Beijing: China Theatre Press.

Wang Ling. 1998. Chinese Version of A Doll's House. – Playbill.com (http://www.playbill.com/news/article/37974-Chinese-Version-of-A-Dolls-House-Premieres-in-Beijing-Apr-1). Accessed 16 September 2011.

Wu Xue. 1956. Some Thoughts on the Production of *A Doll's House* ("Nuola" yanchu so xiang dao de). – *Literary and Arts Bulletin* (Wenyi bao), 16, 41.

Zhao Dan. 1980. *The Gate of Hell* (Diyu zhi men). Shanghai: Shanghai wenyi chubanshe.

INTERLITTERARIA 2015, SUPPL. 1: 211–224

Victims and Perpetrators: Two Novels on the 1942 Novi Sad Atrocities

JOHN NEUBAUER

Abstract. Unspeakable matters inevitably generate discourses that try to grasp the unfathomable. The horrors of the Holocaust and the enormous body of writing about it are evidence for this. Are some discourses better suited for the task than others? Instead of adding yet another text to the many theoretical answers to this question, the present essays takes a single case, the 1942 Novi Sad atrocities, and sets different discourses against each other. First I confront history making and history writing with fiction, and in the second one, I juxtapose two different kinds of Holocaust perspectives, namely a victim perspective in Aleksandar Tišma's novel and a perpetrator one in that of Tibor Cseres. Unexpectedly, the perpetrator novel deals with people locked up while victim perspective is linked to a free survivor.

Keywords: Holocaust, cultural memory, the unspeakable, facts and fiction, victims and perpetrators

At the end of Aleksandar Tišma's *The Book of Blam* (1971), the protagonist attends a concert in the imposing Novi Sad synagogue, which had been converted into a concert hall because the decimated Jewish community could no longer deliver the required quorum. Listening to the music before the intermission, Miroslav Blam is carried away by playful sounds that evoke images that are not irrevocable (210). In the intermission, he encounters, however, the old Funkenstein, who survived Bergen-Belsen by playing music for those taken to their execution, upon the camp commander's order. After the intermission, Blam can no longer listen to Dvořák's *Serenade*: constantly feeling observed by an invisible eye, he finds the music, the people, the converted synagogue, and himself shams. All these lies try to cover up the truth of existence. Once outside, he foresees his future execution, which, in contrast to his Holocaust attitude, he will not try to escape (226).

For Blam, music can no longer be what it was for many romantics, namely a divine language that speaks of an unspeakable divine world. His father Wilim, who adhered to an "enlightened atheism", preferred the cosmopolitan "incense" of cafés to the tradition-laden synagogue music. Like the rest of the family except

DOI: http://dx.doi.org/10.12697/IL.2015.S1.16

for Miroslav, Wilim was murdered by Hungarian soldiers in the Novi Sad 'razzia' of 1942. In the post-war world, Miroslav is unable to find companions with whom he could communicate. His inability to speak about his self-contempt and the unspeakable horrors of his experiences, imposes upon the novel an omniscient narrator, who tells the stories of the Jews and the Serbs of Novi Sad, focusing on the 1942 razzia.

Miroslav Blam's inability to talk emblematically expresses the problems of everybody who wishes to evoke and consider the horrors of the Holocaust. Though we have developed by now many verbal and non-verbal modes of communication to let the unspeakable speak to us via Holocaust effects (see Ernst van Alphen), I am sceptical about most of them, and this is one reason why I tried to avoid writing about the Holocaust. I agree with Blam that even music is unable to convey authentically the horrors of the Holocaust, and while I admit that music with filmic or other images that can be heart-rending, I often feel that such representations manipulate the audience.

As Tišma seems to suggest in his *Pre mita*, the imagination may be given a limited freedom in poetic and novelistic attempts to speak about the Holocaust:

> The evil that has accumulated in our days can be cleansed only by means of extended catharses, for which art is an excellent field, and the artist, who has the ability to activate and motivate evil, is an excellent mediator ... to muffle evil with silence, or with black-and-white declarations (which is the same), amounts to sweeping it under the rug, enabling it to survive latently, to kill, and to wait for the moment to break out. (6–7 quoted in Gvozden 97; my translation)

I hope to show the emotive and intellectual power of fiction about the Holocaust with two novels on the Novi-Sad razzia of 1942. The first is Tišma's *The Book of Blam*, while the second one is Tibor Cseres's *Hideg napok* (1964). Unfortunately, I am unable to compare novelistic and filmic representations, for I have not seen András Kovács's 1966 film *Hideg napok* and *The Book of Blam* has not been adapted to the screen.

A few preliminary words about the much-discussed differences between fiction and historical studies. Archival academic research, family histories, personal recollections, witness accounts, and other forms of historical documentation are indispensable for any kind of discourse on the Holocaust. Recollections – as opposed to documents from the time of the events – are not purely factual, for time wreaks havoc with memory. Indeed, it has become so difficult to separate neatly facts and fiction that many relevant works consciously characterise themselves now with terms that merge the two. 'Autofiction', for instance, is a term that writers use for hybrid texts that fuse autobiography and fiction. Such texts admit that autobiographical narratives are hardly ever purely factual, for they are produced by a personal consciousness that often records, voluntarily or involuntarily, factual inaccuracies. Even the Nobel-Prize-winning Elie Wiesel had to revise some of his Holocaust recollections in later editions.

Looking at historical studies, we should note a major restriction: historians may enter into the thoughts of their historical characters if these have somehow been made public. However, the moment they present non-documentable psychological attitudes and opinions, they engage in fiction. Dan Porat's recently published *The Boy: A Holocaust Story* (2010), contains, for instance, dozens of authentic photographs, of which the most famous one shows a little Jewish boy facing SS guns with hands up. This, and many other ones, was taken from the report *Es gibt keinen jüdischen Wohnbezirk in Warschau mehr!* (published in English in 1979 as *The Stroop Report: The Jewish Quarter of Warsaw Is No More!*), which Jürgen Stroop, the SS leader of the German forces that put down the uprising in the Warsaw Ghetto, sent to Heinrich Himmler in May 1943. Porat meticulously and conscientiously traced, as far as he could, the stories behind the photos, and he reconstructed the life stories of several victims and perpetrators (including that of Stroop), but he did not shy away from filling some gaps with plausible fiction – which some people resent, for they prefer to keep fact and fiction apart. Publicly recorded statements are reliable facts, but we must always ask how far from the actual events the recording occurred. The speaker may have seen things very differently in other moments of his or her life. Furthermore, we always have to ask whether the documentation adequately presents the full range of relevant materials.

As Dorrit Cohn has shown in her book of 1978, the minds of fictional characters are 'transparent' for narrators who are outside the fictional world. Once the narrator participates as a character in the fictional world, if he or she is an 'internal' narrator, the minds of the other fictional characters should again become inaccessible – although there are several imaginative devices that can overcome this categorical division. Nevertheless, as a rule, fiction offers recipients richer material for empathy (or hatred). Fiction can portray unexpressed and inaccessible psychological processes, including pain and suffering, love and hatred.

These all too general and selective introductory remarks are meant to support my suggestion that fictional works can be effective for evoking and discussing the Holocaust. This is particularly true, I believe, in the specific historical case I have chosen, the Novi Sad razzia of January 1942, which is complex and sensitive because it involves Serbs as well as Jews, i.e. nationalism as well as anti-Semitism. It differs, for instance, from Anne Frank's case, where genocide was operating against Jews but not against the Dutch. The twofold mass murder in Novi Sad partly explains why Hungarian and Serb historians, politicians, and citizens still disagree on crucial matters of responsibility.

The topic has contemporary relevance. In June 2013, the Hungarian President, János Áder, apologised to Serbia's national assembly for Hungarian crimes committed against innocent Serbs in Vojvodina during World War II. This was a prearranged response to the declaration of the Serbian parliament a few days earlier, which condemned the post-war massacre of Hungarians in Vojvodina. The Serbian retribution is the subject of *Vérbosszú Bácskában* (1991), another book by Cseres. In *Hideg napok*, the question whether the Serbs will eventually take revenge is raised twice but only in passing (84, 147).

I know not how these two atrocities were reported in the Serbian media, but I have read the Hungarian language version of the Wikipedia about them, and found that it was obviously written from a Hungarian perspective. The article suggests (which is probably true) that Serbia was pressured by the EU to admit the Serbian post-war revenges, which the Hungarian Wikipedia text characterises as "a heinous crime" ("*mérhetetlen gaztett*") without attaching a comparable adjective to the earlier Hungarian atrocities. The Hungarian text reports that Áder remembered the razzia victims with piety ("*kegyelettel*") but does not say that the President excused himself on behalf of his nation for the Hungarian murders. Similarly biased reports in the Hungarian Wikipedia show that random facts do not constitute truth. Emblematic, is the case of gendarmerie captain Sándor Képíró, who appears in the Cseres novel and has received renewed international attention in recent years. Képíró was condemned by a Hungarian court in 1944 but was released when the German troops marched into Hungary on March 19 of that year. A post-war Hungarian court sentenced him to 14 years in prison, but, again, in absentia, for Képíró had already fled to Austria, and then to Argentina. He lived there, presumably under a false name, but returned to Hungary after the political turnover, when he was assured that the court verdict had been annulled.

Reports date Képíró's post-war trial to 1946 or 1948. The date is important, for if the verdict of 14 years in prison was made in 1946, defenders of Képíró cannot claim that János Nagy, a former Hungarian soldier from Képíró's platoon, provided the decisive evidence under torture by the communist secret service. The communist secret service had no such power in 1946. Képíró himself never admitted that he participated in executions or any illegal activity. Under pressure from the Wiesenthal Center in Vienna he was once more brought to trial in May 2011 in Budapest, at age 97, but a Hungarian court ruled in July of that year that Képíró was not guilty. He died in September 2011, and several YouTube videos about his funeral are accompanied by vicious anti-Semitic blogs. The case is not finished – and perhaps will never be. Talking about 1942 in Novi Sad is not just commemoration but also participation in contemporary politics.

Hideg napok (1964)

Cseres's novel appeared a year after Hannah Arendt had published her book on the 1961 Eichmann trial in Israel, titled *Eichmann in Jerusalem: The Banality of Evil*. Eichmann resisted the pressure to admit his guilt; Arendt claimed that he enthusiastically joined the Nazis because he was unable to think independently. Her title suggests that perpetrators like Eichmann are subservient rather than bloodthirsty or inhuman. The interpretation is still controversial, especially after the recent film on her and the Eichmann trial.

Trials interrogate perpetrators, but they seldom succeed in finding convincing motivations and personality characterisations. This may be one reason why Cseres includes no interrogation in *Hideg napok*, contrary, for instance, to Arthur Koestler's *Darkness at Noon*, where interrogations and internal reflections alternate in the life of the jailed protagonist. Cseres puts four fictional Hungarian participants of the Novi Sad razzia in a cell, apparently as part of the trial that took place during World War II. However, there are no interrogations, the four men are ignorant of the accusations against them, and they wonder why they had been jailed together. The setup is obviously a fictional and hypothetical construction, which should yield information unavailable to judges and historians. Unlike the witnesses in Akira Kurosawa's film *Rashômon* (1950), the cellmates in Cseres's novel do not argue with each other about jointly experienced individual events or the meaning of the witnessed razzia as a whole.

The most astonishing jail conversations with a perpetrator are not fictional but historical, recorded by Kazimierz Moczarski in his *Rozmowy z katem* ('Conversations with an Executioner', 1977). Moczarski, the leader of the Western-led Home Army in the Warsaw Uprising of 1944, was sentenced to ten years in prison by the communists because of his Western filiation, and with unbelievable maliciousness he was placed in a cell with Jürgen Stroop, the SS liquidator of the Warsaw Ghetto. Predictably, Stroop never showed any guilt feelings, but driven by an urge to talk about himself, he told his life in installments to Moczarski, who listened without criticism, in order to get Stroop's 'full' story. Stroop was executed in 1952, while Moczarski was released from prison in 1956, and he recalled the conversations subsequently. They appeared in 1972 in installments and in 1977 as a book. Later research confirmed the accuracy of what he wrote down.

In contrast to Stroop, the cellmates of Cseres are preoccupied with the atrocities and their role in them. We are watching a group dynamic between four people, all of whom (just like Eichmann) deny any guilt. The fictional figures do not speak under oath, and they incriminate the speaker only in the eyes of those in the cell (including themselves); they speak relatively freely and informally, although they do not like each other and they suspect that one of them is a spy. The dynamics of the conversation is heavily influenced by military and social hierarchies, which are slightly negated by their remarkably similar personalities. All of them are obsessed by sexual violence (79–80), and they have little interest in or empathy with others, including their cellmates. They express no guilt, and their remarks do not lead to meaningful confessions.

The most bloodthirsty fictional figure of the novel, corporal Dorner, is not in the cell. His worst atrocities are recounted by corporal Szabó, who served under him. Next to Sándor Képíró, the two highest and most vicious historical officers, Major-General József Grassy and Lieutenant General Ferenc Feketehalmy-Czeydner, also appear briefly in the novel, but we do not hear what happened to them. They actually fled to Germany to avoid Hungarian prosecution, joined the SS, and returned to Hungary in March 1944. The Americans arrested them after the war, handed them over to the Hungarians, who then turned them over to the Yugoslav authorities. Grassy was executed in Novi Sad and Feketehalmy-Czeydner in Žabalj.

The four fictional cellmates, Ensign Pozdor, lieutenant Tarpataki, major Büky, and corporal Szabó tell each other about their experience of the razzia but systematically play down their responsibility in it. They seldom respond to the others. The two opposing and most problematic figures are Büky and Szabó. The latter, the only plain soldier in the group, has no money, is of lower-class origin, and unmarried. His extensive reports are in an uneducated language. Büky, in contrast, is a well-to-do married man who became angry with Major-General Grassy because he was forbidden to bring his wife and child to Novi Sad. This is, however, no proof of his family attachment. Having found comfortable accommodations in the home of a Jewish travelling salesman, he praises his hostess so highly in his letters to his anti-Semitic wife in Győr that she becomes jealous, and not without reason. The hostess invites Büky once for dinner, he keeps inviting himself afterwards, and then becomes sexually aggressive. He tells his cellmates: "She pretended she was afraid to resist" (31), implying that he didn't really have to rape her. To claim marital loyalty, Büky hypocritically assures his cellmates that his devotion to his wife and son did not diminish thereby. On the first evening of the razzia, the husband was back home. A Hungarian neighbour came to fetch a bucket of water from their well and was shot dead when returning, because he disobeyed the curfew. Büky relates the event to his cellmates with apparent disengagement (34), but telling them about the *disznótor*, a pig-killing feast, at the house the next day he indicates that he had a growing desire for Milena, the Serbian wife of the concierge.

Büky claims that the inhabitants regarded him as the guardian angel of the house (59–60), but the alleged angel soon became helpless. Next morning, a man with a bloody turban was brought to his office; his family had been murdered the previous day, and, having miraculously survived the deadly bullets, he now wanted a report on the event (which Szabó had described already to his cellmates as Corporal Dorner's atrocity). Büky refused to believe the story but prepared a draft report. When Grassy dismissively tore it up, Büky angrily accused him, not of the planned murder of the man (which was, indeed, carried out by Dorner: (97–98), but because he considered the separation of husbands and wives as "unlawful". That thousands of Serbs and Jews are unlawfully killed at the same time doesn't disturb him at all.

Szabó's detailed account of Dorner's atrocious killings heats up the atmosphere of the cold days in the prison cell. When he relates that he refused to save a little boy of seven from death row, Büky repeatedly prevents him from continuing (99). According to the narrator (100–101), he desperately murmurs in the cell that they are all murderers, but, as we shall see, this is a very personal matter, not a sign of his humanism. When the other cellmates also refuse to listen to Szabó's account of how Dorner's unit went berserk, Büky picks up the thread of his story by recalling that during the razzia it suddenly struck him that his wife and son may be in town (101). What would he do with them?

The genocide generates a drama in the cell. Büky speaks of Germans who first participated in the razzia but then moved over to the other side of the Danube with some reliable witnesses who could testify that they were not guilty (111–112). What's the point? Finally, he is unable to withhold his secret from his puzzled cellmates. Jealousy did drive his wife and child to Novi Sad just before the start of the razzia. His son became a beloved playmate of the girls in the house, and even his wife found a certain bond with the Jewish and Serbian mothers. Büky tried to send away all these women and children with the next train, but they had to return because trains were no longer leaving. Returning home later, Büky found his dead host in front of the house, dressed in Bücky's own uniform. Apparently, he was killed while unsuccessfully trying to protect his family with a trick. However, the women were picked up by Hungarian soldiers, only the three children were left behind. Büky started a frantic search around town for his wife, but had to console himself with the meagre hope that she may have left with the Germans (125–126).

Szabó knows what really happened and readily pours it out, not in search of the 'truth' but as a means to hurt Bücky. There were only 15–20 people left to be murdered at the Danube when a high official arrived with the order to stop the massacre. Dorner protested and was shot dead (133–134). The previous hour was even more dramatic. The last killings were so intensive that the machine guns broke down, and Szabó went to the nearby pub to fetch a carriage-pole that would keep the hole in the ice open and help push the victims into the icy water. While the machine gunner relaxed in the pub playing with mostly Jewish children, the adults were lined up outside in underwear to march towards the deadly hole. Three women begged for help, claiming that their husbands were Hungarian officers, and one of them could even cite the names of a whole unit, but since the other two did not speak Hungarian she was distrusted. Szabó took pleasure looking at their full bodies, while one of his colleagues dragged the Hungarian-speaking woman to the pub, raped her, and forced her back into the row. When one of the other women was shot, the Hungarian woman threw herself onto the rapist's boots, kissing and hugging them while begging for clemency. When Szabó lustfully describes how the iron hook of the carriage-pole tore her underwear, Büky becomes indignant and delivers a deadly kick to Szabó (138) because he realises that the infinitely humiliated women was his wife.

Once Büky is led away, the remaining two cellmates, Pozdor and Tarpataki, avoid questions of guilt and engage in trivial chatting. Pozdor notes that blowing holes in a frozen river was neglected in their military training, while Tarpataki wonders how the authorities knew that so many of the 3390 victims were older people (146). Pozdor then wonders whether the highest perpetrators considered that revenge might come. He cynically adds that if that should happen, the Hungarians will have to face fewer potential revengers after the razzia. Tarpataki can only spit at this (147).

When new cellmates are added, the razzia becomes a non-topic. Did the military commander himself not say at the end of January: "Gentlemen. Not a word about this!" (147)? The razzia remains an *unbewältigte Vergangenheit*, a past that has not been morally worked through. Indeed, when Cseres wrote his novel in 1964, the term was applicable to much of Europe, especially Eastern Europe. *Hideg napok* was an early and particularly courageous attempt to initiate a serious Hungarian self-questioning in order to come to terms with the past, because it focused on the country's perpetrators. As Tišma recommends in the passage quoted above, Cseres avoided a 'black and white' story by not putting in the cell the worst criminals, the real historical perpetrators of Képíró, Grassy, and Feketehalmy-Czeydner, and the fictional Dorner. The cellmates share the social prejudices and anti-Semitism of their leaders, and go along with it. In a banal way they reveal the "banality of evil". Judging by what they say and display in the cell, their greatest sin was indifference, lack of independence, and lacking courage to protest. Only Büky confronts his superior, Grassy, but only because

Grassy has not allowed his family members to join. Grassy's apparently capricious deviation from the military rules was obviously part of preparing the razzia, and Büky's family drama paradoxically justifies the decision.

Hideg Napok has not received the attention it deserves, though it has been republished several times in Hungarian and was translated into many languages, including Serbian, German, English, and French. The cellmates do not adhere (or do not want to appear to adhere) to inhuman ideologies. Because they are guilty, but not the blackest figures, looking at them closely raises questions they themselves suppress. Why did they not exercise any genuine self-criticism? Why did they not feel guilty? Why were they not ready to come to terms with their own pasts? The novel's jail cell is a laboratory that fails to produce the medication that would induce proper healing.

Knjiga o blamu (1971)

Moving to *The Book of Blam*, we change from perpetrators to a surviving protagonist who suffers from the guilt that perpetrators ought to have. Although January 1942 in Novi Sad is still in focus, Tišma's fictional world is radically different. The Hungarian book digs up the events from personal memories in a prison cell that is suspended in a temporal and spatial vacuum, whereas *The Book of Blam* embeds the razzia historically, geographically, socially, and psychologically. The wider context makes things more complex but hardly more transparent.

The opening of Tišma's novel provides a diagonally opposite setup to *Hideg napok*, where the cell goads the characters to speak. Blam has an overview of Novi Sad's centre from the corridor of his building, popularly known as Mercurius. The narrative present is post-war Yugoslavia, where Blam need not fear razzias and their consequences. In *Hideg napok*, the discussion of the perpetrators leaves hardly any space for the narrator, whereas the protagonist in *The Book of Blam* is so reluctant to talk that an external narrator has to speak for him most of the time. He tells us at the outset that Blam is reluctant to give his address as Mercurius. Vacillating "between pleasure and annoyance, because he dislikes being pigeonholed" (2), Miroslav correctly but rather misleadingly, gives his address as "Old Boulevard 1" – an outdated name that indicates that he lives in the past rather than the present.

Why this desire to remain incognito, to live behind a mask, to hide away in a mansard apartment that is all but inaccessible? Since Miroslav's family was wiped out by the Holocaust, one's first impulse is to ascribe it to his Jewish heritage, and, more concretely, to the German/Hungarian persecution of Jews during the 1933–1945 period. As I read it, however, Blam's timidity and shyness does not result from his Jewish persecution or from his sense of guilt that he has, unjustifiably, survived. Several scenes show that Blam was nearly autistic in his early, pre-persecution childhood.

Blam's only sibling, his young sister Estera, shows that timid inaction was no inherited family trait either. She dies as a resistance fighter, contradicting Hannah Arendt's view that the Jewish East-European middle-class failed to resist the aggressors. Tišma's narrator devotes several pages to Estera as a school child (88–90), to her activities as an underground resistant fighter, and to her death (126–132), yet she dominates Miroslav's mind only briefly, after her unexpected murder (136). He takes a similar distance from the other victimised action-oriented figures. Next to Estera, the most active figure is Ljubo Čutura, who had initiated Blam as a schoolmate into a courageous harvesting of hawthorn fruits (13–15) and defended him against an anti-Semitic teacher (48–49). As a partisan he seeks asylum with Blam shortly before he is caught and murdered (137–144, 184–188). As we shall see, Blam is similarly unable to follow the deadly path of Slobodan Krkljuš, the brother of his childhood friend Aca.

Among the perpetrators, we find, next to the unnamed killers of Estera and Čutura, people who rent rooms in the Blam house, including the charming philanderer Pedrag Popadić. Helping the family to find a doctor to carry out an abortion on a girl whom Miroslav made pregnant, Pedrag gets into intimate conversations with Miroslav's mother, and finally seduces her. When he brings to his room another woman, a dramatic confrontation reveals the affair to everybody. Pedrag is allowed to reoccupy his old room after a brief military service, but when he becomes editor of the *Naše novine*, a new fellow-traveller newspaper under Hungarian rule, he moves to the Mercury and offers Vilim Blam a job in the advertising section (88). At the end of the war, he tries to change horses but is immediately executed for having been a fellow traveller.

Miroslav's post-war ambling through the former Jewish quarter of Novi Sad offers the narrator the opportunity to describe the neighbourhood and the history of its former inhabitants, nearly all of whom were murdered on the spot or transported to death camps (22–26). Miroslav survived the razzia in relative safety and did not witness its worst atrocities. His survival was not due to careful planning but to his ill-considered and malfunctioning marriage to a non-Jewish woman, which he did not foresee as a lifesaver. He got to know Janja at a dance school and she consented to go with him to the movies – which she did every time a boy asked her. The sexual desire that ignited in Miroslav when he once saw her in peasant clothes never rekindled later, but nevertheless he proposed to her and the parents ultimately consented to the marriage for Miroslav had a higher social standing. During the war, Miroslav once saw from a tram how Janja and Pedrag Popadić were kissing, but this (and everything else important for him) he cannot discuss with her.

Considering the timespan of Tišma's book, the events of the razzia come relatively late, in the eleventh of the fourteen chapters. This is the only chapter, in which the narrator mainly adopts perpetrator perspectives, which are broader here than in *Hideg napok*. The chapter opens with an 'objective' topography of the city on the Danube, a horseshoe-shaped spider web (150–151), which is then shown in the hands of the unnamed Hungarian officers preparing the house-to-house razzia. The narrator follows several units combing particular districts. The first one, led by second lieutenant Géczy (152–157), strictly follows the rules the first day and arrests only two Serbs who came to the city for a visit. The narrator tells us that young Géczy brought his wife to Novi Sad and hurried to the first razzia day from a warm conjugal bed (152). Whether bringing his wife was officially authorised remains unclear, but the presence of a wife suggests that Tišma may have been familiar with Cseres's novel. In any case, Géczy is severely reprimanded in the evening by an unnamed general, presumably József Grassy, who orders him to round up "one-hundred criminals" the next day (153). To overcome inhibitions, Géczy, as all others, is served rum for breakfast. His murdered innocent victims that day include Vilim Blam and his wife (156). Miroslav, who already lives a baptised life with Janja in the Mercurius building, is checked by police lieutenant Nándor Varga (166–169), who keeps to the rules and gladly takes Pedrag Popadić as his guide through the building. Miroslav comes through 'clean'.

The most tragic event of the razzia in Tišma's book is also on the banks of the frozen Danube at the dramatic moments around the order to stop the killing (161–166). The gendarmerie officer here is a magyarised German, who regards the razzia as a "natural" way to eliminate all non-Hungarian and non-German elements (161). Though the Krkljuš family has the needed papers, the old couple and their son Slobodan are picked up and delivered to a spot from where they, with many others, have to walk to their executions on the Danube. On the way, an older man stumbles and falls in the snow; when Slobodan tries to help him to his feet both are shot dead – just minutes before the higher officer arrives and orders an immediate stop to the killing. All victims are sent home and the Krkljuš parents never get the chance to say goodbye to their dead son in the snow. Blam retains a rather meaningless contact with his childhood friend Aca, the brother of the murdered Slobodan. The parallels and contrasts with the murder of Büky's wife at the Danube in the Cseres novel are striking.

Since Tišma's narrator does not tell the story in a continuous chronological line, we shuttle between the present as seen by Blam, fragmentary recollections of his childhood and youth, stories and topographical descriptions supplied by the narrator, and scenes imagined by Blam. Put together, we get something like a temporal and spatial mosaic, which does not congeal into a consistent image. Tišma's novel, like that of Cseres, remains a puzzle of many pieces that each reader will have to configure. Precisely this lack of thesis is what offers readers opportunities to reflect and discuss.

Tišma was born to a Serbian father and a Hungarian-speaking Jewish mother. He studied economy and French language and literature in Budapest during World War II, and graduated in German at the University of Belgrade. Like Cseres, he was not in Novi Sad during the razzia. Both of them acquired some (never fully reliable) documentation for their novels, although their focus is ultimately psychological. Cseres chose dramatic concentration against epic breadth, while Tišma offers within a broader social and geographical representation a still narrower dramatic focus, a deeply disturbing and moving psychological study of Miroslav Blam.

The identity of the authors is related in complex ways to their fictional figure(s), which have the same nationality as their author. By portraying some of his countrymen as perpetrators, Cseres obviously intended to initiate a national self-questioning that could have led to a *Vergangenheitsbewältigung*, a reconsideration of Hungarian responsibilities for the past. This did not happen for two reasons: the communist regime did not feel responsible for crimes committed under Horthy, and it had no interest in reconciliation with Tito's Yugoslavia.

The puzzling fact of Tišma's novel is that Miroslav, a member of the victimised Jewish community, feels intensely guilty after the war, almost like a perpetrator. We know that Miroslav Blam and his problems were to a considerable degree autobiographical for Tišma. As he wrote in his diary on April 8, 1971, *The Book of Blam* jolted him out of security into the insecurity of his "most problematic theme, Jewishness" (*Dnevnik* 535). Further diary entries from September 1972 indicate that writing the novel felt like acquiring a new identity, perhaps comparable to the new identity that Miroslav acquired in the concert hall: "Like a hermaphrodite, whose organism took a long time to decide between femininity and masculinity, I became a Jew only now" (*Dnevnik* 562).

The emblem of Tišma's new Jewish identity became that little Jewish boy in the famous photo mentioned above. As he wrote in his diary on September 13, 1975, he was that little boy with the jockey cap and hands high up, but he escaped his fatality (*Dnevnik* 596). "*The Book of Blam* was published with the photo of my bent profile and with the explicit explanation of the publisher; this work finally illuminates my Jewish being" (*Dnevnik* 563). The Polish writer Jaroslaw Rymkiewicz explored the historical identity of the boy in his novel *Umschlagplatz* (1988), and also identified with him:

> We have the personal data of the kid: Artur Siemitetek, the son of Leon and Saranée Dab, born in Lowicz. Artur is my age, both of us were born in 1935. We stand next to each other, he on the photo made in the Warsaw ghetto, I on the platform of Otwock. ... It seems that we wear the same cap. Mine has a brighter shade and is also too big on my head. The boy wears leggings and white socks. I smile nicely on the Otwock platform.
>
> The little boy's face in the photo, taken by an SS commandant, is expressionless. "You are tired" I say to Arthur. Very likely it is difficult to stand with raised arms. I know what we should do. I raise my hand and you should put your one down. Perhaps they don't notice it. Wait, I have a better idea. We both raise our hands. (Quoted in Gvozden 96)

Identifying this way with the little Jewish boy, Rymkiewicz expresses empathy and humanity. The authors of the two discussed books also had their identities at stake: Cseres questions certain heavily ingrained Hungarian identities, while Tišma may be said to be moving towards an identity that was dormant in him. The Holocaust reshaped identities – and continues to do so.

John Neubauer
johnneubauer329@gmail.com
Keizersgracht 734F
1017 EW Amsterdam
NEDERLAND / THE NETHERLANDS

References

Alphen, E. van. 1997. *Caught by History: Holocaust Effects in Contemporary Art, Literature and Theory.* Stanford: Stanford UP.

Arendt, H. 1963. *Eichmann in Jerusalem: The Banality of Evil.* New York: Viking Press.

Cohn, D. 1978. *Transparent Minds. Narrative Modes for Presenting Consciousness in Fiction.* Princeton: Princeton UP.

Cseres, T. 1964. *Hideg napok.* Budapest: Magvető. [Adapted by András Kovács in a film with the same title in 1966.]

Cseres, T. 1966. *Hladni dani.* Subotica, Beograd: Minerva.

Cseres, T. 2003. *Cold Days.* Budapest: Corvina.

Cseres, T. 1991. *Vérbosszú Bácskában.* Budapest: Magvetö. [Trans. as *Titoist Atrocities in Vojvodina 1944–1945; Serbian Vendetta in Bácska.* Buffalo & Ontario: Hunyadi, 1993. *Krvna osveta u Bačkoj.* Zagreb: AGM, 1993.]

Gvozden, V. 2005. Aleksandar Tišma és a Holocaust-effektus. – *Tiszatáj* (January), 82–98.

Moczarski, K. 1977, *Rozmowy z katem.* Warsaw: PIW.

Porat, D. 2010. *The Boy: A Holocaust Story.* New York: Hill and Wang.

Rymkiewicz, J. 1988. *Umschlagplatz.* Warsaw: NOWA.

Stroop, J. 1979. *The Stroop Report: The Jewish Quarter of Warsaw Is No More!* New York: Pantheon Books.

Takács, M. 2009. Trauma, narrative theory and literature in the interpretation of Tibor Cseres' *Hideg napok*. – *Orientation in the Occurrence*. Ed. István Berszán. Cluj-Napoca: Komp-Press: Korunk, 391–98.

Tišma, A. *Pre mita*. Banjaluka: Glas, 1989.

Tišma, A. 1998. *The Book of Blam*. Trans. Michael Henry Heim. New York etc.: Harvest Books. [Trans. of *Knjiga o blamu*. Belgrade: Nolit, 1971.]

Tišma, A. 2001. *Dnevnik: 1942–200*. Sremski Karlovski: Izdavačka knjižarnica Zorana Stojanovića.

Zločini okupatora u Vojvodini, 1941–1944 [Crimes of the Occupational Forces in Vojvodina 1941–1944]. Belgrade: Napredak, 1946.

Baltic History through the Lens of 20th-Century Drama[1]

BENEDIKTS KALNAČS

Abstract. The paper focuses upon the representation of history in 20th-century Lithuanian, Latvian and Estonian drama. It opens with a discussion of the main issues peripheral societies and cultures face when interpreting their past and present and then delineates why the representation of history is relevant for the Baltic countries in general and of special importance to Lithuania. Contrary to Estonia and Latvia, which did not have a similar past upon which to call for inspiration and courage, medieval Lithuania became one of the largest countries in Europe, and later on, in association with Poland, formed an important Central-European power until the late 18th century. In the period that followed, however, the ban on the Lithuanian script delayed the rise of modern national consciousness, and, in the 20th century, representation of history again became of major importance for Lithuanians, as it did for Estonians and Latvians, especially under Soviet rule. The paper thus tackles 20th-century reflections upon the historical past of the three Baltic nations. The analysis focuses on the independence decades of the 1920s and 1930s as well as the period of Soviet rule stretching across the second half of the 20th century. Both periods are scrutinised in detail as well as being approached comparatively. In the final part of the paper, the representation of the more recent historical past is dealt with as it becomes possible to discuss topics previously forbidden by the Soviet authorities.

Keywords: Lithuanian, Latvian, and Estonian literatures, Baltic drama, Baltic history, representation of history

In 2009, in a series of state supported events, Lithuania celebrated a millennium since the word 'Litua', designating the historical Lithuania, first appeared in written form. The festivities included a large exhibition and the publication of a book of historical materials and interpretations that contained a welcoming introduction by Valdas Adamkus, president of Lithuania. (Šapoka 2009) The primary source for the festival events was a medieval chronicle, the so-called

[1] This research has been supported by the European Social Fund within the project 'Cultures within a Culture: Politics and Poetics of Border Narratives' (Nr. 1DP/1.1.1.2.0/13/APIA/VIAA/042).

DOI: http://dx.doi.org/10.12697/IL.2015.S1.17

Quedlinburg Annals, which recounted the martyrdom of a Christian missionary named Bruno. The name 'Litua' was mentioned for the first time in this chronicle. During the early 21st-century celebrations, the rich and at times glorious history of the Lithuanian people again came to the fore, but at the same time the festival activities clearly underscored a characteristic shared by all three Baltic countries: their history has largely been written by foreign invaders. Even if the political presence of the Lithuanian state played a crucial role beginning with the reign of Mindaugas in the 13th century, almost all of the historical documentation was produced in languages other than that of the indigenous people. To an even greater extent, the historical presence of the Estonian and Latvian tribes has almost exclusively been documented in foreign language sources. Only much later, during the period of national awakening, did the story of the Baltic peoples start to be shaped by native historians and, to a considerable degree, also by writers who supplemented historical facts with stories and legends that became fundamental to the national self-consciousness of the respective peoples.

Thus, while the representation of history was important for identity formation in all three Baltic cultures, historical dramas in particular played a prominent role during the late-19th and early 20th-century national awakening movements. The representation of history, however, proved to be especially important for Lithuanian culture, where the 19th century was a troubled time that limited political, economic, and cultural development due to the extensive russification of the country. The instinct for national self-preservation, however, remained intact, and national history often provided a means for spiritual recovery and pride.

Moreover, in the first truly modern dramatic texts that explored historical topics, Lithuanian authors were also keen to raise issues of national and individual identity. This trend was visible throughout the 1920s and 1930s. Later, during the period of Soviet rule, new efforts to redefine the historical experience of the Baltic peoples began in the second half of the 1950s. This paper mostly focuses on uses of history in Lithuanian drama while constantly keeping in mind parallel developments in the other two Baltic countries, especially during the last decades of the 20th century.

History vs. reality in independent Lithuania

In the early 20th century, all three Baltic countries were gradually moving toward independence, which was declared in 1918. Historical circumstances, however, allowed the newly declared nation-states to stabilise their status only after the independence wars. Before 1918 there were many similarities in the thinking of Estonian, Latvian and Lithuanian supporters of the national idea, but also considerable differences. In the Lithuanian provinces, for example, as historian Andrejs Plakans observes, the most significant and continual skirmish was between "those who envisaged a future Lithuania without any Polish influence and those who insisted that some form of Polishness was inescapably a part of the Lithuanian national ethos. The latter thinking, of course, was anchored in the historic existence of the Polish-Lithuanian Commonwealth." In contemporary discussions, Plakans concludes, "the distant and more recent past collided" (Plakans 2011: 283).

Especially after its territorial expansion in the 14th and 15th centuries, the lands of the Lithuanian Grand Duchy were multicultural and multilingual. Diverse peoples lived side by side and several languages were used in official communication. Even if the population of the historical core areas, such as Samogitia (Žemaitija) and Aukštaitija, remained predominantly Lithuanian, quite often the upper classes were polonised, especially in the period following the so-called Union of Lublin in 1569 when the Polish element increasingly dominated the Commonwealth. However, similar trends were visible from the time of the early agreement of mutual cooperation between Poland and the Lithuanian Grand Duchy (Union of Krėva in 1385), despite the fact that the two nations waged many famous battles together. As in the case of the glorious victory over the Teutonic Order near Tannenberg in 1410, the Lithuanian forces and their leaders played a determining role in the military operations. For example, in his portrayal of the battle, 19th-century Polish artist Jan Matejko clearly puts more stress on the military bravery of the Lithuanian duke Vytautas than upon the Polish king Jogaila, who himself was of Lithuanian origin.

These historical relationships became a topical issue when the declaration of an independent Lithuanian state on February 16, 1918 was followed about a year later by harsh combat with territorial neighbours. Severe battles ensued with the rising Polish state, which attempted to use the unstable political situation to pursue its own interests in securing what it believed to be its rightful boundaries to the south, east, and west. As Plakans notes, Poland's aspirations in the east included the old territories of the Polish-Lithuanian Commonwealth, which brought Polish expectations into direct conflict with those of the Lithuanians. (Plakans 2011: 305) In 1920, these aspirations resulted in the occupation of about one fifth of the territories the Lithuanians not only considered to be theirs (including the ancient capital of Vilnius, which remained under Polish control until the beginning of World War II) but which had also already been identified as such during the armistice between Lithuanians and Poles. To a considerable extent, this development stimulated revivalist thinking in the Lithuanian population and intensified feelings of nostalgia.

More or less direct references to these events appear in the most important Lithuanian drama texts of the independence period, among them, *Skirgaila* by Vincas Krėvė-Mickevičius, first published in 1922, and *Milžino paunksmė* (*The Shadow of the Giant*, 1932) by Balys Sruoga. In an apt remark, the Lithuanian researcher Aušra Martišiūte notes that at this time Lithuanian drama was infused with philosophical reflections on history, and, without doubting the heroism of the legendary characters, it also scrutinised the dramatic intensity of their feelings. (Martišiūte 2006: 160)

Skirgaila, written by Vincas Krėvė-Mickevičius (1882–1954), provides one of the most fascinating examples of this shift. Born in Dzūkija, the region of Lithuania famous for its folklore heritage of songs and legends, Krėvė-Mickevičius studied at the universities of Kiev and Lviv (in present-day Ukraine) between 1904 and 1908. Since tsarist law prohibited his return to his native country, Krėvė-Mickevičius's interest in Oriental culture took him to the Caucasus where he lectured in Baku between 1909 and 1920. After Lithuanian independence, he returned in 1920 and became professor at the Lithuanian University in Kaunas (1922–1940) and then in Vilnius (1940–1943). For many people, the early 1920s were a time of pride mixed with disillusionment about the historical realities of the newly established state. Fully aware of the importance of the changes, Krėvė-Mickevičius faced his own uncertainty about the events evolving around him in his depiction of Skirgaila, the main character of his drama. He places him in a position that emulates his own contradictory feelings: the play tackles the persisting conflict of pagan and Christian identities in Lithuania.

It is interesting to note that the coexistence of different religions was strongly felt even when Lithuania was the last remaining pagan country in Europe. During the reign of Grand Duke Gediminas (who ruled from 1316 to 1341 and who founded the city of Vilnius in 1323), Lithuania became one of the major powers in East-Central Europe. According to historian Andres Kasekamp, it was "a pagan realm which ruled over a majority Christian population". As a result, one Orthodox and two Catholic churches for eastern and western merchants existed side by side with a pagan temple erected by Gediminas on the ruins of Mindaugas' cathedral. The temple housed the idol Perkunas, the god of Thunder and chief of Lithuanian deities, and was a structure that mimicked Christianity, since Baltic pagan worship was typically conducted outdoors in sacred groves or at sacrificial stones. (Kasekamp 2010: 21–22)

The events depicted in *Skirgaila* evolve slightly later, between the years 1386 and 1392, which ushered in crucial transformations in the history of the Lithuanian Grand Duchy. These changes are linked to the accession to the Polish throne of the Lithuanian duke Jogaila. The duke had married the Polish princess Jadwiga as a result of political manoeuvres and attempts by the Polish nobles to stabilise their state as well as to make the powerful Lithuanian Grand Duchy a reliable ally. The marriage took place in 1385, and a year later Jogaila became the king of Poland. While the wedding pact has been viewed as a controversial document by later historians, at the time it was considered "a state alliance and an act of union" (Kiaupa 2005: 59). The union established the Jagiellonian dynasty that ruled over much of East-Central Europe for the next two centuries.

Although Jogaila appointed his brother Skirgaila viceroy in Lithuania (Kasekamp 2010: 25), political tensions between the Polish and Lithuanian parts of the new state persisted, partly because of the aspirations of the Lithuanian duke Vytautas, the cousin of Jogaila and son of Kęstutis (who might have been a victim of Jogaila's plotting while trying to secure a more powerful position for himself). Vytautas (who, on the same occasion, barely escaped a murder attempt himself) later became Jogaila's political adversary. His activities led to a civil war that ended with a compromise in 1392 when Vytautas was offered the viceroyship (and somewhat later was named the Grand Duke of Lithuania). In a parallel move, Skirgaila was pushed out of his native land and dispatched to rule over Kiev; he died during this period of enforced obedience in 1397.

In Krėvė-Mickevičius's play, the character of Skirgaila, portrayed during his term as a viceroy, is already plagued by hesitations and doubts. The play opens as Skirgaila hosts several Polish and German knights, a duty he assumes in the changed historical circumstances resulting from the Christianisation of Lithuania after Jogaila becomes King of Poland. In contrast to earlier times, when participating in the almost yearly campaign against the Lithuanian heathens had become a virtual rite of passage for European knights (Kasekamp 2010: 23), both the Poles and Teutonic knights were now viewed as Lithuania's political allies. While Krėvė-Mickevičius portrays Skirgaila as a reliable political leader who overtly fulfils his duty in his homeland, he also shows that Skirgaila has not come to terms with the new situation. He is tempted to imitate the ostensibly good manners of the medieval knights even though he cannot abandon his own pagan identity. The feeling of being 'not quite' like the knights motivates Skirgaila to consciously provoke his guests during the official celebrations. As the events evolve, Skirgaila himself becomes a victim of the complicated plotting by false friends who care only about their own interests. The play thus connects to a situation often experienced by small states in the 20th-century world. Feelings of betrayal certainly haunted many Lithuanians after they lost the battle with Poland in the early 1920s.[2]

2 The first version of this drama, initially published in 1922, was written in Russian, and only a couple of years later a somewhat altered Lithuanian version appeared. This also demonstrates the cosmopolitan experience of the writer, while at the same time a conscious awareness of his own nationality develops in the course of the play.

In addition to religion, history also became a topical issue as Lithuanian theatre rapidly matured. In the early 1930s, its development was closely linked to the innovative work of the young director Andrius Oleka-Žilinskas. One of his most creative productions was based on *Šarūnas,* a drama completed by Vincas Krėvė-Mickevičius in 1912. Produced in 1930, the stage version by Oleka-Žilinskas received recognition and attention in both the Lithuanian and Latvian press. It was staged at the Lithuanian State Theatre in Kaunas, and Oleka-Žilinskas chose the young poet Balys Sruoga as one of his closest collaborators. They later worked together on productions staged at the Theatre of the Young, a company started by students of Oleka-Žilinskas. Sruoga's first play, *Milžino paunksmė,* was staged there in 1934.

Sruoga (1896–1947), like his older colleague Krėvė-Mickevičius, had a good grasp of the international literary scene. During the 1910s, he studied at the University of Moscow and later in St. Petersburg. Even more importantly, Sruoga joined the literary circle of Russian symbolists, in which his compatriot, the poet Jurgis Baltrušaitis, played a significant role. After World War I, Sruoga went west to study at Munich University, where he became well acquainted with expressionist tendencies. As a result, he gained a solid understanding of modernist art and confidence regarding his position in the rising theatre scene in Lithuania. When he started his work at the Lithuanian university in Kaunas, where he was active from 1924 to 1940, Sruoga initiated a seminar that "outgrew its stated purpose and became a sort of discussion club for young literati, budding playwrights, actors, and theatre critics" (Blekaitis 1986: 211).

Most of the scripts Sruoga completed during the late 1930s and 1940s featured a historical background that foregrounded "periods of peril" rather than "moments of glory" (Blekaitis 1986: 213). In them, the main characters are trouble-ridden and split personalities whose inner contradictions are clearly linked to the historical context within which they have to act. In his first drama, *Milžino paunksmė,* which was written on the occasion of the six-hundredth anniversary of the death of Grand Duke Vytautas the Great, Sruoga took a somewhat different approach. The play is also set in the early decades of the Polish and Lithuanian union while the specific events unfold between 1427 and 1430. The play ends with the funeral rites for Vytautas but nevertheless the strong presence of the hero in Lithuanian history is the focus of attention.

One of the most innovative elements of *Milžino paunksmė* is the author's decision not to present Vytautas on stage. When Sruoga submitted the play to the committee planning the official celebrations to mark the anniversary of Vytautas's death, the committee neither awarded it a prize nor recommended it for production (since it did not conform to the traditional way of celebrating a great personality (Martišiūte 2006: 242)). In the play, Sruoga made Jogaila the main protagonist; Vytautas remains godlike, "omnipresent but invisible", in the words of Blekaitis (1986: 214). Historians attribute a change in popular consciousness to the period depicted in the play and point out that the compatriots of Vytautas, while remaining generally open and tolerant, vigorously embraced the idea that Lithuanians had created the new state and that Lithuanians not only ruled it but also were responsible for its destiny (Kiaupa 2005: 77).

In Lithuanian culture, Jogaila is usually classified as a young and unprincipled person. In *The Shadow of the Giant,* however, his character is that of an experienced sceptic who doubts his ability to make an impact on historical events and, consequently, withdraws in resignation. This passive stance is a conscious one. Jogaila strives to avoid actions that might harm his Lithuanian compatriots. Turning a deaf ear to the more radical propositions of his counsellors at the court in Cracow, Jogaila thus indirectly supports Lithuanian sovereignty, which is symbolically embodied by the powerful figure of Vytautas. Psychologically, this portrayal forms a bridge to later Soviet dramas, especially those written by Juozas Grušas, who uses historical plots to point to the limited possibilities for anyone to act according to individual intentions during Soviet rule.

Another innovative aspect of Sruoga's play is provided by the fact that he often focuses on seemingly private incidents instead of great public happenings. This approach emphasises a sense of 'otherness' not only in the opposition between the public and private self but also in relation to the different preferences of Jogaila as a Polish king and, in Sruoga's interpretation, as a lively Lithuanian patriot. To a great extent the playwright's subjective vision corresponds to historical reality since Jogaila's position at the time was especially difficult because he was forced to take into account the frequently conflicting interests between Lithuania and Poland and to manoeuvre between them (Kiaupa 2005: 77). As a consequence, Jogaila's split identity comes to the fore as a determining feature of his character.

Written during the brief interwar period of independence, the plays by Krėvė-Mickevičius and Sruoga underline the constant psychological tensions that have an impact upon the Lithuanian people, even during times of relative peace and self-determination. The reading and theatre public appreciated the interest of both writers in topical issues of Lithuanian history as well as their keen awareness of the sensibilities of the nation during the interwar period.

The recontextualisation of history

During the years of Nazi occupation, when it was more or less possible to point toward historical parallels of contemporary events, history sometimes appeared on the horizon of the playwrights' interests. During the first post-war decade of

Soviet rule, on the other hand, authorities were keen to suppress any reminder of the national history of the once independent Baltic nations. The play *Herkus Mantas* (1957), by the Lithuanian dramatist Juozas Grušas (1901–1986), was one of first and most important examples of how history and memory, beginning in the late 1950s, became prominent in cultural life and particularly in literature. The fate of the Old Prussians, who had already been extinguished from the stage of history, was an especially relevant topic since it implied the possibility of a similar scenario connected to Soviet colonial practices. The interest in history and memory remained popular for some time, although the visions of playwrights differed to a great extent. The plays by Grušas and Justinas Marcinkevičius (1930–2011), another important Lithuanian dramatist, published and performed during the 1960s and 1970s, provide an especially telling example.

The early plays of Marcinkevičius essentially conformed to the requirements of socialist realism. (Mitaitė 2009: 191) In the course of his career, however, his creative output changed substantially as he began to pay considerable attention to issues of national culture, for example, in his narrative poem *Donelaitis* (1964). In the years leading up to the restoration of Lithuanian independence, Marcinkevičius was one of the most popular playwrights. His poetic voice became elegiac, perhaps, as Mitaite notes, "because the individual realises the transience of existence and his kinship with everything alive" (Mitaitė 2009: 191).

While Marcinkevičius's poetic trilogy, *Mindaugas* (1968), *Katedra* (*The Cathedral*, 1971), and *Mažvydas* (1977), bears clear resemblance to earlier models of Soviet writing, at the same time it speaks to the soul of the nation and addresses critical questions to contemporary rulers. Retrospectively, the author himself has commented on his concern with national identity in his treatment of such historical events as the formation of the state of Lithuania in the 13th century, the beginning of Lithuanian letters in the 16th century, and the unity of art and spiritual power represented by the construction of the Vilnius Cathedral (completed 1801). (Marcinkevičius 2005: 5) The main protagonists in all three are well known historical persons, such as the architect Laurynas Stuoka-Gucevičius (1753–1798), Martynas Mažvydas (1510–1563), who wrote the first Lithuanian printed text, a catechism issued in 1547, and Mindaugas (?–1263), the first king of Lithuania who was crowned on July 6, 1253 (a day celebrated as a national holiday in contemporary Lithuania).

Each play in the trilogy features a strong personality, a man who struggles to fulfil his aspirations, faces numerous opponents, and is morally superior to most of the others around him. A closer look at the trilogy, however, reveals that Marcinkevičius consistently challenges the stereotypes of the Soviet period and even risks breaking some of its prevalent rules. First of all, he revives the cultural tradition of verse drama which abandons the (socialist) realism model and establishes a link with earlier Lithuanian texts, such as those by Balys Sruoga. Secondly, Marcinkevičius applies the ostensibly Soviet system of historical development not only to Lithuanian history but also to the formative stages of the Lithuanian nation. He thus reverses certain prevalent expectations by depicting the long span of centuries as a continuous battle for self-determination against foreign powers. The Soviet colonial discourse that features a strong and powerful man as a creator of history is therefore challenged on a deeper level by an anti-colonial discourse that describes an endangered nation's endless struggle.

In their book *Post-colonial Drama: Theory, Practice, Politics* (1996), Helen Gilbert and Joanne Tompkins propose a model for approaching postcolonial narratives that applies to Marcinkevičius's dramatic poems. In their view, the following features are characteristic of postcolonial performance: a focus on "acts that respond to the experience of imperialism, whether directly or indirectly; acts performed for the continuation and/or regeneration of the colonised (and sometimes pre-contact) communities; acts performed with the awareness of, and sometimes the incorporation of, post-contact forms; and acts that interrogate the hegemony that underlies imperial representation" (Gilbert and Tompkins 1996: 11). When applied to the dramatic texts of Marcinkevičius, this approach confirms the contradictory nature of his poetic dramas. For example, despite using the model of historical representation that correlates to Soviet ideology with its notion of historical progress as the result of social transformations (thus embodying the hegemony of the narrative of power), the author simultaneously challenges his initial stance by featuring Lithuanian historical characters as the main protagonists and as creators of their own visions. By so doing, Marcinkevičius re-creates the historical narratives of the Lithuanian people, including that of their own statehood, which clearly opposes the dominant doctrine of Soviet internationalism.

The double-faced nature of the dramatic poems has produced extended discussions about the position of the creative output of Marcinkevičius in the context of Lithuanian letters. Clearly, the reception of his work differs among scholars working in Soviet Lithuania, in exile, and in independent Lithuania (where a recent tendency has been to take a rather more critical stance). However, if we do not restrict our focus to the official rhetoric of Soviet criticism, the analysis provided by critics of diverse backgrounds overlaps to a significant extent.

In his introduction to the English translation of *Mindaugas* (Straumanis 1986), exile critic Rimvydas Šilbajoris pointed out the contradictions and dilemmas faced by any author working in a totalitarian system. In his view, Marcinkevičius struggles to reach an almost impossible middle ground: specifically, "to build his nest somewhere between the horns of this dilemma: he proclaims his allegiance to the Soviet system while at the same time addressing its victims in a heartfelt voice of loyalty with their deepest sufferings and aspirations" (Šilbajoris 1986: 147).

Thus, Marcinkevičius must somehow try to embrace both "the aspirations and cruelties of his State. His record as an artist is one of an inspired and eloquent failure to achieve this impossible thing; yet, in trying, he has become one of the country's most important and accomplished writers," concludes Šilbajoris (1986: 147). Somewhat later, exile critic Audrius Vilius Dundzila expresses a related thought in more straightforward terms, contending that Marcinkevičius's Mindaugas is "a veiled version of the Communist Party in Lithuania", a character popularly viewed as an autocrat who "both participated in Stalinist terror and later protected Lithuania from massive russification. Mindaugas is a Soviet Lithuanian cadre who benefits himself while serving the state" (Dundzila 1990: 48).

Vytautas Rubavičius, a critic who directly experienced the Soviet years, points out that the author's voice in Marcinkevičius's dramatic poems is not free for it must embody both the actual circumstances and the necessity to adapt. What is more, Rubavičius contends, because the past experiences of those living in the colonial empire also have to be addressed seriously in the context of the future, contemporary judgments should not simply take an oppositional or subversive stance with regard to previous opinions. (Rubavičius 2006: 85) Critic Aurimas Švedas makes a similar point when he states that the works of Marcinkevičius generate diverse responses to Soviet ideological and historiographic claims as the author both reinforces Soviet ideology and provides a challenge to it; he simultaneously supports and negates the official claims about the perception of history. (Švedas 2013: 55) Thus, the very fact that Marcinkevičius picked topics Lithuanian historians were not permitted to tackle was an important breakthrough in the representation of history, even if the texts themselves only mildly challenged the Soviet ideological discourse.

Indeed, one of the most intriguing questions to ask is how these texts were received by the public and what impact they had on popular minds. For example, Rubavičius notes that Soviet Lithuanian author Eduardas Mieželaitis first published the poem *Man* (*Žmogus*, 1961) in Russian translation and only later in Lithuanian because he wanted to ensure the poem's success on the so-called all-Union scale by conforming to party lines and thus also benefit himself financially. (Rubavičius 2006: 92) Do the dramatic poems of Marcinkevičius fit into the same pattern? And what did these texts and their metaphors mean on the level of personal experience? Šilbajoris suggests that Mindaugas's entire endeavour is a physical metaphor: it is "a clay model of Lithuania, to which he adds a piece, physically and symbolically, every day" (Šilbajoris 1986: 152). Even more strikingly, at the end of another of Marcinkevičius's dramatic poems, *Mažvydas*, the protagonist and the creator of the first Lithuanian catechism utters the word 'Lietuva' at the very point when, together with assembled Lithuanian peasants, he starts to read from the book he has just completed. For me this scene became one of the most striking early theatre experiences during the guest performance of the Lithuanian Drama Theatre in Riga in the early 1980s. It was, arguably, a breakthrough to a different level of self-awareness at a time when almost every manifestation of national identity as a substantial part of individual integrity was strictly kept out of the public space.

To a considerable extent, the success of Marcinkevičius's work was embedded in his ability to create emotionally charged scenes and complex characters. Šilbajoris even claims that the protagonists of the dramatic poems are consciously built on contradictions. (Šilbajoris 1986: 149) The same principle might be applied to the general structure of *Mindaugas*, which allocates an important role to the portrayal of two chroniclers with irreconcilable points of view, one called Black and the other White. Because their words and actions are ambiguous, the validity of their statements is both outside and inside the horizons of the verbal universe in which they have been created; the chroniclers are thus both freed from and limited by the confines of the play. (Ibid.)

The dominant position of Mindaugas is juxtaposed to the virtually outlawed position occupied by his beloved Morta, the wife of his ally Vismantas. Morta gives birth to Mindaugas's son but is constrained to silence by virtue of the circumstances. When Morta goes mad, the juxtaposition of the heroic narrative about Mindaugas with that of Morta as 'the other' points to the fact that there are many more contradictions in life than usually expected or allowed by Soviet ideological prescriptions. Whatever the approach, Marcinkevičius's trilogy to a great extent displays individuals acting within the framework of canonical socialist values while at the same time the texts at least marginally challenge the existing political order.

Another approach, one that offers a more radical deconstruction of the socialist realism canon, can also be attributed to texts from the 1970s that use more subtle artistic means to challenge established political and aesthetic presumptions. In them, scepticism towards the socialist realist models manifests itself both in the rewriting of historically established stories and in the use of irony, paradox and grotesque to diminish the importance of earlier messages. The play *Barbora Radvilaitė* (1972) by Juozas Grušas, which in many respects stands in opposition to the heroic trilogy of Justinas Marcinkevičius, is a case in point.

Juozas Grušas wrote both prose works and plays. He studied Lithuanian and German literatures at the Lithuanian (later renamed Vytautas Magnus) University in Kaunas, graduating in 1931. He worked as an editor while also serving as chairman of the Lithuanian Writers' Society in 1937–1938. Grušas started his literary career in independent Lithuania, but kept silent during the early years of Soviet rule. Then, in 1957, he wrote *Herkus Mantas*, which became one of the texts that marked the beginning of the so-called Thaw in Lithuanian literature. In subsequent years, Grušas was one of the most prolific Lithuanian dramatists.

Among his most important works was *Barbora Radvilaitė*, a play that draws on 16th-century historical sources to set up a subtle dialogue with Lithuanian cultural tradition and bases its plot on a complex historical background. After the coronation of Alexander, the Grand Duke of Lithuania, as the king of Poland in 1501, the titles of king and grand duke were always held by one and the same person. (Kasekamp 2010: 29–30) This practice signalled the increasingly closer relations between Lithuania and Poland, a trend that continued when Alexander was succeeded by his brother Sigismund (the Elder) in 1506. On the other hand, during the 15th century the leadership of the Grand Duchy had been monopolised by a ruling elite of about twenty noble [Lithuanian] families who owned the largest landed estates. (Ibid.) Understandable tensions arose between the Lithuanians and Poles. This political background played a substantial role in the relationship between Sigismund Augustus (1520–1572), the heir to the Polish crown, and Barbora Radvilaitė (1520–1551), an offspring of one of the most prominent families of the Lithuanian nobility. Following her early death, Radvilaitė became a legendary character of Lithuanian history and was especially popular from the 18th century onward.

The plot of Grušas's play unfolds in the 1540s and centres on the secret marriage of Sigismund Augustus and Barbora in 1547. While the world of kings and aristocrats is still the focus of attention, the characters are portrayed in highly personal terms and in circumstances that only marginally relate to history. Nevertheless, historical realities are decisive in the lives of the protagonists and the play builds upon the tradition of Lithuanian historical drama that foregrounds the tensions between Lithuanian and Polish characters, such as the plays by Krėvė-Mickevičius and Balys Sruoga. Lithuanian scholar Reda Pabarčienė has pointed out the substantial parallels between *Barbora Radvilaitė* and an earlier unfinished version of the same story by Sruoga in the 1940s. (Pabarčienė 2006) Some aspects also link the work of Grušas to Marcinkevičius's dramatic trilogy; both plays foreground historically crucial turning points and depict their protagonists as they reflect on transpiring events.

Barbora Radvilaitė represents an important step in the development of Lithuanian dramaturgy during the Soviet period. There are, however, at least two substantial differences between the texts of Grušas and Marcinkevičius. First of all, the world inhabited by Grušas's characters is less safe and its characters are not portrayed carrying out heroic deeds. Despite their aristocratic family backgrounds, they are not in a position to decide their own fate. Instead, their political and personal decisions are determined by others, with the result that they are helpless before an unpredictable future. The grand narrative is no longer possible, as demonstrated by the doubts and deep inner contradictions of the protagonists. Heroes understand each other best through sensual communication, such as dancing; their environment is so unpredictable that they often cannot grasp the meaning of their own words.

Another important feature of Grušas's text is suggested by the title of his play. Its focus is a woman, Barbora Radvilaitė, rather than a male bravely paving his way into the future. To a great extent, the twists and turns of Radvilaitė's fate are dictated by the politically and morally colonising power, which ostensibly is superior both in social standing and gender. This aspect absorbs additional meaning when compared to Grušas's earlier work, *Herkus Mantas,* in which a heroic male attempts to challenge the advance of world history. If compared to the works of Marcinkevičius, the plays by Grušas take a much more radical and ironic view of reality. In the Soviet period, these texts inevitably co-existed with dramas much more respectful toward the prevailing ideology.

The dissolution of the glorious narrative of Soviet military victory

The 1980s witness yet another challenge to the socialist realist canon. Its basic premises are inverted as attitudes toward recent history change substantively. Topics earlier considered taboo themes, such as the mass deportations of the indigenous population carried out by the Soviet authorities in 1941 and 1949, and the prevailing narrative of World War II as 'the Great Patriotic War', acquire more tragic and human features. Authors start to portray the consequences, such as the departure of a substantial portion of the Baltic population, and they depict everyday scenes from the war period, thus challenging the black and white contrasts characteristic of Soviet history-writing.

The Estonian scholar Jaan Undusk has asserted that Soviet historiography lost its moral grounding because it was impossible to change the dominant ideological message, except for incorporating factual material acquired in the process of research. (Undusk 2006: 130) This contrast constituted the main difference between history written in exile and in the Soviet Union. The rise of historical consciousness in the Baltic communities abroad led to the production of scholarly and literary works on historical topics. Such efforts were almost impossible under Soviet rule because the ideological prescriptions underlying interpretation could neither be avoided nor challenged. According to theatre researcher Piret Kruuspere, even as late as the 1970s, historical generalisation in literature or theatre was only possible in an indirect and implicit manner. (Kruuspere 1999: 83) Even as more reasoned discussions about the earlier history of the Baltic countries gradually broke through existing barriers, the narrative of the victorious Soviet war machine remained the most important staple of communist ideology. Despite the fact that direct colonial rule ended twenty-five years ago, discussions about World War II memorials erected in the Baltic countries during Soviet times continue to be the most emotionally loaded of topics, and any actions the democratically elected governments of the Baltic states might take provoke a menacing reaction from Russian politicians as well those in the local population who still adhere to imperial ideology whenever they feel their interests threatened.

Two case studies demonstrate the inversion of the traditional heroic narrative of World War II in the 1980s and indicate the rising self-esteem of the indigenous population of the Baltic countries. In 1982, the Estonian dramatist Jaan Kruusvall (b. 1940) wrote *Pilvede värvid* (*The Colours of Clouds*), which initially attracted publicity in exile and later was approved for production in Soviet Estonia. Together with *Vaikuse vallamaja* (*The Parish House of Silence*, 1987) the play marked Kruusvall's most important literary expression of the spirit of the times. Piret Kruuspere has pointed out that the 1980s marked a rise in the direct approach to social and historical problems: for a brief time, she writes, Estonian theatres "functioned almost as lecture rooms, where supplemental lessons in national history were given" (Kruuspere 1999: 86). Kruusvall follows this thread in *Pilvede värvid*, albeit in a somewhat qualified respect.

Written at a time when documentary drama was at the peak of popularity, *Pilvede värvid* nevertheless manages to propose an original aesthetic approach, one well suited to the topic of hidden and taboo history. The events take place on an Estonian coastal farm during the autumn of 1944, as the war front approaches a small fishing village and everyone awaits further developments. The local inhabitants face the dilemma of deciding whether to flee or remain. The Estonian researcher Anneli Saro argues that "the play is exceptional in Soviet literature because the almost archetypal Estonian family it depicts has clearly positive connotations, and initially lacks any connection with the Soviet army and ideology" (Saro 2011: 73). Even while suffering from the hard labour and food shortages of the German occupation, people living on the farm never express any hopes about the Soviet army as a liberator – a central figure of speech in Soviet rhetoric. The members of this family are apolitical: they have no allegiance to either of the warring empires, do not want to choose sides, and admit that the war doesn't make sense to them. (Ibid.)

In her discussion of the play and its production at the Estonian Drama Theatre, where, after premiering in 1983, it was performed more than 250 times, Saro points toward a crucial quality of the production directed by Mikk Mikiver: "One of the main characteristics of the production was silence – silence or unspoken words at the end of the sentences, between sentences, between characters and between scenes. In the early 1980s, these moments of silence acted like empty signifiers, which were filled by the audiences according to their personal or collectively shared experiences." (Saro 2011: 74)

What we notice first of all in *Pilvede värvid* is thus a revised interpretation of history, one that challenges the established patterns of representation and allows a glimpse into the depths of collective memory. Instead of yet again experiencing the official Soviet rhetoric of military heroism, the audience confronts the enormous suffering of people caught up by the cruel events; instead of recovering one's land (as the 'liberation' narrative suggests), the author focuses on the loss of the land. Instead of focusing on the brotherhood of nations (the cliché most stubbornly preserved in Soviet ideological descriptions), the tragic dissolution of a family stands metonymically for the fate of the Estonian nation, singled out as the object of history and virtually helpless as it is torn apart by alien powers.

The Latvian dramatist Gunārs Priede (1928–2000) follows the same pattern of thought in his play *Centrifūga* (*Centrifuge*), written in 1984 after he saw a production of *Pilvede värvid* at the Baltic theatre festival in Vilnius. *Centrifūga* deals with the events taking place during the same period of time, the autumn of 1944, in the German occupied western part of Latvia. At the time, Priede was already an experienced dramatist who had repeatedly challenged the ideologically imposed limits of representation. In *Centrifūga*, however, he directly addressed events of the war that were deeply engraved in his own memory, taking the experiences of a close relative as the model for the play's protagonist, Irma. The plot centres on the fate of people of diverse nationalities who are united by their efforts to save the life of a prisoner of war. Priede challenges another of the great Soviet narratives, that of the subjugation of all interests to the task of destroying an enemy. The protagonists refer to "our small war" and their generous and humane actions are deeds of salvation that contrast sharply with the conventional image of a heroic and unified Soviet nation consciously waging political opposition to invaders.

In these plays, the dissolution of one of the greatest of Soviet narratives – that of the victorious patriotic war – anticipates the inescapable social changes about to shatter the whole order of Soviet society. Both *Centrifūga* and *Pilvede värvid* substantially contributed to the inversion of the traditional Soviet perception of World War II. These texts served as beacons of a different way of thinking about historical and contemporary events and pointed toward the direction the Baltic societies of the 1980s were moving with incredible speed. Their appearance at a crucial moment of societal transformation underscores the enormous relevance of the historical themes preserved throughout the 20th century.

Benedikts Kalnačs
benedikts.kalnacs@lulfmi.lv
LU Literatūras, folkloras un mākslas institūts
Mūkusalas iela 3
LV-1423 Rīga
LATVIJA / LATVIA

References

Blekaitis, J. 1986. Introduction to *Kazimieras Sapiega*. – A. Straumanis, ed., *Fire and Night. Five Baltic Plays*. Prospect Heights: Waveland Press, 211–217.

Dundzila, A. V. 1990. King and power. – *Lituanus*, 36, 1, 39–48.

Gilbert, H., Tompkins, J. 1996. *Post-colonial Drama: Theory, Practice, Politics*. London & New York: Routledge.

Kasekamp, A. 2010. *A History of the Baltic States*. Basingstoke: Palgrave Macmillan.

Kiaupa, Z. 2005. *The History of Lithuania*. Vilnius: Baltos lankos.

Kruuspere, P. 1999. Estonian Drama at the End of Millenium: Memory and Identity. – *Naujos idėjos ir formos Baltijos šalių literatūrose*. Vilnius: LLTI, 83–93.

Marcinkevičius, J. 2005. *Trilogija ir epilogas*. Vilnius: Lietuvos Rašytojų sąjungos leidykla.

Martišiūte, A. 2006. *Pirmasis lietuvių dramaturgijos šimtmetis*. Vilnius: LLTI.

Mitaitė, D. 2009. Justinas Marcinkevičius. – E. Eglāja-Kristsone, A. Mihkelev, V. Gasiliūnas, eds., *300 Baltic Writers: Estonia, Latvia, Lithuania*. Vilnius: LLTI, 190–193.

Pabarčienė, R. 2006. Komparativinis detektivas: Juozo Grušo *Barbora Radvilaitė* – Balio Sruogos *Barboros Radvilaitės* transkripcija? – *Žmogus ir žodis*, nr. 2, 49–61.

Plakans, A. 2011. *A Concise History of the Baltic States*. Cambridge: Cambridge University Press.

Rubavičius, V. 2006. A Soviet Experience of Our Own: Comprehension and the Surroundind Silence Notes. – V. Kelertas, ed., *Baltic Postcolonialism*. Amsterdam: Rodopi, 83–104.

Saro, A. 2011. Estonian Historical Drama of the 1980s: A Form of Dissidence. – E. Baliutytė, D. Mitaitė, eds., *Baltic Memory: Processes of Modernization in Lithuanian, Latvian and Estonian Literature of the Soviet Period*. Vilnius: LLTI, 71–79.

Straumanis, A., ed. 1986. *Fire and Night. Five Baltic Plays*. Prospect Heights: Waveland Press.

Šapoka, M., ed. 2009. *Millenium of Lithuania. Millenium Lithuaniae*. Vilnius: Lithuanian Art Museum.

Šilbajoris, R. 1986. Introduction to *Mindaugas*. – A. Straumanis, ed., *Fire and Night. Five Baltic Plays*. Prospect Heights: Waveland Press, 147–153.

Švedas, A. 2013. J. Marcinkevičiaus drama *Mindaugas* sovietinės ideologijos, istorijos politikos ir istoriografinių konjuktūrų lauke. – *Colloquia*, 30, 34–55.

Undusk, J. 2006. History Writing in Exile and in the Homeland after World War II. Some comparative aspects. – C. Hasselblatt, ed., *Different inputs – same output? Autonomy and dependence of the arts under different social-economic conditions: the Estonian example.* Maastricht: Shaker, 127–144.

Speaking to Strangers to Speak about Oneself. Walt Whitman in Johannes Semper's World[1]

KATRE TALVISTE

Abstract. This is a study of an early work on Walt Whitman by Johannes Semper, an Estonian translator and literary critic. His brochure *Walt Whitman* (1920) contains an essay on the American poet's life and work, as well as a number of Estonian translations of his poems. Semper's book is largely based on a similar one published a few years earlier in Russian by Korney Chukovsky, but still clearly represents Semper's own understanding of poetry and his personal interpretation of Whitman's work. This look at Semper's reading of Whitman serves as the basis for a reflection upon the relationship between original and translation, and upon self and otherness in individual literary practices as well as in the literary tradition as a whole, especially in a small literature.

Kewords: Walt Whitman, Johannes Semper, Korney Chukovsky, translated poetry, translation history, Estonian literature, small literatures

Sinule,

Võõras, kes sa vastu tullen äkki tahaksid kõnetella mind, miks ei tohiks sa seda siis teha?
Ja miks ei tohiks ma sinuga kõnelda?

Walt Whitman

Walt Whitman obviously never wrote this poem, in this particular form, in this language. When it first appeared in this Estonian translation, in 1920, all of the target public probably wouldn't have been able to read it in English – German and Russian were the main foreign languages for native Estonian speakers at that time. Today, the global and local linguistic situation have changed and this poem in its relative simplicity and brevity would probably be accessible to most of the Estonian readers in the original, perhaps even more so than its first Estonian version written in a language characteristic of its time, rather unusual in the eyes of today's reader.

This accessibility would most likely be an illusion. The obvious foreignness that comes from reading in another language and the impression of understanding

1 The research was funded by the Estonian Insitutional Research Funding grant *Estonian Literature in the Paradigm of Comparative Literary Research* (IUT 20-1).

DOI: http://dx.doi.org/10.12697/IL.2015.S1.18

the text don't necessarily match the understanding a native reader would have, or the strangeness the native reader might perceive despite the text being in his or her own language. With my limited knowledge of Whitman's reception in America, I can't say how exactly this observation might apply to this particular poem, but in general terms, it is the most persistent problem that follows all translators and translation scholars, if their scholarship is founded on some kind of experience. Semantic meanings can be learnt or figured out, expressions can be found to match them, but the understanding (or lack thereof) of these meanings in their original context isn't as easily acquired. An honest translator tries to get a feeling of how a text works in its original environment, but also realises that its functioning in its new environment ultimately remains his or her responsibility – never an exact equivalent, always dependent on the translator's own individual and cultural world in ways the original never intended and wouldn't have been able to be.

Johannes Semper's translations and interpretation of Walt Whitman's poetry constitute a fascinating case in this respect. In 1920, Semper, a young promising Estonian literary critic and poet, published a brochure *Walt Whitman*. It contains an essay about the American poet's life and work, followed by a selection of poems. Later, Semper scholars have pointed out that the brochure is not "as much a fruit of independent study of Whitman, as a reflection of interpretations of other writers" (Andresen 1979a: 220), the other writers being mainly Korney Chukovsky (Siirak 1969: 118), the eminent Russian critic and poet who had published several collections of Whitman's poetry in Russian.

A few parallels between Semper and Chukovsky should be noted before looking more closely at Semper's essay about Whitman. Chukovsky, about ten years Semper's senior and a passionate anglophile since his early days, had discovered Whitman in 1901. Wanting to share his enthusiasm with his fellow countrymen, he applied himself to translating Whitman's poems. His first collection of translation was published in 1907, creating enough interest to be reprinted in several editions, but as he recalls later, he considered the first version so inadequate that he made a new one in 1913 (Chukovsky 1966: 5–6, 1969: 5–6). Chukovsky's journey into Whitman's world rather closely resembles Semper's discovery of another poet: Émile Verhaeren. Semper, who was early on drawn to French-speaking cultures, discovered Verhaeren and was promptly fascinated by his work around 1910, and spent almost two decades struggling to come up with translations that would convey the reasons for his enthusiasm. Like Chukovsky with his book *Мой Уитмен* (*My Whitman*, 1966), Semper also returned to Verhaeren in his later years, reworking some of his earlier translations and adding a couple of new ones.

With Whitman, Semper didn't revise his work later nor does he seem to have experienced considerable translator's frustration in the early days, although the concentration of Whitman's work was intense enough to leave traces in Semper's own poetry. Whitman is usually referred to as an equally important source of influence beside Verhaeren at that time (Andresen 1979b: 251, Siirak 1969: 122) and Semper's decisive turn to free verse in the early 1920s certainly confirms that, although other poets, especially the German Expressionists, undoubtedly played a role in that development. Whitman clearly was important to Semper, for a time, although in a different way from Verhaeren, but also through the mediation of another poet to whom Whitman seems to have been what Verhaeren was to Semper. This similarity in rapport, however hard to establish in a rigorously academic way, is significant. Literary translation is a close and intimate relationship, and it can take many different forms in the life of a translator. Not all authors inspire such a strong personal need for translation as Whitman and Verhaeren did, respectively, for Chukovsky and Semper, and not all authors who do keep haunting their translator with a strong sense of inadequacy. Semper's case would support the supposition that it only happens when a translator encounters a stranger in whom he perceives something profoundly his own, perhaps lacking or unnoticed so far, and then realises that he needs to considerably develop his abilities and resources before being able to express, to himself and to others, what this missing piece of his world is.

Semper's essay on Whitman offers a chance to observe and more formally describe this search for completing otherness, perhaps for the very reason that Semper's relationship with Whitman remained less personal, apparently borrowed from Chukovsky. Content-wise, the borrowing is obvious. Semper uses paragraphs sentences and quotes directly taken from Chukovsky's text. In addition, his sources are clearly the same as Chukovsky's, although he doesn't list them as correctly as Chukovsky does.[2] Semper's text is shorter, he skips several anecdotes Chukovsky shares with his readers, giving instead a brief resumé of the event related. For instance, Chukovsky recounts a colourful incident of Whitman tending to a wounded soldier and nearly infecting himself with gangrene (Chukovsky 1919: 22), which Semper simply renders with "Physically weakened (from over-exertions during war-time), he lives till 1892. He died on March 26." (Semper 1920: 10)

Semper has also changed the general thematic structure of the essay. Chukovsky opens with a journalistic attention-grabber – an advertisment Whitman had published for an early and unsuccessful novel, which Chukovsky uses as an introduction to Whitman's biography, character and works. In Semper's telling, the author's character precedes life events, but, more importantly, the

[2] The basis for comparison and source for Chukovsky's translations here is the fourth edition of his book (Chukovsky 1919).

whole presentation of Whitman is preceded by Semper's own reflection on the communicative and social functions of poetry. His opening thesis is that poetry is essentially a solitary pursuit, but in some cases, such as Whitman's, it is a means of reaching out to others, even strangers (Semper 1920: 5).

This is characteristic of Semper's literary criticism, and particularly obvious in texts with a relatively descriptive purpose, such as the essays on various foreign authors. No matter how, and how accidentally, a journey into another author's creative universe began for Semper, by the time he invites readers to join him in the discovery, he has developed a conceptual context for it, a problem to be solved or at least explored along the way.[3] In *Walt Whitman*, his opening paragraphs represent a crucial moment in the development of his critical thought. About a decade into his literary career, he is focused on the question (functions of poetry in modern times) that had inspired some of his first critical reflections (Semper 1912), and still thinks in youthfully rigorous oppositions: the higher, better, and essentially aesthetic universe of poetry is opposed to the banal, materialistic universe of everyday life in the modern human society. However, the choice of Whitman as his object of study and translation, undoubtedly contributed to the evolution of Semper's critical and poetic thought towards what it gradually became during the 1920s: a refusal of empty aestheticism in favour of perception of poetry as a cognitive and ethical device meant to structure human experience with its multitude of aspects (individual and social, sensual and spiritual, emotional and intellectual, etc.), all of which are equally valuable, hierarchised perhaps by personal perception, but not by preconceived notions.

The ability to perceive the world and one's self in this synthetic, all-accepting manner, is the main reason both Semper and Chukovsky admire Whitman. They describe him as the poet of joy and optimism, a pantheist and democratic spirit who has equal admiration for nature and culture, life and death, good and evil, the smallest individual beings and the universe as a whole. Semper's selections of poems follows his essay clearly stems from this way of reading. He has chosen, in the following order, eleven sections of *Songs of Myself*, three from *Children of Adam* (*From Pent-Up Aching Rivers, I Sing the Body Electric* and

[3] Some of his introductions have also changed over time, from edition to edition, if the initial problem has lost relevance. With the Whitman essay, this is not the case, but it is interesting to note, as yet another parallel with Chukovsky, that Chukovsky's opening for the book *My Whitman* (1966) did change with time: in its second edition, in 1969, he begins the study of Whitman's poetry with a reference to space travel become reality (Chukovsky 1969: 10), which obviously was not yet relevant when the first edition was published in 1966. The enthusiasm for space travel was universal, and practically mandatory in the Soviet Union, but in this case it actually develops a long-present theme in Chukovsky's interpretation.

A Woman Waits for Me), two from *Calamus* (*I Hear It Was Charged Against Me* and *For You O Democracy*), the fifth and the ninth section of *Salut au monde*, *Song of the Open Road*, *Out of the Cradle Endlessly Rocking*, the third section (*Beat! Beat! Drums!*) from *Drum-Taps*, two parts of From Noon to Starry Night (the final section of *The Mystic Trumpeteer* and *Excelsior*) and five short poems (*Beautiful Women*, *Transcriptions*, *Europe*, *To a Certain Cantatrice* and *To You*) regrouped under the title *Mitmesugust* (*Miscellaneous*).[4] This ensemble powerfully expresses exaltation with life in its corporal and sensual reality, and on a quieter, but clear tone a passion for human solidarity, social justice and enthusiasm for the modern world. Chukovsky's guidance in discovering this poetic world is obvious from partial similarity of the selection itself and especially from some details. For example, Semper's version of *From Pent-Up Aching Rivers* follows Chukovsky's rather than Whitman's syntax. Whitman's text is actually a long and complex adverbial phrase finally followed by the subject, verb and object in three final verses:

> From pent-up aching rivers,
> From that of myself without which I were nothing,
> From what I am determin'd to make illustrious, even if I stand
>   sole among men,
> From my own voice resonant, singing the phallus,
> Singing the song of procreation,
> Singing the need of superb children and therein superb grown
>   people,
> [...]
> From the night a moment I emerging flitting out,
> Celebrate you act divine and you children prepared for,
> And you stalwart loins.
> (Whitman 2004: 252, 254)

4 Some of the longer texts and excerpts have been partially translated, with omission of several verses. Neither Chukovsky nor Semper refer to the precise edition of *Leaves of Grass* they have used. Pending further study, we can assume that Semper's translations are based on the 1881 or the death-bed edition. One of the clearest indications is a verse from section 24 of *Song of Myself*: *Walt Whitman, üks kosmos, Manhattani poeg* (Whitman 1920: 39) that translates the final version of this self-identification (*Walt Whitman, a kosmos, of Manhattan the son*, Whitman 2004: 214). The versions of this verse dating from earlier editions are syntaxically different enough to be unlikely to be translated in this concise manner (see Karbiener 2004: 796 about the evolution of this verse).

Such an extreme syntax always constitutes a challenge for the translator. Chukovsky has chosen to simplify Whitman's phrase by rendering the introductory verses syntaxically more independent and semantically more decided:

> Запружены реки мои, и это причиняет мне боль,
> Нечто есть у меня, без чего я был бы ничто, это хочу я
> Прославить, хотя бы я стоял меж людей одиноко,
> (Chukovsky 1919: 86)

Semper follows the exact same path:

> Sulet on mu jõed ja see teeb mulle valu,
> Mul on midagi, ilma milleta oleksin null,
> See, mida otsustin ülevana kiita, kui veel inimeste keskel seisaksin üksikuna,
> (Whitman 1920: 48)

'My rivers are pent up and it causes me pain, / I have something without which I would be nothing' is an image solidified in a way that a translator is often compelled to choose. Concretisation of images is an inevitable part of the translation process, but reconstruction of the original ambiguity in the translated text is not a given, either because the translator fails to find a way to make it work, or because the translator ends up being more convinced by one possible interpretation than by others. These two situations are always a matter of the translator's (or any reader's) perception; texts are not objectively divisible into ambiguous and unambiguous elements. Translators are expected to decide the meaning every step of the way, and the end result doesn't always reveal how much hesitation, interpretative effort, collegial counsel or literary examples went into the creation of a particular phrase or image. However, syntaxic structures and semantic ellipses of high individuality, such as in Whitman's poem, are likely to require a lot of interpretative effort with various possible outcomes, and if a quasi-identical outcome is reached by two translators, the notion of influence can, for once, be applied with certainty and, moreover, with an actual meaning to it. Semper has closely followed Chukovsky where it has been helpful to him in making sense of Whitman's text. English was far from his first foreign literary language, and the text in question is a challenge for any translator, as is obvious from Chukovsky's own effort of taming it.

In several other aspects, Semper's reading of Whitman differs from Chukovsky's. He is far less interested in religious and political interpretations, and clearly more fascinated by the themes of body and sexuality. Chukovsky's Whitman is first and foremost a poet of general human values and abstract spiritual quests, Semper's Whitman – a poet of individual, sensual, unique experience. In addition, the modern urban and technological environment plays a more important and more positive role in Semper's interpretation of Whitman than it does in Chukovsky's reading. Semper's choice of sections 5 and 9 of "Salut au monde", a poem Chukovsky hasn't included at all in his selection, underlines the importance of this aspect for him. These sections (*I see the tracks of railroads of the earth, / I see them in Great Britain, I see them in Europe...* – Whitman 2004: 298; *I see the cities of the earth and make myself at random a part of them...* – Whitman 2004: 301) all but express his own fascination with the modern environment, especially the speed of movement and communication it has brought, and his passionate need to experience as much of the world as possible and to feel at home in its diversity. Semper did indeed travel and live abroad a lot, so his claiming railroads and places from all over Europe as his in his poems is based on considerable empirical experience, as opposed to Whitman's mostly imaginary one. But one original and fundamentally important common characteristic that probably drew Semper to Whitman in the first place, no matter with whose support and mediation, is their conviction that the empirical and imaginary experiences are not as different as they are sometimes considered to be. Experience is what happens in a person's mind, senses, emotions and surroundings; parts of it always originate from imaginary sources created and nourished by texts, not actual objects. The authenticity of experience is not determined by the material reality of the object, but rather by the integrity and intensity of the subject's relation to it.

The same can be said of literary criticism and translation, to return to Nigol Andresen's observation about the lack of originality in Semper's book on Whitman. Indeed, objectively it is mostly a compilation of borrowed elements. Some sources of inspiration, knowledge and poetics are fairly obvious, others would undoubtedly be revealed by further study. As was suggested by Jaan Undusk (2014), there probably were also German sources that influenced Semper's understanding of Whitman; and if Semper followed up on some of Chukovsky's own suggestions of translations and influences in other European languages, he may have found other substantial inspiration for constructing his Whitman. My objective here was not to determine what these sources of inspiration are or even to comprehensively describe the one source that was Chukovsky. It was to reflect, on the example of the interaction between Whitman's, Chukovsky's and Semper's world, on the impossibility of being alone in the universe – either material, intellectual, poetic, or any other kind. The elements used in construction of any individual universe come from contact with others, originality and individuality lies in the construction process and in the subject involved in that process. Semper's *Walt Whitman*, an often forgotten or easily dismissed early work, rather peripheral apparently in Semper's own eyes and in later studies, is excellent modelling material for this issue. Far from being among the books first thought of when thinking of Semper's contribution to Estonian literary scholarship, criticism and translated literature, and indeed far from being a truly independent creation, it is still unmistakeably 'a Semper', clearly representing the same subject, who about a decade earlier discussed the role of lyrical poetry in the modern world and would, a few years later, write the poems of *Viis meelt* ('*Five Senses*', 1926) and finally find his voice in poetic translation. Whitman seems to have been part of the process rather than an object of interest in his own right, a stage in Semper's search for himself.

A blatant instrumentalisation of the Other, on one hand. On the other hand – an honest attempt to not remain the same, to grow into something new as a result of contact with the Other. From the perspective of great and influential monolingual cultures, this transformative power of contact between subjects, individual or collective, has come to be viewed as something ethically and politically suspicious, perhaps because the reciprocity of the transformation doesn't clearly manifest itself in that type of environment. Actually, it doesn't necessarily manifest itself in any environment – small cultures, small literatures living in constant presence and awareness of others may also perceive the contact as monodirectional. In their case, this perception often translates into concern about unwanted influences from the Other (a concern that echoes through Estonian literary history as well, and a concern Semper was perhaps less willing to heed than many, although he was quite as capable of occasionally feeling and expressing it as his contemporaries). As Western culture has grown to value otherness, this fear has somewhat decreased, but seems to be replaced by a mirror-image concern felt by great literatures – a fear of not being touched at all by otherness, of not being able to transform. Whitman can be described as an example of this incapacity, yet Whitman can also constitute a reassuring example of the inevitability of transformation, if looked at from a different perspective, for instance from far away.

A central poet to a central literary tradition in Western literature, Whitman has remained, despite the onetime efforts of Johannes Semper and a later translation by Boris Kabur (Whitman 1962), a rather peripheral figure in a peripheral literary tradition. In Estonia, Whitman has the quality of an abstract and distant symbol, nothing like the very real, personally engaging presence that is perfectly perceptible on his home ground. The impression, of course, is a subjective one, but at least purposefully sought out and observed as the most readily available object of comparison. When travelling briefly in the footsteps of Whitman (from New York to Washington D.C. via Long Island and Camden, in December 2014), even the briefest encounters with people, from museum curators to hotel receptionists, showed that something about Whitman mattered to them, or at least that Whitman was something to relate to, while at home my Whitman expedition provoked a series of hesitant admissions of having possibly heard the name, many happy moments of recognition from references to modern American fictional characters quoting Whitman, and several discoveries of Whitman's poetry.[5] It is not just the matter of original versus translated literature. There are translated authors in the Estonian literary tradition who function in a totally different way, quite comparably to the most meaningful original ones. (Back when I was working on Baudelaire, everybody said, "Ah, I see".) The point is not to idealise a situation where a great poet is not really read, but to shape a concrete, albeit minuscule example of the multitude of Whitmans existing in World Literature. The one read and remembered in his original culture will never be adequately accessible to other literatures elsewhere – the texts can be translated, but the experience and environment that first inspired them and continues to surround them don't travel as easily. Even when reading Whitman, an Estonian reader doesn't read a poet whose verses (s)he may encounter anywhere in the everyday urban space, on a façade of a public building, for example, and to whom other readers sometimes refer as *Walt*.

This makes a significant difference, especially since the practices of quoting lyrical poetry in public spaces and occasionally referring to major poets by their first names (if entitled by personal or professional familiarity) exist in Estonia as well. We may not know Whitman very well, but there is something very familiar in the way a poet's person and work function as a foundation of a cultural and historical identity. This relates to another faraway perspective to consider Whitman from: as present as he may be in today's culture, he is not our contemporary. Strictly speaking, he wasn't Johannes Semper's either, but due to historical circumstances, their generations in their respective countries had many similar experiences, especially in their early years. Both moved personally from a rustic childhood environment to a modern, industrial and technological, urban setting, and through a rather tumultuous flow of intellectual and ideological currents. In other words, both actually lived the advent of modernity when it reached their lifespace, and both essantially welcomed that most overwhelming otherness of their time, the otherness that came from within the culture rather than from another, foreign place.

Briefly, Whitman's case is well suited to illustrate that the otherness is always there, impossible to extinguish and impossible not to tame in some way,

5 "At home" doesn't refer to academic and/or literary circles, where there are probably more awareness and experience with Whitman's work, but to a variety of enthusiastic recreational readers able to enjoy literature in several languages and curious about other cultures.

although, depending on circumstances, it is more or less possible not to notice or to purposefully ignore it. When that purpose is set aside, small literatures may have an advantage in exploring the situation, because it is much more obvious in their case. The smaller the literature, the larger the world, and the more impossible to ignore its presence. Encountering strangers, constructing one's self in relation to them and with elements borrowed from them is not an option, it becomes the only experienced form of existence and almost the only imaginable reality. In this reality, the dual notion of *World Literature – Comparative Literature* takes on a specific function: it allows for a distinction between an object and a discipline. Not that the distinction is systematically applied or even perceived in the same way by everybody, but it matches the duality of the situation. There's the undeniable and rather overwhelming presence in the world of literature neither written nor available in one single language and within one single culture. And there's an academic discipline whose task it is to deal with that presence and that diversity. Small and large literatures represent different types of experience of otherness and foreignness, and so do literary scholars coming from these different types of traditions, as is clearly demonstrated by the articles and essays brought together in this volume. As comparativists, we all obviously agree that otherness is something to be valued, but we look for it and relate to it differently, according to how we are originally used to experiencing otherness. There's the dream and desire for the distant Other, perceived as elusive and fragile; and the matter-of-fact curiosity for, and sometimes wariness of, the ever-present Other, perceived as immense and inexhaustible. Walt Whitman represents the first model, Semper, the other.

Perhaps we should look more closely into possible combinations of these two perspectives – try not to forget the difference of the original Other from the one we construct for ourselves in order to make sense of the world, but also remember that the original Others are never really waiting our permission to be themselves, they just are, whether we are aware of them or not, and they may even be busy constructing their images of us, if they happen to be aware of us (which is not always the case). In a way, everything we are aware of, belongs to us, as Walt Whitman belongs to the readers who affectionately call him by his given name, or as he belonged to Johannes Semper, who 'took' him from Korney Chukovsky (without any of them really taking anything away from others). I believe the true ethical challenge doesn't reside in denying individual readers or whole literary traditions the practice of rewriting or retelling the world of others as their own, it resides in understanding that whenever somebody does so they speak about themselves, not others, which is always a legitimate thing to do, but if we search for a way of learning about others, that can only be found in listening, and speaking in turns, as suggested by Whitman (2004: 177) in a short poem that seemed significant enough to Semper to use to introduce and to conclude his journey into Whitman's world – he quotes it at the beginning of his essay and has chosen it to be the final piece of his selection:

TO YOU

Stranger, if you passing meet me and desire to speak to me, why should you not speak to me?
And why should I not speak to you?

Katre Talviste
katre.talviste@ut.ee
Kultuuriteaduste ja kunstide instituut
Tartu Ülikool
Ülikooli 16
51003 Tartu
EESTI / ESTONIA

References

Andresen, N. 1979a. Johannes Semper väliskirjanduse vahendajana. – N. Andresen, *Terendusi*. Tallinn: Eesti Raamat, 217–233.
Andresen, N. 1979b. Johannes Semperi noorusluule. – N. Andresen, *Terendusi*. Tallinn: Eesti Raamat, 234–252.
Chukovsky, K. 1919. *Uot Uitmen: poeziya grjadušej demokratii*. Peterburg: Izdanie Petrogradskogo Soveta Rabočih i Krasnoarmejskih Deputatov. = Чуковский, К. 1919. *Уот Уитмен. Поэзия грядущей демократии*. Петербург: Издание Петроградского Совета Рабочих и Красноармейских Депутатов.
Chukovsky, K. 1966. *Moj Uitmen*. Moskva: Progress. = Чуковский, К. 1966. *Мой Уитмен*. Москва: Прогресс.
Chukovsky, K. 1969. *Moj Uitmen*. Moskva: Progress. [Revised and completed edition.] = Чуковский, К. 1969. *Мой Уитмен*. Москва: Прогресс.
Karbiener, K. 2004. Endnotes. – Whitman 2004, 787–818.
Semper, J. 1912. Lüürik ja meie aeg. – *Noor-Eesti IV*. Tartu: Noor-Eesti, 146–167.
Semper, J. 1920. *Walt Whitman*. Tallinn: Varrak.
Siirak, E. 1969. *Johannes Semper*. Tallinn: Eesti Raamat.
Undusk, J. 2014. Discussion at the workshop *Johannes Semper ja prantsuse vaim*. Tallinn, June 4.
Whitman, W. 1920. Valik luuletustest. – J. Semper, *Walt Whitman*. Tallinn: Varrak, 33–64.
Whitman, W. 1962. *Rohulehed*. Tallinn: Eesti Riiklik Kirjastus.
Whitman, W. 2004. *Leaves of Grass. First and "death-bed" editions*. New York: Barnes & Noble Classics.

About the Authors

ARTURO CASAS, credited as Professor, is Senior Lecturer of Literary Theory and Comparative Literature at the University of Santiago de Compostela (USC). His main research interests include the work of Rafael Dieste and his cultural and political activities during the Second Spanish Republic and the exile, contemporary aesthetic and literary thought, systemic studies on culture and literature, the methodology of literary history, and the Galician poetry of the 20th and 21st centuries. He has edited the poetry of Uxío Novoneyra (2010) and Salvador García-Bodaño (2014), and, as a co-editor, also the multi-authored volumes *Performing Poetry: Body, Place and Rhythm in the Poetry Performance* (2011) and *Resistance and Emancipation: Cultural and Poetic Practices* (2011). He leads the Research Centre for Emerging Cultural Processes and Practices, founded in 2010 at USC. He has published in collaboration translations of Estonian, Irish, Italian and Arabic poetry.

DOROTHY FIGUEIRA is Distinguished Research Professor in Comparative Literature at the University of Georgia, USA. Trained in both comparative literature and the history of religion, she is interested in the intersection of religion and literature. Her research includes: *Translating the Orient* (1991), *The Exotic; A Decadent Quest* (1994), *Aryans, Jews and Brahmins: Theorizing Authority through Myths of Identity* (2001), *Otherwise Occupied: Theories and Pedagogies of Alterity* (2008), and *The Hermeneutics of Suspicion* (2015). She has held positions at Cornell University, SUNY, the University of Illinois; she has been a visiting professor at Indiana University, the University of Lille, and Jadavpur University (Kolkata). She has been the recipient of several Fulbrights to India. She holds degrees from the Ecole Pratique en Sciences Sociales, Harvard University, the University of Chicago. She has served as president of the ICLA. Professor Figueira has also served as editor of *The Comparatist* and is currently editor of *Recherche littéraire/Literary research*, the review journal of the ICLA. She has edited several books including most recently with Marc Maufort, *Theaters in the Round* (2011), and *Literary Cultures and Translation: New Aspects of Comparative Literature* (2015) with Chandra Mohan.

GERALD GILLESPIE is Professor Emeritus of German Studies and Comparative Literature at Stanford University (1974–), after prior service at the University of Southern California (1961–64) and SUNY Binghamton (1965–74). He has been a research fellow at the University of Pittsburgh, the University of Paris, and Cambridge University, and a guest professor at the University of Pennsylvania, New York University, the University of Minnesota, Peking University, the University of East Anglia, the University of Munich, and the University of Hagen. Corresponding Member of the Berliner Wissenschaftliche Gesellschaft and Honorary Professor of International Studies at Liaoning University (China). Selected publications: *Evolution of the European Novel* (1987, in Chinese); *Garden and Labyrinth of Time: Studies in Renaissance and Baroque Literature* (1988); *By Way of Comparison: Reflections on the Theory and Practice of Comparative Literature* (2003); *Proust, Mann, Joyce in the Modernist Context* (2003, 2nd ed. 2010); *Echoland: Readings from Humanism to Postmodernism* (2006); as editor, *Comparative Literature, World Literature* (1990); *German Theater before 1750* (1992); *Romantic Drama* (1994); *Visions in History* (1995); *Ludwig Tieck's "Puss-in-Boots" and Theater of the Absurd* (2013); *The Nightwatches of Bonaventura* (2014); as co-editor, *Powers of Narration* (1995); *Narrative Ironies* (1997); *Mallarmé in the Twentieth Century* (1998); *Romantic Prose Fiction* (2008); *Intersections, Interferences, Interdisciplines: Literature with Other Arts* (2014); *Contextualizing World Literature* (2015). Earlier books concerning German Baroque and Romantic literature, and the Spanish dramatist Valle-Inclán. Numerous articles on European and New World Romanticism and Modernism, narrative, textual theory and criticism, and the global development of comparative literary studies. Has held Fulbright, Max Kade, American Philosophical Society, Mellon, Guggenheim, and NEH Senior fellowships, and other awards. Editorial and editorial(-advisory) board posts: *Int. Archiv f. Sozialgeschichte der deutschen Literatur, Comparative Literature, Recherche Littéraire, German Life and Letters, Utrecht Publications in Comparative Literature, Synthesis, Literary Imagination, KulturPoetik*. Has served as General Secretary (1979–85), Vice-President (1985–88), and President (1994–97) of the International Comparative Literature Association; Chair, ICLA Commission on Structures (1986–91) and Research (1991–94, 1998–2000); Council member, Association of Literary Scholars and Critics (1998–2001).

JEANNE E. GLESENER is Associate Professor in Luxembourgish Literatures at the University of Luxembourg. Her PhD in comparative literature focused on the aesthetics and the reception of contemporary migration literature in Great Britain, Germany and Luxembourg. Her main research interests are Luxembourgish literatures and contemporary European migration literatures. Her current fields of research include writing literary history in intercultural and multilingual contexts, small literatures in Europe and the history of Luxembourgish literatures. Recent publications include articles on multilingual and intercultural Luxembourgish literatures, the location of small literatures in World Literature and the Francophone Luxembourgish novelist and poet Jean Portante.

JAVIER GÓMEZ-MONTERO is Professor of Literature and Romance Studies and director of the Department of Romance Languages and Literature at Kiel University (CAU), Germany, and director of the Centre for the Study of Spanish Renaissance in its European context (CERES: www.uni-kiel.de/ceres). Since October 2007, he has also been in charge of the Centre for Galician Studies (CEG: www.uni-kiel.de/ceg). Moreover, he directs the Literary Translation Workshop (TTL) at Kiel University and edits a publication series at Verlag Ludwig. He has published several studies on cultural anthropology and works on The Way of St. James, as well as on anthologies of literary texts about it. From 2010 until 2012 he coordinated the Intensive Programme (IP) URBES EUROPAEAE (www.uni-kiel.de/urbes.europaeae), as well as activities related to the two projects Cultures and Languages on the Route of Santiago de Compostela (www.camino-eu.com/) and University and School towards a European Literary Canon (www.uni-kiel.de/elica) in Germany, both supported by the Education, Audiovisual and Culture Executive Agency (EACEA) of the European Union. Prof. Gómez-Montero's research focuses on modern and contemporary poetry, Renaissance fiction, and the works of Cervantes.

HARVEY L. HIX earned his PhD in Philosophy from the University of Texas (USA) and currently teaches in the Philosophy Department and the Creative Writing MFA of the University of Wyoming. His recent books include a poetry collection entitled *I'm Here to Learn to Dream in Your Language* (Etruscan Press, 2015), an art/poetry anthology, *Ley Lines* (Wilfrid Laurier University Press, 2014), and a collection of the poetry of Juhan Liiv, *Snow Drifts, I Sing* (Guernica Editions, 2013), translated with his long-standing friend and collaborator Jüri Talvet.

MARKO JUVAN is a literary theorist and comparatist, head of the Institute of Slovenian Literature and Literary Studies at the Research Center of the Slovenian Academy of Sciences and Arts (ZRC SAZU), and professor of Slovenian literature at the University of Ljubljana. Juvan presented papers at conferences throughout Europe, in the US, Canada, South Korea, Japan, and Australia. He was visiting professor at the universities of Brno and Zagreb and lectured at the universities of Budapest, Munich, Hamburg, Prague, Reykjavík, Vienna, Ghent, and Novi Sad. Between 2007 and 2011 he was a member of the Executive Committee of the European Network of Comparative Literary Studies (REELC/ENCLS), and from 2008 to 2014 he was a member of the Committee on Literary Theory of the ICLA/AILC. Since 2013 he has served on the Section Committee for Literary and Theatrical Studies of the Academia Europaea. In addition to numerous articles and edited volumes in Slovenia and abroad (for example, *World Literatures from the Nineteenth to the Twenty-first Century*, a special issue of the *CLCWeb: Comparative Literature and Culture*, 2013), his recent book publications include *History and Poetics of Intertextuality* (2008), *Literary Studies in Reconstruction* (2011), and *Prešernovska struktura in svetovni literarni sistem* ('The Prešernian Structure and the World Literary System', 2012).

BENEDIKTS KALNAČS is Deputy Director of the Institute of Literature, Folklore, and Art at the University of Latvia, Riga, and Professor at the University of Liepāja. He is co-editor of *300 Baltic Writers: Estonia, Latvia, Lithuania* (Vilnius, 2009), *Back to Baltic Memory: Lost and Found in Literature 1940–1968* (Riga, 2008), *We Have Something in Common: The Baltic Memory* (Tallinn 2007), *Ibsen in Poland and the Baltic Nations* (Oslo, 2006), and editor and author of several books in Latvian, most recent among them *Postkoloniālā Baltijas drāma* (Riga 2011).

LIINA LUKAS is Associate Professor for Comparative Literature at the Institute of Cultural Research and Fine Arts at the University of Tartu. Her research interests are Estonian–German literary contacts, Baltic-German literature and early Estonian literature. She heads the Research and Web Project of Baltic Literary Culture – EEVA, supported by the Estonian Science Foundation, which studies and offers, in digital format, international access to old cultural texts, written or published in the Baltic cultural space (www.utlib.ee/ekollekt/eeva). She is a member of the Board of the International Vladimir-Admoni-Doktorandenschule at the University of Latvia; chairwoman of the Goethe-Gesellschaft in Tartu; member of the Estonian Association of Comparative Literature, member of the Estonian Literary Society, member of the International Association for German Studies, member of the Academic Advisory Board of *Interlitteraria* and a member of the Editorial Board of the yearbook of German studies *Triangulum*.

JOHN NEUBAUER is professor emeritus of Comparative Literature at the University of Amsterdam, Corresponding Fellow of the British Academy (FBA), and co-editor of the comparatist journal *arcadia*. His publications include *Symbolismus und symbolische Logik* (1978), *The Emancipation of Music from Language* (1986), and *The Fin-de-siècle Culture of Adolescence* (1992). He was co-editor of *The Reception of Laurence Sterne in Europe* (2004), of the four-volume *History of the Literary Cultures of East-Central Europe* (2004–2010), and of *The Exile and Return of Writers from East-Central Europe* (2009). His present interests include music and language in the nineteenth century, theories of literary history, and adaptation in the arts and evolution.

ALFREDO SALDAÑA is Professor of Literary Theory and Comparative Literature at the University of Zaragoza (Spain). His main research interests are philosophy of culture, aesthetic theory and contemporary literature, with a special attention for poetry. Among his works are the essays *Modernidad y posmodernidad: filosofía de la cultura y teoría estética* (1997), *El poder de la mirada. Acerca de la poesía española posmoderna* (1997), *El texto del mundo. Crítica de la imaginación literaria* (2003), *Hay alguien ahí* (2008), *No todo es superficie. Poesía española y posmodernidad* (2009) and *La huella en el margen. Literatura y pensamiento crítico* (2013). He has also published books of poetry: *Fragmentos para una arquitectura de las ruinas* (1989), *Pasar de largo* (2003), *Palabras que hablan de la muerte del pensamiento* (2003), *El que mira las palabras* (2004), *Humus* (2008) and *Malpaís* (2015).

DOROTHEA SCHOLL is Assistant Professor at the department of Romance languages and literatures at the University of Kiel. Her fields in research include Franco-Canadian Literature, Renaissance and Baroque literature, romanticism, symbolism and the avant-garde, with special regard to the interrelation of arts and literatures and of ethics and aesthetics. She has published about 50 articles on these themes. She is the author of *Von den "Grottesken" zum Grotesken. Die Konstituierung einer Poetik des Grotesken in der italienischen Renaissance* (Münster 2004). She has edited *La question du baroque* (Œuvres & Critiques XXXII, 2, 2007) and *Romantisme et réception du romantisme au Canada francophone* (Œuvres & Critiques XXXIX, 2, 2014) and is the co-editor of *Bibeldichtung* (Berlin 2006) and of *Literatur und Moral* (Berlin 2011).

MONICA SPIRIDON is professor of literary theory, semiotics, and twentieth century European culture at the University of Bucharest, Romania, specialising in comparative literature, literary theory, and European studies. She is the author of seventeen books of literary theory, comparative literature, and an east-Central European intellectual history of the twentieth century published in Romania and abroad. She authored numerous academic studies in scholarly periodicals and about two dozen chapters in books published in Germany, Italy, Greece, The Netherlands, France, Portugal, Brazil, Iceland, Cyprus, Slovenia, Estonia, The Czech Republic, Great Britain, Hungary and the United States. She was a member of the ICLA Executive Council (1997–2003), president of the ICLA *Research Committee on Eastern and South-Eastern European Literature* (2000–2010), Vice-president of the ICLA (2010–), founder of the *European Network of Comparative Literary Studies* (ENCLS) and member of its Executive Bureau (2003–2007). Since September 2010, she has been a member of *Academia Europea.*

LIISA STEINBY (until 2007 Liisa Saariluoma) is professor of Comparative Literature at the University of Turku, Finland. She is the vice-president of the International Herder Society 2015–2016. She has published eleven monographs and ca 90 articles on different aspects of the modern novel or literary theory, among others a comparative study on the postmodern novel (*Der postindividualistische Roman*, 1994), a monograph on Thomas Mann (*Nietzsche als Roman. Über die Sinnkonstituierung in Thomas Manns "Doktor Faustus"*, 1996), two on the eighteenth-century German novel (*Erzählstruktur und Bildungsroman. Wielands "Geschichte des Agathon", Goethes "Wilhelm Meisters Lehrjahre"*, 2004; *Wilhelm Meisters Lehrjahre und die Entstehung des modernen Zeitbewusstseins*, 2005), and *Kundera and Modernity* (2013). Edited volumes include, among others, *Bakhtin and His Others. (Inter)subjectivity, Chronotope, Dialogism* (with Tintti Klapuri, 2013), and *Narrative Concepts in the Study of Eighteenth-Century Literature* (with Aino Mäkikalli, in press). Her main interests concern the problematics of modernity in the novel comprising the period from the eighteenth century to the present, as well as the questions of the theory of art and the epistemology of literary studies.

KATRE TALVISTE is a part-time senior researcher at the University of Tartu, the managing editor of the Estonian Association of Comparative Literature's journal *Interlitteraria* and an editor of school textbooks for literature at the Avita Publishing House. Her main research interests are the history of translation and the pedagogy of literature. She has published the books *La poésie estonienne et Baudelaire* (2011) and *Laulmine iseendast ja teistest. Mõtteid tõlkivatest luuletajatest* (2013), as well as various articles.

KWOK-KAN TAM is a Fellow of the Hong Kong Academy of the Humanities and also serves as the current Head of the International Ibsen Committee, University of Oslo. He is Chair Professor and Dean of Arts and Social Sciences at the Open University of Hong Kong. He received his PhD in Comparative Literature from University of Illinois at Urbana-Champaign. He worked at the East-West Center, Honolulu, as Postdoctoral Fellow in the 1980s and as Fellow in the 1990s. He was Professor and Reader of English at the Chinese University of Hong Kong before he moved to the Open University of Hong Kong in 2007. He has published widely on Ibsen, comparative literature, modern drama, Chinese film, and world Englishes. Among his many books are *Culture in Translation: Reception of Chinese Literature in Comparative Perspective* (OUHK Press, 2012), *Englishization in Asia: Language and Cultural Issues* (OUHK Press, 2009), *Ibsen and the Modern Self* (*Acta Ibseniana* VII, Oslo, 2010), *Gender, Discourse and the Self in Literature: Issues in Mainland China, Taiwan and Hong Kong* (CU Press, 2010), *Englishization in Asia: Language and Cultural Issues* (2009), *English and Globalization: Perspectives from Hong Kong and Mainland China* (CU Press, 2004), *Ibsen in China: An Annotated Bibliography of Criticism, Translation and Performance* (CU Press, 2001), *Soul of Chaos: Critical Perspectives on Gao Xingjian* (CU Press, 2001), *Politics of the Subject in Modern Chinese Literature* (Oxford, 2000), *A Place of One's Own: Stories of Self from China, Taiwan, Hong Kong and Singapore* (Oxford, 1999) and *New Chinese Cinema* (Oxford, 1998).

JAAN UNDUSK, a graduate of Tartu University (PhD 1986), is since 2000 the director of the Under and Tuglas Literature Centre, a research institute of the Estonian Academy of Sciences in Tallinn. Among his interests are the philosophy of language and literature, German life and letters in the Baltics, the rhetoric of history writing. He has written a large number of articles and essays on Estonian, Baltic German and German authors, as well as translated works of Friedrich Nietzsche, Emmanuel Lévinas, Meister Eckhardt, Thomas Bernhard and others. As a writer, he has published a novel, plays and short stories. In 1995 he was awarded the International Herder Prize for literary research by the Vienna University. He is a member of the Estonian Academy of Sciences (2007) and Baltic History Commission in Göttingen (2008).